D0331263

More Advance Praise for Uncharitable *and Dan Pallotta*

"For those of us who have labored in the trenches of the nonprofit world, this book comes like a rainstorm to a parched land. For too long society has demanded that the nonprofit sector put traditional operating procedure ahead of innovation. . . . Dan and his team have raised unprecedented sums to help treat devastating human disease. Our lab received $100,000 for research from one of his company's events. The findings from that research allowed us to secure over $20 million more in federal grants. Those who would take issue with doing things in a new way will have to reconcile their reservations with those results."
—Peter Anton, M.D., Professor of Medicine, and Director, Center for HIV Prevention Research, David Geffen School of Medicine at UCLA

"Dan is a pioneering individual of tremendous vision. A decade ago, he reinvented the concept of charitable fundraising—and his ideas now promise to reengineer the entire non-profit industry. The lines between the private sector and civil society already are blurring, but the momentum of Dan's ideas will accelerate this fusion. *Uncharitable* is a must read for people seeking careers in social enterprise or attempting to drive meaning into their work."
—Jonathan Greenblatt, Co-Founder, Ethos Water, and CEO, *Good* Magazine

"Do the norms and values that have defined the way charity has been undertaken for centuries continue to make sense in the current age of globalization, mass marketing, and technology? Dan Pallotta makes a convincing case that the time has come to rigorously measure strategic impact rather than overhead ratios, be more competitive in regard to mass communications and marketing, and more adequately invest in administrative systems and program support."
Charles MacCormack, President and CEO, Save the Children

"Charitable non-profits exist to leverage our country's prosperity for the benefit of those in need, and yet too often non-profits reject the tools and the techniques that have made that prosperity possible, shortchanging their noble causes in the process. With passion and logic, and drawing on his own deep well of experience, Dan Pallotta shows how the power of capitalism can be marshaled to the cause of compassion."
—Yuval Levin, Ethics and Public Policy Center, and former Associate Director of the White House Domestic Policy Council and Coordinator of National AIDS Policy

"America needs the smartest and most creative people operating its multi-billion dollar nonprofit sector. To attract them, we must be competitive in compensations, business management and fundraising ideas. Nonprofits who see themselves 'poor as a church mouse' do their mission and supporters a disservice."
—Morris Dees, Founder and Chief Trial Counsel, Southern Poverty Law Center

"Dan Pallotta's book is a brilliant take on the absurdities that constrain the potential of our fastest growing sector—the nonprofit world in America. He raises questions that every executive director asks him or herself every week, but finds no public discourse on. Dan has put together a timely manifesto that outlines the only direction that makes sense—embracing true entrepreneurial initiative and challenging the paradoxical split in America that sets business free but straitjackets charities."

—Torie Osborn, Senior Advisor to Los Angeles Mayor Antonio Villaraigosa, and former Executive Director, Liberty Hill Foundation, National Gay & Lesbian Task Force, Los Angeles Gay & Lesbian Community Services Center

"As the chairman of a nonprofit policy institute, Dan Pallotta has clarified for me the explicit and many implicit constraints under which we operate. My thanks."

—William A. Niskanen, Chairman, The Cato Institute

"Dan Pallotta writes a commanding and compelling vision of what charities and nonprofit organizations are capable of becoming if freed to fully embrace free enterprise thinking and action. He would have us break permanently from the notion that spending money in the service of raising money for deserving social causes is a sin. Anyone who cares about the vexing social and health problems facing society should pay close attention to the brilliant ideas percolating in this groundbreaking book."

—Everette J. Freeman, President, Albany State University

"I have long considered Dan Pallotta a wise and visionary man with much to contribute to our world. This book proves it. His insights into charities and non-profits are as brilliant as they are unexpected and unorthodox. It has always seemed to me that the impulse in our culture to give to worthy causes is a manifestation of what is best about us as people and as a society. This book explains how we limit the effectiveness of our organizations and undermine the realization of our purest dreams and our highest hopes. It is essential reading for anyone who cares about non-profit organizations or the money they give to them. I truly believe that following the wisdom in this book would lead us to impacting on the problems of our world in a genuinely amazing way."

—Judith Light, two-time "Best Actress" Emmy-Award Winner, and AIDS Activist

"*Uncharitable* is the most courageous and necessary of all of the recent books that have been written about philanthropy and the nonprofit sector. Dan Pallotta understands that being faithful to those that charities are designed to serve requires more than generosity and good management. It requires taking risks, confronting antiquated notions of politically correct charity, and most of all remembering that nonprofit efficiency should be a means to an end not an end in itself. *Uncharitable* charts a new path that if followed could finally create the incentives needed to unleash the enormous potential of nonprofits to change the world."

—Bill Shore, Founder and Executive Director, Share Our Strength

UNCHARITABLE

Civil Society: Historical and Contemporary Perspectives

SERIES EDITORS:

Virginia Hodgkinson Public Policy Institute, Georgetown University
Kent E. Portney Department of Political Science, Tufts University
John C. Schneider Department of History, Tufts University

For a complete list of books that are available in the series, visit www.upne.com.

UNCHARITABLE

How Restraints on Nonprofits
Undermine Their Potential

DAN PALLOTTA

TUFTS UNIVERSITY PRESS
Medford, Massachusetts

Published by University Press of New England
Hanover and London

Co-sponsored by Jonathan M. Tisch
College of Citizenship and Public Service

TUFTS UNIVERSITY PRESS
Published by University Press of New England,
One Court Street, Lebanon, NH 03766
© 2008 by Tufts University Press
Printed in the United States of America
5 4 3 2 1

All rights reserved. No part of this book may be reproduced in any form or by any electronic or mechanical means, including storage and retrieval systems, without permission in writing from the publisher, except by a reviewer, who may quote brief passages in a review. Members of educational institutions and organizations wishing to photocopy any of the work for classroom use, or authors and publishers who would like to obtain permission for any of the material in the work, should contact Permissions, University Press of New England, One Court Street, Lebanon, NH 03766.

Library of Congress Cataloging-in-Publication Data
Pallotta, Dan.
Uncharitable : how restraints on nonprofits undermine their potential / Dan Pallotta.
p.   cm. — (Civil society : historical and contemporary perspectives)
Includes bibliographical references and index.
ISBN 978-1-58465-723-1 (cloth : alk. paper)
1. Nonprofit organizations—Government policy. I. Title.
HD2769.15.P35 2008
338.7'4—dc22   2008037289

University Press of New England is a member of the Green Press Initiative. The paper used in this book meets their minimum requirement for recycled paper.

To Jimmy

&

to Freeman, who taught me how to make an argument

All great truths begin as blasphemies.

— GEORGE BERNARD SHAW

CONTENTS

INTRODUCTION

All successful revolutions are the kicking in of a rotten door.
— JOHN KENNETH GALBRAITH

The fact that charity exists at all is a testament to the tenderness of the human soul. We feel for others. When someone else is suffering, we suffer ourselves, and we have a powerful and emotional need to help. The very fact that charity is an emotional subject is further testimony to our love for one another. On the question of whether or not humankind is basically good, this reality speaks for itself.

The system we have for channeling this inner charity is itself called "charity," and just as we all have a desire to make a difference, we have all been taught by this system how best to do it. But as we look around at the persistence of poverty and need, of disease and suffering in a world of unimaginable affluence and productivity, we have to ask ourselves, Does the system work? Is it the best system we could have? What other systems are available? It is to these questions that this book is addressed. The possibility that there is another system that could take our love for one another and leverage it into social progress on a scale we have never even considered must be examined.

Like most people, I never asked questions about our system of charity. Why would I? Who was I to question a system that had been around for centuries? It never dawned on me to ask questions about it. Then I spent two decades working inside the system. During that time an observation was gathering momentum—this system doesn't work. Another observation was gathering momentum about a system that does.

This book is about those observations. Specifically, it is about eradicating the nonprofit beliefs that are the basis of our system. This book advocates a reversal of almost everything we have been taught about doing good, in order that we might achieve good on a scale not previously imagined. It is about freeing charities—and all of the good people who work for them—from a set of rules that were designed for another age and another purpose, and that actually undermine their potential and our compassion. It is about giving charity equal rights with the rest of the economic world and allowing it to use the system everyone else uses to get things done—free-market capitalism.

Whenever I told people I was writing a book about freeing charity to use the tools of capitalism they would nod their heads, believing they were in total agreement, and proceed to say that we absolutely need to put *more* restraints on charity. This response was consistent. It made me realize something else—that the only way most of us can even *conceive* of improving charity is by constraining it *further*. I could see that this belief was so ingrained that it had compromised my friends' hearing—literally. Our nonprofit ethos is a kind of religion on which we have been raised, and it doesn't easily suffer the bigger picture. In fact, like most religion, it obscures the bigger picture. *Suffice it to say, this book is not about adding constraints. It is about removing them, in the interest of the bigger picture.*

For example, after explaining to a friend that we need to let charities hire the most talented people in the world, he wholeheartedly agreed and then said something that didn't logically follow: "It makes me angry to see people making high salaries in charity." "Even if they're worth it? Why?" I asked. "Because it's supposed to be nonprofit," he replied. Right there he gave expression to the entire problem. His logic was internally consistent but externally nonsensical. Still, I understood where he was coming from. Twenty years ago I felt the same way. In fact, I remember thinking it was unconscionable that a charity event producer I knew about was making a profit "off of," as I thought of it at the time, people's compassion. "Nonprofit" means you don't seek gain for yourself. So when someone wants a high salary, of course it makes us angry. It is a violation of the fundamental basis of the system.

But what if the fundamental basis of the system is the *problem*? What if a system that frowns on self-interest turns out to be an inferior way of serving the interests of others? What if a system that allows people to satisfy *their own* self-interest as well as the interests of others turns out to be a much more effective way of helping those in need? In other words, what if the whole system should not *be* nonprofit in the first place? Then my friend's logic, and the whole of society's, is rotten to the core, and everything we have come to believe about helping the needy is as well.

From a system that starts with an illogical premise will come a series of illogical rules. Such is the nature of the nonprofit dilemma today. For instance, the great suffering masses of the world would no doubt benefit from the full-time services of the brightest graduates coming out of the nation's top MBA programs. However, society's nonprofit thinking refuses to allow them to earn anywhere near the kinds of salaries they can command in the for-profit sector. Predictably, then, they head off to the for-profit sector, steering clear of its nonprofit stepsister. People continue to die as a result. This we call morality.

The same is true of the issue of investment capital. If we allowed investors to make as great a financial return by investing in their favorite charity as they can by investing in Toyota, they would send investment capital to their favorite charity. That charity would have money with which to experiment and to grow. Alas, society's nonprofit commandment prohibits this. So all the investment capital goes to the for-profit sector. Our favorite charities are starved for new capital. This we call benevolence.

Same with advertising. No doubt, the Leukemia Society would take in more donations if they paid for advertising on the Super Bowl. Our nonprofit mindset prohibits it, on the grounds that it is wasteful and that people should give without having to be asked. So Budweiser advertises on the Super Bowl instead and reaps the sales bump that might otherwise have gone to the Leukemia Society. This we call charity. The very system we have cherished as the hallmark of our compassion in fact undermines it.

The more I began to write about these irrationalities, the more I was haunted by an obvious question. From where could this erroneous thinking possibly have come? We are not irrational by nature. In the depths of our hearts, we want to do whatever will most help the needy. How could we possibly have become religious about a belief system that undermines those we most want to help?

I began looking for the answer by studying the earliest formal constructions of charity in America, beginning with those of the early Puritan settlers to New England. Having grown up in that region, I was familiar with the Puritan gestalt, and the nonprofit gestalt felt uncannily similar. I am not a historian, but nevertheless I found what I was looking for. It was as fundamental as things can get. It was the Puritans' religious belief that human beings are evil, that we are obnoxious in the eyes of God, and that the self is depraved. Logically, this meant that the self had to be negated. Charity became the monument to this belief, a compensation for human depravity. From that core belief grew a complex array of rules and secondary beliefs designed to preserve it. As a result, the merchants, farmers, and carpenters of the world got an economic system that indulged self-interest—they got free-market capitalism. The needy got a religion—charity—whereby the merchants, farmers, and carpenters could do penance for their self-interest. By and large, that is still what the needy have today.

Most of the efforts to improve the current situation are careful not to offend the underlying religion. Thus, they are necessarily complex, and can only hope to have an impact at the margins, if at all. But this is not a complicated problem to solve. Remove the error, and you remove the problem. What we are left with is this shocking reality: that the way to alleviate suffering on earth is to use the same system that satisfies every other human need and that heretofore has been prevented from doing so by the religion. That system is free-market capitalism. If we surrender our nonprofit dogma, we bring economic freedom to the causes and charities we love, and we make rapid progress toward solving the most vexing problems facing humanity. It is to this radical thesis that this book is addressed.

To understand the current problem we have to start with a problem that originated almost four hundred years ago, so the first chapter begins with a contingent of ships carrying some of the earliest Puritans to the New World. The second half of the chapter deconstructs their ideas about profit and charity. *A journey into Puritan history might sound worse than a root canal, but for me it ended up feeling more like a therapy session— "Oh, this is why I think that way." I hope it will have the same effect on you.* The more light we can shed on what we do and how we got in the habit of doing it, the closer we will get to an epiphany about why it doesn't work. The more we understand why it doesn't work, the more eager we will be to move on from these antiquated ideas and begin dreaming of the amazing and humane new world we could create with our own ideas, relevant to our times, not to the seventeenth century.

I learned about all of these irrationalities the hard way. A horrible thing happened after creating one of the most successful charitable fundraising event operations in history. *We went out of business.* From 1994 to 2002, the AIDSRides and Breast Cancer 3-Day events that my company created raised more than half a billion dollars and netted more than 300 million dollars in unrestricted funds for dozens of AIDS and breast cancer charities—more money, raised more quickly, for these causes than any private event operation had raised in history.[1] As a result of our innovative approach to fundraising, Harvard Business School commissioned a case study of our methods in 2002.[2] That year, our most successful ever, we netted $81,985,303—more than half the annual giving of the Rockefeller Foundation—in unrestricted funds for a variety of causes. *Then we went out of business.*[3] More about that in the case study at the end of the book.

The ideas in this book came to me while our business was becoming more and more effective. I watched critics attack us, with logic they would never apply to the for-profit sector, simply because our methods challenged convention. Remarkably, this seemed to matter more to them than the results we were producing. The tragedy of seeing all the good we were achieving attacked in the name of an allegedly superior morality that would rather allow people to suffer than employ new ideas that could help them led me to write this book.

I am not an academic. I am an activist and an entrepreneur, with all of the passion and impatience those roles imply. If there is any value in this book it is not academic. It is simply that it is able to say what most people inside the nonprofit sector are unable to, for fear of losing their livelihood or the livelihood of their institutions and the clients they serve. Its purpose is to be a voice of reason and truth for those whose voices are silenced by fundamentalism and oppression inside the sector. I am not constrained by these burdens. One of the ironic luxuries of losing everything you built is that you are free to tell it like you see it. If our business were still operating, I could not have written the book.

It is my hope that this book will give definition to a new cause—the challenge of transforming the very meaning of charity itself—and that it will ignite a passionate movement inside and outside the sector on its behalf. More plainly put, I mean to create an uprising, a movement that questions all of what we have been taught—every rule, every constraint, every sacred cow—everything and anything that stands in the way of our ability to eliminate suffering and need. The nonprofit sector is being suffocated by a morality imposed from the outside and reinforced from within. It is based on methods instead of outcomes, and it is killing people. I don't believe there is any cause more important than the eradication of this *thinking,* because it stands in the way of eradicating many of the great problems confronting humanity.

UNCHARITABLE

CHAPTER I

The Morality of Outcomes

Confusion of goals and perfection of means seems, in my opinion,
to characterize our age. — ALBERT EINSTEIN

Six o'clock on the morning of April 8, 1630. After ten days of
southwest winds and stormy seas, the weather has finally turned
fair, with a slight wind from the east and the north. John Winthrop, "brave leader of Christian tribes" and future governor of Massachusetts, is at last able to set sail for the New World from Yarmouth,
England, aboard the 350-ton *Arbella* with fifty-two seamen and twenty-
eight brass cannons on its gun deck headed for Salem, Massachusetts.
Winthrop leads a contingent of four vessels, with seven others to follow
three weeks later, the first of seventeen that will carry one thousand pas-
sengers to Massachusetts in 1630. Some two hundred die on the eight-
week journey. On the occasion of this voyage, Winthrop delivers a sermon entitled "A Modell of Christian Charity" that makes famous the
symbol of "a City upon a Hill," an image he drew from the gospel of
Matthew.[1] It begins, however unintentionally, by institutionalizing inequity, poverty, and the need for charity itself:

> God Almightie in his most holy and wise providence hath soe disposed of
> the Condicion of mankinde, as in all times some must be rich some poore,
> some highe and eminent in power and dignitie; others meane and in [sub-
> mission . . .] soe that the riche and mighty should not eate vpp the poore, nor
> the poore, and dispised rise vpp against their superiours, and [shake] off their
> [yoke].[2]

An honest study of the sermon reveals it to be a heartfelt plea for unity
and humanity, made impossibly complex by the oppressive religious
dogma and class and racial prejudice of the times. It is a message of
love delivered to a people taught to detest their nature. Therefore, it

essentially ignores the daunting reality of self-interest by mandating self-deprivation. It is part vision, part rulebook for maintaining social order three thousand miles away from the institutions that normally enforced it.

It establishes benevolence toward one's fellow man as mandatory and formalizes it in a "covenant" with God. It warns that if these people abide anything less than "a strickt performance of the Articles contained in it," then "the Lord will surely breake out in wrathe against [us and] be revenged of such a [perjured] people and make [us] knowe the price of the breache of such a Covenant."[3] The entire scene is a contradiction lost on its cast: a community of aspiring benevolence headed to a strange land to build God's new world by appropriating it from its natives—determined to "possesse it."[4] If they keep their covenant, that possession will be their reward from God.

These people, their beliefs, anxieties, and contradictions will create the basic construction for charity and philanthropy in America. Winthrop and his fellow Puritans were Calvinists, guided by the teachings of sixteenth-century French theologian John Calvin, who believed man was depraved—totally and hereditarily. This is important, because this belief would become the primary driver of their ideas about charity. The following startling passage is from Calvin's definitive work on Christian theology, *Institutes of the Christian Religion:*

> Original sin, therefore, seems to be a hereditary depravity and corruption of our nature, diffused into all parts of the soul, which first makes us liable to God's wrath . . . we are so vitiated and perverted in every part of our nature that by this great corruption we stand justly condemned and convicted before God . . . even infants themselves, while they carry their condemnation along with them from the mother's womb, are guilty not of another's fault but of their own. For, even though the fruits of their iniquity have not yet come forth, they have the seed enclosed within them. Indeed their whole nature is a seed of sin; hence it can only be hateful and abhorrent to God. . . . For our nature is not only destitute and empty of good, but so fertile and fruitful of every evil that it cannot be idle . . . the whole of man is of himself nothing but concupiscence.[5]

"Concupiscence" means "strong sexual desire, lust." No wonder he used the term—Calvin was twenty-six years old at the time he wrote this.[6]

The Puritans were certainly not the first to believe in original sin, but they were the first to formalize a construction of charity. That original sin was the centerpiece of their worldview then becomes critical. *Love of one's fellow man was to be motivated by hatred of oneself.* Internal inconsistency doesn't get more inconsistent than that. It is impossible that a system with that basis could exploit the full potential of humanity's love. Indeed, it is remarkable that it motivated any. If we are to accept the modern enlightened view that we are all one, then hatred of oneself is nothing more than hatred for another. The absence of love for oneself leaves no love for anyone else.

At the same time they were meditating on depravity and eternal damnation, the Puritans were fulfilling God's will by killing and enslaving Indians and executing suspected witches. It is in this overall context that their model of Christian charity must be understood. Their City upon a Hill was soaked in the blood of its natives. Their construction of charity did not exist apart from their fear, their need for perfection, or their belief in their own unworthiness. This book is about building a world without intimidation or limitation by their anxieties or ghosts. Its purpose is not to demonize them, but to free us of their demons.

The possibilities that stand before us deserve such a deconstruction. In fact, it is long overdue. We are the first generation to hold in our hands the possibility of ending hunger on the earth. Our children can know a day without cancer or multiple sclerosis. We can be alive on the morning when church bells ring in unison the world over because a cure has finally been discovered for AIDS. We stand on the precipice of a possibility not known to any of our ancestors—a world free of most of the suffering that has plagued humanity since the beginning of time. Our greatest moral question is whether we will make this imagined world a reality. The most important question we can ask at this juncture is, What stands in our way? I believe the answer is simple—it is our inherited definition of morality itself.

Nonprofit Ideology

The word "profit" comes from the Latin noun *profectus* for "progress" and the verb *proficere* for "to advance." Thus, the term "nonprofit" means, literally, nonprogress. It is a dangerous unconscious statement of intent, or lack of it. No advance. No progress.

This is not a simple case of mistaken meaning. The Puritans' conviction that the self was depraved required that it be negated, whether it wanted to profit, progress, or advance. Charity, as they constructed it, became the epicenter for this negation. To these roots we will return.

Even on the basis of the modern understanding of profit—as in financial surplus—the nonprofit sector suffers from the distinction of being the only sector whose name begins with a negative, as Harvard Business School Professor Allen Grossman has noted. It apologizes for itself before it begins. It seems to understand only what it is against and is rudderless with respect to what it is for. It is from this starting position that we attempt to transform society or, put more accurately, do not attempt it, under the false impression that we do.

All of this is the opposite of what we intend. We give money to charity because we *do* want progress. We want things to change, not stay the same. Somewhere in the depths of our hearts we have a desire to make a difference. We all want our lives to matter. In an often dreary world, each dollar we give is a sign that we have not yet lost hope. In the midst of our busy lives, each contribution is a sign that we have not forgotten about all those who live in poverty, despair, and abandonment. Out of this basic charity *inside* of us has grown a charity *outside* of us—a multibillion-dollar industry employing millions of people who work to turn our contributions into positive change. We put our trust not just in individual charities, but in the *system* of charity itself to take our offerings and make of them a better world.

But that system doesn't seem to be giving us what we are after, or what we should be after. So we have to ask ourselves, Why do things seem to stay pretty much the same? Why have our cancer charities not found a cure for cancer? Why have our homeless shelters not solved the problem of homelessness? Why do children still go hungry on the streets of America? Why have the pictures of the starving children in Africa not changed in five decades? Why, in this age of incredible affluence, do we seem unable to close the gaps that divide those who live in comfort and those who suffer?

Many people want to blame charities themselves. "They are inefficient. The money never goes to the people it's supposed to. People who work for charity are lazy." A study released in 2008 by Ellison Research showed that "most Americans believe non-profit organizations and charities are not financially efficient enough in their work."[7] A 2004 Brookings Institution study found that "nearly one out of three respondents expressed little or no confidence in charitable groups, and only 11% said they believe that charities do a very good job of spending their money wisely."[8] Seventy percent of people surveyed in a 2008 NYU study said that charities "waste a 'great deal' or a 'fair amount' of money."[9] I can't subscribe to this myopic point of view. I am in awe of the work that our charities do. I am in awe of the people who work for charity. Day in and day out they give their hearts and souls, making huge sacrifices, and working under the most difficult circumstances and the most oppressive economic restraints. They don't deserve to be scapegoated in this way. We should be singing their praises.

Some people want to claim we're a selfish or apathetic society—that we care more about flat-screen televisions than we do about the poor. I don't subscribe to this point of view either. American individuals, corporations, and foundations gave away $295.02 billion in 2006. Of that, $222.89 billion, or 75.6 percent, came from individuals.[10] About 65 percent of all American households with an income of less than $100,000 donated to some type of charity, and nearly 100 percent of those with incomes greater than $100,000 did.[11] A 2006 British study put American charitable giving, quite conservatively against other studies, at 1.67 percent of gross domestic product—still more than double the figure for the next-closest nation.[12] Our charitable infrastructure is the largest on earth. These are hardly signs of an uncaring people. They are signs of the opposite.

Still others say that hunger and disease are inevitable and that they will always be around no matter what we do. I subscribe to this point of view least of all.

We might find out something about why our current ideas aren't working by comparing them with ideas that are. Why are we so successful at making sneakers, iPods, entertainment, and countless discretionary products, and at selling them too? Why does the for-profit sector consistently attract those in the upper percentiles of the world's best business schools? Why does the for-profit sector attract all of the investment capital? How does it monopolize the world's advertising? Why do businesses grow to be huge while charities, particularly those working on behalf of the world's most needy citizens, remain quaint and small? As of 2004, about 72 percent of America's nonprofits had annual revenues less than half a million dollars.[13] And while the nonprofit sector may account for about 5.2 percent of U.S. gross domestic product, by at least one account as of 2004, spending for "public and societal benefit" amounted to only 5.5 percent of that, or just 0.39 percent of America's gross domestic product.[14] Spending on "human services" amounted to 13.6 percent of the total nonprofit sector account, or just 0.71 percent of America's GDP.[15] Why do the organizations dedicated to our greatest needs have the fewest resources?

The answers to these questions will have us questioning the fundamental underpinnings of the world of charity as we know it, right

down to the notion of whether it should be a separate world at all. They
will challenge the assumptions on which that world is based and confront both its methods and its ends. They will reveal the damage done
by principles that have never been questioned. They will uncover what
is uncomfortable to confront.

Our system of charity doesn't produce the results we are after because there is a flawed ideology at work. Its error flows directly from the
Puritan belief in human depravity. The principal tenets of this ideology
go something like this:

- People who want to work in the nonprofit world should be more
  interested in the good they can do than in the money they can
  make. Those who want material abundance do not have the concerns of the needy at the forefront of their minds.
- Charities should not take risks. They are taking risks with earmarked funds. They should be cautious.
- Charities do not have the luxury to think about the future. Donated money should be spent immediately to alleviate the suffering of others.
- Charities should not waste money on expensive advertising. It is
  money that could otherwise go to the needy.
- Charities should not make mistakes. A mistake means a charity is
  wasting money and waste is immoral.
- No one should seek to earn a profit in charity. Profitmaking is for
  the for-profit sector.
- Charities should maintain a low overhead percentage. This is the
  only way to know that any good is being done. Low overhead is
  moral. High overhead is immoral.

The canon to which these mistaken ideas belong is what I refer to as
nonprofit ideology. It is a dysfunctional mentality based on deprivation.
Our loyalty to it keeps us from getting what we are really after.

*Let me be clear that by "nonprofit ideology" I do not mean the nonprofit sec-
tor. I do not mean nonprofit organizations or the people who work for them.
Nor do I mean the wonderful ideals of a better world that the people who work
in the sector strive after every day. By "nonprofit ideology" I mean the oppressive set of rules that the whole of society has forced on these good people and organizations—the severe restraints we impose on them that keep them separated from the dreams that brought them into the sector in the first place.*

That said, there are other tenets that come from the observation of the
natural behavior of human beings and the fundamental laws of nature.

They are not contrived but predictable. Their validity has been established by nearly three hundred years of capitalist productivity, and if we are serious about curing breast cancer, ending poverty, and advancing the cause of humanity, they warrant our attention:

- If we allow charity to compensate people according to the value they produce, we can attract more leaders of the kind the for-profit sector attracts, and we can produce greater value.
- The more that charities take calculated risks, the better the chance that they will break new ground.
- The more we allow charities to invest in the future instead of only the current fiscal year, the more they will be able to build the future we all want.
- Advertising builds consumer demand. The more that charities are allowed to advertise, the better they can compete with consumer products for the consumer's dollar, and the more money they can raise for the needy.
- The more mistakes a charity makes in good faith, the faster it will learn and the quicker it will be able to solve complex problems. This is the only path to solving problems—one must "fail upward."
- Profit is the key to investment capital. If people could make the same return from investment capital in charity as they can in for-profit investments, charity would raise massive additional investment capital.
- A charity's overhead percentage doesn't give you any data about the good it is doing in the world. If charities focused more on solving the world's problems than on keeping overhead low, more of the world's problems would get solved.

But this is not what we have been taught. Instead, we have been force-fed a set of ideas about doing good that actually accomplish the opposite. They prevent real progress.

Our logic has been sacrificed to ideology. That which we have been taught is good in us—selflessness, the willingness to deprive ourselves—prevents us from doing real good in the world. That which we have been taught should upset our moral compass—profit, capitalism, the free market, the desire for personal material gain—is in fact the fuel that could power stunning change in the world. They could achieve morally superior outcomes.

Our charity is conducted within a context that measures morality by loyalty to the religion—loyalty to the means. It is not conducted within a context of what will produce the best end result and what will not. It is not conducted within the ultimately moral context. Predictably, then, we are taught to feel good or bad on the basis of things that don't make an impact or that unexpectedly make a negative impact, like modest executive salaries, donated equipment, donated advertising, low spending on administration and "overhead," instead of on the basis of the real moral questions, like whether hunger is being ended or cancer is being cured. *We have been taught to judge morality by tactics without regard for the morality of the outcomes.*

For example, we are told by a charity that 80 percent of our donation goes to the cause. The newspapers tell us this is good, simply because it sounds frugal, but regardless of what charitable good is actually being done. Nevertheless, the charity wears that number on its sleeve and takes on a dangerous air of sanctimony.

We learn that someone has made a great deal of money in some charitable endeavor. We are taught to feel morally outraged, regardless of how much benefit the person has achieved. We learn that some charitable director's salary is modest. We are taught that this is good, regardless of the fact that she may be making little progress—regardless of the fact that someone who commanded a salary three times higher could make ten times the difference. What an inferior satisfaction is the good feeling we get from a modest executive salary compared to the feeling we would have if we ended hunger on this earth. Gold stars over church bells. We have settled for scraps.

We are told that a charity's office equipment was donated instead of purchased. We are told this is good, regardless of the fact that the charity has to spend more time fixing broken computers than serving the needy. We learn that a charity's experimental fundraising event funded with donor contributions has failed. We are taught that this is morally reprehensible, regardless of what was learned or what breakthrough was being attempted. Over and over again, the morally inferior choice is labeled superior.

An ambitious reporter puts a sentimental photo of a child with leukemia in the newspaper and asks, "How can you be so cruel as to want to earn a profit from his situation?" I put up the photos of a million others like him and ask, How can you be so shortsighted as to deny me and a thousand others the monetary incentive it would take to devote our life's work to helping these children? You have just robbed them of our talents. What if your moral compass is wrong?

Ironically, by *denying* charity the tools of capitalism while *allowing* the for-profit sector to feast on them, we place charity at a severe disadvantage to the for-profit sector, on every front and at every level. The hands of charity are tied, while the for-profit sector scoops every penny off the economic table. Charity is segregated from the rest of the economic world. And this apartheid is the result of its own ideology. It is in the *name of charity* that capitalism is banished. Indeed, charity could not be undermined with more homage paid to charity.[16] But the principal beneficiary of this charity is the for-profit sector. The poor are left to take some solace in the fact that charity observed all the discrimination with great frugality.

It is a further irony that we prohibit charity from using the tools of capitalism to rectify the very disparities some would claim capitalism creates. *We allow people to make huge profits doing any number of things that harm the poor, but prohibit anyone from making a profit doing anything that will help them.* Want to make a million selling violent video games to kids? Go for it. Want to make a million funding the cure for childhood leukemia? You are a parasite. *The illogic is breathtaking. The ramification is even more so. If free-market ideology could rectify the disparities some claim are created by free-market practices, isn't the nonprofit ideology that obstructs it the problem in the first place?*

The Illusion of Permission

As if this were not enough, the cultural pretense of the past decade is that capitalism in charity *is* encouraged. One of the cruelest and most dangerously disingenuous messages being preached to the nonprofit sector today is that it should act more like business—cruel because we don't allow it to, and dangerous because it creates the illusion that we do, preempting any initiatives for change under the guise of its already being under way.

When charities are told to act more like businesses they are, by and large, being told nothing more than to be more efficient, as if efficiency were a substitute for vision. The term is used in the narrowest sense— read: less money spent on overhead, with no understanding of what "overhead" really is and what it really isn't. Whoever believes that this and this alone is what it means to act like a business never ran a successful one. Great businesses grow on great vision. Efficiency is a secondary matter. How the business people who sit on the boards of our charities have allowed an obsession with efficiency to become conflated with what it means to act like business is one of the great mysteries of modern economic history.

No one in authority is suggesting that we give the nonprofit sector the far-reaching freedom we *really* give to business. There is no new movement demanding that the nonprofit sector place efficiency a distant second to a great vision. It is simply not a discussion that is happening. It is sacrilegious to question the importance of efficiency.

No one is suggesting we open the floodgates of market-based compensation and high-stakes risk taking to charity. No one is suggesting we let charity use our donated dollars to pursue a daring dream, even if it might fail. While business advertises, charity is taught to beg. While business motivates with a dollar, charity is told to motivate with guilt. While business takes chances, charity is expected to be cautious. We measure the success of businesses over the long term, but we want our gratification in charity immediately. We are taught that a return on investment should be offered for making consumer goods, but not for making a better world.

Overlooking Critical Distinctions Separate from the preaching that charity should act more like business, there are a growing number of innovative social entrepreneurs and philanthropists who really *are* experimenting with capitalism to address some of the most vexing social problems of our time. The misleading notion is advanced that this means capitalism has come to charity. But it is being labeled something that it isn't. These reports overlook an important distinction, confusing change occurring in experiments *outside* the sector with some new freedom being given to those *inside* it. Alternatively, they confuse innovative program approaches with the ability of charities to use the tools of capitalism to *expand* those approaches. Or they confuse new measurements of effectiveness with new freedoms to achieve it. But in reality, the 700,000 active charities in America that we are asking to change the world are not being given new freedoms in any of these categories. Great as these new approaches are, they do not address the most critical issue—releasing charities from their anachronistic restraints.

New Philanthropists The new fortunes being made in technology have given rise to a slew of large new grant-making foundations. This is wonderful, but the erroneous leap is made that it signals the merger of capitalism and charity. The reality here is often simply that new capitalists are entering the world of philanthropy, often saddled with the same old ideas about the need for low overhead and low salaries. The only things new about it are the names and faces. Andrew Carnegie was a capitalist turned philanthropist. It didn't mean he integrated the two. We can have an entirely new generation of philanthropists and still be left with seventeenth-century charity.

I was at a meeting with the leaders of Google's new philanthropic efforts where bird flu was being discussed. It is hard to think of a more forward-thinking player than Google. Its foundation is actually funding for-profit social action initiatives (with Google money, which comes with a lot more freedom than funds donated by the public). But for this particular project, which *was* to be funded using traditional mechanisms, it was said that there should be no impression that anyone was earning a profit. But this is the heart of the matter. If there were no opportunity for profit in business, there would *be* no Google. Even great corporate spirits like Google are indoctrinated in these old ideas. Why else would they abandon the profit motive on this most important of all endeavors? But where there is no incentive, how can there be any result that rises to a level any higher than a quaint gesture? *The sick and the poor are dying of quaint gestures. Do we really think it is comforting to the mother of a child who has just died of bird flu to be told that at least no one earned a profit in the failed effort to save her son?*

Flexible Philanthropy That said, a few of these new foundations are giving money to charity with fewer restrictions. Some, to their great credit, understand the need for charities to invest in infrastructure. This alone doesn't mean they have opened the gates to capitalism without restriction. Nevertheless, it is encouraging. Much is made of it in the elite literature studying the cutting edges. But the grants of a handful of innovators on the periphery do not cut the restrictive strings attached to the roughly $300 billion donated annually to charity by society-at-large.[17] The fact that a few lucky grantees are receiving some money without strings attached from a forward-thinking foundation doesn't mean the local soup kitchen, or even those few lucky grantees, will be getting any new freedom from the donating public, which doesn't read the social entrepreneurship articles coming out of think tanks. And none of the new philanthropic efforts are putting up funding to change the donating public's mind. These few foundations are changing the way *they* give, but no one is trying to change the way *everyone* thinks about giving.

Venture Philanthropy There is also a new phenomenon being explored and practiced by some foundations and donors called "venture philanthropy," based loosely on the venture capital funding model of the for-profit sector. Venture philanthropy seeks to measure the effect of a dollar on the actual social problem a charity is established to address, rather than, or in addition to, measuring overhead. In other words, it is focused on the effectiveness of a charity's programs. These efforts are worthwhile, but they don't remotely address the real problem. Finding good charitable programs has never been the problem. The problem has been finding the capital to expand them on a mass scale. It is not for lack of knowing how to feed the hungry that people starve to death. It is for lack of half a trillion discretionary dollars.

We can "venture" into as many cutting-edge pilot program ideas as we want, but until we allow charity to venture into big-league risk-reward and other economic incentives, it won't ever have the capital to apply them on any meaningful scale. A little capital to experiment with programs is hardly the same thing as the freedom to practice capitalism, and a little capital is all venture philanthropy has right now, as compared, not only to the scale of the need, but also even to the size of the donation pool on which nonprofit ideology has its grip. The expansion of venture philanthropy thinking won't change that. It may result in existing funders adopting new measurements, but it won't result in new capital. The current venture philanthropy model isn't trying to find, or even claiming that it is trying to find, a path to the capital we need.

Moreover, there is an unintentional cruelty at work in the demand for charities to be more effective. It is a bit of the blood-from-a-stone syndrome. How can charities become more effective overall if we won't let them use the tools everyone else in the economic world uses as the fundamental *basis* for effectiveness? It is no blessing to throw a charity a million dollars to achieve a result and then tell it that it must apply the same set of seventeenth-century rules that have heretofore left it incapable of achieving the result in the first place. The demand for a crop won't produce anything if you deny a man a plow. It doesn't matter if we change what we're measuring. If we don't change the rules, charities will never be able to measure up.

Micro-Finance What about Grameen *Bank's* micro-financing, for which Muhammad Yunnus won the Nobel Prize? It has brought *billions* in capital to the poor. Isn't that capitalism applied to charity? It is capitalism applied to poverty, but it doesn't bring new economic freedom to the nonprofit sector in the United States. Grameen *Bank* operates in Bangladesh, outside of a traditional American nonprofit context. In the United States, there is a separate and independent Grameen *Foundation* that works to replicate the Grameen model. Grameen *Foundation* in the United States is nonprofit. *It can use the the tools of capitalism to help the poor, but, like every other American nonprofit, it cannot use them to help itself. It cannot use them to increase its scale. It is a revolutionary model for helping the poor bound by our draconian rules for growth.* It is like telling the Wright brothers that their new airplane is a great idea, but they must limit its use to the inside of the hangar.

For example, Grameen Foundation can give people the capital they need to build businesses, but it cannot raise capital in the stock market to increase its ability to provide it. If it were to purchase the services of a high-priced CEO to help mastermind a massive expansion or undertake a major ad campaign to bring in new long-term revenues, either one of which would raise its short-term overhead, our nonprofit mindset would come down on it like a guillotine. Donors would be outraged. So much for the tools of capitalism come to charity. It is a tragic irony of our system that Grameen Foundation's own annual report must go to great pains to reassure donors about how low it keeps its overhead—the very measurement that is the cornerstone of the old ideology and the embodiment of its restraints.[18] If we permitted Grameen Foundation in the United States to spend more on "overhead" it could turn its millions in annual lending[19] to billions, and we could instead be reading about how low we are keeping the level of global poverty.

Social Business What about some of the for-profit businesses that are being started to address social problems? They are amazing. I think they point the way to a new future. But we do charity a disservice when we mistake them for a signal that new economic freedom is coming to charities themselves. The simple fact is they are happening *outside* of the nonprofit sector. A 2008 article on the front page of the business section of the *New York Times* entitled, "A Capitalist Jolt for Charity," writes of a philanthropic couple who were donating millions to an inner-city literacy charity.[20] But, ironically, in order to expand the work, "the once-struggling venture has morphed into a primarily for-profit enterprise." They said that "this needs to be a large business to have a really significant impact. . . . We couldn't do what we're doing as a nonprofit."[21] This is hardly sign of a movement to rescue the nonprofit sector from its ideological prison. It is quite the opposite—a recognition that no rescue party is coming. It is a common-sense strategy on the part of some very smart people to stay away from the prison altogether. But at some point we have to start addressing what's going on inside the gates, because that's where all the donations end up. Three hundred billion dollars in annual giving (not to mention hundreds of millions more in fees from services) and millions of professionals are trapped there, unable to unleash their full potential because of their confinement. Average donors aren't telling them they can use those billions to morph into for-profit companies in order to escape.

A 2007 article in the *Atlantic Monthly* describes the ways Bill Clinton's foundation is helping to organize markets to bring low-cost AIDS drugs to developing countries and characterizes this on its cover as the reinvention of charity. But Bill Clinton himself says in the article, "This is not charity." Bill Clinton's deal making with AIDS pharmaceutical companies is extraordinary, no question about it. But it will not change the fact that an AIDS charity will still be crucified if it tries to attract a pharmaceutical executive with the same kind of pay package Pfeizer can offer him. It is ironic that the very same article that pronounces the reinvention of charity and the embrace of the profit motive closes by saying that many of the young employees of Clinton's foundation will go on to decades-long careers in "non-profits."[22] It is precisely this basis that needs reinvention.

Moreover, examples like this often exist in celebrity or affluent bubbles. The influence Bill Clinton has to do things in a radical new way is not enjoyed by a mid-level nonprofit executive who has to comply with the rules as they are in order to keep her job. Furthermore, the permission a billionaire has to do things in his own way, with his own money, doesn't signal an endorsement of these practices by the system-at-large, or sanction their use with the donating public's money. Let the first hunger crusader be paid a multimillion-dollar salary, and the ensuing media crusade will soon inform us that the reinvention of charity is not close to being under way.

If a high-profile captain of business went down to skid row in Los Angeles and said, "I can get all these homeless people into housing within ten years, but I want to be paid fifty million dollars to do it," he'd be vilified. But the long-term economic benefit of this achievement would be worth far more than $50 million. If he said, on the other hand, "I want to be paid fifty million dollars to sell five hundred million dollars worth of movies"—a few of them even about matters of social concern—his praises would be sung on the cover of *Time* magazine.

Literature Finally, with respect to the trade literature, there is an illusion that a new discussion is happening about changing charity, but in reality the discussion is about helpful ways to cope with the system as it is. One sees well-meaning and often very helpful management book titles with phrases akin to "Making Your Nonprofit Better," "Better Results for Nonprofits," and "Taking Nonprofits to the Next Level." Good as they are, they concede the fundamental validity of the nonprofit basis of the system even in their titles. Some border on celebrating it. We are having a discussion about how to make the best of an abusive spouse, when what we need is a new mate altogether.

Grace

We have soldiered along for centuries without questioning the ideology that underpins our notions of charity. We have done as we have been told, without asking why. Even the most radical among us have been moralized, coerced, or otherwise hypnotized into conformity. Here we have an ideology around which evangelical fundamentalists and radical feminists alike can rally. Here we have a doctrine on which there is precisely no difference of opinion between Ralph Nader and Dick Cheney. We have debated everything from the death penalty to gay marriage to the existence of God, but we have not questioned our approach to charity or any of the rules by which we have been forced to conduct it. It is a religion with no unbelievers.

It is time to start questioning it. It is time for a transformative conversation, heated and controversial though it may be, to replace the impotent one we *have* been having about how to manage within the existing dysfunction. We need a conversation worthy of our true intelligence and potential. A conversation about setting charity free. Free to experiment. To risk. To make mistakes. To think in the long term. To envision. To build. To spend. Yes, to spend. To dream. And to make those dreams real, in the same way Nike and Nintendo and all the other free-market enterprises do, and in pursuit of goals far less urgent. To achieve this we need full liberation, not moderation of the existing prison. We must liberate charity, without qualification, to use the same tools of capitalism and the free market that we allow business to use and that some claim have created the very disparities charity is supposed to rectify.

Our expectations of charity have grown enormously, but our understanding of it has remained primitive. Centuries ago the role of charity was narrow—to bring food or clothing to the sick or the needy in one's own village, on a face-to-face basis, or, in many cases, to convert souls. *Over time, however, we have thrust upon charity the responsibility for solving the world's greatest and most complex macro problems, from curing cancer to ending hunger.*

Charity has made the transition from individual to industry, but *our thinking* has not. The thinking that applies to helping one's neighbor will not suffice for solving the world's great problems. Micro beliefs are not relevant to macro issues. Indeed, beliefs that may make sense and may even work at the micro level can be nonsensical and disastrous on the macro level.

The word "charity" comes from the Greek *charos,* for "grace" or "love." It is a far cry from "nonprofit." To be charitable in the twenty-first century means to abandon charity as we know it. It is to summon the grace and the love to embrace a new idea, one that we have constructed ourselves, based on what *we* want to accomplish.

Hernando De Soto declares in *The Mystery of Capital* that "capitalism stands alone as the only feasible way to rationally organize a modern economy. At this moment in history, no responsible nation has a choice."[23] The nation of charity is no different. Isolated acts of individual kindness are no match for world hunger. Capitalism and the free market are the only engines that can solve problems of that magnitude, and we must summon the love and the grace to let them.

A Model of Christian Charity

Where does this nonprofit ideology come from, and how does it perpetuate itself? At a tactical level, there is a system that teaches us to think and behave this way. It is fragmented, without central control, not entirely intentional, and largely not even conscious of itself. It consists of the media, government regulating agencies, grant-making foundations, and various charity "watchdog" agencies. Together they constitute an arbitrary substitute for a thoughtful system of education on the subject. We receive no formal education in charity. Our schools teach math and English, woodshop and typing, but nothing about charity. Consequently, we learn everything we know about it, accurate or otherwise, through the dribs and drabs that come at us randomly through this system—the media is the principal spigot.

Ironically, one of the most important components of the system is the very group it undermines—that is, the roughly 700,000 active charities in America themselves (of the 1,064,191 registered with the IRS as of 2006).[24] For fear of being ostracized, they try to conform, through often counterproductive self-sacrifice and, in some cases, accounting contortions, to unrealistic standards set by the watchdogs and the media. This conformity has the circular effect of validating the underlying ideology and the standards that enforce it. More and more charitable organizations choose a morally inferior path because they are rewarded for it or, at least, not penalized. The quest for this pseudo-morality, instead of the quest to end hunger and cure cancer, becomes the primary objective.

The most important component of the system is, of course, society at large—each of us—which, without understanding the damage that it does, demands of charity that it be faithful to the ideology.

Why have we not changed our thinking? Because we believe what has become familiar. As John Kenneth Galbraith said, "People approve most of what they best understand . . . economic and social behavior are complex, and to comprehend their character is mentally tiring."[25] Moreover, the system is oppressive. Threatened by any possibility of real change, it suppresses discourse. It intimidates with a moral stick. It discourages thought, inquiry, truth, and possibility. This is doubly dangerous, because nonprofit organizations are supposed to be society's agents of change. Instead, they are coerced into a kind of servitude to the status quo. It is a frightening sight to behold—an otherwise fearless, countercultural gay activist, nose rings, tattoos and all, ready to take on the Pentagon, cowering at the sound of an efficiency-rating agency's footsteps.

The New England Puritans

Where did this system get its beliefs? Our rules and ideas about charity began their journey into formalism with Puritan constructs. These constructs placed reason and results second to a host of other priorities, including self-sacrifice, self-denial, self-accusation, suffering, self-criticism, and the salvation of the soul. To understand charity in America today one has to understand its Puritan roots, and the Puritans' Calvinist beliefs, especially their commitment to "a view of human depravity."[26] Historian Amanda Porterfield writes in "Protestant Missionaries: Pioneers of American Philanthropy":

American Protestant missionary work provided the organizational and intel-
lectual context out of which many other forms of American philanthropy
have emerged. . . . American Protestant missionary history developed from
the religious worldview of the New England Puritans, and especially from
their desire to be part of God's new Israel and its manifestation in North
America.[27]

Most forms of early Puritan charity involved face-to-face giving and
assistance that typically came hand in hand with efforts to convert souls
to Christianity. Over time the features changed, but the influence remained. Porterfield adds:

In the early twentieth century, the progressive side of this tradition of missionary activism and world reform was transmuted into scientific forms of
philanthropy that helped to shape . . . the agendas of numerous private agencies dedicated to education and social reform. Thus, Calvinist patterns of
thought and behavior proved to be relevant and adaptable to different situa-
tions and cultural contexts.[28]

Historian Stephen Innes, in *Creating the Commonwealth,* writes,
"New England represents the only historical case in which Calvinist,
sectarian Protestantism was institutionalized at the very founding of
the social order."[29] Historian Perry Miller notes that, among all the
"isms" that have influenced American culture, from rational liberalism
to frontier individualism, "Puritanism has been perhaps the most conspicuous, the most sustained, and the most fecund," and that its force
has been "accentuated because it was the first of these traditions to be
fully articulated, and because it has inspired certain traits which have
persisted long after the vanishing of the original creed."[30] Miller asserts
that "without some understanding of Puritanism, it may safely be said,
there is no understanding of America."[31]

Winthrop's Sermon

What was the Puritans' construction of charity? John Winthrop's famous sermon, "A Modell of Christian Charity," provides a record. His
words reverberated in other sermons for another century and a half.[32] "A
Modell of Christian Charity" has been cited and recited by presidents,
preachers, poets, and teachers ever since. It is a cornerstone of the
American liturgy. It outlines the City upon a Hill that Winthrop hoped
to build—"one in which godly men and women, united by mutual

respect and love, labored together to better discern and advance God's will."[33] Winthrop scholar Francis J. Bremer writes, "To realize his ambition he would have to confront and overcome New World nature and natives, threats from abroad, and challenges from heretics and zealots within the community."[34] The principles by which he beseeched his fellows to live were designed to help him achieve that.

Some historians argue that by "Christian Charity" Winthrop meant Christian love, not literally almsgiving. This is rebutted by the fact that the sermon very specifically addresses almsgiving. Moreover, Winthrop didn't use the word "love"; he used the word "charity." Whatever he may have *meant* became flattened over time by what he actually *wrote* and *said*. Therefore, "A Modell of Christian Charity" is as important for the definition it gave to the word "charity" as the definition it gave to the underlying mentality.

The sermon disgraces self-interest and profit: "But if our heartes shall turne away soe that wee will not obey, but shall be seduced and worship . . . other Gods our pleasures, and proffitts, and [serve] them; . . . wee shall surely perishe out of the good Land whether wee passe over this vast Sea to possesse it."[35] It can hardly be a coincidence, then, that the charitable industry is distinguished not by the good works that it does, or the urgent nature of its mission, but by which way it sways on the question of *profit*. This would otherwise seem an arbitrary feature on which to focus. Why not the "urgency sector" or the "compassion sector"?

Innes writes that in Winthrop's view man's tendency toward materialism was not inherent in his nature, but was both the cause and consequence of Adam's fall from grace; Winthrop believed that only after Adam's fall "was universal love replaced by self love" (self love being a negative quality) and that after his fall "men and women in their corruption acquired an insatiable acquisitive propensity. Thus the economic motive, what became the drive to expand capital, originated in Adam's sin. For Calvinists, it could only be kept in check by the (unmerited) infusion of divine grace."[36]

The problem was that at the same time Winthrop was disparaging profit and self-interest in his model of charity, he and his fellow Puritans were dependent on them for the economy they were about to build. They believed profit to be good at the same time they believed it to be bad. Charity offered a way to compartmentalize this frustrating contradiction. The sermon was not entitled "A Model of *Economic Development*." They needed no lectures on that, as we will see below. It was designed to *compensate* for their model of economic development. It was designed to compensate for their self-interest. As a by-product of disparaging profit, it drew a dividing line that was essential to the Puritan construction of society itself. Charity was its name. The notion was this: on one side of the line, we will deny our self-interest and that will make our self-interest acceptable on the other. Charity gave Puritans the psychological permission to engage in their natural self-interest. Self-deprivation and charity were therefore made synonymous.

Ironically, *in the very same sermon,* Winthrop writes, "It is not only lawful but necessary to lay up" (accumulate wealth) in order to "have ready upon such occasions, as the Lord shall call for them" goods to give to the needy. He adds, "A man must lay up for posterity, the fathers lay up for posterity and children, and he is worse than an infidel that provideth not for his own."[37]

Innes writes that on the eve of the voyage on the *Arbella,* Winthrop himself "underscored the opportunities for fishing, fur trading, and commercial husbandry, as well as 'making pitch, Tarr, Pottashes, and sope ashes'" and that Winthrop "expressed the hope that the 'Trade of Furres' alone 'may be Brought out of that Continent to the valew' of no less than '£30,000 per annum at least.'"[38]

The Puritans were the developers of America's early capitalism. Winthrop and his fellow travelers established their new settlement as a corporation—the Massachusetts Bay Company. Innes suggests that they "were bearers of a culture that was already capitalist when they arrived in the New World."[39] "The Puritan migrants to New England were drawn predominantly from the most commercial regions of the mother country."[40] Their settlement in Massachusetts became the New World's first capitalist commonwealth.[41] It succeeded because "it freed the economy of anachronistic restraints; and it recognized the link between land ownership and productive labor."[42] In other words, the link between self-interest and productivity. Innes adds that "Massachusetts settlers became the leading commercial people on the continent from the mid-seventeenth century onward."[43]

In commerce, the Puritans glorified profit making. To understand how much, one has to understand the concept of "calling," which was the underpinning of their social ethic. They believed that each person was born with a calling, whether that was to be a tailor or a ship maker, and that it was one's duty to God to find and follow that calling with great discipline and energy for the greater good. "Living in the Puritan commonwealth meant working to support it with a relentlessness that may indeed have been historically aberrant."[44] The Puritans took this idea so seriously that they actually passed a law in 1642 that threatened to take away people's children if they were not "brought up in a legitimate calling."[45] This pursuit was one way they measured morality. It was not just neighbor-to-neighbor assistance or the conversion of souls that defined it. The degree to which one pursued one's calling with vigor was also a definition of virtue, because it could contribute to the community good, but also because it produced excess wealth, which could be given to the poor.

The Puritans believed financial success was given by God;[46] that outward success was a sign of their rightness with God and that if they pursued their calling with discipline and fervor, they would be rewarded with material success; and that by cleaving to God they would infallibly gain prosperity.[47] Max Weber, in his famous thesis on the relationship of capitalism to Puritanism, writes "indeed, that a particularly high level of profit could be the direct *product* of religious [uprightness]."[48] He wrote that the degree to which one's calling was pleasing to God depended on "private economic *'profitability.'* For if the God that the Puritan sees as acting in all the fortunes of life reveals to one of his children the opportunity to make a profit, then there is purpose in this."[49] Innes observes, "There were complaints of a peculiarly calculating sort of profit-seeking in New England, as distinguished from other parts of America, as early as 1632."[50]

However, in order for the pursuit of wealth to be considered moral, it had to be pursued with total denial of self, yet another critical way that morality and self-deprivation became conflated. Profit seeking had to be devoid of self-interest: "People should devote themselves to profitmaking—*without* succumbing to the temptations of profit."[51] Innes describes the central tension as "the need to show 'diligence in worldly business and yet deadness to the world,'"[52] and writes that "profit seeking was fine—indeed it was morally imperative—so long as it was grounded in communal necessity."[53] No wonder they had to compartmentalize it. The practical difference between accumulating profit for oneself and not accumulating it for oneself was so subtle that, as historian Stephen Foster put it, it "could be grasped only by a mental contortionist."[54]

At the same time Winthrop was demonizing profit in a sermon about charity, one of his contemporaries and a highly regarded Puritan minister, John Cotton, was espousing it when he talked about commerce: "For a man to [take] all opportunities to do be doing something . . . and loseth no opportunity, go any way and bestir himselfe for profit, this will he doe most diligently in his calling."[55] In 1632, Winthrop's trading partner predicted that "'we shall raise good profit not only by our fishing trade . . . but by hemp, flax, pitch, tar, potashes, soap ashes, masts, pipe staves, clapboard (and iron we hope).'"[56]

Perry Miller, in his definitive work *The New England Mind: The Seventeenth Century* writes of the Puritans that "devotion to business, accumulation of estates, acquisition of houses and lands: these were the duties of Christians" and that one should "employ their estate 'so that, it should become a larger estate.'"[57] Richard Baxter, a Presbyterian divine at the time said it all:

> If God show you a way in which you may lawfully *get more* than in another way . . . if you refuse this, and choose the less gainful way, *you [violate] one of the ends of your calling, and you refuse to be God's steward . . . you may labor to be rich for God,* though not for the flesh and sin.[58]

But there was a problem. Materialism and "worldliness" were *inescapable* by-products of the prosperity they created. The Puritans feared that as people became more prosperous they would become less moral. The Puritan concept of calling "always tempted him to get out of his place, to strive to grow richer, and eventually seek profit for himself and not for God and community."[59] According to Miller, "The more everybody labored, the more society was transformed. The more diligently the people applied themselves . . . the more they produced a decay in religion and a corruption of morals, a society they did not want. . . . The wrong thing was also the right thing."[60] Making matters even more complicated, they had a *duty* to pursue the wrong thing. Innes adds that "industry, temperance and self-discipline might well lead to the temptations of wealth, but a Puritan who foreswore these virtues was no longer a Puritan."[61] Miller captures the contradiction:

> While the ministers were excoriating the behavior of merchants, laborers, and frontiersmen, they never for a moment condemned merchandizing, laboring, or expansion of the frontier. They berated the consequences of progress, but never progress; deplored the effects of trade upon religion, but did not ask men to desist from trading; arraigned men of great estates, but not estates.[62]

These contradictions created an enormous philosophical and psychological ambiguity. Innes writes, "Industriousness and frugality brought wealth, which in turn brought temptation and worldliness. . . . At the core of the Puritan ethic was a tension that was at once extraordinarily productive economically and tremendously difficult psychologically."[63] How were the Puritans to deal with this tension? Innes summarizes their solution:

> The Bay Colonists established a market economy and erected a moral-cultural system and civic society to supplement and control it. They authorized a regime of private property and freedom of contract but endeavored to see that it was checked and balanced by moral witness and civic restraint. Preachers such as Thomas Shepard (1605–1649) never tired of reminding the saints that self-interest was "a raging Sea which would overwhelm all if [it] have not bankes." . . . The saints attempted to bridge what Emile Durkheim called the "duality of human existence," the co-existence in the same person of interest-motivated and altruistic-motivated action.[64]

Charity, as Winthrop was outlining it on the *Arbella*, was to be an essential component of the "moral-cultural system" the Puritans would use to "supplement and control" the market economy. Innes observes, "The Puritan covenant provided an essential counterweight to capitalist development."[65] He adds, "If, as Henry Adams later opined, 'resistance to something' is the defining New England trait, its sources likely lie in the early colonists' tortured attempts to prevent the Protestant ethic from turning into the spirit of capitalism."[66] The resistant label "*non-profit*" makes sense in this context.

Innes concludes that the Puritans were successful at creating an oxymoron—moral capitalism. *But in doing so, they necessarily denied its reciprocal—capitalistic morality.* Winthrop believed that "piety and profit . . . could go hand in hand."[67] But by sentencing charity to be a mediating influence on commerce, the Puritans made this only half-true. They left out the half that now consists of some 700,000 active charities and the millions of people who work for them. The Puritans were not saying you can (a) make money in business and give it to the poor *and* (b) make money directly assisting the poor. They drew a line that implicitly said that you could make money on this side of it but not the other. Your piety could come from your wealth, but your wealth could not come from your piety. They didn't actually say this. They didn't have to. By making charity a penance for making money, it became axiomatic. *How could you possibly make money helping the poor if helping the poor was your penance for making money?*

So in the Puritans' universe, charity is necessarily segregated. It cannot use the same tools as commerce. It cannot use self-interest or profit as motivation. That would destroy its ameliorative and redemptive purpose. Charity satisfied the need for a sanctuary of economic morality. As Innes states, "The belief that surplus wealth should be put to socially benevolent purposes—shared with the community and the church—helped restrain the Protestant ethic from turning into the [modern] spirit of capitalism."[68] At least in their minds. While the Puritan concept of "the calling" also made one's work holy and redemptive, it created wealth. Since wealth could not be focused on oneself, charity's redemptive quality became unique. "Sin entered not through acquisitiveness, but through *self-regarding* acquisitiveness."[69] Charity became a separate universe, necessarily devoid of self-regard, to which the Puritans could travel to demonstrate their goodness. This universe survives today. A corporate titan can do any number of things in his capitalist compartment that a moral purist might find immoral, then redeem himself by making a large gift to charity. But all of this is artificial.

The Puritans knew that self-interest worked. They knew that a free market, rather than a restrained market, worked. And they knew that the accumulation of capital worked. They watched it transform their society. Instead of allowing the tools of capitalism to work wonders in the application of their benevolence, they prescribed a benevolence based on self-denial, free of capitalist methods, to compensate for their capitalist tendencies. They created two worlds where there was only ever one. This forced on them the artificial notion that the way to solve the problems of one world was somehow different than the way to solve the problems in the other. Miller describes the Puritan period accurately as "a chapter in the emergence of the capitalist mentality, showing how intelligence copes with—or more cogently, how it fails to cope with—a change it simultaneously desires and abhors."[70]

We continue to live in these two worlds today. Capitalism is permitted in one and not the other. Despite the knowledge that every great commercial achievement in history has succeeded because of one set of methods, we prescribe an opposite set for this other world of suffering and need. They don't work.

Hernando De Soto begins *The Mystery of Capital* by quoting the following inquiry, which is relevant here:

> The key problem is to find out why that sector of society of the past, which I would not hesitate to call capitalist, should have lived as if in a bell jar, cut off from the rest; why was it not able to expand and conquer the whole of society? . . . [Why was it that] a significant rate of capital formation was possible

only in certain sectors and not in the whole market economy of the time?"—
Fernand Braudel, *The Wheels of Commerce*[71]

By abhorring the realities of their own nature, the Puritans cut charity off from the very market incentives that would go on to build the
nation's entire system of commerce and that indeed built their own.

This dividing line was not entirely abstract. Winthrop's sermon pre-
scribes two different laws for governing economic exchange: "the Way
of Justice" and "the Way of Mercy." He says that a person should take a
different economic approach when bargaining with the needy as opposed to bargaining with an economic equal. (For instance, one should
not ask for repayment of a loan from a man who cannot afford to repay
it—in such a case, the non-needy were expected to give the money
freely.) But the application of the same law today is unjust. In Puritan
times, people gave directly to the needy, without using brokers. This is
no longer possible on any meaningful scale. Charity is no longer an exchange between the non-needy and the needy. It is an exchange between
the *non-needy* (donors) and the *non-needy* (the charity work force) to
provide services *to the needy*. It is an exchange between equals to help the
needy. It is no different than the exchange between those who buy cars
and those who make them. A law that was meant to provide an economic discount to the needy in face-to-face transactions is now improperly exploited to expect nonprofit sector workers to provide a wage discount to wealthy donors (and other non-needy donors), who are in
essence buying a service from them, which they use their labor to provide. The donating public (including its most wealthy members) expects the nonprofit work force to extend to it the law of mercy. But it
was never intended that such a law be applied in this way.

Beyond his rejection of profit, Winthrop pronounces suffering and
need as inevitable. As cited above, "God almightie . . . hath soe disposed
of the Condicion of mankinde, as in all times some must be rich some
poore. . . . All men being thus (by divine providence) rancked into two
sortes, riche and poore."[72]

It is logical that the Puritans would overlook capitalism, the free market, self-interest, and indeed anything else as models for eradicating
poverty. They never imagined that the condition could or should be
eradicated in the first place. What residue from that worldview limits
our imaginations today? Is it possible that we don't look to the models
that could eliminate problems because we can't imagine them being
eradicated either?

I referred earlier to the irrationality of a system that blames capitalism for the inequities in our society but refuses to let charity use capitalism to rectify them, the illogic of being willing to pay people good money to do things that might hurt the poor, but not to do things that might help them. It is as if they are not entitled to or deserving of the resource it would take to pay them. Again, there is a feeling that some kind of economic segregation is also at work here. The segregation makes sense if Puritanism is at its root. Not only does it satisfy the rule of self-sacrifice, it satisfies a need to keep the segregation in place. Richard Gross writes in "Giving in America: From Charity to Philanthropy" that "Winthrop's vision of charity was premised on the existence of inequality; differences and distinctions among men were immutable parts of the divine order. Indeed, such diversity was essential to God's benevolent design."[73] Bremer captures the irony in describing a contemporary portrait of Winthrop:

> [It] shows a man who dressed well, as befitted his station. His upper garment, a silk doublet, was black—a sign not of puritanism but of wealth, since it was a difficult and thus expensive color to achieve with natural dyes. It was accented with an elaborate linen ruff trimmed with lace and with linen cuffs, both the ruff and cuffs likely made from lawn, a particularly fine and expensive form of linen. In his one hand he is holding a silk glove.[74]

In 1651, the Massachusetts General Court, upset that "men or women of meane condition, educations, and callinges should take upon them[selves] the garbe of gentlemen," banned the wearing of such clothing by anyone with an estate worth less than £200.[75]

What would such people have done had poverty been eradicated? Their construction of the world would have disintegrated. They needed the poor as an object of their benevolence. This is how God constructed the world. Winthrop's sermon says that the division between rich and poor exists so that God might "[exercise] his graces" in the rich—"theire [love,] mercy, [gentleness, temperance] etc.," and might develop "in the poore and inferiour sorte, theire faith patience, obedience etc."[76] If this is not our influence, why then has a system that ensures the ability to make a benevolent gesture not been abandoned for one that ends the need for a gesture in the first place? Businesses make commitments to daring goals on a regular basis. What charity can we name that says we will end such-and-such problem by such-and-such date? This kind of vision was not part of the Puritans' construction, even as they were imagining visions of a City upon a Hill. It does not seem presently to be part of ours.

No self-interest and inevitable suffering. This is the essence of the Puritans' construction of charity as it applies to us today. Some will say the essence of Winthrop's sermon was love. It was trying to be, but it too was impossibly undermined by its context and the rules that context demanded. And so our love is undermined by its legacy.

Beyond the Sermon—Self-Sacrifice

Beyond what Winthrop wrote, Puritan beliefs offer additional insights. Self-sacrifice and suffering were cornerstones of the Puritan philosophy. Self-accusation was the "central" phrase of New England literature.[77] In Innes's conclusion to *Creating the Commonwealth* he writes:

> In no other colony could the most industrious women and men, who throughout their lifetimes had striven to "improve [their] Time and Talents for God's glory," daily lacerate themselves with accusations of "selfishness, sensuality, unbeleef, inordinate love to creatures, etc." and the overwhelming conviction that they were—"and ever have been"—the most "unproffitable" of the Lord's servants.[78]

Renunciation of self-pride was an important feature of American missionaries. "Self-criticism was central in this mythology."[79] Porterfield notes:

> American missionary thought involved a strong investment in self-criticism that was rooted in the biblical concern about the need for awareness of sin and, more specifically, in the Puritan preoccupation with self-assessment. This investment in self-criticism required individuals to actively search out "prideful" motives in themselves and renounce them.[80]

Feelings or demonstrations of self-love were considered sinful. Laurence Friedman and Mark McGarvie point out that "Puritan society required the subordination of individual or selfish interests to the good of the whole."[81] It should come as no surprise centuries later that the residue of such beliefs would be a prohibition on monetary incentive or anything that smacks of concern for self.

Efficiency

The Puritans were notoriously preoccupied with efficiency. This revealed itself most conspicuously in their obsession with the methodical use of their time.[82] It was Benjamin Franklin (himself an important figure in

American philanthropy and the son of a strict Calvinist father) who wrote, "Remember, *that time is money*."[83] According to Innes:

> Anglo-American Puritanism in particular, "saturated its believers with an acute sense of the dangers of idleness, enjoining them to guard against the misspence of time and to improve the passing moment, each of which, in the end, had to be accounted for in heaven."[84]

He quotes the Reverend Joseph Hall declaring that "'nothing is more precious than time.' Nothing shall 'abide a reckoning more strict and fearfull.' The Almighty 'plagues the losse of a short time, with a revenge beyond all times.'"[85] Small wonder that we focus today on "efficiency measures" in charity, which purportedly tell us which charities are wasteful and which are not, rather than focus on which charities are or are not alleviating suffering or making real, measurable improvements in their communities. When combined with the tendency toward self-accusation, these roots may also explain why the nonprofit sector is so quick to police itself with these measures and chastise itself and its own when they are not strictly met.

Moreover, the Puritans were notoriously frugal. It is irrational that, as a matter of principle, we would think it morally superior for a charity to have a computer donated rather than to buy one, especially if the donated computer reduces productivity. But it makes sense if we are captive to Puritan traditions.

Male Domination

Puritan culture was dominated by men. Howard Zinn writes that the first colonies were "controlled by priests, by governors, by male heads of families."[86] This left women with responsibility for much of what was then considered charity. Innes makes note of "women's role in exercising charity (personal responsibility for one's neighbors)."[87] Women also disproportionately filled the pews of local churches, which meant they were disproportionately being reminded of their depravity and of their need to be self-depriving on behalf of others. "From the 1660s onward, church membership in most New England towns became progressively feminized; no first-generation church admitted more men than women in any single decade from the 1660s to the end of the century."[88]

Porterfield describes how these factors affected women's involvement in early forms of charity: "The missionary proved her worthiness to be educated through her willingness to suffer on behalf of others.

This commitment to self-sacrifice compensated for the elevation in status associated with advanced education and new opportunities for employment."[89]

Innes makes a critical point: "By the closing decades of the seventeenth century, women members outnumbered men by more than two to one in New England congregations, and ministers were taking note of this in rhetoric that later would be associated with the doctrine of separate spheres."[90] The doctrine of separate spheres was a system:

> Crafted in the early nineteenth century from the Revolutionary-era notion of republican motherhood. Men, physically and mentally strong, were destined for the world of "war, work, and politics"; women, naturally weaker but morally purer, were meant for the home, "marriage, motherhood, domestic joys and charities."[91]

History records the overwhelming influence of women in building the nation's charitable infrastructure. Kathleen McCarthy, in "Women and Political Culture," writes that around the time of the Revolution, women

> Exercised significant economic roles under the mantle of what would now be termed *nonprofit entrepreneurship*. After the Revolution, small groups of elite women began to test the boundaries of revolutionary egalitarianism by creating charitable institutions of their own.[92]

Toward the end of the eighteenth century, "women's charities and asylums began to appear in the larger seacoast cities like Philadelphia and New York, providing charity and employment for poor women with families and asylums for dependent children."[93] It is telling that in the index to *Charity, Philanthropy, and Civility in American History,* edited by Friedman and McGarvie, the listing with the second-largest number of subheadings is "Women." That with the most is "Philanthropy" itself.[94]

This further solidifies the notion of a segregated civil society; not only does the Puritan influence divide charity from the rest of the world along economic distinctions, it divides it by gender as well. A 2002 *Chronicle of Philanthropy* article reported, "Seven of 10 workers at independent-sector organizations are female."[95] Moreover, and more important, it establishes the for-profit sector as dominant over charity—superior, patriarchal. Charity is subservient to a male-controlled construction of society. Here a chastity belt becomes a particularly powerful symbol. It must be more than coincidence that the Puritans were

Calvinists and that Calvin's primary influence was St. Augustine of Hippo, whose *Confessions* reads like a twelve-step sexual inventory and is primarily a book of self-criticism for the indulgence of the sexual aspects of his nature. How uncanny too that the words "charity" and "chastity" bear such a striking resemblance to one another. The origin of "chastity" is Middle English—from the Old French *chastete,* which in turn derives from the Latin *castus,* for "morally pure."[96] There, too, is our means-based definition of charity, exactly. How sad that the meaning of "charity" is grace, but the meaning we give to it is the definition of "chastity."

This construction, as expected, takes form today in all the ways we have been describing—it is perfectly analogous to a male-dominated relationship: charities cannot take chances, they cannot have the same level of compensation as business, they must be supervised and measured by their efficiency, and we must always be on the lookout for how they spend our money. The fact that we will not allow charities to use the same *tools* as business may be explained in large part simply by the fact that we perceive and regard them as female, and apply to them, and to the suffering masses of the world, all of the same discriminations we apply to women.

Conversion Anxiety

One of the most important Calvinist beliefs was that of election—that God had preordained which individuals He would save and which He would not. The elect were actually referred to as the "saints." Human beings could not change their destiny. They could live a virtuous life consistent with that of someone they believed was predestined to be saved, but they could never really know if they were one of the chosen, and no amount of good behavior could change God's original choice. Calvin wrote:

> God once established by his eternal and unchangeable plan those whom he long before determined once for all to receive into salvation, and those whom, on the other hand, he would devote to destruction . . . with respect to the elect, this plan was founded upon his freely given mercy, without regard to human worth; . . . but . . . he has barred the door of life to those whom he has given over to damnation.[97]

The anxiety of not knowing whether one was one of God's chosen people—"conversion anxiety," as it is called—was overwhelming. To calm this anxiety, people had to prove that they were at least worthy: "the *failure* to strive was conclusive evidence that one had not yet been offered saving grace."[98] Again, charity provided a sanctuary and a means. The fulfillment of one's obligation to others was one of the "preconditions for elect status."[99] Porterfield writes, "As the Puritan tradition developed in America, strenuous self-sacrifice in the cause of missionary work was a favored means of trying to reach this bar."[100] The legacy of this anxiety may demystify a host of our illogical restrictions on charity, from limits on compensation to prohibition on profits or investment return, even to limits on the resources a charity can use to get its job done.

An ironic side effect of the doctrine of election was that it allowed wealth to become a potential indicator that one had been elected. Wealth was evidence of divine grace. What once in the Catholic church had been a sin, suddenly, for Calvinists became a sign.[101] But in order to be elected, one also had to disavow any interest in self or any wealth acquired out of self-interest. So election contributed to, if it did not create, the central Puritan psychological dilemma.

As we try to understand how we got to a system that is more concerned with the morality of tactics than the morality of outcomes, Porterfield offers the following profound conclusion about Puritan-inspired missionaries:

> Motivated by the effort to master anxiety about their own unworthiness . . .
> many nineteenth-century missionaries seemed to measure benevolence more
> in terms of their own heroic acts of self-sacrifice than in terms of what the
> people they served said they needed or wanted.[102]

We might do well to keep this finding in mind when we take a closer look at charity in contemporary America.

One might argue that the Puritans were influenced by things more powerful than, or as powerful as, their anxiety—that their desire to do good was as real in their hearts as it is in ours. That may well be true, but we cannot know how distracted they were by what was on their minds. You don't have much time to explore the impulses of your heart when you are constantly consumed by a fear as fantastic as that of eternal damnation. These were the same people who executed women suspected of witchcraft. In fact, Cotton Mather, an influential Puritan minister from Massachusetts, described by historian Robert Bremner in his classic *American Philanthropy* as "the chief exponent of do-goodism in Colonial America" and "one of the commanding figures in the history of American philanthropy," is best remembered for his persecution of witches.[103] Three of the five judges at the Salem witch trials were members of his church.[104]

Furthermore, the Puritans believed that in "giving" the gift of Christ to Native Americans, they were entitled to take their land. Again, Winthrop wrote "A Modell of Christian Charity" while on his way to the New World "to possesse it."[105] Howard Zinn writes that Winthrop:

> Created the excuse to take Indian land by declaring the area legally a "vacuum." The Indians, he said, had not "subdued" the land, and therefore had only a "natural" right to it, but not a "civil right." A "natural right"did not have legal standing.[106]

As governor, John Winthrop wrote dispassionately of a pilgrim attack on the same Naragansett Indians, stating that "they had commission to put to death the men of Block Island . . . to take possession of the Island [and to demand] some of their children as hostages, which if they should refuse, they were to obtain it by force."[107] This he believed was God's will. Winthrop used Indian slaves himself.[108] The Reverend Cotton Mather, in describing a pilgrim raid on a Pequot Indian village in which the wigwams were burned to the ground, writes, "It was supposed that no less than 600 Pequot souls were brought down to hell that day."[109] A century of the decimation of Native American tribes hardly argues for the overpowering influence of Puritans' hearts over their beliefs. At the very least, it has to make us question whether we want our system of charity based on theirs.

Conclusion

Throughout the late 1700s and into the 1800s, the Puritans' personal and religious forms of charity gave way to more professional and, in some cases, secular efforts. In these later years distinctions developed between those aspects of Protestant missionary work related to the salvation of souls and those related to issues of social justice. This process reached a climax in 1932 with a report funded by John D. Rockefeller entitled "Re-Thinking Missions," which definitively separated the two areas. But liberal Protestants did not abandon their commitment to charitable enterprise. According to Porterfield:

The liberals simply stepped out of the evangelical confines of missionary work and into new philanthropic agencies funded by the Rockefeller, Ford, and Carnegie Foundations, or into academic research in anthropology or religious studies, or into development programs funded by the U.S. government.[110]

She concludes:

> The American pioneers of scientific philanthropy came out of a culture saturated with an energetic commitment to world reform that had its roots in Calvinism and Protestant Christianity. Whereas they turned away from the business of preaching repentance for sin, escape from hellfire and damnation, and acceptance of Christ as a personal savior, these liberal philanthropists were like missionaries in deriving power and prestige from their efforts to reconstruct the world.[111]

The values by which the Puritans were guided are the root of the history of *our* charity. That history offers no evidence of any *fundamentally* intervening influence since. While one could argue that the dogma has been significantly tempered, the context is still there. One can modify one's view that the world is flat—"Well, it is not as flat as we originally thought"—but that is quite a distance from believing that the world is round. Indeed, such modifications make the basic context more palatable, which is perhaps more dangerous than outright extremism. They keep the system in place under the pretense of its being gone. To say that it might be okay to pay someone working for a charity a little more money is hardly opening the gates of the free market. The Puritan beliefs have become less extreme and less dramatic, to be sure, but they have not been fundamentally transformed. There has been no movement toward the rejection of self-sacrifice as the road to social change. Indeed, it is still the road prescribed.

To conclude this brief history, it is clear that the Puritan fingerprint is all over our present convictions about charity. I have not written an exhaustive history of philanthropy. This has been an inquiry to see if the shoe fits. I believe it does. It fits all too well. It must be more than coincidence that our charity is based on self-sacrifice and that anyone who tries to profit in its context is considered wretched. If not, it is certainly odd that society does not brand as "shameful" the making of a profit by the sale of carbonated sugar water to children in the impoverished nations of sub-Saharan Africa, or the sale of health insurance at a profit to the impoverished elderly in America, or the sale of computers at a profit to children in the American ghetto in need of an education.

We must find a different path. We have had to deconstruct the Puritan ethic in nearly every feature of our society, from science to business to issues of equality and civil rights. It is time now to deconstruct it in this most moral of endeavors. Galbraith wrote of the whole of economics in 1958:

> We are guided, in part, by ideas that are relevant to another world; and as a further result, we do many things that are unnecessary, some that are unwise, and a few that are insane. The affluent country which conducts its affairs in accordance with rules of another and poorer age also foregoes opportunities. And in misunderstanding itself, it will, in any time of difficulty, implacably prescribe for itself the wrong remedies.[112]

Our current situation is the result of the uncorrected obsolescence of old ideas.[113] The Puritans could not have foreseen charity's expansion to the status of industry. It wasn't until the late eighteenth and early nineteenth centuries that economic thought began to take its modern form.[114] The Puritans didn't relate their personal beliefs to any theory of macroeconomics. We cannot afford such a luxury in the twenty-first century. Our personal beliefs create our macroeconomics, whether we realize it or not. The micro belief that compensation in charity should be limited has macro implications. When held by a critical mass of people, as it now is, it has a macro effect. The Puritans lived in an age when poverty and suffering were inevitable. We live in an age where these problems can be solved. They lived in an age when the donor, so to speak, gave directly to the needy. We live in an age when the donor hires others to provide services on behalf of the needy. The ideology that sufficed for one age will not work for another.

The Puritans' gift to us was a strong ethic of charity. Our system for charity is more developed than that of any other nation on earth. But they also gave us the beginnings of another gift—capitalism. Our task is to reconcile these two and build a new construction for addressing the world's most urgent needs. It is time for a charity born of reason. Does this mean that our charity must be devoid of feeling? That there is no place for love? No. Why must the presence of self-interest mean there is no love in our hearts? This is a Puritan idea. Its time has passed.

CHAPTER 2

The Foundations of Our Misconstruction

Reality is that which, when you stop believing in it, doesn't go away.
—PHILLIP K. DICK

Economic Apartheid

Consider the following contradictions. Sony can make a profit from a Bruce Springsteen album that heightens awareness of the plight of migrant workers, but no one can earn a profit working for a charity trying to help the migrant workers of whose plight we want people to be more aware. Profit is eschewed as an incentive in charity, but charities invest the retirement funds of their employees in the stocks of for-profit companies in order to produce economic incentives. No one can earn a profit investing in a charity soup kitchen, but Campbell's can make a profit selling the charity its soup. A supermarket can make a profit selling food to the poor, but a poverty charity cannot use profit to attract people to help end poverty. Foundations must be nonprofit, yet they generate the money they give to charity by investing their endowments in the stocks of for-profit companies.

In four hundred years, the myth of this other world that the Puritans created has become stronger, not weaker. As charity has grown larger and more complex, new constraints have been applied that have only had the effect of solidifying the compartmentalization.

This chapter deconstructs the nature and effects of this myth in the twenty-first century in five critical areas: compensation, risk taking, long-term vision, advertising, and capital investment. The first section is introductory. It previews the nonprofit versus for-profit discrimination in each area and shows how all five areas converge to completely separate the causes we love from the rest of the economic world. The rest of the chapter examines each area in depth and uses real-world examples to document the debilitating effects of their underpinnings. The objective is to get at the bottom of things. It is to come to know our beliefs and how we practice them—across the board—to see why they don't work and to explore what will.

Compensation and Capital Investment

The for-profit sector is allowed to compensate people on the basis of their value. The nonprofit sector must limit compensation to some arbitrary threshold based on emotion and gut feeling. The for-profit sector can pay investors a financial return on their money; the nonprofit sector cannot. These rules come as much from our mythology about what charity is *not* as from our ideas about what it *is*. The myth is that charity is people helping other people and that the for-profit sector is people helping themselves. One world helps others; the other does not. One is benevolent; one is not. One permits economic self-interest, and the other does not. This is the residue of the Puritan "law of mercy." The myth of two worlds legitimizes the need for a separate compensation standard (sacrificial wages) in the labor market and a separate investment return standard (none) in the capital investment market. However, the perspective is grounded in a fiction.

The fallacy is that the for-profit sector does not help people. If we shut down the global oil conglomerates tomorrow, we would soon find a world in need of a great deal more help than it is in need of today. If not for the for-profit companies that make bicycles, my company could never have conducted the AIDSRides to raise money for charity. If not for the for-profit electric companies, we could not power any of our charities. Worse, we would have need for a great deal more charity in a world without heat, light, or the ability to communicate or produce food. Who would say that Google hasn't dramatically helped the world by providing instant access to most of the world's information? Who would say that the Toyota Prius isn't helping to make the air cleaner? Helping people is what the for-profit sector does. It satisfies needs. It's just that it doesn't do it for free. Benevolence comes from the Latin *bene* and *volent*, for "well-wishing." It does not mean "donate." Because the for-profit sector doesn't help for free doesn't mean that it fails to provide a social benefit. The for-profit sector simply doesn't regard the presence of self-interest as being at odds with meeting need. Indeed, it regards the two as essentially connected.

Adam Smith said it first, in *The Wealth of Nations:*

> But man has almost constant occasion for the help of his brethren, and it is in vain for him to expect it from their benevolence only. He will be more likely to prevail if he can interest their self-love in his favour, and [show] them that it is for their own advantage to do for him what he requires of them. Whoever offers to another a bargain of any kind, proposes to do this. Give me that which I want, and you shall have this which you want, is the meaning of every such offer; and it is in this manner that we obtain from one another the greater part of those good offices which we stand in need of. It is not from the benevolence of the butcher, the brewer, or the baker, that we expect our dinner, but from their regard to their own self-interest. We address ourselves, not to their humanity but to their self-love, and never talk to them of our own necessities but of their advantages.[1]

In this way, most of the needs of the world are met. This is good in and of itself. But there is other goodness at work here as well. Self-interest is not satisfied by money alone. People also want challenging work. They want to fulfill their potential, pursue their dreams, and leave their mark on the world. The butcher gives us our dinner not just because we give him money, but because he enjoys being a good butcher. Most great entrepreneurs are driven at least as much by their passion as they are by a desire to make money. The satisfaction of the desire to make a difference, married to the satisfaction of self-love, makes for a powerful combination that embraces two aspects of our nature at the same time. It finds full expression in a for-profit, free-market ideology. On this point, Billy Shore, in *Revolution of the Heart,* excerpts examples of visionary companies studied in the best-selling business book *Built to Last:*

> "Contrary to business school doctrine, we did not find 'maximizing shareholder wealth' or 'profit maximization' as the dominant driving force or primary objective through the history of most of the visionary companies. [. . .] Profit is like oxygen, food, water, and blood for the body; they are not the point of life but without them, there is no life." This is not to say the visionary companies don't seek profits. They do. But the research demonstrates they are equally guided by a sense of ideology, values and purpose beyond just money making.[2]

In terms of the labor market and the capital investment markets, free-market capitalism is superior to nonprofit ideology for addressing human needs and producing tangible social benefit because it appeals to, rather than constrains, our authentic nature. If one market allows us to be fully who we are, and the other restrains us to be half a person, to which market will the majority of people bring their talents? To which market will the world's most talented business leaders gravitate? To which will they bring their capital?

Advertising

How we approach advertising depends on what we think charity has to offer the consumer. Here again we compartmentalize. We believe that the for-profit sector sells products and services to consumers that satisfy the needs of self, whereas charity provides services to consumers that satisfy the needs of others. This is inaccurate. Charity also satisfies the needs of self.

First, by providing services that alleviate and/or solve social problems, charity provides a benefit to all of society, self (donor) included. The end of poverty would mean more productive resources in the world, more consumers, and higher standards of living for all. The eradication of disease would mean fewer resources spent on health care and more resources used for productive purposes that would also raise the standards of living for all. It is not just the needy who would benefit. All of us would.

Second, in many cases, and in almost all cases involving large gifts from affluent donors, corporations, and even foundations, donors get valuable recognition for their gifts. This is more commerce than philanthropy, and there is a large market for it, from the naming of buildings to advertisements in dinner programs. A donor whose name is on the top of a $25 million building as a result of a $5 million gift is getting value for her dollar, not all that different from the value consumer brands get from the money they pay for naming rights to major sports arenas. A donor whose name appears in a $1,000 full-page dinner program advertisement read by a captive audience of affluent peers is also making a trade.

Third, by offering the consumer a service that satisfies the needs of others, charity satisfies a need of the consumer. The need to alleviate the suffering of others is a natural human need. In satisfying that need, charity satisfies self-interest. Adam Smith's *Theory of Moral Sentiments,* which he wrote in 1759, seventeen years before the publication of *The Wealth of Nations,* begins with the following unequivocal observation:

How selfish soever man may be supposed, there are evidently some principles in his nature, which interest him in the fortune of others, and render their happiness necessary to him, though he derives nothing from it, except the pleasure of seeing it. . . . That we often derive sorrow from the sorrow of others, is a matter of fact too obvious to require any instances to prove it; for this sentiment, like all the other original passions of human nature, is by no means confined to the virtuous and humane, though they perhaps may feel it with the most exquisite sensibility. The greatest ruffian, the most hardened violator of the laws of society, is not altogether without it.[3]

Indeed, the notion that Puritan charity was without self-interest is refuted by the fact that Puritans relied on self-interested motives themselves: helping one another ensured survival, reciprocity helped ensure that you would be helped when you needed it, and conspicuous giving elevated social status.

That we have this wrong—that we believe charity offers a service just to others and not to self—is important. It means that the nonprofit obsession with asking people to be "selfless" pitches the whole bargain backward. Charity is not selfless. Charity is great for the self.

Moreover, what charity has to offer the consumer is not much different from what the for-profit sector has to offer the consumer. It may differ in the way that, say, ice cream differs from music or, to come closer to the mark, the way that ice cream differs from a spiritual best seller, but it is the same in that it speaks to various self-interests—improving our standard of living, alleviating the suffering of others, and elevating our own social status.

Let us look at how *differently* the two sectors, each with essentially the *same* offer, market their products and services to the public. First, in terms of methods, the for-profit sector drives consumers to their maximum point of consumption through advertising. It recognizes a powerful correlation between advertising and demand. In fact, to the extent that they have the money, consumer brands keep on advertising as long as the last dollar produces a penny of benefit. They only stop when they have saturated the market with their message and their incremental dollar produces zero net benefit. In this way they build demand for their offer, whether it is a cellular phone, ice cream, or a spiritual book. This is founded on a simple principle—that people are not omniscient, and they do not know what you want from them unless you tell them.

Charity, by contrast, operates on the reverse principle. It discourages the expenditure of donor dollars on paid advertising, under the false notion that such expenditure amounts to taking money from the needy. This conclusion can be quickly dismissed if, for example, I spend $50,000 in donor funds on a newspaper ad that delivers $500,000 in donations for the needy. Nonetheless, the belief persists. It is a by-product of the false Puritan belief in our depravity and in the charitable act as penitential. A dollar that goes to advertising robs me of the penitential satisfaction I get from a dollar that goes directly to the needy. Therefore, paid advertising is labeled wasteful, slick, or extravagant. It is true that charities engage in substitute forms of advertising and market-ing—direct mail appeals, face-to-face relationship building with the wealthy, and so on. Yet even these methods are discouraged beyond a point. Fundraising "efficiency" standards strictly govern the degree to which charities can engage in these activities. When that limit has been reached, they are sentenced to silence, even if substantial incremental benefit has been left on the table.

Furthermore, starting from the mistaken position that charity is ex-clusively about others, and is therefore selfless, nonprofit ideology de-mands, or at least expects, that consumers be at their maximum readi-ness to give out of the goodness of their hearts, without need for any persuasion from advertising, without any appeal to self-interest. When they don't, its only recourse is to complain about the apathetic state of humanity. This is unrealistic. I am not immoral if my failure to give to the fight against genocide in Darfur is based on the fact that I don't know what is happening there or I don't know how money could help.

Of less importance, but still significant, is the issue of message. The for-profit sector, once again, appeals directly to our self-interest. It en-deavors to persuade us that this product or service will work to our ad-vantage. For the most part, charitable messaging tends to avoid such ap-peals, focusing instead on guilt or shame through the use of overwhelming statistics on suffering that make us feel power*less,* instead of power*ful.* One of the most powerful marketing messages I have ever heard concerning helping others appealed directly to self-interest. It was ascribed to Rabbi Harold Kushner: "Being kind to others is a way of being good to yourself." Charities seldom explore this kind of message.

So in the ultimately important consumer market, and on the ques-tion of advertising, free-market ideology once again trumps nonprofit ideology because it recognizes, instead of ignores, self-interest. To which market will I send my dollar—the one that makes me aware of its offer or the one that doesn't? The one that shows me the benefits of my purchase or the one that overwhelms me with a feeling of helplessness?

Risk Taking and Long-Term Vision

The duality here is simple. The for-profit sector says that experimentation should be allowed. Not only does it tolerate failure, it *values* it—even encourages it—in the interest of breakthrough and advancement. It is called research and development. Nonprofit ideology says that failure is immoral because money comes from donors who intended their dollars to go directly to the needy. Astonishingly, in all my interactions with charities over the years, I have never come across a research and development department for new revenue models. The notion that failure is immoral does not take into account the value of what was learned and what future achievements will come down the road. This is the opposite of how business looks at failure.

There is an issue of self-interest at play here as well. The for-profit sector recognizes the need for people to challenge themselves. Nonprofit ideology demonizes failure because society demonizes it. We must remember that nonprofit ideology is not something the nonprofit sector concocted. It is something the whole of society did. That aside, again, free-market ideology trumps nonprofit ideology because it recognizes the whole of our nature. To which market will I bring my creativity—the one that will give me the resources to explore it or the one that will not? Which market will lead to greater progress—the one that explores new ideas or the one that does not?

On the question of long-term vision, nonprofit ideology discourages it, under the theory that donations were made so that they could be distributed immediately. The notion that a dollar invested in a ten-year plan is not a dollar going to help the needy is irrational on its face, but the fact that it is not going to the needy *now* obscures the value it will produce down the road. Capitalism, on the other hand, is a patient calculator of value. If it takes ten years to create a profitable enterprise, it will wait. Which ideology is likely to produce the better long-term result?

The Sum Effect

Charity has been separated from the rest of the economic world, denied important economic rights, and forced to operate under a counterproductive set of rules. That it is denied economic rights in any one of the five areas we have just discussed is bad enough. That it is denied them in all five leads to extreme economic isolation and puts the causes we love

Table 1

For-Profit Rule Book	Nonprofit Rule Book
Compensate according to value. No limits on financial incentive.	*Don't* compensate according to value. Strictly limit the use of financial incentives.
Effect: Attracts top talent for life.	Effect: Discourages top talent.
Buy advertising until the incremental benefit is zero.	*Don't* advertise unless the advertising is donated. Dollars spent on advertising could have gone to the needy.
Effect: Saturate the market with your offer, build maximum demand.	Effect: Minimal ability to build demand.
Manage and reward risk.	*Don't* take risks. Donated dollars are earmarked for programs.
Effect: Discover new opportunities for growth.	Effect: Discover few opportunities for growth.
Invest in the long-term.	*Don't* invest in the long-term—must meet short-term "efficiency" standards.
Effect: Builds long-term value.	Effect: Institutionalizes problems.
Unlimited permission to pay return on investment to attract capital.	*No* permission to pay return on investment to attract capital.
Effect: Trillions of dollars of capital.	Effect: No surplus capital.

at a severe disadvantage to the rest of the economic world. A simple side-by-side comparison brings the overall sum of the inequity into focus (see table 1).

There is a disconcerting snowball effect to all of this. The more that capitalistic enterprises are able to hire the world's best talent, the better they become at attracting capital. The better they become at attracting capital, the more money they have to spend on building demand. This increases revenue, which gives them more money to spend on building demand, attracting even more talent and raising more capital. What we cling to as an ideology of benevolence is in fact an ideology of inequality and injustice. Charity is in a one-legged footrace with a competitor in a Ferrari. The competitor is in the Ferrari when he acts fairly, according to a pure capitalistic model. When he acts unfairly, or monopolistically, he is in something more akin to a jet, and the whole system multiplies the injustice.

There Is No Need for a Separate Nonprofit Ideology

Capitalism works. It demonstrates a superior ability to meet human needs. It produces dramatic results by embracing both sides of our nature—the desire to satisfy self-interest *and* the desire to contribute to others. It allows us to contribute to the world and contribute to ourselves at the same time. Its effectiveness does not vary with the nature of the need. It can produce hospitals, food, and drugs just as well as it can produce toys and candy bars. *Ergo, there is no need for a separate nonprofit construction. Humanity already has an effective method for solving problems and producing social benefit.*

A report on venture philanthropy by Community Wealth Ventures for the Morino Institute concluded:

> Non-profit organizations exist in a culture of dysfunction—limited capacity and modest outcomes pervade critical organizational elements such as strategic planning, staffing, training, management, financing and performance measurement. This dysfunction makes success highly improbable and calls into question the sustainability of organizations unable to adequately capitalize future growth.[4]

We don't need selfless means to achieve an end that benefits others or a charitable ideology to achieve a charitable end result. We have conflated the end result with the operational ideology that ought to produce it. We don't do this elsewhere. *We don't expect entertainment executives to be entertaining in their business affairs or agriculture executives to be vegetarian.* We expect them to be capitalistic. Why should charity be any different?

I am not saying we don't need charity. I am saying we don't need a separate set of rules for its conduct. We need to help the poor. We need all the good people and organizations that are presently trying to help them. We just don't need a different ideology for doing it. We need to cure disease. We don't need a different set of rules for doing it. Indeed, to the extent we *are* curing disease, it is largely on the basis of for-profit ideology. "If it uses capitalism, then it isn't charity" is the obvious rebuttal. It all depends on how we define charity. If we define it as self-deprivation, then no. But if we define it as the alleviation of suffering, how could we call it anything else? What is *not* charity is anything that stands in the way.

We have artificially constrained the natural process for satisfying certain social needs by creating a separate set of rules that intentionally prohibit it. Nonprofit ideology disrupts the natural tendency of people to solve problems. People see the urgent needs of the world's most helpless citizens, but they are denied the proper economic incentives (and other critical tools) to make them willing to devote their lives to meeting them. So they do their little bit for charity by writing a check a few times a year or volunteering their time, and then go off to a playing field where the rules better serve their whole being. Free-market capitalist ideology isn't the problem. Nonprofit ideology is. It demands that 100 percent of our motivation come from only part of our nature—that all assistance to the needy be motivated only by our benevolence, and none of it by our self-interest. No wonder then that charity cannot produce the whole result we are after.

It is a fortunate feature of the human race that its members have diverse passions. If everyone wanted to be a violinist and no one a farmer, we would have a problem. Thankfully, if we survey a hundred people, we will discover a hundred different passions. Some want to be doctors, some teachers, some farmers. Some are passionate about solving scientific problems and some about solving social problems. It is also true that we almost all want to do well for ourselves. Unfortunately, many of the people who might have the best ideas for eradicating hunger end up going to the for-profit sector. Their interest is thwarted by a set of rules that requires more selflessness than human beings naturally possess. There are as many people ready to go out and end world hunger and cure cancer as there are people willing to go out and sell soda and sneakers, but we need to even the playing field so that the ones who want to end world hunger can afford the same kind of home as their peers selling soda.

My own company was a case in point. It was a for-profit enterprise using free-market methods to meet a need—namely, the need for more funding of AIDS and breast cancer services. It was successful at fulfilling that need. It demonstrated a new way of raising money. But as the case study at the back of this book shows, nonprofit ideology wanted no part of this. It didn't want someone earning a growing profit, even in the face of growing dollars for the needy. It didn't want to see an "empire" built, even though empires are what we need to meet the massive scale of the problems that confront us. The free market was showing a way to get the job done. Nonprofit ideology rejected it.

There is an obvious question. The for-profit sector succeeds because it has things to sell people who in turn have enough money to buy them. Where is the economic incentive to end poverty? The poor don't have any money to pay people to end poverty. Where will the money come from? The answer is, it will come from all of us. How will we be motivated to give it? We will be motivated by our self-interest and our natural love for one another. But these motivations must be adequately aroused.

Ayn Rand wrote eloquently about the reality of this love and our error in mischaracterizing it:

> By elevating the issue of helping others into the central and primary issue of ethics, altruism has destroyed the concept of any authentic benevolence or good will among men. It has indoctrinated men with the idea that to value another human being is an act of selflessness, thus implying that a man can have no personal interest in others—that to *value* another means to *sacrifice* oneself—that any love, respect or admiration a man may feel for others is not and cannot be a source of his own enjoyment. . . . Today, a great many well-meaning, reasonable men do not know how to identify or conceptualize the moral principles that motivate their love, affection or good will, and can find no guidance in the field of ethics, which is dominated by the stale platitudes of altruism. . . . A "selfless," "disinterested" love is a contradiction in terms: it means that one is indifferent to that which one values.[5]

It is a fortunate reality of the universe that we have a desire to help others in need, in the same way that we have a desire to be entertained. BBC News reported in 2006 on experiments described in the journal *Science* indicating that "infants as young as 18 months show altruistic behaviour." One of the studies' authors said that "the results were astonishing because these children are so young—they still wear diapers and are barely able to use language, but they already show helping behaviour." This without the benefit of a sermon by John Winthrop. The studies further suggest that altruism "is a strong human trait, perhaps present more than six million years ago in the common ancestor of chimpanzees and humans."[6]

If we don't believe in such a natural goodwill, then giving must be obtained by coercion. If we do believe in such a natural human instinct, it can be appealed to in the same way the free market appeals to our other desires. In the same way we exploit our love of entertainment, we can exploit our love of love itself.

However, to the extent that we do *not* capitalize on our inherent goodwill, we lose its benefits. This is true of most of our desires. I love music. I also love movies. If the music industry were prohibited from advertising its new offerings, but the movie industry were free to advertise as much as it wanted, I would see a lot more movies than I would buy music. This is precisely the present problem. It is why we appear to be less than charitable. Charity competes for the consumer's discretionary dollar in the same marketplace as Coca-Cola, NFL Football, Sony, L'Oreal, and all the other consumer brands. It is a fallacy that charities compete only with one another. They compete with anyone and everyone else who wants our dollar. Money is fungible. *We don't have one currency for charity and another for consumer goods.* Fifteen dollars that goes from my pocket to a movie ticket and a box of popcorn could just as easily have gone from my pocket to the American Foundation for AIDS Research. If the movie industry is free to advertise but charity is not, I am going to see a lot more movies than I am going to give money to charity.

Society's aversion to letting charity advertise is a commitment to the self-fulfilling prophecy that human beings are depraved and selfish. The less you advertise, the more you prove it.

If we allow charity to use free-market practices, we will see an increase in the money being raised, more effective solutions, and a circular reinforcement that will further increase investment in solving the great problems of our time. We will be able to "buy" the services of people who want to find solutions, at a price that gives them the incentive to do so, just as we buy the services of people who plant flowers on our streets to make the world more beautiful and satisfy our aesthetic desire. Why haven't we done so up until now? Because there is no free market for buying and selling the solutions to these problems.

Charity, in this reimagined construction, can be rightly defined not as a separate world, not as a cut-off sector of people, but as an integral part of our nature—a motivation of all people. In the same way the free market responds to our natural physical thirst with a thousand beverages, the free market can capitalize on and respond to our natural desire to help those most in need with a host of intelligent solutions, each of them free to use a set of rules that optimize effectiveness. There will no longer be one sector of people, too small to get the job done, disproportionately giving of themselves under a set of rules that diminish their effectiveness, trying to solve by themselves problems that are the responsibility of the entire world.

I am not saying that this "liberated charity" will be a panacea. But I am saying that it will be infinitely more potent than what we have now. Will it be able to solve every problem? I don't know. Will the government have a role? Of course. But given that government often provides assistance through contracts with charity, the present system will contaminate any added value government seeks to provide. The current ideology has denied us the opportunity to exploit the true potential of our goodwill. *For all we know, that potential is unlimited.*

In summary, the issue here is tragically simple. The free market is a self-correcting system. Driven by people's self-interest and the natural desire to make a contribution, it seeks out unique needs and satisfies them. One of the most powerful needs it will seek to satisfy, and profit from, is our natural desire to help one another. It only stops working when it is interfered with. When we attempt to correct a self-correcting system, we undermine it. The solution is the problem. So the question is, Why did anyone ever try to correct it in the first place? Because of the belief that human beings are depraved. If we are depraved, then we need correction—hence the development of a correcting mechanism. But if our nature is truly good, or even just not depraved, all of our society is founded on a false principle. *We don't need a separate construction to correct for capitalism. We need capitalism to correct for our irrational construction of charity. Put another way, capitalism isn't the problem. The lack of it is.*

The First Error—Constraints on Compensation: Charity and Self-Deprivation Are Not the Same Thing

Our Present Construction

We have been taught all our lives that charity and self-deprivation are the same thing, that the best way to help others is to give up something ourselves. This notion doesn't survive logic. Under such a theory, our ability to help others is limited to what we have to give away. If, on the other hand, we work at making more for ourselves, we will have much more to give away and will provide a social benefit through our labor as well. Indeed, if we sell everything we have and give it to the poor, we will be poor ourselves—we will become a part of the problem. Jewish ethics advocate that charitable giving should be limited to about 20 percent of wealth, so that the givers themselves do not become impoverished and thus a burden to the community. Jesus, on the other hand, proposed an unsustainable model. He could imagine selling all one had and giving it to the poor because he had miraculous powers that enabled him to manifest bread and fish whenever he wanted them. What are the rest of us without such powers to do? He walked around from house to house as a guest. If all his hosts had sold everything they had and given it to the poor, where would he have stayed?

Real charity must be defined by what does the most good for others, not by what brings the most deprivation to self. A construction truly based on the need to do as much good for others as possible will not concern itself with whether or not someone profits in the process. It will be focused on whatever will produce the greatest outcome for those in need. By contrast, a construction based on self-deprivation will be concerned *first* with whatever produces the greatest self-denial and *last* with whatever produces the greatest results for those in need. John Winthrop, for instance, does not mention the objective of eradicating poverty. He says it will always be with us.

The ideal of charity as self-deprivation is narcissistic. Its objective is the confirmation of one's own goodness. It is necessarily self-centered—sanctimonious. It cares more about its own survival than about real grace. It is incapable of envisioning complex solutions to the external problems of others because all of its vision is focused inward. It doesn't care as much if an external problem gets solved as it does about the degree to which it is able to continue to sacrifice self in the name of the problem. Indeed, a solution to an external problem is problematic because it will extinguish the object of self-sacrifice. As if this were not bad enough, the self-denying ideal is further satisfied, if not more easily satisfied, by imposing itself on others. Idealists, in this sense, confirm their own goodness by the degree to which they are diligent judges of the self-depriving behavior of others. They gain further self-assurance on the basis of those judgments; that is, your impurity reassures me of my purity; your depravity, of my virtue. It is ultimately selfish because it is willing to impose itself on others regardless of the fact that such imposition may serve only to undermine relief for those in need.

That this is immoral is axiomatic. A person who wants to be paid more and more money to produce more and more good will be prevented from doing so by those who want to impose on her their moral imperative of self-deprivation. Whose price is more dear?

Rand wrote in *The Virtue of Selfishness:*

Since nature does not provide man with an automatic form of survival, since he has to support his life by his own effort, the doctrine that concern with one's own interests is evil means that man's desire to live is evil—that man's life, as such, is evil. No doctrine could be more evil than that.[7]

Self-interest is real. It can no more be annihilated than energy can. It cannot be banished by decree. It will mutate and find its way in through a back door. The pseudo-moral purist represents that mutation. No one acts more in his own self-interest. He has an insatiable need for moral superiority. In return for it, he trades nothing but the "flapping of his gums."[8] He is willing to transfer the entire cost to the needy, who pay for it with their lives. The laborer asks only for his fair market salary and is willing to pay his way by earning it with the entirety of his labor, and assist the needy to boot. The moral purist has the audacity to call him selfish. He has to. What a trick—the most dangerous kind of selfishness disguised as the most noble kind of love. And he teaches us to preach his sermon for him when he's not around. But he has nothing to offer the needy but despair.

In the following excerpt, Princeton economist Paul Krugman writes about the moral purist's objection to globalization, on the grounds that it makes the wealthy wealthier, even though it also raises wages for the poor. The characters are different, but the message is the same:

> But matters are not that simple, and the moral lines are not that clear. In fact, let me make a counter-accusation: The lofty moral tone of the opponents of globalization is possible only because they have chosen not to think their position through. While fat-cat capitalists might benefit from globalization, the biggest beneficiaries are, yes, Third World workers. After all, global poverty is not something recently invented for the benefit of multinational corporations.[9]

Our construction today finds expression in a chastising and pervasive narrative. The best way to deconstruct our approach is to briefly deconstruct the narrative's principal beliefs.

"People who want to make money in charity are doing it off the backs of the needy." This is a distortion. We don't say that Thomas Edison made a fortune off of the *dark*. He made a fortune off of the *light bulb*. He made the light bulb off of his *knowledge*. He acquired his knowledge by his *hard work and the time and energy he put into it*. He made his money off of the value he added to the world.

The more a person profits by making light bulbs, the more light bulbs he will make. The more he profits by making a better light bulb, the more he will try to make a better light bulb. Similarly, the more a person can profit from making the world a better place through what we call charity, the more she will try. In such a case, it cannot be said that she is making money by exploiting the needy. Under a fair market arrangement where a person is being paid an amount correlated to the value that her time and talent adds, that is nothing more than a fair exchange—fair, simply because that person could take her time and talent to the for-profit sector and exploit it for the same amount. She is making money "off" her value. It is illogical to say that she is making money "off" the needy.

I am as opposed as the next person to paying people in charity higher salaries gratuitously. If a person isn't providing any value, he shouldn't get a penny. Throw him out. Ironically, it is the flip side of our irrational construction of charity that keeps dead weight employed in charity. In the same way that we *demonize* someone being paid a lot for *not* being properly self-denying, we *tolerate* someone producing zero value simply because he *is* properly self-denying, or at least talks a good self-denying game. But what is the person sacrificing who is getting paid and producing no value? His value is negative. He is ripping the needy off—even while he is demonizing the guy getting paid for producing positive value, all the while screaming at him, "Shame on you." Shame on *him*. If we fix the construction, we can solve both problems at the same time. As soon as we start paying people on the basis of what they're worth, productive people will start flowing in and unproductive people will start flowing out.

Furthermore, this notion of people making money "off" the needy points the lens at the method instead of the outcome—at the self instead of the result—and thereby does a disservice to the result. It focuses our attention on what an individual person is getting paid instead of what a person is producing on behalf of the needy. In fact, it ignores what the person is producing because of its emphasis on what she is being paid. If someone raises $100 million for the needy and we are conditioned to focus only on the $1 million she was paid, we are necessarily going to devalue the result the person produced or ignore it entirely.

We have to focus on the result, because it is with the result that we are ultimately concerned, or should be. The questions that should be uppermost in our minds are market questions: What result got produced? Was the payment worth the result? And is there another supplier that could produce the same result for less money? Instead, we have been trained only to ask how much the person was paid, and if the amount rises above a figure that triggers some artificially instilled gag reflex—usually, these days, three or four hundred thousand dollars—we want to crucify the person, without knowing a thing about the value he's produced or what salary he could have commanded with his talent in another market. In this way we devalue artificially. The needy are the ones paying the price.

"There has to be a limit to the amount of money people can make in charity." Such a limit would serve nothing but tradition and would, and does, hurt the needy. This is very simple. To place a limit on compensation is to place a limit on outcomes. If a limit were placed on the amount of profit the stockholders of the Edison Electric Light Company could make, there would be a limit on the innovation they would be willing to fund and pursue. There would be less innovation. Similarly, limits on compensation for alleviating social problems only limit the degree to which people finance, work on, and innovate on behalf of those problems. To believe otherwise is to cling to the futile wish that people will do more just because of the cause itself, and it is to leave the needy at the mercy of a wish instead of reality.

The temptation to place a limit on salaries is based on a fear of moving fully into the free market. If we cling to an old way of thinking, under the guise of a new way of thinking we will be worse off than if we simply stay the course. To impose an artificial limit, even if it is ten times higher than what we presently tolerate, is to solidify the principle of artificial limits per se. These are precisely what define the current paradigm. This kind of moderate approach will kill the whole enterprise. There is nothing moderate about it. It is the old way of thinking masquerading as the new. It is not a transformation.

A compensation limit not correlated to value is necessarily artificial. It is based on something other than the thing for which compensation is being provided—in this case, a feeling, an emotion, an ideal. What is wrong with idealism? Nothing, unless we are worshiping the wrong ideal. Given the choice between two ideals—self-sacrifice or the end of world hunger—I choose the latter. A market approach is the best way to get us there. An artificial compensation limit interferes with it.

A hypothetical example: we agree that people should be able to make more money in charity if they provide more value, but it should be no more than a million dollars a year, no matter what. The result: we have just eliminated from the game most of the CEOs, CFOs, COOs, and many of the senior vice presidents of every one of the Fortune 500. Their talents have now been lost to the needy because of our restriction. The for-profit sector, having no such restriction, continues to enjoy their value. We are right back where we started.

A comment by a charity professional in *Chronicle of Philanthropy* typifies the two-world construction and parrots a counterproductive attitude: "'The nonprofit sector is not the for-profit sector. . . . I don't think we need to pay someone $350,000 to get the best and the brightest.'"[10] One has to ask what world this person is talking about. You couldn't get Bill Gates for $350,000 a *week,* let alone $350,000 a year. You couldn't get Richard Branson or Michael Dell or a thousand other business superstars for anywhere near that kind of money. Is there one kind of "best and brightest" who is worth only $350,000 a year and should work for the needy, and another kind of "best and brightest" who is worth many times more and should not work for the needy?

"People who want to make money in charity are obscene." Is it not more obscene that we would allow people to continue to die of AIDS because we would restrict from the market, on grounds of obscenity, the people who might be able to eradicate it? Is it not more obscene that we would pay a soccer player $50 million a year to generate $500 million a year in ticket and merchandise sales and television royalties but *not* pay someone $50 million a year to engineer the elimination of world hunger, the value of which would be inestimable? The example is not hypothetical. The *Week* contained the following report in January 2007:

> BECKHAM: CAN HE SAVE U.S. SOCCER?
>
> The Los Angeles Galaxy, a team in the U.S.'s struggling professional league, surprised the world last week by signing David Beckham, "the world's most recognizable athlete," to a five-year, $250 million contract. The overseas soccer cognoscenti were quick to point out that at 31, Beckham isn't the player he once was—and that he was famously overrated to begin with. But who cares? What Major League Soccer needs more than anything is a massive injection of glamour and publicity, commodities that Beckham—model-handsome and married to former Spice Girl Victoria "Posh" Adams—brings in droves.[11]

The point is not that it is obscene for David Beckham to get paid $250 million. It is obscene that our society would prohibit a charity from paying a fraction of that amount to the people who might be able to help us end world hunger or cure AIDS. It is obscene that a paper asks, "Who cares?" about this but refers to a charitable professional making 2 percent of the same amount as a "scam artist." The double standard is what is obscene.

"Those who work for charities should do it out of the goodness of their hearts." And if they don't? If it is more than they are willing to sacrifice? What would the needy say about the goodness of *our* hearts for unilaterally denying their talents to them on the basis of our moral ideals, without even consulting them?

If people are expected to give to charity simply out of the goodness of their hearts, why do we have tax exemptions? Shouldn't we give as much whether we are able to save money on our taxes or not? If people should work for charity simply out of the goodness of their hearts, why pay them anything at all? Why not require that they be ascetics? We don't, because we know that if we did no one would work for charity. We recognize already that the goodness of one's heart is limited and that productivity is correlated in some fundamental way to economic incentive. The fact that there is a competitive employment market at all in the nonprofit sector contradicts the notion that people who work for charity are motivated only by their hearts, or that we really expect them to be. Why, then, rely exclusively on the goodness of their hearts to create incremental progress?

Goodness of heart is only one of the things that motivates us. When we demand that it be the *only* thing that motivates us, we only shortchange the needy. For instance, I assert that the more profit someone can make solving the world's problems, the more he will try to figure out ways to solve them. Someone else, however, might say that's not true, that some people are motivated not by profit, but by the goodness of their hearts, and they will try to solve the world's problems no matter what. That may be true, but then the question is, are there enough of them? We needn't look very far for the answer. Most of the great problems we *have* solved are in the domain of commerce, where the profit motive is promoted, and most of the great problems we have *not* solved are in the domain of charity, where it is prohibited. If profit and goodness in partnership produce the greatest results, we should take away the dividing line that now separates them and allow them to marry.

"People who want to make money in charity don't have the needy up-permost in their minds." *Most* people do not have the needy upper-most in their minds. Our concern for the needy lives alongside a variety of desires and needs. The fact that someone wants to capitalize on her full economic value does not negate the possibility that she also has love in her heart. These impulses coexist. We have too many real-world ex-amples of this to take any other notion seriously. The existence of War-ren Buffett alone shatters the proposition entirely. Here again, we con-front the Puritans' irrational construction. You can make money and help the needy, but you cannot help the needy and make money. The tragedy of the current construction is that the thinking of people like Warren Buffett has been dedicated entirely to the for-profit sector throughout most of their working lives. How many great leaders have been lost to the cause of solving our greatest problems because charity approves of only half of their nature?

"People who donate to charity make a sacrifice, so the people who work in charity should too." Making a onetime donation to charity is an en-tirely different thing from making a lifetime donation of one's entire economic future. It is irrational to apply the same standard to the two propositions. It is presumptuous for a person making a donation to charity to use that to dictate to someone else the standard by which he should live the rest of his life. When you ask me to give up my eco-nomic potential in the name of charity, not only do you ask me to give up a potential lifestyle, but you ask me to involve my family in the deci-sion as well—the schools my children will be able to go to, the life I will be able to provide for them, and for my spouse, the places to which we will be able to travel, the retirement I will be able to enjoy, the age at which I will be able to enjoy it, the estate I will make available to my heirs, and, ironically, how much money I might be able to give to char-ity. If I say no to this, if I say I am unwilling to give it all up—I am going to dedicate my life to business—am I immoral? Of course not. Why then would it be immoral of me to ask for that same lifestyle while dedicating my life to charity?

We have conflated two different markets: the labor market and the gift-giving market. We want the same ideology to apply to both: if I make a sacrifice in the gift-giving market, you should make a sacrifice in the labor market. The problem is that sacrifice is defined differently from one market to the next. In the gift-giving market, a sacrifice can be defined by as little as a $25 contribution. In the labor market, it starts at salary cuts in the $25,000 to $50,000 range at the middle-management level or with a salary cap of $300,000 to $400,000 at the leadership level, which cap might represent a cut in pay from earning potential in the for-profit sector by many millions of dollars. The price of sacrifice in the gift-giving market is low enough to stimulate widespread charitable giving. The price of sacrifice in the labor market is far too high to stimulate adequate supply.

There is another critical issue related to the Puritan law of mercy mentioned before. It involves the question of whether the donor is making a sacrifice at all. The spirit of the Puritan law has been carried over to the present. But it is misapplied. It now says that a nonprofit employee should conform to a different law than a for-profit employee, because the former deals with the poor. But this is not true. The nonprofit employee is bargaining with the donor, who is not poor. The donor wants to hire the employee to provide a service on his behalf to the poor. The employee is therefore bargaining with an equal (or usually someone of far greater wealth) and should be under no moral obligation to provide a discount on her labor. The donor is buying a service. That service provides him with a double value. First, it satisfies his desire to help others. Second, it makes the world in which he lives a better place. He benefits from this. To say that he has made a sacrifice is true only in the sense that he has given up one thing of personal value for another thing of personal value. In this sense, it could be said that he makes a sacrifice when he buys a camera. He has given up his ability alternatively to buy a new pair of shoes with the money instead. In any case, he wants something from the nonprofit employee, and the employee should have a right to set her price, without the introduction of any regulation or constraint based on morality.

"People who work in charity made the choice to do so, so they made a choice to sacrifice as well." Yes, they did make a choice to work in charity. But if sacrifice is the price of the choice, we have to ask how many other talented people made a different choice. That is the point. By tying charitable vocation to sacrifice, we are driving people into the for-profit sector. Moreover, there is significant evidence that the nonprofit sector work force suffers from a high incidence of turnover and burnout as a result of the take-it-or-leave-it choice we offer them. How is this the best way to serve the needy?

One could say, "Well, if they're not happy, that's their problem." But it isn't. It's *our* problem. What kind of productivity do we think we will get out of an unhappy work force? Smith's observation on the subject is visionary:

> The liberal reward of labour, as it encourages the propagation, so it increases the industry of the common people. The wages of labour are the encouragement of industry, which, like every other human quality, improves in proportion to the encouragement it receives. A plentiful subsistence increases the bodily strength of the labourer, and the comfortable hope of bettering his condition, and of ending his days perhaps in ease and plenty, animates him to exert that strength to the utmost. Where wages are high, accordingly, we shall always find the workmen more active, diligent, and expeditious, than where they are low.[12]

One could also say that if these people aren't happy where they are, they should leave. That's not much of a solution. If they all left, who would operate our charities? If they won't leave because they need the money, we simply have a labor pool forced into servitude by their economic needs. This is neither sustainable nor effective. There may be a small supply of people who simply won't leave because their hearts won't let them, but then all we have is a small supply of people, and people at that who resent the fact that their good heart costs them a lot of money. Why should people pay a premium for a good heart? It becomes a curse.

"I've made a sacrifice to work in charity, so others should as well." If a person has made the decision to work for a charity at a lower wage than he could make in the for-profit sector, and expects in return the moral authority to impose a moral standard on others, there is no sacrifice at work. If I have made a sacrifice just so I can dictate morality to others, I haven't made a sacrifice. There is no gift. What I am doing is commerce, a trade of money for some kind of moral authority, which, ironically, nullifies the moral authority. Therefore, there is no basis for asking others to make a sacrifice.

Beyond that, there is once again the following question: What if the applicant says no and heads toward the for-profit sector? She is then in a moral safe zone. Once again, it makes no sense that, in a case where two people are earning a relatively significant salary, each producing the same economic value, the one doing the charitable work should be judged less moral than the one not.

The Present Double Standard

In 2007, the IRS completed a salary investigation of various nonprofit organizations. In conducting the study, it "sought to apply a law enacted in 1996 that gives the agency the authority to fine charity officials for receiving salaries and other benefits that are deemed excessive, as well as to penalize trustees who approve the compensation."[13] Can any of us imagine the for-profit sector allowing the IRS to weigh in on its compensation levels? This is an assault on individual liberty that towers over anything we might have feared in the Patriot Act. The assumption is that the government knows better what bargain one entity can make with another than the entities themselves and that it has a right to intervene to assert its superior judgment.

The Supreme Court's opinion in the *Riley* case concerned the issue of the "reasonableness" of an outside professional fundraiser's fees. It is profound and on point:

> The State's additional interest in regulating the fairness of the fee may rest on either of two premises (or both): (1) that charitable organizations are economically unable to negotiate fair or reasonable contracts without governmental assistance; or (2) that charities are incapable of deciding for themselves the most effective way to exercise their First Amendment rights. Accordingly, the State claims the power to establish a single transcendent criterion by which it can bind the charities' speaking decisions. We reject both premises.[14]

In 2002, there was a firestorm in the San Francisco media over the compensation of the James Irvine Foundation's CEO, Dennis Collins. Irvine is one of the largest foundations in America and one of the largest contributors to social welfare in California. The furor over Collins demonstrates the striking double standard that exists between compensation in the nonprofit and for-profit sectors.

According to the foundation's website in 2008, since its founding in 1937 it had made more than $900 million in grants to over three thousand nonprofit organizations.[15] By 2001, Collins's last full year at Irvine (he retired in January 2002), he had been president of the foundation for fifteen years.[16] It had close to $1.3 billion in assets and made grants of $62.6 million. Over the preceding five years, its assets had grown by close to $300 million, and its annual grant making had grown by over $27 million.[17] The following is taken from an article that appeared in the *San Jose Mercury News:* "CEO's Rewards at Non-Profit—The Irvine

Foundation spent millions of dollars on its longtime president, Dennis Collins, from a compensation package that reached $717,000 one year to lavish retirement fetes and gifts."[18]

The article doesn't make any scientific attempt to judge his compensation on the basis of his value, positive or negative. The figure of $717,000, in and of itself, is enough to merit a story. (In fact, Collins's salary for the year was $350,629; the remainder was deferred compensation.)[19] There is no acknowledgment of its irrelevance in the absence of a benefit analysis. Equally disconcerting is that the paper doesn't expect the reader to want to see such an analysis. More striking is how ordinary the $717,000 figure would be in the for-profit sector. No business reporter would be able to generate the slightest sensation over a number so small there, where debate rages only when numbers rise above $50 million. The negative sensation is disconcerting in light of the fact that the story acknowledges that during Collins's tenure the "grant budget grew to $73 million from $12 million" and that "its program staff won national awards."[20]

Furthermore, the article makes it sound as if he were earning millions of dollars each year, rather than cumulatively over his fifteen-year tenure at the foundation. He was fifty-eight when the article was written.[21]

The article states: "This spending ultimately hurt California residents, for the San Francisco–based foundation is dedicated solely to the welfare of California, from enriching the arts to helping poor immigrants in the Central Valley."[22] Here an investment in a professional is *necessarily* something that "hurt California residents." How can any analysis claim that an expense hurt the outcome without doing a corollary analysis of the outcome? The most basic business tools are forgone in the current climate. The measurement of means overrides all concern with the result.

The article then states:

> Compensation: In 2000, Irvine's chief financial officer alerted the board that Collins' 1999 compensation was so high that he could face sanctions if the IRS audited the foundation. The board ordered a study, which showed that while his base salary was in line with heads of similar foundations, his retirement income was not. That made his total compensation 78 percent higher than the average, and 29 percent higher than the next highest paid executive. The board did not reduce his pay package.[23]

How do we know what value those other executives were producing? How are their salaries relevant in the absence of that information? And what basis would the IRS have for sanctions in the absence of a benefit analysis?

A nonprofit executive is quoted as follows:

> "These kinds of numbers really disappoint me," said John Gamboa, executive director of the Greenlining Institute, a non-profit group dedicated to increasing investment in low-income areas, which received Irvine grants in the past, but not in 2001. "There are so many little groups that are struggling, that need this money. I'm disillusioned and dismayed."[24]

It is true that many little groups are struggling. And it is true that they need money. But why do they need *this* money? Why do they need the very money that is being invested to try to help them? Why don't they need the money that was paid to the head of Coca-Cola? Why is *their* struggling always tied to the salary of the CEO of the agency trying to help them? Why must the poor and the charities that are trying to help them always be pitted against one another as competitors for limited dollars while the real competition—business—is out making an unlimited fortune? Robin Hood used to take from the rich and give to the poor. We tell charity to give to the poor by *taking* from the poor.

The Morino Institute paper hits the nail on the head:

> According to Chris Letts, Allen Grossman and William Ryan, co-authors of *High Performance Nonprofit Organizations,* in the for-profit sector, organizational capacity is valued as the primary means for succeeding in the marketplace. . . . The relationship between programs and organizational capacity is strikingly different in the non-profit sector. The two are considered almost as competitors in a zero-sum struggle for limited resources. Money invested in organizations is considered lost to direct service.[25]

A 2007 article in the *Stanford Social Innovation Review* observed the behavior of nonprofit organizations with respect to simply providing their own employees with a living wage; in other words, the article focused not on the issue of more lucrative executive compensation, but on the issue of the sheer ability of the line staff to survive:

> And what happens when local folks come together to campaign for a living wage, as they have in dozens of cities all across America? Guess who's often on the front lines of the opposition? You've got it—nonprofit organizations. In 2002 *The Chronicle of Philanthropy* reported that "The Salvation Army of Eastern Michigan argued against a living wage referendum that raised the hourly wages for employees" in 1998. The Salvation Army official quoted in

the article said, "Conforming to the law would drain cash and require cutting services to homeless people." The Montgomery (Maryland) County Council witnessed similar nonprofit recalcitrance in the face of living wage legislation, continued the *Chronicle* article. "A wage bill that included charities lost in the council in 1998 largely because nonprofit groups refused to back it," Council Member Phil Andrews was quoted as saying.[26]

Finally, the *Mercury* article on Irvine reports, "Legal experts suggest Collins's compensation should be examined by the IRS and the state attorney general."[27] The CEO of Oxford Health Plans, a private health insurance company, made more than $717,000 *every four days* in 2002. And that doesn't include $25 million in unexercised stock options.[28] And Oxford Health Plans is supposed to be helping sick people who are struggling too. But we don't see anyone asking the attorney general to get involved there.

In any event, the attorney general's office "did not challenge the board's procedure in setting Mr. Collins's pay."[29] All in all, there was an unbelievable volume of activity and commentary on a salary package that, in a for-profit setting, would be completely unremarkable.

In the summer of 2004, a Senate Finance Committee memo offered two hundred ideas for revising nonprofit regulation. According to the *Chronicle of Philanthropy:*

> The Senate memo suggested that the government might want to force foundations that pay their executives $200,000 or more to submit information to the IRS justifying that decision. It also said that the IRS might want to set a rate for how much nonprofit groups should spend on a typical meal, travel, or lodging, just as the government does for its employees.[30]

The nonprofit sector is treated like a child, incapable of managing its own affairs.

Macro data substantiate this double standard. The *Chronicle* reported in 2002:

> The median salary for chief executives of nonprofit organizations is $42,000—less than what private companies typically pay people in jobs carrying far less responsibility, such as computer programmers, construction managers, and dental hygienists, according to a new study by the Urban Institute, a think tank in Washington. The institute's analysis was based on informational tax returns filed by nearly 55,000 nonprofit groups in 1998.[31]

We have all heard sensational stories about the head of a charity being paid hundreds of thousands of dollars. It is true that there are some chief executives in charity who are paid six-figure and even seven-figure salaries, but they are few and far between. In 2004, the *Chronicle* identified fifty-two charities that paid their leaders more than $1 million.[32] This in a country with 6.5 million millionaires.[33] Of the fifty-two people the *Chronicle* reported were paid more than a million dollars, forty-two worked for large hospitals (they are not constrained by society's construction of charitable ethics because, by and large, they don't have to rely on society's donations to operate), making the number of people earning that much at charities as we traditionally conceive of them a statistical zero. By contrast, according to the 2004 edition of the *Wall Street Journal*/Mercer Human Resource Consulting CEO Compensation Survey, the *median* annual "direct compensation (base salary, annual bonus, and the present value of long-term incentives)" of for-profit CEOs at 350 large U.S. companies "rose 17.1% to $7.0 million in 2004, mirroring the median 17.4% increase in total shareholder return (TSR) in 2004."[34]

There is an additional double standard even within the nonprofit sector itself. In 2004, it was reported that the *nonprofit* New York Philharmonic paid its conductor $2.28 million for "14 weeks with the orchestra and an annual tour."[35] A 2004 *New York Times* article noted that at least twenty-three college football coaches (working for either government-sponsored or nonprofit schools) earned over $1 million, noting, by the way, that "it's not a question of whether a baseball player or coach is worth that much. The issue is what is market value."[36] This is a revealing subcompartmentalization. A market approach is allowed even within the nonprofit sector when the emotional sympathy for the needy is absent; high salaries can be paid to entertain high society, but the moment a picture of a starving child is introduced, all the rules change. The needy's own images work against them. They give rise to all of the feelings of guilt and shame at the base of the Puritan construction and, of course, our own. In the name of charity, we place the needy second to football, symphonies, and the entire world of commerce under the mistaken notion that, by refusing to allow people to make money "off of them," they are being placed first.[37]

Tables 2 and 3 take a look at how America's highest-paid CEOs in the health insurance business compare with America's highest-paid CEOs in health charities, one of the highest-paying segments of the charitable sector, for the year 2002.

Table 2

Highest-Paid CEOs in Private Health Insurance, 2002

Name	Company	2003 *Compensation ($)*
Norman C. Payson	Oxford Health Plans	76,000,000
Leonard D. Schaeffer	Wellpoint	21,800,000
Allen F. Wise	Coventry	21,700,000
R. Channing Wheeler	United Health	9,600,000
John W. Rowe	Aetna	8,900,000
Total		$138,000,000

SOURCE: Families USA, "Private Health Plans That Service Medicare Provide Lavish Compensation to Executives," "FamiliesUSA.org: The Voice for Health Care Consumers" website, June 24, 2003, http://www.familiesusa.org/resources/newsroom/press-releases/2003-press-releases/press-release-private-health-plans-that-service-medicare.html, accessed April 19, 2004.

The top five CEOs in for-profit health insurance made approximately seventy-four times what the top CEOs in America's health charities made. It is an upside-down world that prioritizes the affordability of disease this high above its eradication. The differences are even more striking if we compare the health charity CEOs with the highest-paid CEOs in all of business, where the CEOs of Occidental Petroleum and Yahoo took in $322 million and $174 million, respectively, in 2006.[38] It is true that the head of a $5 million charity should not be paid as much as the head of a $5 billion corporation, but that is not the issue here. What is at issue is the arbitrarily mandated imbalance in compensation between people asked to produce equal value. The American Red Cross, one of the largest nonprofits in the country, had expenses of almost $4 billion in its 2005 fiscal year, which included the flow of donations following Hurricane Katrina, while its CEO's compensation was $493,616.[39] How many CEOs of $4 billion for-profit corporations would be attracted by that salary? And, of course, there were no stock options. Even more telling, that salary was more than that of any other social service leader.[40] The *Chronicle* reported that the top executives of the twenty social service groups in its 2005 study of the leaders of nonprofit organizations earned a median of $197,208—more than thirty-five times less than their for-profit counterparts in the *Wall Street Journal*/Mercer survey for 2004.[41]

In 2007, the New York Yankees paid its players a total of about $189 million, presumably to win the World Series.[42] The Yankees did not win

Table 3

Highest-Paid CEOs in Health Charities, 2002

Name	Charity	Compensation
William Neaves	Stowers Institute	$717,324
Peter Van Etten	Juvenile Diabetes Foundation International	$460,000
Richard Murphy	Salk Institute	$451,882
Robert Beall	Cystic Fibrosis Foundation	$441,239
John Seffrin	American Cancer Society	$415,000
Total		$2,485,445

NOTE: Large non-profit hospitals are not included; as I stated earlier, these institutions are an inapposite comparison. They do not rely on the generosity of the public for their survival, and so are not nearly as constrained by our beliefs. That being said, according to the *Chronicle of Philanthropy*'s 2004 report on top salaries in charity, the highest was earned by Sidney Kirschner, CEO of Northside Hospital in Atlanta. He was paid $2 million in 2002. Even this inapposite comparison supports the point. His salary was thirty-eight times lower than that of the top private health insurance company CEO in the for-profit sector (Harvy Lipman and Elizabeth Schwinn, "52 Top Executives Are Paid at Least $1-Million," *Chronicle of Philanthropy. The Newspaper of the Nonprofit World* online, June 24, 2004, http://philanthropy.com, accessed August 5, 2004).
SOURCE: "Managing: Results of the Salary-Survey Search." *Chronicle of Philanthropy: The Newspaper of the Nonprofit the World* online, 2003, http://philanthropy.com, accessed March 18, 2004

the World Series in 2007. But we don't see anyone seeking retribution. Contrast all of this with our attitude toward charity. The *Chronicle of Philanthropy* ran the following story in October 2003:

> Jon Van Til, a professor of urban studies at Rutgers University at Camden who studies nonprofit compensation and other issues, said that he had spoken to donors who give small amounts and are "shocked" and "absolutely befuddled" by recent reports of the high pay packages earned by some charity executives. Prospective donors who see a charity leader's income rising while their own stays flat may be less inclined to give to that charity, he said. Mr. Van Til suggests that charities that pay their executives more than the President of the United States—who currently makes $400,000 a year—should lose their tax-exempt status.[43]

Yet again, an arbitrary figure is proposed without any correlation to productivity or results. The comparison with the presidency is simply not pertinent. Is the charity executive going to be permitted to travel for four years on Air Force One, live in the White House, have a staff of dozens of secretaries, chefs, butlers, and assistants, and achieve instant global celebrity that can later be monetized as multimillion dollar book deals and speaking tours? Bill Clinton received an estimated $10 to 12 million advance for his biography.[44] He netted $40 million in speaking fees from 2001 to 2006—about $10 million in 2006 alone.[45] Is that the pay limit being proposed?

As if all this were not irrational enough, consider the logic at work when the for-profit sector is at its worst:

WHERE ONE IS ALLOWED TO DO GREAT

- Selling expensive sneakers to poor kids in the ghetto
- Overseeing a fast-food chain that irradiates beef
- Managing a global conglomerate that makes violent movies for children
- Acting in such a movie
- Supervising advertising for a company that encourages children to eat and drink more sugar
- Supervising the marketing of cigarettes to the rural poor

WHERE ONE IS NOT

- Doing anything related to helping the world through a charity

An Inadequate Supply of Saints

One of the products of the Puritan missionary movement was the Mount Holyoke Female Seminary, founded in 1837 in Massachusetts. It was "an important center for the advancement of both women's education and missionary training in the nineteenth century."[46] Porterfield observes:

> In an effort to participate as fully as possible in this broad river of benevolence, tuition at Mount Holyoke was kept to a minimum by making students responsible for all the cooking, cleaning and washing; by furnishing rooms with donated furniture; and by employing teachers with "so much of a missionary spirit" that they would gladly accept "only a moderate salary."[47]

Nearly two hundred years later, 1,932 nonprofit executive directors from eight cities participated in a 2006 survey entitled "Daring to Lead." According to the study, "Three quarters don't plan on being in their current jobs five years from now. And most don't see themselves leading another nonprofit organization. . . . Frustrations with boards of directors and institutional funders, lack of management and administrative support, and below-market compensation add stress to a role that can be challenging even in the best circumstances."[48] Forty-nine percent of the respondents planning to leave in the next year "have low satisfaction with their compensation."[49]

The same study indicated that "nearly two in three executives believe they have made a significant financial sacrifice to do this work, with executives at small and mid-sized organizations most likely to believe so. . . . On a 6-point scale, 39% of executives under 40 years old rate their sacrifice as a 6, as do 37% of executives in their 40s, and 32% of executives in their 50s and 60s."[50]

Paul C. Light, now professor of public service at NYU, writes that the nonprofit sector has "the most dedicated workforce in the nation. It is a workforce that comes to work in the morning motivated primarily by the chance to do something worthwhile."[51] However, he cautions that this work force cannot be taken for granted. "Gone are the days when the nonprofit sector could count on a steady stream of new recruits willing to accept the stress, burnout, and the persistent lack of resources that come with a nonprofit job."[52]

A 2006 story in the *Wall Street Journal* chronicled the loss of non-profit university endowment managers to the for-profit sector: "University endowments are facing a brain drain as successful money managers itching for bigger paychecks quit to start their own investment funds."[53] The heads of the Stanford and Harvard University endowments are examples; both left their nonprofit positions for for-profit ventures.[54]

All of this is sobering in light of present market conditions. The Bridgespan Group, in a 2006 study of nonprofits (excluding hospitals and colleges), said, "Over the next decade, these organizations will need to attract and develop some 640,000 new senior managers. . . . By 2016, these organizations will need almost 80,000 new senior managers per year."[55] The need for new leaders is due partly to the retirement of the baby boom generation and partly to the growing number and size of nonprofit organizations. This is the number of new managers required just to keep the world's most urgent problems from becoming more urgent, not the number required to eradicate them.

Emmett Carson, former president and CEO of the Minneapolis Foundation, articulated the problem in a speech at Georgetown:

Today's image of the nonprofit sector as largely relying on volunteers or underpaid, hard-working professionals, for whom compensation is neither required nor sought because of their unwavering commitment to a particular cause is increasingly untrue and problematic. . . . These paid employees have every right to expect that they will be able to afford a decent place to live, have adequate health insurance, and a comfortable retirement.[56]

If we continue to demand that the people who work for charity do it out of a sense of sacrifice and missionary zeal, and that they fulfill our expectation of them as saints, where will the people come from to fill these vacancies and do this work? The Bridgespan Group report advised:

Today nonprofit organizations struggle to attract and retain the talented senior executives they need to fulfill their missions. Over the coming decade, this leadership challenge will only become more acute. . . . Nonprofits have neither the size nor the resources to develop large numbers of managers internally, as their for-profit counterparts do. The sector also lacks robust management-education and executive-search capabilities. . . . The projected leadership deficit results from both constrained supply and increasing demand.[57]

The last sentence is interesting. It describes an *Alice in Wonderland* economy where everything is upside-down—where the cause of the deficit is assigned to low supply and high demand. In an ordinary market, such a condition would not last. As any student of high school economics knows, low supply and high demand would quickly conspire to raise prices, increasing the supply. In the for-profit sector, you wouldn't predict the outcome of such a condition to be a continuing deficit of supply, but rather a satisfaction of such a deficit by an increase in price. However, in this case, because of a different set of rules the demand is *in*effectual—a sad reality. It does not interact with supply to raise wages in the normal way because of the regulatory effect of moral prohibition on increases in price (i.e., compensation), which creates an *un*natural price. Consequently, it does not bring an adequate number of new people into the market. There is another, unregulated market to which they can go (the for-profit sector) that will pay the price they seek.

One thing is clear: while it may be saints we are demanding, there aren't enough of them. Shall we allow people to suffer as a matter of principle because the demand is not met? What kind of principle is that?

The institutional knowledge of any organization's human resources represents one of its most valuable capital assets. In the case of charities, it may be the only capital asset they have. It has real, perhaps singular economic value. When that value is not allowed to accrue, because of a revolving-door effect induced by below-market compensation, there is real economic loss. In the interest of saving money in the short term, these organizations are hemorrhaging it in the long term. How is that efficient?

Mutually Exclusive Choices

We impose mutually exclusive choices on the brightest, most passionate, most creative young minds and spirits coming out of America's finest universities, as well as on everyone else: they can either fulfill their personal dreams or they can help further the dreams of the world, but they cannot do both. We ask them to choose between their personal security and their desire to assist those who suffer, their dreams for the world and their dreams for themselves. We tell them to pick a part of their nature and leave the other part behind. How is this charitable to anyone? How can we ask people to give up on the vision they have for their personal lives and expect them to come up with a vision for the world? What great dreamer dreams only half a dream? A 2006 story in the *Chronicle of Philanthropy* reported, "College debts are one reason that many recent graduates are intimidated by the big gap between the starting pay at charities and at businesses. The average entry-level job at a nonprofit group pays 22 percent less than at a for-profit."[58]

On the critical issue of nonprofit leadership, the problem becomes more acute. As of 2006, tuition at the nation's top business schools hovered around $40,000; the University of Chicago's was $41,600, Wharton's was $44,795, and Harvard's was $39,600.[59] This excludes room and board, other fees, personal expenses, and lost wages. Table 4 is from *Business Week*'s annual MBA survey for 2006, which listed *total costs* for the two-year MBA program, including lost wages, at the five top schools in the country. The figures are frighteningly high. Also summarized are the salary premiums graduates could expect to obtain as a result of their investment, as well as the number of years it would take them to recoup their investment with those salary premiums.

Table 4
Total Cost for MBA Programs

School	Cost ($)	Salary Premium ($)	Years to Pay Back
MIT	324,305	21,499	15.08
Stanford	328,062	22,351	14.68
Harvard	345,401	23,921	14.44
Wharton	328,748	25,775	12.75
Berkeley	291,805	24,239	12.04

SOURCE: "The High Price of Admission: 2006 MBA Programs," *Business Week* online, http://bwnt.businessweek.com/bschools/06/mba_payback.asp, accessed January 28, 2007.

Business Week puts the average annual 2006 salary for graduating MBAs at the top thirty schools just shy of $100,000, with those graduating from schools like MIT's Sloan achieving median pay of $110,000, and those from Harvard $105,000 per year.[60] These figures apply to the first year out of school. The average age of these students when they graduate is about twenty-eight.[61] Again, by comparison, the 2002 median salary for *all* chief executives of nonprofit organizations, each presumably much older, was $42,000.[62]

The gap becomes more extreme as these MBAs progress through their careers. In 2003, *Business Week* surveyed 1,496 of those who had graduated from business schools in 1992.[63] For Columbia MBAs ten years out of business school, the *median* combined annual salary and bonus was $350,000; for Harvard MBAs it was $380,000; for Stanford MBAs it was $400,000.[64] This is at an approximate age of thirty-eight, with most graduates having another thirty to forty years of earnings increases ahead of them. The highest reported salary for the group, for just that year, at that approximate age, was $2,005,000.[65]

By contrast, in 2004, the mean salary for the *top executives* at America's foundations, presumably significantly older than thirty-eight, was $110,000.[66] A *Chronicle of Philanthropy* story that came out in 2001, just two years before the *Business Week* survey, reported that the average salary for a *chief executive* at a small medical charity with an annual budget of $500,000 or less was $51,097. The average compensation for a *chief executive* of a $5 million–plus medical research charity was $232,658, while the average pay for the "top executive at an antihunger charity in that budget range was $84,028."[67]

This gap widens when we compare large charities with large companies. A *Chronicle* story reported that the median 2006 compensation for the *leaders* of the nation's 249 *largest* nonprofits was $315,969, about seven times less than the $2.4 million median salary for chief executives of the 500 biggest American companies in 2005 as reported by *Forbes* and twenty-two times less than the median compensation in a narrower sample of 350 top corporate leaders by the *Wall Street Journal*/Mercer survey.[68] When you narrow the sample more, the difference becomes far more pronounced. *USA Today* reported that "median 2005 pay among chief executives running most of the nation's 100 largest companies soared 25% to $17.9 million."[69] These are the kinds of compensation levels to which many of the top business school graduates aspire. On what basis will we ask them to work for $315,000 a year when they get to their top earning years? *It's far less expensive for them to simply donate that amount to charity each year.* And on what basis do we ask a thirty-eight year-old business school graduate who has a $400,000 earning potential at that age, and who has invested several hundred thousand dollars in professional training, to work for an anti-hunger charity at $84,000 a year? The compensation figures shown in table 5 for the nation's five highest-paid 2006 corporate leaders are sobering, considering that salaries for the head of the American Cancer Society and Red Cross were a little more than $400,000 a few years before.[70]

Moreover, it is not just huge salary cuts we are asking of those in this talent pool. We are asking them to come to work in a sector where they will not be able to allow their organization to take calculated risks, invest in the long term, build demand through advertising, recruit other executives at competitive salaries, attract surplus capital in an investment market, or make any mistakes. With all of that factored in, it is not even a choice between personal security and altruism. It is a choice between personal security and frustration. The Morino study concurred:

> This organizational disposition creates a cycle where nonprofits are resource constrained, talent poor and frustrated in their growth and development. Those who work in nonprofit organizations, and have sacrificed and dedicated their careers to helping others, deserve better.[71]

Unless we are ready to pass judgment on the bright young minds who pursue a comfortable lifestyle with *no* impulse to work for a charity (and I am certainly not willing to do that), how then can we pass judgment on students who *have* the impulse to do charitable works but,

Table 5

2006 Compensation for Highest-Paid Corporate Leaders

Company	Executive	Total Salary and Bonus ($)
Capital One Financial	Richard D. Fairbank	280,083,843
KB Home	Bruce Karatz	163,934,209
Cendant	Henry Silverman	133,261,147
Lehman Brothers	R. S. Fuld, Jr.	119,539,850
Genentech	Arthur D. Levinson	109,431,444

SOURCE: "Special Report: Executive Compensation," *USA Today* online, April 10, 2006, http://www.usatoday.com/money/companies/management/2006–04–07-ceo-total.htm, accessed January 29, 2007.

when faced with the choice between doing well for themselves in business or doing good through charity, choose to go into business. It is not that they are not altruistic. According to the *Harvard Business Review:*

> Studies show that more than 90% of current Harvard Business School students are on the boards of a variety of nonprofit organizations. And polls of HBS classes suggest that the overwhelming majority of those students will stay meaningfully involved with nonprofits after graduation. One recent study found that four-fifths of all HBS graduates are involved with nonprofits, with more than half serving on boards. And when you exclude graduates in their early career-building years (generally up to ten years after graduation), the numbers jump even higher.[72]

How much value could be added if we gave these people the incentive to come on full-time? It is not an indictment of their moral character that most in this position choose the lifestyle they have been conditioned to want instead of committing their lives to the service of humanity. Rather, it is an indictment of the poor choice we have given them.

It is from the by-products of this choice that we will build the leadership for solving the world's most urgent problems. It is at the mercy of this choice that we leave the poor and the needy, women with breast cancer, people with AIDS, the homeless, the environment, and all of the other causes about which we care so much.

The ramifications of this choice are real. Thomas J. Tierney, cofounder of the Bridgespan Group, wrote in the *Stanford Social Innovation Review:*

Today, many nonprofit organizations struggle to attract and retain the talented senior executives they need to convert dollars into social impact. Searches for chief executive, operating, and financial officers often turn up only one to three qualified candidates, compared with four to six for comparable private-sector positions. The experience of a large nonprofit seeking a seasoned executive to guide its national expansion is typical: Only a single qualified candidate even considered the position. Like many other organizations in the nonprofit realm, this agency was one person away from a leadership crisis.[73]

The alternative that we offer these people is a poor one, because it robs charity of them in their prime. We tell them to go off and make their fortunes outside of charity—to use all of their creativity to sell sneakers and soda and hamburgers, to use all of their drive and ambition manufacturing golf clubs and video games, to use all of their managerial talents managing portfolios and investment bankers—and then, when they have achieved their ideal lifestyle, when they're sixty or sixty-five—about the time they're so exhausted from pursuing their fortune that they have no energy for anything else—we invite them to do charitable works.

This is not a solution. If we want people studying and trying to solve the great social problems of our times, we ought to set up a system that allows them to dedicate their lives to it, from the time they get out of college, without having to sacrifice their personal dreams. We do this in every other field of endeavor. People dedicate their lives to things, and this is how they develop wisdom in their fields. We ought to construct choices that encourage them to engage the great social problems of our times for their entire lifetimes, so that we have sages and elders in this most important of all arenas.

An Abusive Mixed Message

We live in a world that tells us at every turn we should make more money, that money is power, freedom, and the measure of one's worth. It is not just at our selfish interests that these messages are aimed. They are aimed also at our benevolence and our fears. We see messages everywhere telling us that money allows us to better educate and protect our children, provide our families with better health care, provide our parents with a better retirement—even that money is the key to making a difference in the world. These messages come at us from every angle: advertising, the news media, the publishing sector, the entertainment industry, our own family and social systems, and, most ironically, the philanthropy of the wealthy themselves whose ability to spread compassion is directly related to the money they have accumulated. We then tell people who work in the charitable sector that they should *not* want to make money. We expect them to be supernaturally immune to societal indoctrination.

It is a cruel mixed message: Donald Trump tells them, "You need to be wealthy," and charitable ideology tells them, "You need to be poor." The *Wall Street Journal* tells them, "You need to look out for yourselves," while the nonprofit Puritan ethic tells them, "You need to be concerned about others." Worse, their own self-interest tells them, "I want to be more comfortable," and charitable ideology says, "You should sacrifice your comfort for the comfort of others." If you were in a romantic relationship with someone sending these kinds of mixed signals, your friends would tell you to walk out.

In a perfect illustration of this phenomenon, an issue of *Worth* magazine ran two ironic stories, both featured on the cover. The first was about the "25 Most Generous Young Americans."[74] By definition they would have to be among the twenty-five most affluent young Americans. The table of contents elaborates, "These 25 under 46 are making the world a better place with a combination of youthful energy, money, and star power," and features a full-page photo of Andre Agassi as one of the young benefactors.[75] *Forbes* reported Andre Agassi's 2004 earnings at $28.2 million.[76] Everything about it says you should want to be wealthy like these people, because then you can be more generous.

Who do we think of as the most charitable people in the world? Billionaires and millionaires—Bill Gates, Bono, Ted Turner, Michael Jordan, Oprah, Al Gore, among others. Whose names do we see engraved on the hospital benefactor wall? Not people of middle-class station. Money is humanity.

The second *Worth* article is entitled, "100 Best Charities (and 10 Worst)." To determine the best charities, *Worth* "took a three-year average of the percentage of . . . total revenue . . . allocated to programs, administration, fundraising and reserves."[77] One of the things that typically lowers a charity's score in such a measurement is the amount of money it pays its chief executive. So there is an inverse correlation set up between high salaries and high grades. This is ironic in light of the fact that *Worth* magazine is a testament to opulence. The very same issue contains a feature section entitled, "SelfWorth." Its subtitle reads, "Lifestyle Investments and Luxury Escapes." The section contains an ad for the "crème de la crème of high rise condominium living, unrivaled in all of Las Vegas" with a photo above it featuring a plate of beluga caviar with the headline "Life is just a bowl of beluga." The next page features an article on a car called the "Saleen 7," which has a $395,000 price tag.[78]

The message is clear: *you* should want beluga caviar and a condo in Las Vegas, but if a charity pays someone else enough to eat beluga caviar or buy a condo in Las Vegas, *you* should not give to it.

Consider some of the advertising slogans that surround us:

"A diamond is forever" (DeBeers).

"Because you're worth it" (L'Oreal).

"Life takes Visa."

"The ultimate driving machine" (BMW).

"Never follow" (Audi).

"Life, liberty, and the pursuit" (Cadillac).

"Like nothing else" (Hummer).

"What are you made of?" (Tag Heuer).

"Miele. Anything else is a compromise."

"The passionate pursuit of perfection" (Lexus).

"Beauty without rules" (Tiffany & Company).

"Four Seasons Hotels and Resorts. When Life Feels Perfect."[79]

To those who want to work for a charity, society flips these messages around: "A diamond is for *everyone else*," "Because you're *not* worth it," "Always *follow*," and "*No* life, *no* liberty, just the pursuit of wealthy donors."

Advertising body copy goes even deeper into the psyche:

- "Horsepower is what sends you against the back of your seat. . . . Rather than leveling off after an initial burst of acceleration, the all-new 306-horsepower Infinity G rewards you with a seemingly endless progression of power . . . Infiniti."[80]
- "There was a time when I couldn't see the road ahead. So I hit the accelerator, and the whole world opened up. *My dream is to expand my horizons.* It is much brighter out here than I expected. Lincoln. Reach higher."[81]
- "It's just the way it used to be. When film stars danced, as white-gloved waiters poured champagne and elegantly dressed couples

found romance in the largest ballroom at sea. A most civilized adventure. Queen Mary 2. Cunard. The most famous ocean liners in the world."[82]

- "Intrigue your senses. We invite you to feast. To captivate not only your palate, but your eyes as well. To dine in a manner not easily forgotten; to release your inner sous-chef; to indulge the notion to have breakfast appear daily on your private verandah. We invite your senses to be delighted, time and time again, in ways large and small . . . Holland America Line. A Signature of Excellence."[83]
- "The New Range Rover for 2007—Starting at $77,250. Unequaled and uncompromised, the new Range Rover for 2007 remains the benchmark of luxury and refinement. Even while Range Rover stands as a classic icon, it never stands still."[84]
- "The best service anticipates your needs. And we understand you need to arrive refreshed and ready wherever business takes you. That's why we offer the most flat beds worldwide . . . we think you'll find our business class like no other. British Airways."[85]

Should the people who want to work in charity not even *want,* let alone be able, to *have* their senses intrigued too? Expand their horizons? Go on a civilized adventure? Arrive refreshed? The message is, if you work in that sector, don't even dream about these things; it is immoral for you to want the salary it would take to afford them. In any other field of endeavor, you can dream of rising beyond your station, but not in charity. No matter how high you rise, you are never supposed to want any of this, because it means you don't have the needy uppermost in your mind.

The conditioning is pervasive. Even in a spiritual magazine like *Yogi Times: Lifestyle for the Modern Yogi* (glossy and upscale), we find an article like "The Sutras of Holistic Wealth," with advice that tells us:

Living a prosperous life is a habit that must be cultivated from within. We each have a choice whether to train ourselves to become abundant in every area of our lives, including our finances, or to settle for our current results. . . . Are you satisfied with how many assets you have? Stocks? Bonds? Real estate? . . . In order to improve your financial results, you will need to make managing, investing, saving, and increasing your income a daily focus for at least three percent of each day. The language, awareness and habits of wealth building will become a part of who you are and what you attract into your world each day.[86]

This is preceded by an ad that says, "Free Wealth & Success Workshops with Financial Guru Vanessa Summers."[87] It is followed by an ad for Hästens handcrafted beds ("How Much Is Great Sleep Worth?") that can cost as much as $40,000.[88] I am not saying any of this is wrong. Abundance is healthy. I'm saying it's cruel to acknowledge this to the world at large while simultaneously discouraging it in the nonprofit sector.

Advertising also consistently warns us about compromising. If you don't buy this or that, you are compromising yourself, compromising your spouse, your children, and their safety. Someone who is consistently told he cannot buy the uncompromising this or that, unless he has the spiritual strength of Buddha, can only be left with a sense of a compromised self.

Moreover, consider the people society celebrates, from the parade of $20-million-a-picture movie stars, receiving awards at the Oscars, dressed in Armani and donated Harry Winston jewelry, to millionaire and billionaire football stars, rock stars, and dot com entrepreneurs. Doctor Phil is a millionaire. Barack Obama is a millionaire. Ralph Nader is a millionaire. The people who play average Joes on TV all seem to be real-life millionaires. No one who wants to work for a charity is supposed to aspire to any of this. As if this were not bad enough, we are then presented with campaigns that show the celebrities we are supposed to admire wearing the products we are supposed to buy, from Tiger Woods wearing Tag-Heuer to Yo-Yo Ma wearing a Rolex. The charitable work force is neither supposed to aspire to their status or want the products they endorse.

Oprah Winfrey, speaking at a *charity fundraiser* for Beth Tfiloh Dahan Community School, told the audience:

> I have lots of things, like all these Manolo Blahniks. I have all that and I think it's great. I'm not one of those people like, "Well, we must renounce ourselves." No, I have a closet full of shoes and it's a good thing. . . . I was coming back from Africa on one of my trips. . . . I had taken one of my wealthy friends with me. She said, "Don't you just feel guilty? Don't you just feel terrible?" I said, "No, I don't. I do not know how me being destitute is going to help them." Then I said when we got home, "I'm going home to sleep on my Pratesi sheets right now and I'll feel good about it."[89]

You can be inspired by this, as many of Oprah's viewers are, unless you intend to spend your life working for a charity.

The mixed message reaches a pinnacle of cruelty inside the sector itself, where the very nature of fundraising puts the charitable *professional,* who is not supposed to be economically focused, face to face on a daily basis with some of the wealthiest members of his community. The relationship is necessarily subservient. The professional is dependent on the wealthy donor for her own livelihood. She is confronted head on with the fact that the person who has pursued his self-interest has a greater financial capacity to be charitable than the professional herself and has greater say over charitable policy than the professional who spends her life in the field. As if that were not difficult enough, the billionaire who spends 1 percent of his time on charity and 99 percent of his time building wealth we call a "philanthropist." The three-hundred-thousand-aire who spends 100 percent of his time working on charity and 0 percent of his time building real wealth we call "obscene." What ambitious, talented, self-respecting Stanford MBA is going to say yes to this proposition?

No surprise, the marketing messages aimed at present and future business leaders also associate your arrival in society with money—just a lot more of it. The following advertising messages appear in *Elite Traveler*—"The Private Jet Lifestyle Magazine":

- "Freedom. Fueled and Waiting. Fractional Jet Ownership Designed Around You. Bombadier Flexjet offers you the finest fractional jet ownership experience and the freedom to indulge life's passions. . . . When you want to fly, simply call us. In as little as six hours, your aircraft is fueled and waiting. So is your freedom . . . Bombardier Flexjet."
- "To most, this lifestyle is off limits. To you, it's without limits. Unprecedented exclusivity has arrived . . . Sumptuous. Opulent. Luxurious . . . With superbly conceived world-class amenities and a discreet staff to indulge your every whim . . . 26 oceanfront condominium residences . . . pre-construction value from $4.9 million to over $8.5 million. Luxuria, Boca Raton, Florida."
- "Participating in Solstice is a life-defining moment—an awareness that traditional second home ownership can be limiting. . . . Within Solstice, you enjoy flexible and unlimited access to a growing collection of one-of-a-kind, six million dollar second homes in the world's best locations. Solstice. Luxury Residence Collection."
- "Explore the world's oceans in Deluxe Accommodations, Penthouse Suites with butler service or Exclusive Yacht-Style Cruising . . . you might even Charter your own vessel . . . Cruise Specialists. Dedicated to Luxury Travel."
- "The Turnberry Doctrine: There's no reason to spend a moment of your life settling for less than the best. This is our newest way of

saying, 'If you have the means, we have the ways.' Turnberry Ltd. The people who wrote the book on private club lifestyles."
- "Superiority Complex. Bellagio, Las Vegas. Embrace extravagance."[90]

One need not be among the superelite to be on the path of these offerings. I received a glossy twenty-page brochure from the UCLA Alumni Association. The cover read, "Around the World by Private Jet." Inside was a description of a spectacular trip from Machu Picchu to the Great Barrier Reef to Tibet to the Pyramids and places in between. The price tag—$49,500 per person.[91] Presumably, the trip and the catalogue were assembled by nonprofit workers for whom the trip is wildly out of reach.

The following Smith Barney ad in the *Robb Report* makes the correlation between wealth and humanity for this group explicit. In one paragraph it summarizes perfectly the whole of what we are taught:

> I am working wealth. Earn your first dollar by your labors. Get up early, work late. Get up the next day and do it again. Keep doing it, even after the dollars start adding up. Smile at challenges. Curse at idleness. Be true to your dream. Don't stop until you achieve it. Then dream another dream. And work to achieve that. Pass on your values. Not just your assets. Give your family a better life. And the world a better life, too. . . . Leave signs of significance. . . . We at Smith Barney would like to say one thing to you. WELCOME. Working Wealth. Smith Barney.[92]

We expect potential nonprofit leaders to be immune to these messages or to have more moral fortitude than the rest of those in their peer group who will be able to afford these things. If they do not have that fortitude, the message is that we don't want them in the sector. By and large, they oblige.

This brings up the question of the way, in this age of affluence, we define how much consumption is too much. This is a subjective question. How do potential nonprofit leaders (or any other potential nonprofit job candidates) answer it? How do Harvard MBAs answer it? By what standard do they measure their success? If feeling successful is mandatory for their entry into the charitable leadership market, this should be a question that concerns all of us. Galbraith wrote in 1958:

> People are poverty-stricken when their income, even if adequate for survival, falls radically behind that of the community. Then they cannot have what the larger community regards as the minimum necessary for decency; and they

cannot wholly escape, therefore, the judgment of the larger community that they are indecent. They are degraded for, in the literal sense, they live outside the grades or categories which the community regards as acceptable.[93]

Just as middle-class people can feel degraded by comparing their life-styles to ones they cannot afford, those in the upper classes can feel degraded by an elite environment they cannot afford but their peers can. This may reflect some spiritual deficiency. Be that as it may, it is a disease that is widespread, and we have to deal with it as a reality. It does the needy no good for us to preach to these men and women that they shouldn't feel degraded. They will never put themselves in a position where they might feel degraded in the first place. Ours, then, is little more than a luxurious opinion. All it does is discourage an entire class of business leaders from applying their talents to the issues we ask charity to address.

Summary

All of this creates a perfect storm of deprivation. First, the constraints on charity send much of the world's greatest talent into the for-profit sector. Second, the people who do come into the nonprofit sector are unlikely to stay long enough to create critical institutional consistency and knowledge. Third, they endure so much personal financial stress that it is hard to imagine how they could have very much imaginative reserve left to envision solutions to the world's greatest problems, let alone to execute them. Fourth, because they themselves are not affluent, they travel outside circles of affluence, where mutually beneficial cross-promotional and synchronistic business initiatives are so often cooked up. In the end, all of these things come together to create a dynamic failure of possibility. The for-profit sector continues to thrive, and the nonprofit sector continues to struggle. And it all occurs in the name of charity.

The Second Error—Prohibition on Risk: Punishing Courage, Rewarding Timidity

Experimentation and Risk

In 1986, Ken Kragen, at the time the manager of pop singers Kenny Rogers and Lionel Ritchie, among others, had a vision of a grand-scale charity and community-building event called Hands Across America. The dream was to have a line of people holding hands from the West to the East Coast on a Sunday afternoon in May, with each participant making a contribution to fight hunger and homelessness. Hands Across America was the template, in many ways, for the charitable mega-event. Against an ambitious goal of $50 million, it raised $34 million. Expenses came in at about the amount predicted. According to the official website, Kragen's efforts "resulted in at least a billion more from the US government and private organizations. . . . Most importantly [they] opened the door for the media to report on the plight of these people. Something they rarely did until then."[94] President Reagan, not previously considered a friend of the homeless, held hands in the line at the White House. Ken Kragen was forty-nine at the time, had a Harvard MBA, and volunteered all of his time and effort to the project.

Nonetheless, the fact that the event was new and unorthodox, and fell short of its goal, triggered the predictable reaction. ABC News reported, "Critics have said the heavily hyped event failed as a fundraiser because it cost $17 million to produce and fell far short of its goal of raising $50 million to feed the hungry."[95] *Time* magazine wrote about the "slick video for the project's rather schmaltzy anthem,"[96] and the *New York Times* reported:

> One year ago, Hands Across America was billed as the unassailable charity event of the 1980s. . . . But there were lots of gaps in between, and a lot of people did not send in their pledges, resulting in a net of only $15 million for the hungry and homeless after all costs were paid. . . . Organizers have found themselves on the defensive because the cost of mounting the event was $14 million to $16 million. Even though the cost was known in advance, its size in relation to donations hurt credibility.[97]

Another *New York Times* story, headlined "Hands Across America Faces Costs and Delay," reported that "only about half the $41.6 million raised by Hands Across America will be given to the needy because of high administrative costs" and singled out costs for "such things as toll-free telephone numbers," as if charity shouldn't use toll-free telephone numbers.[98] It went on to pass judgment by saying, "Guidelines of the Los Angeles Social Service Department . . . say at least 70 percent of the proceeds of a fund-raising event held by a not-for-profit foundation should go to the charitable cause."[99] An Associated Press story quoted a Los Angeles Social Services Department investigator saying, " 'Something is wrong' " and " 'It could be mismanagement or anything.' "[100]

The *Los Angeles Times* (the event's headquarters were in Los Angeles) wrote no fewer than twenty stories on the event, often focusing in minute detail on finances and shortfalls against the $50 million goal. The paper began six months before the event raising suspicions about things as specific as the amount of rent the project was paying for offices in a "Century-City high-rise."[101] On June 12, a 1,100-word story reported that the event "appears to have been a fundraising disappointment" and that "operating overhead alone will total about $12 million."[102] Five days later, a 2,223-word story reported that the project's accomplishments "have received mixed reviews."[103] According to the article, an "issues analyst" for a San Francisco hunger organization stated that "the fund-raising shortfall raises serious questions about Hands Across America's parent organization" and asked, "'What kind of organization is behind this?'"[104] The article quoted the head of a local food bank stating, "'That is a disappointment. . . . 'I'm sure this is going to give everybody involved cause to reflect. . . . [The financial shortfall and high overhead] will have an impact on how people approach these things in the future. . . . I would think that when people are approached again, they are going to proceed with real skepticism (about projects) that require a real big front-end investment.'"[105]

The article continued, "The essentially middle-class media event failed to measure up to its lofty expectations for other reasons" and quoted a local resident saying, "On Sunday, May 25, 1986 I was not only part of an historic human chain, but I was part of human disappointment."[106]

Two months later, on August 25, the *Los Angeles Times* reported:

> An article which appeared Aug. 16 in the *Cleveland Plain Dealer* said that only about half the Hands Across America income would actually be spent on the homeless and hungry—the avowed purpose of the mega-event. . . . The *Plain Dealer*'s article recycled the information over the nation's news wire services and raised anew the question of the high Hands Across America overhead. The *Plain Dealer* quoted George Delianedis of the City of Los Angeles Public Social Services Department as saying he would be watching Hands Across America expenses "real closely." Delianedis is an investigator with the department.[107]

Marty Rogol, executive director of the project (whose salary was $68,000), said:

> The amount of confusion caused by [the *Plain Dealer*] article is phenomenal. . . . I had one person asking if it was true Marty Rogol embezzled money from Hands Across America. One reporter called me from New Jersey asking

if we were going to shut down because we couldn't meet our expenses. It's unbelievable.[108]

The *Los Angeles Times* article went into minute detail, exploring specific cost figures for everything from insurance premiums to "direct-mail expenses," "cost accountants," "executive staffing," and "catalogues," among other things, adding that "a more detailed line item breakdown of Hands expenses will be completed and made public by mid-September."[109] Consider this against the lack of any investigative journalism of the record $40.6 billion profit that Exxon reported at the end of 2007.[110] The story reports Kragen and Rogol saying that "they were spending most of their time dealing with fallout from the *Plain Dealer* story."[111]

About a month later, a 2,702-word story in the *Los Angeles Times*, reacting to how much good organizers said the project had done, noted, "But reporters keep coming back to the money. . . . Why had it cost more than $16 million to put on the 15-minute national event?"[112] It then pointed out that the accounting firm that audited the event was "earning a $7,500-a-month retainer," as if this were relevant in any way. *When was the last time anyone wrote twenty stories asking why it cost $200 million to make a ninety-four-minute movie?*

A few months later, someone commented in a *Los Angeles Times* op-ed piece, "I think of the Hands Across America offices in Century City, and the distance, emotional as well as physical, from there to Skid Row. . . . I wonder if the people in those offices have any real conception of poverty."[113]

With character assassination like this, who in his right mind would ever want to take the initiative to spearhead an effort like this again? Indeed, the *Los Angeles Times* reported that Ken Kragen, apparently coming to his senses, said after the event, "'I've got to get back to making a living.'"[114] If the lack of competitive compensation were not enough to keep a bright young MBA out of the nonprofit sector, surely this kind of harassment would.

Hands Across America never happened again. None of what was learned could be applied to a sequel. All the capital contained in that institutional knowledge was lost. The "disappointing" millions that went to the homeless from that event never went to the homeless again. The annual revenue stream that could have been generated was annihilated after its first year. By any logical standard, that would have to be defined as the most disappointing outcome of all.

Overall, our company's experience was identical. The two highest-profile events that turned out to be disappointments were met with an investigation by the Pennsylvania attorney general and became the subject of a class-action lawsuit. Any disappointment became a target of suspicion and character assassination. For instance, the thirty-three event campaigns we produced between 1994 and 1998 netted, on average, 56 percent of donor contributions for charitable services.[115] This was exceptional considering the logistical complexity of the events and the velocity and volume of our fundraising. But a 1998 article in San Francisco's *Bay Area Reporter* focuses on four events that had returns below 50 percent, using characterizations like "unmitigated disaster," "we got screwed," "moral compass broken," and "make money for themselves and [do] not provide help for people with AIDS."[116] *POZ,* a for-profit magazine geared to the HIV-positive community, used expressions like "fiasco," "dismal," and "respectable fundraisers cringe at these kinds of scams."[117] But by the end of 1998, after just five years of staging the events, we had netted $57.33 million in unrestricted funds for charity.[118]

Worse than this was the lack of genuine interest in the data. One newspaper published an editorial that said we "blamed the disturbingly low ratios of net proceeds vs. high production costs on everything from Mother Nature to low gay support to logistical problems."[119] Presumably the right explanation would have been that we were just horrible people. There was no thoughtful consideration of the legitimacy of factors we were citing.

We met with similar hostility on a series of specialized, particularly challenging rides called the AIDS Vaccine Rides we designed specifically to raise funds for vaccine research. We financed these with our own bank financing, and I put my home up as collateral to obtain it. Our first ride across Alaska netted $4.16 million for three leading U.S. research institutes.[120] Based on that success, we launched two more of the events the next year, one across Montana and one across the Canadian border in New England. But too few riders signed up to reach our revenue targets. This necessarily made our fixed costs a larger percentage of the revenue. Still, the three events netted *another* $4 million in critical unrestricted funds for AIDS research. But percentage returns were low. The criticism of us was merciless, as described in the case study which appears later.[121] One of our AIDS Vaccine charities, which had received more than $2 million in unrestricted funds from our efforts in two years, sent us the following letter under enormous pressure from AIDS activists. The tension between reason and our distorted definitions of morality is palpable:

> It is with great sadness that I write to inform you that [we] cannot continue our participation in your AIDS vaccine events in 2002 and later. This decision is based on the disappointingly low rate of return to the vaccine research institutions for the events that took place in 2001. An institute like ours simply cannot morally justify engaging in fundraising activities with such high costs. . . . Let me also take this opportunity to express our gratitude for the funds you have raised on our behalf in 2000 and 2001. This form of unrestricted research support has considerably expanded our vaccine development effort, which is now moving along nicely. We will always be indebted to you and your colleagues at Pallotta TeamWorks.[122]

Eight million dollars had been netted in two years for unrestricted vaccine research—money that was nonexistent before the events. It is nonexistent again. Would the activists pressuring the charity say it is now somehow more moral that no money is going to AIDS vaccine research from those events?

As a result of this potential liability, charities rarely undertake initiatives whose outcomes are not predictable. On those rare occasions when they do and they fail, the results are often swept under the rug out of fear of a witch-hunt—blended in with their entire organizational accounting to obscure specifics, rendering inaccessible any data from which others could learn. *The charitable data stream on experimentation is dry.*

Even if staff were inclined to experiment, funding for anything bold and daring is hard to come by. New initiatives require spending precious discretionary unrestricted dollars. This typically requires board approval. Board members tend to be extremely risk averse. Their participation on the board is driven by a variety of motives, not the least of which are prestige and community standing. They typically do not sign on to accept the potential liability to their reputations that presently comes with a high-profile disappointment. Government funding is notoriously conservative. Foundation funding is no different. A *Harvard Business Review* article by Christine Letts, William Ryan, and Allen Grossman entitled "Virtuous Capital: What Foundations Can Learn from Venture Capitalists" notes, "Perhaps the most striking difference between venture capital firms and foundations is how they manage risk."[123] The Community Wealth Ventures report produced for the Morino Foundation summarizes the article's observation on risk: "VC firms take risk and are rewarded accordingly. Rather than being avoided, risk is managed. Foundations avoid risk because they are not rewarded one way or the other for taking risk. Accordingly, foundations compromise the likelihood of measurable returns."[124] Similarly, individual major donors are unlikely to fund initiatives that are less than a sure bet.

A 2003 story in the *Chronicle of Philanthropy* described the ironic behavior of entrepreneurs:

> Megagifts—donations of $10-million or more—are a critical component of American philanthropy. Such donations accounted for more than $29-billion of the donations that charities received from 1995 to 2000, according to "Mega-Gifts in American Philanthropy," a new report by the Institute for Jewish & Community Research. . . . A lot of the donors of big gifts are entrepreneurs, and even though many spent their lives taking risks in business, they generally do not give money away in the same fashion. . . . Most of the gifts were for projects that can be considered safe or risk-averse.[125]

In every other field of endeavor, people are encouraged to make mistakes. "If at first you don't succeed, try, try, again" is the cheer to every sector but charity.

On its face this sounds reasonable. We don't want our dollars wasted on experiments. We want them to go to the needy. But we assume that dollars are being wasted if they don't go directly, immediately, and visibly to the needy. We assume that experimentation is necessarily wasteful. All of our common sense tells us otherwise. If we give the notion a second thought, we can see that it's counterproductive to any hope of progress. If charities cannot make mistakes, they cannot learn. If they can make only small mistakes, they can never learn anything great. They are sentenced to an eternity of small contexts.

It is important to draw a distinction between what we allow charities to do with the whole dollar we donate and what we allow them to do with that part of the dollar we believe is "going to the cause." We don't explore very much what a charity *does* with the part of a dollar that goes to the cause. The average donor simply wants to know what percentage *goes* to the cause. Consequently, many donated dollars, particularly in the case of disease research, are in fact used for experimentation without fear of reprisal. But what I'm talking about are the limitations donors, government, and foundations place on the *amount* of dollars a charity can raise for scientific research in the first place when we prohibit them from experimenting with *fundraising* or with ways to build capital or to broaden the appeal of the cause itself. It's one thing for a scientist to conduct an experiment that "fails"—that is still categorized as a dollar that went to the cause. There is no reporting mechanism that addresses it. But if a charity "fails" with a bold new fundraising idea, the dollars expended are categorized as *not* going to the cause and are applied to overhead. We don't do this with science or business. Because charities don't want to get bad grades on overhead percentages and because they don't want to be seen as spending donor dollars on "failures," they often avoid initiatives that are bold in this critical area. They don't spend money on research and development for *development* itself.

What kind of experimentation am I talking about? It could be the use of donor dollars to buy a restaurant franchise that could produce a steady annual revenue stream. If the experiment "failed," the data might be used to explore another area or to open another type of restaurant (that also might "fail"). It could also be the use of donor dollars to launch a targeted ad campaign on television designed to bring in new donors, which might include a few expensive ads during a prime-time television show. If those "failed," the data might be used to adjust the media buys, to buy new ads, and so on. Eventually there might be enough data to test a Super Bowl ad that could bring in millions in donations (but that also might "fail").

Mark Kramer, the former chairperson of the Jewish Funders Network, in a *Chronicle of Philanthropy* opinion piece entitled "Venture Capital and Philanthropy: A Bad Fit," writes:

> The tools of the venture capitalist will not work in philanthropy. . . . For all venture capitalists' vaunted wisdom and experience, the companies in which they invest fail far more often than they succeed. The rule of thumb is that one out of ten investments will be a home run, two to three others will break even or make a modest profit, and more than half will fail outright, with the entire investment lost. In the venture-capital world, those dismal odds work because one success can bring such phenomenal results that it compensates for all the failures. For example, $10,000 invested in the Internet search service Yahoo when it began four years ago would be worth $35-million today. Get that one right, and the other nine investments are never even noticed. Can those odds work in philanthropy? It is difficult to imagine a foundation board that would be pleased if half of its grants went to organizations that failed, and only one out of ten went to organizations that surpassed their goals. In philanthropy, there is no simple way to measure social benefits like monetary returns, no comparable calculus that justifies the waste of rare and precious humanitarian dollars on nine programs that accomplish nothing in the hopes that one will succeed on a substantial scale."[126]

Kramer asks whether the odds can work in philanthropy, where foundations have little tolerance for failure. First of all, to sacrifice progress on the altar of perfectionism is public relations, not philanthropy. As for whether the odds can work in philanthropy, as in "love of humanity," I can tell you they do. An approximately $500,000 initial investment by the Avon Foundation in the Breast Cancer 3-Days turned into $194.4 million in net unrestricted funds for their programs. A $50,000 initial investment in California AIDSRide turned into $20 million in net unrestricted funds for AIDS for the Los Angeles Gay & Lesbian Center. In both cases, it was our first attempt, not our tenth. But even if it had been our tenth, even if $4.5 million had been spent on nine "failures" up until that point, how can any rational analysis call an attempt at a $194.4 million end result a "waste of rare and precious humanitarian dollars"? This is yet another example of focusing on means instead of outcomes. Furthermore, that one out of ten venture projects will succeed is not a "hope." By Mr. Kramer's own admission, it is a statistic.

I mentioned earlier that venture philanthropy doesn't address the real problem, which is the need for capital, because venture philanthropy only seeks to identify new program approaches. I didn't say that it doesn't work at identifying new program approaches. I think it does, to a great extent. But what if venture philanthropy looked beyond programs to revenue models? A venture philanthropy model focused on finding new revenue models—which is in reality what venture capital funding does in the for-profit sector—one willing to take financial risk in pursuit of breakthrough fundraising approaches, could amount to a revolution. It could unveil an unimaginable array of new revenue streams heretofore unknown and untested. *On that point, it has always seemed unbelievable to me that foundations would rather fund programs over and over and over again instead of fund experiments in fundraising. If foundations nurtured new revenue models, charities could generate their own revenue for programs. The tens of billions that foundations give away every year to programs could instead be used as start-up capital for new fundraising events, campaigns, charity-owned businesses, and more. It could be leveraged to generate hundreds of billions more in permanent revenue streams to fund programs. Instead, its leveraging potential is permanently annihilated by program expenditure itself. In this sense, current practice only institutionalizes charities' dependence on foundations.*

The fact that venture capitalism isn't accepted doesn't mean it is a bad fit or that it will not work. It could fit for the needy. It could work for the poor. In the end, this is all that matters. That foundations don't have the stomach for risk is an indictment of ideology, not the fundamental validity of venture capitalism and experimentation.

Imagine if there were a similar measure in the for-profit sector that explicitly categorized research and development costs as a negative or that otherwise penalized the sector for experimentation. All we need do is look at any business achievement born of boldness and erase it from the landscape. Anything not certain to succeed would have to go—from the telephone to the combustion engine and anything that stood on their shoulders. There would be nothing left.

We have *built* our society on the backs of bold gambles, experimentation, mistakes, failures, and learning. How could we possibly *improve* society for its most needy citizens without doing the same?

The business model for the motion picture industry is germane. An annual report for MGM states:

> The film production aspect of our business is non-linear. Some pictures will be successful, and certainly some will not. . . . Overall, the year 2002 yielded mixed results in film performance for the Company's MGM Pictures unit and specialty film division United Artists (UA). Although the Studio's films underperformed in the first six months, winning releases in the second half of the year prompted a dramatic comeback, leading to another profitable overall film slate. MGM finished out the year in strong fashion.[127]

"Failure" is built into the motion picture business model, and the movie studios have many of them. Think of all the movies that went straight to DVDs at Blockbuster without ever making their way into movie theaters, much less a profit margin. Movie studios can't know which movies are going to be hits and which are going to fail. If they knew which ones were going to fail, they wouldn't make them. A movie cannot be tested in a focus group before it is made. It can only be tested after it is made and after the money has been put at risk. Then and only then can a studio know if people like it. Often they don't. Sometimes they do. If "failure" were prohibited in the motion picture industry, there wouldn't *be* a motion picture industry.

What is true of the motion picture industry is true of most of the consumer products industry. There are always more unsuccessful new product launches than there are successful ones. The history of failure far exceeds the history of success. In the end, after whatever available data are considered, businesses make nine-figure decisions on the basis of a guess. But we don't allow our charities to make guesses. One cannot get very good at guessing if one is never allowed to do it.

Aren't we turning the odds against the needy in a much larger way if we do not take risks? Aren't we in fact *guaranteeing* only that their condition will remain the same, except for small incremental improvements from time to time? The odds of a breakthrough in a well-considered experiment will always be greater than zero. The odds of a breakthrough by trying nothing are *guaranteed* to be zero.

If a charity tries something bold and fails, but learns from its effort and applies the lessons learned to a new endeavor that succeeds, that helps the needy. Why, then, do we think of it as wasted? Why do we think it did *not* help the needy? Because we can't see the result down the road. Boldness paid off over the long term, but the window we are asked to look through is only open for a year. The Morino Institute points out:

> For entrepreneurs who seek to introduce venture capital–like disciplines to philanthropy, investment criteria goes hand-in-hand with risk taking. For the purposes of this report, we are equating risk with willingness to fund capacity building. A funder who invests in an organization's future capacity will have no assurances of success and will have no immediate measures of accomplishment. This funding strategy contrasts to that of a traditional foundation which funds service delivery programs. Capacity funding might produce great outcomes down the road, as Letts et al. argue, but there is no proven correlation in the nonprofit sector between capacity building and improved service delivery. One might have to wait for years before seeing results, just as a venture capitalist expects only three of 10 investments to succeed and [is] uncertain of results when investing in a venture.[128]

Our short-term focus fails us. "What percentage of my donation went to the cause?" is a question that enforces that focus. It is based on a single twelve-month period and is therefore incapable of giving us even a glimpse at the value the "failure" may provide down the road, in a year or two or three. It punishes those who exercise courage and rewards those who are timid.

If we abandon the illogical idea that a dollar we give today can only help the needy if it is used today, then we can let go of the idea that there should be a guarantee that a dollar we give today will be used today. We can be more generous with how our generosity is applied. We can give a charity the flexibility to do what it believes is best. Then "failures" will be seen as progress, and we won't feel that any promises to us have been broken. Our whole opinion of charity can become elevated, and a charity itself can have the freedom to dream and the confidence to know it has our confidence. From this great things can come.

If we change our attitudes, we can have our cake and eat it too. We can give money to a mix of charitable endeavors, some bold and some cautious, instead of perpetually demanding caution exclusively. Charities themselves can provide a mix of options, from bold to cautious, and advertise the benefits of each, making the case for specific experimentation directly and forcefully to the public. Over time, some charities will become known for their boldness, others for their conservatism, in the same way that different for-profit enterprises do. Investors will put money in a mix of both. The market will be free instead of restricted. From this great solutions can emerge.

The opportunity cost of those nonprofit sector dreams we have discouraged is inestimable. But it is not the only loss. A system that creates barriers to vision not only loses visions. It loses visionaries. It loses them coming and going, from the inside and the outside.

An organization constrained to seek certainty perpetually relives the past, trying the same old things over and over again and boring employees to death. It will never attempt anything breathtaking that might stimulate the imagination or open the door to wonder and possibility. It is exiled from the future. It operates in an environment that not only discourages ideas that have already been imagined, but discourages the development of new ideas.

Most people come into the nonprofit sector full of hope. They come because they want to change things. They soon realize that they are in an environment that wants no part of that. It cannot risk it. Their bold ideas are discouraged. They become imprisoned in a domain of predictability. It is one thing to tell people that a charity doesn't have the resources to try out their ideas. It is completely another to tell them that even if it did, it wouldn't risk implementing them. What hope does that leave people? What incentive do they have even to try? On this point, Paul C. Light wrote:

> Unfortunately, many non-profit organizations see innovation as an unnatural act. They erect needless barriers to new ideas, frustrate collaboration, deny employees permission to make mistakes, withhold the resources needed to experiment, and create a climate of fear that silences all but the most courageous. . . . Slowly but surely, they become towering monuments to the status quo they once sought to challenge, drifting from year to year with no real sense of purpose or commitment. Even a moribund organization can innovate once, however. Just find a heroic leader willing to try a new approach in spite of bureaucratic nitpicking, impatient clients, scarce

resources, sometimes-hostile coverage in the press, and antiquated management systems. Once the heroes are worn out or leave, however, the innovations quickly perish.[129]

We think that a charity should have the luxury of paying people less because they get fulfillment from helping people. But if people cannot try out their new ideas for helping people, then even that incentive is gone. Such an environment is suffocating to anyone, whether she is in it or thinking of entering it. If we are not incubating ideas or idea makers, we will have no ideas about how to address the problems we face, and no people with the incentive to come up with them.

Some might say that this is an indictment of those working in the nonprofit sector. It is not. There are plenty of talented people in the sector. It is simply that the sector won't be able to hold onto them. If it cannot encourage their best thinking, it cannot encourage them to stay. People want to make a difference. They want to fulfill their potential. The best of them will not stay, nor should they, in an environment that very nearly expressly prohibits them from doing so.

The Third Error—Discouragement of Long-Term Vision: The Need for Immediate Gratification Institutionalizes Suffering

That the need for immediate gratification makes disappointments look like failures or that it stifles innovation is not the only problem. It also discourages long-term planning, even when it is not particularly risky. In business we encourage long-term thinking and investment. In charity, we encourage the opposite. A study by the Princeton Survey Research Associates bears this out:

> *Donors expect their money to be used for current programs.* When Americans donate money to a charitable organization, they expect the bulk of their contribution to go toward current programs, rather than be put in reserve. In total, 63% of Americans have such expectations—including nearly half (46%) who assume that *all* of their contribution will be used to fund current charitable work.[130]

Mark Rosenman, a professor at Union Institute and University, writes in the *Chronicle of Philanthropy:*

> Organizations that work for long-term change instead of short-term deliverables would find it nearly impossible to raise the money they need. . . . The

sad truth is that charitable dollars are overwhelmingly directed to providing services to meet immediate, often pressing, needs, to remedy problems but not to solve them. Much too little attention and too few resources are spent on efforts to seek fundamental change.[131]

After the September 11 attacks, the Red Cross attempted to set aside for future catastrophes some of the enormous quantity of donations that poured in. The outcry was so significant that the organization's president had to resign. The *New York Times* reported:

> The American Red Cross was widely criticized for saying it would hold back some of the donations it received for Sept. 11 victims as a reserve fund for future disasters. Although that is standard procedure among disaster relief agencies, the fuss made other charities cautious about the way they disbursed funds earmarked for Sept. 11.[132]

In the midst of the controversy, an Associated Press report headlined "Some Money Raised for Red Cross' Liberty Fund to Go to Long-Term Plans" noted:

> Philanthropic watchdog groups are expressing concern over the Red Cross' intention to use some donations to an account earmarked for victims of the terrorist attacks for other broad-based needs. . . . A portion of that money will go to broad-based activities such as a blood reserve program, a national outreach effort and a telecommunications upgrade.[133]

The *New York Post* reported that "Red Cross president Bernadine Healy quit yesterday amid growing criticism that the charity was spending too much of the $500 million it had raised since Sept. 11 to build its empire rather than help victims."[134] And according to the *New York Times*, "Senior [Red Cross] agency officials were criticized by members of Congress and legislators in New York who accused the agency of cynically using the Sept. 11 tragedies to address long-term fund-raising goals."[135]

Another criticism leveled at the Red Cross was that it did not make it clear that some of the funds donated might be used for long-term purposes and preparedness for future disasters. The Red Cross countered, "We believe very much that we are honoring donor intent."[136] The Associated Press reported that of the $550 million that had been raised to date, $50 million would be used "for a blood readiness and reserve program that would increase the group's blood inventory from two or three days to 10 days," $26 million would be used for "nationwide community outreach," and $29 million would be used on "relief infrastructure, including telecommunications, information systems, database management, contribution processing and other overhead costs."[137]

That some degree of controversy might have arisen may be understandable. That it rose to the level of a national scandal is remarkable. This was a disaster-relief organization setting aside funds for future disaster relief. If an "empire" was being built, it was only for the purpose of better addressing the next disaster, which could have come at any day.

In a classic reenactment of Puritan contrition, the Red Cross pleaded for forgiveness. It appointed former U.S. senator George Mitchell to oversee the fund. In a *New York Times* story, Mitchell said, "To its credit, the Red Cross acknowledged its mistakes and changed some of its policies that were mistaken."[138] According to another story, the Red Cross "reversed course . . . and said they would donate all the money raised by the fund to those directly affected by the attacks."[139] It had the feeling of an incident Innes recounted from John Winthrop's journal in which a miller and some of his hands began repairing a leaky milldam on a Saturday afternoon and continued working into the night past the Sabbath, when work was prohibited. Tragically, the next day, the miller's daughter drowned. "Called to stand in contrition before his church, the father, 'freely in the open congregation, did acknowledge [his child's death] as the righteous hand of God for his profaning his holy day against the check of his own conscience.'"[140] In a demonstration of its commitment to self-restraint and nonprofit ideology, in 2007 the Red Cross appointed the former commissioner of the IRS as its new executive director.[141] Wouldn't the world's premier aid organization want an expert in providing aid at its helm instead of an expert in compliance?

That the Red Cross reversed course should not come as any great comfort to us as we think about the possibility of a future attack. It is disconcerting at best to know that they have an inadequate telecommunications system and a two-day blood supply.

The problem doesn't end with blood supplies and phone systems. It pervades every level of nonprofit operation. Consider what the public reaction would be upon learning that $100,000 in donor funds went to pay an executive search firm to find a charity's future leader or if $50,000 went to send an employee to business school in an effort to develop a future leader from the inside, instead of those funds going directly to the needy. Thomas Tierney wrote in the *Stanford Social Innovation Review:*

> Unlike businesses, most nonprofits cannot cultivate their own supply of future leaders. Successful companies routinely invest enormous amounts of

time and money attracting talented junior managers and developing them into leaders. Most nonprofits (even larger ones) are too small to provide meaningful career development opportunities for their employees. Most cannot afford the huge investment in recruitment and human resources that such development requires—especially when boards, funders, and donors view such expenditures as wasteful overhead. . . . Nonprofits also lack the human resources infrastructure available to for-profit organizations. Business schools supply a steady stream of next-generation leadership to the private sector. The executive search industry has grown from modest beginnings a few decades ago to a multibillion-dollar business. . . . These services exist because profit-making businesses can amply reward those who help fill their leadership supply needs. Without extra time and money to invest in finding talent, nonprofits simply cannot compete with the for-profit world when it comes to finding capable leaders.[142]

Les Silverman and Lynn Taliento, in the *Stanford Social Innovation Review,* wrote about the results of a "virtual conversation among 11 nonprofit executives who have also held senior positions in the for-profit world—that is, crossover leaders."[143] Among those were David Chernow, leader of Junior Achievement Worldwide, and Richard Schlosberg, who was CEO and publisher of the *Los Angeles Times* before serving five years as president of the David and Lucille Packard Foundation. On the subject of building capacity for the future they write:

"I see undercapacity all over the nonprofit sector," [said Schlosberg]. Many good managers in the nonprofit sector would agree on the need for capacity building, but simply can't get donors to support it. "In the for-profit business," says Chernow, "you spend an enormous amount of money on that training. Here, if we went out to corporations and foundations to give us money to develop capacity in our organization and to build leadership, it's not as readily accepted. It's hard to get that kind of investment."[144]

That the current construction suffocates big ideas that take years to manifest is only one part of the problem. The other part is all of the good three- and four-year ideas that the construction undermines. For example, the percentage of overhead on our California AIDSRide rose from an average of about 40 percent from 1994 through 2000 to about 50 percent in 2001.[145] One of the reasons for this sudden shift was that in 2001 we decided to make significant investments for the future that required spending a good deal of money in the present, all of which needed to be allocated to overhead. For instance, we had been spending a lot of money renting equipment for the events. This included large hydraulic stages for the ceremonies, sound systems, circus-like dining tents capable of seating five hundred to a thousand people, mobile modular units for command centers, and other things. This equipment was expensive to rent. Early on, we knew that we could buy it for the same amount that it would cost us to rent it, in some cases, for just one year. That meant we would have the equipment for years to come and could control the annual expense to provide it at the events.

We also invested in a state-of-the-art customer service center, so that when calls came in from our advertising, we wouldn't lose any of them, and we would have a high-quality staff in a central place trained to educate and inspire callers about our events so that more people would register. This call center, and all of the computer and telephone equipment that went with it, was an expensive investment in the short term, but we believed it would mean more riders and walkers over the long term and more money going to the charities.

Again, both of these long-term investments—designed to improve the percentage of overhead in the long term—necessarily caused a short-term spike in 2001, for which we were immediately criticized. The system has no tolerance for something like that. The typical donor response to high infrastructure costs is, understandably, for example, "I'd rather just give the money to the homeless myself. That way 100 percent of it goes to them." It's understandable because we are all conditioned to focus on the short-term. But it is time we began to realize that the infrastructure required to feed a homeless person for a day is entirely different from the infrastructure required to create systemic improvement, or to end homelessness for everyone for good.

Using the famous example of "Amazon.com," consider how a short-term focus puts charity at a disadvantage with respect to pursuing bold long-term visions. Amazon's strategy was to sell books at cost or at a loss so that it could eventually dominate the market. The investment community had a high enough tolerance for the strategy to make it feasible for Amazon to raise the capital to pursue it. It operated at 100 percent of cost or more for over six years. Amazon was founded in 1994.[146] In January 2002, Amazon posted its first net profit—$5 million, or one penny per share.[147] Amazon has remained profitable ever since, with net profits of $35 million in 2003, $588 million in 2004, and $359 million in 2005. In 2005, Amazon entered the Standard & Poors 500 index, replacing AT&T.[148] After the initial proof of the concept, there was no longer an issue of risk taking. The opportunity was there to make money almost from the start. The *Seattle Post Intelligencer* quoted one early Amazon investor, Nick Hanauer:

> "What few people understood was that the reason they didn't make money was that for the previous five years every time there was a trade-off between making more money or growing faster, we grew faster," said Hanauer, whose $40,000 investment in Amazon once was valued at $250 million. "It wasn't that there weren't lots of opportunities to make money. It was just that we had consciously foregone [*sic*] those opportunities to reach scale and make it impossible to duplicate what we had done. And voila!"[149]

Imagine if we launched a charity to fight hunger based on the "Amazon.com" model, where the opportunity for short-term use of funds was consistently passed up for a bolder long-term vision. Or imagine the example of a vision to create the largest charity on earth capable of generating the largest annual revenue stream in history for hunger-relief and development projects with the ambitious goal of ending hunger in Malawi within fifteen years. The strategy would be to spend the first five years raising tens of millions of dollars for the cause (from the donating public). None of those funds would go directly to help the hungry. The present efforts of other hunger charities would, however, continue. The newly raised funds would be used to create a critical mass of constituents in years 6 through 10 via an annual mass advertising and outreach campaign of $50 million. In those same years, no funds would go directly to feed the hungry; instead, they would be used to finance the ad campaign and develop the war chest for the execution phase with the goal of raising $2 billion. Years 10 through 15 would constitute the execution phase of the project in Malawi. For ten years, hundreds of millions of dollars would be raised without any of it going directly to the hungry.

The system would work against such a model in every way. If charitable programs were defined as feeding the hungry, the percentage of donations reported as going to the cause would be zero. The model would be extremely vulnerable to media sensationalism. The media would report to the public that none of the dollars being raised were going to feed the hungry. There would be a public outcry. The founders would be crucified. Investigations would ensue.

The scenario is not just easy to imagine. It is predictable. It is difficult to imagine anyone with the intelligence to pull it off not being intelligent enough to stay away from it.

Consequently, the great, forward-looking ideas remain ideas, never to see the light of day. The great, forward-thinking idea makers go into other areas of endeavor. This is not how business works, and it's not how our charities should be forced to work. As long as charities have to live or die by the answer to questions about short-term percentage returns, they will always forgo long-term investment for short-term improvement in their percentage of overhead. Short-term expectations create nothing but long-term suffering and injustice.

The Fourth Error—Discouragement of Paid Advertising: If You Don't Advertise Here, Your Competition Will

The Present Inequality

The *Los Angeles Times* this morning contains eight full-page, ten half-page, and twenty quarter-page advertisements. Not one of them is for a charity. The *New York Times* has ten full-page ads. Not one for a charity. This week's *Time* magazine has twenty-eight full-page ads. Not one for a charity. *People* magazine has fifty-three full-page ads. Not one from a charity. Two, from Sprint and Pantene, mention corporate marketing promotions for a cause. *USA Today* online has ads for AT&T, Microsoft, and Scott Trade. CNN online has ads for General Motors and Blockbuster. *Real Simple* online has ads for Hewlett Packard and CBS. The bus that just drove by has an ad for a new TV show called "Rules." No ads for a charity.

YouTube ranks the 2007 Super Bowl commercials. The asking price for a thirty-second spot was $2.6 million.[150] Fifty-one ads are listed. One is from a pharmaceutical company talking about the risk of heart disease. Not one of the ads listed was purchased by a charity to market a charitable purpose.

The discrepancy cannot be laid at the door of the differences in scale between the basic needs the for-profit sector satisfies and the more discretionary desires (the desire to help others) satisfied by charity. The majority of these ads are not, by and large, for the basic necessities of life. They are for lipstick, DVDs, magazines and newspapers, investment services, diamond watches, dating services, sodas, candy bars, beer, cruise lines, comfort pharmaceuticals, and so on. Coca-Cola, Ford, Revlon, Budweiser, Snickers, Chevy, E-Trade, Sprint, and Lunesta are all represented, but not hunger, AIDS, leukemia, education, suicide prevention, or any of the other pressing issues of our time that *do* involve basic necessities, life and death.[151]

Similarly, at any shopping mall in the nation we find Banana Republic, Sunglass Hut, the Apple Store, Abercrombie & Fitch, American Girl, Quiksilver, Barnes & Noble, Häagen-Dazs, Crate & Barrel, and a dozen other for-profit retailers of discretionary consumer goods, all with dazzling window displays. Not a single retail outlet for our charitable interests. If ever a charity opened a store alongside these consumer products retailers and paid the kinds of rents they pay for a premium shot at consumer pedestrian traffic, the leaders of the organization would be run out of town on a rail.

The following contrasting data paint a sad picture of reality. *Advertising Age* reported in 2006 that State Farm Mutual Auto Insurance Co., the *lowest spender* on its list of the nation's top one hundred national advertisers, spent $338 million on U.S. advertising in 2006.[152] A 2003 *Chronicle of Philanthropy* story on the nation's community foundations, by contrast, reported:

> Three in four community foundations expect to spend as much or more money this year to market and advertise their organizations. . . . More than half of the respondents said they favored inexpensive marketing methods, such as sending e-mail to prospective donors or establishing a Web site. . . . Almost half of the funds said they spent less than $25,000 on marketing and advertising during their most recent fiscal year.[153]

Another *Chronicle* story on the American Cancer Society reported:

> The American Cancer Society has been "a little bit outrageous" in its push to pass anti-tobacco legislation in Congress, the charity's chief lobbyist, Linda Hay Crawford, proudly acknowledges. . . . The cancer society has set up a "war room" to coordinate daily strategy on tobacco bills with other nonprofit groups, conducted public-opinion polls, and paid for a major advertising campaign to try to sway U.S. Senators and Representatives. The cancer society's national office plans to spend about $1-million this year on "Operation Ignite" and other advocacy efforts. . . . "If you are going to do advocacy, you ought to use all the techniques appropriately and legally that your competitors use," says Ms. Crawford. . . . The American Cancer Society hopes its aggressive tactics in the tobacco battle will serve as a blueprint for others involved in future legislative fights.[154]

By contrast, in the same year, the five largest cigarette manufacturers spent $6.73 *billion* on advertising and promotions, according to the Federal Trade Commission—six thousand times more than the American Cancer Society.[155]

Table 6

2006 Budgets for All Purposes *for Popular Charities*

Charity	Total Expenses for All Purposes ($)
Cystic Fibrosis Foundation	180,503,829
Humane Society	86,014,263
Juvenile Diabetes Foundation International	164,261,000
Muscular Dystrophy Association	187,268,796
Public Broadcasting Service	494,480,234
Save the Children	322,445,843
Special Olympics	177,048,432
Unicef	464,665,162
United Cerebral Palsy	434,962,054
United Negro College Fund	151,923,512

SOURCE: Noelle Barton, Maria Di Mento, Candie Jones, and Sam Kean, "The 2006 Philanthropy 400," *Chronicle of Philanthropy: The Newspaper of the Nonprofit World* online, 2006, http://www.philanthropy.com, accessed February 13, 2007.

In 2007, Microsoft spent an estimated $500 million for marketing *the launch* of their new Vista operating system.[156] This amount is larger than, in some cases double or more, the total 2006 expenditures *for all purposes* of ten popular charitable institutions, among the nation's four hundred largest, as reported by the *Chronicle of Philanthropy* (table 6).

In addition to this spending, in 2006 the *Seattle Post Intelligencer* reported that Microsoft would spend "$120 million a year on an advertising campaign to fight its image as 'a huge American company.'"[157] So while charity is unable to spend money on advertising in order to *get* larger, the for-profit sector has so much freedom that it can spend a fortune to convince people it isn't as large as it appears to be. That irony aside, it boggles the mind that a single for-profit business can spend the equivalent of the entire budget of some of the nation's largest charities on a submessage in its overall advertising plan, which plan is but a line item in its overall marketing plan.

It is a testament to the dearth of advertising in the nonprofit sector that the IRS Form 990 on which charities report their expenses does not even include a line item for advertising. Most of the charities themselves don't have a line item for it in their own annual reports. As opposed to the for-profit sector, which has all manner of trade publications with specific advertising data by medium for thousands of for-profit consumer brands, the nonprofit sector data pool on the matter is virtually empty.

The following are the 2005 (unless otherwise noted) advertising and/or marketing budgets for five of the nation's most popular consumer companies compared with advertising expenses reported to the IRS by five popular charities. In order to do an apples-to-apples comparison, I have compiled data that are strictly for the charities' advertising expenditures for fundraising (i.e., bringing in sales), not for marketing services to clients, as that is part of the charitable program being sold to consumers. The disparity could not be more pronounced.

General Motors	$4,353,200,000
AT&T	$2,470,800,000
Walt Disney Company	$2,278,800,000
McDonald's	$1,662,100,000
Estee Lauder	$1,093,000,000 [158]
Save the Children (2004)	$ 6,420,000 [159]
American Foundation for AIDS Research	$7,071 [160]
United Way of America	none stated [161]
Leukemia & Lymphoma Society (2004)	none stated [162]
Amnesty International	$40,038 [163]

The numbers speak for themselves. The difference in scale is equivalent to that between the height of a toddler and the Sears Tower. Yet the difference in interest in cosmetics versus charity is attributed to an apathetic, uncaring public.

A *Stanford Social Innovation Review* article entitled "No Market for Marketing" reported on a 2005 *California Management Review* survey of forty-eight nonprofit marketing managers with prior for-profit experience:

> The U.S. nonprofits in which they now work either do not use major marketing tools (e.g. demand forecasting, demographic segmentation, market share analysis) at all or do so with far less intensity than do for-profit companies. Indeed, the most savvy nonprofits make less use of marketing tools than the least savvy for-profits. The study further finds that most nonprofits do not have a marketing plan, and that many nonprofit executives do not have a marketing perspective. [164]

The survey's authors suggested that:

> Nonprofits' resistance to cultivating market savvy comes from the normal fear many people have of change and novelty. Another barrier is nonprofits' perception of for-profits: "In some circles, business ideas were seen as suspect and potentially contaminating." [165]

Sharon Sutton, managing director for communications and social marketing at the American Institute for Research, concurring with the authors of the article, states, "Even the term 'marketing' is not acceptable to some nonprofits."[166]

The following comment by a charity event producer is representative of that attitude:

> It was our practice to work our tails off to get full-page advertising donated for our campaigns. Only on the rarest of occasions did we spend money to— to buy full-page advertising for fear that in doing so, we create great cost inefficiency in the production of our campaigns and end up being a bit of a betrayal of the very donors that we were seeking to attract.[167]

On a macro level, according to the *Jack Myers Media Business Report,* advertising spending in the United States in 2006 was estimated to be $220 billion, as much as the total amount American individuals donated to charity for all purposes.[168] Much of charitable giving goes to religious and educational institutions (36 percent and 39 percent of the whole, respectively). Of the entire $295 billion donated to charity in 2006, only $49.78 billion went to health and human services. Consumer market advertising expenditures amount to more than four times that total.[169]

Total *marketing* expenditures in the United States, including those for advertising, public relations, promotions, and trade shows, was estimated to be $729 billion, or two and a half times the amount raised by charity in total and nearly fifteen times the amounts given to health and human service charities.[170] A contrasting figure was estimated by an extrapolation study of seventy-one nonprofit organizations' tax returns undertaken by researchers Susan Raymond and Kate Jewell for Changing Our World, Inc. According to one of the organizations' chief strategy officers in 2006: "Itemized examination . . . resulted in an extrapolated estimate of $7.6 billion for the sector."[171] The study doesn't indicate what percentage of these funds were spent on program services rather than revenue generation. I assume it includes them, making it a liberal (if not extremely liberal) figure for comparison with consumer product sales marketing. It also doesn't tell us how much was spent by health and human service charities, as opposed to charities dedicated to the arts, religion, and higher education. *Nonetheless, even conceding the entire amount, $7.6 billion represents about 1 percent of the Myers estimate for total annual marketing expenditures in the United States. One dollar to market charity for every $100 to market consumer products.*

Although Galbraith made the point with respect to services provided by the government to meet social needs, his message is nonetheless applicable here:

> While public services have been subject to these negative attitudes, private goods have had no such attention. On the contrary, their virtues have been extolled by the massed drums of modern advertising. They have been pictured as the ultimate wealth of the community. Clearly the competition between public and private services . . . is an unequal one. The social consequences of this discrimination—this tendency to accord a superior prestige to private goods and an inferior role to public production—are considerable and even grave.[172]

Imagine what would happen if we learned that a charity spent $2.6 million in donor dollars on a Super Bowl ad designed to promote the cause, instead of earmarking that amount directly for aid or research. It would be scandalous. Yet day in and day out, consumer products marketers invest hundreds of millions of dollars that they consider to be every bit as valuable in order to pummel us with messaging about their products. Are they stupid, or do they know something charity does not or is not allowed to fathom?

What about all the money spent on fundraising? Isn't that marketing? In some sense, some of it is. But this does not argue against the inequity. First of all, many fundraising dollars are used to reach out to the affluent, leaving most of the mass market untapped. Second, many of these dollars are used to reach out to existing donors and constituents, leaving new potential donors in the mass market untapped. Third, even if we call all of an organization's fundraising expenses marketing expenses, the amount still doesn't come close to the tsunami that comes at us from the for-profit sector. According to watchdog standards, no more than 35 percent of an organization's donations should be spent on administration and fundraising. If we were generous and said the average organization spends 25 percent of what it raises on fundraising, and then multiplied that by the $222 billion individuals gave to charity in 2006,[173] we would get $55.7 billion, or about 7.6 percent of what was spent on marketing in the United States last year in total.[174] The most important point here is this: charities are conspicuously absent from traditional forms of mass marketing—from television to magazines, from radio to the Internet, from outdoor (billboards) to retail. This means the revenues that could be generated there are absent as well.

Why Do We Discriminate?

We discriminate for two reasons. First, marketing is a long-term proposition, and charity has been defined as a short-term game. Second, we
see advertising as wasteful, because, as Krugman said, "we haven't
thought our position through." Just as a string of clichés narrates our
construction for compensation, a string of clichés narrates our construction for marketing:

"Charities should get all their advertising donated." There are four
problems with this. First, what if they can't? Should they be left hidden
from public view? Second, what if the advertising that is donated isn't
the advertising they need? Should they sacrifice success? Third, the odds
that enough advertising will get donated to put charities on a level playing field with the for-profit sector are precisely zero. Fourth, if advertisers understand the value of advertising enough to be willing to finance
it through *their* donations (i.e., by donating advertising), we ought to
be able to make the case for advertising spending to the donating public
as well.

On the first point, the decision about whether to buy advertising
should be based strictly on a cost–benefit analysis, not on a pseudo-
moral standard based on tradition, because a cost–benefit analysis will
produce the most benefit for the needy. There is only one question that
matters: is advertising likely to produce more value than it costs? This is
a long-term question. If the answer is yes, there need not be further discussion. If the answer is no, same thing. If the answer to the question is
"I don't know" (which is probably the case for 99.9 percent of the charities in America), then another question comes up: how will you ever
know if you don't try it? Which would we prefer, that charity remain
forever in the dark about its true potential, in the name of short-term
aid, or that it find out what its true potential really is? If Coca-Cola had
never advertised, it would never have found out that it is Coca-Cola.
Why sentence charity to such a fate?

Some will say, "Well, we should study it." What is there to study in a
vacuum? We don't make Coca-Cola study it. We let them do it, and
study its resulting profits. It is yet another cruel facet of discrimination
that we expect the nonprofit sector to engage in a study before it spends
a penny on anything while the for-profit sector is out producing real-
world results with no such burden.

Moreover, I can tell you that my company did study advertising, in practical application, for nine years, with tens of millions of dollars, and the results were unequivocal. It works.

On the second point, marketing is a science. It must be executed with precision. If I can get the specific advertising donated, exactly as it is called for in my plan, wonderful. The donation is incremental funding. But if I cannot, I should not be prohibited from executing my plan on ideological grounds. To prohibit me from doing so is to put me at a severe disadvantage to my for-profit competitors, who are bound by no such restriction. If Coca-Cola had to rely on donated advertising as well, it would be a fair game, but Coca-Cola doesn't, so it isn't. A 2007 study found that 32 percent of donated charity TV ads and 40 percent of radio ads run during the dead hours of the night. Moreover, only 2 percent of public service announcements play during prime time—between 8 P.M. and 10 P.M.[175] Why should Coca-Cola be able to pay for prime-time advertising during the most popular television show of the day, while I am left to rely on a thirty-second donated spot at 3:30 in the morning for my charitable cause? If I need heart surgery, it does me no good to receive the donated services of a mechanic. Yet this is what we tell charity—see what the mechanic can do for your heart.

On the third point, there is presently, at least, an *annual* imbalance of $722 billion between what the for-profit sector spends on traditional forms of marketing and what the nonprofit sector spends. That's 1 percent spent by charity, 99 percent spent by the for-profit sector. In order to double the first figure to 2 percent, marketers would have to donate another $7.6 billion in in-kind forms of marketing. In order to bring it up to 10 percent, they would have to donate another $70 billion in in-kind marketing, or roughly 10 percent of their gross revenues, which would probably represent more than half, if not all, of their profits. This is a pipe dream. There is no conceivable way that the marketing industry alone is going to donate the amount of marketing it would take for the nonprofit sector to realize its true market potential.

On the final point, let's say that a full-page ad in a major Sunday newspaper costs $100,000. We will be liberal and say the paper's profit is 50 percent. If the paper donates the ad, it is donating $50,000 worth of value. That is the equivalent of $50,000 in cash. One hundred percent of the donation is going to advertising. The paper is not outraged by that figure. It doesn't believe that its contribution is wasted. It doesn't complain that it is not helping the needy. It knows that it *is,* because it knows the power and value of advertising. The paper's understanding is sophisticated, not crude. If the people who know the most about advertising are not in the slightest concerned about 100 percent of their donation going toward advertising—indeed, they are proud of it—we ought to be able to make the case for spending on advertising to the donating public. At the very least, we should stop apologizing for it.

"A dollar spent on advertising could have been spent caring for the needy." Yes, it could have, and then the needy would always be there, because charity will never find a way to generate the resources it would take to eradicate their need. This is a Puritan-inspired construction of possibility or, more accurately, impossibility. Once again, we must stop being distracted by short-term methods and begin to focus on long-term outcomes. If we allowed charities to begin advertising, we would generate incremental revenues. We would have enough money to do both—address short-term need, at least at the current level, *and* generate the capital necessary to focus on long-term solutions. This assumes that there is a positive correlation between spending on advertising for a cause and revenues from contributions similar to the correlation between ad spending and sales revenues in the for-profit sector. I vouch for this, but will discuss it further just ahead.

"Charity should stay grassroots." The mass market *is* the grassroots, and if we don't advertise in the mass market, we will never *reach* the grassroots. How many nonprofit activists are walking to the bus stop listening to their iPods because Apple targeted them in its marketing? How many shop at the Gap because the Gap has a retail presence (which is a marketing investment)? The for-profit sector is light-years ahead of the nonprofit sector in reaching the grassroots, and any argument that paid advertising is at odds with grassroots empowerment doesn't understand what "grassroots" means. It only serves to advance the hegemony of the for-profit sector. The grassroots are not the ideologically possessed. They are the general public. Either way, consumer advertising reaches both of them.

Advertising and Marketing Build Demand

A 2007 report by Forrester Research found that "76% of marketers had no way to determine their return on investment from their lead [advertising] agencies. Sixty-nine percent said ROI [return on invstment] is too difficult to measure."[176] This is a testament to the deep for-profit sector understanding of the relationship between advertising and demand, and between advertising and revenue. It puts hundreds of billions of dollars a year into an investment whose results it cannot measure. Charity, on the other hand, is required to have an audited study before it can spend a penny.

If advertising and marketing didn't work, American companies wouldn't spend nearly a trillion dollars a year doing it. Indeed, they don't just work; they are, like it or not, the fuel of our modern economy. Without them, it would crumble. They build demand that, in their absence, would not exist. There would be no market for the products, or only a market limited to those who found out about them via word of mouth. No market, no production. No production, no employment. No employment, no survival. In today's world of affluence in the developed nations, there are few things you can get people to do without marketing to them.

One of the contributions for which Galbraith is best remembered is his recognition that demand (or "want," as he sometimes called it) is manufactured by advertising:

> The even more direct link between production and wants is provided by the institutions of modern advertising and salesmanship. These cannot be reconciled with the notion of independently determined desires, for their central function is to create desires—to bring into being wants that previously did not exist. . . . A broad empirical relationship exists between what is spent on production of consumer goods and what is spent in synthesizing the desires for that production. A new consumer product must be introduced with a suitable advertising campaign to arouse interest in it. The path for an expansion of output must be paved by a suitable expansion in the advertising budget. Outlays for the manufacturing of a product are not more important in the strategy of modern business enterprise than outlays for manufacturing of demand for the product. None of this is novel. All would be regarded as elementary by the most retarded student in the nation's most primitive school of business administration. The cost of this want formation is formidable.[177]

David Oglivy, founder of the famous ad agency Oglivy & Mather and called by some "the father of advertising," made his living off of this reality. He put it more crudely, but perhaps more practically in his 1987 book, *Confessions of an Advertising Man,* when he challenged readers to "try launching a new brand of detergent with a war chest of less than $10,000,000."[178] He once wrote an advertisement about advertising itself. Featuring a picture of a cynical, conservative, bow-tied executive, it said:

> "I don't know who you are.
> I don't know your company.
> I don't know your company's product.
> I don't know what your company stands for.
> I don't know your company's customers.
> I don't know your company's record.
> I don't know your company's reputation.
> Now—what was it you wanted to sell me?"
> Moral: Sales start *before* your salesman calls—with business publication advertising. McGraw Hill Magazines[179]

Before the iPod existed, I had no demand for one. How could I? I couldn't conceive of it. So researching, developing, and manufacturing the iPod were the first steps in building demand. The next step was telling me about it—its features, its value, the kind of experience I would have if I bought one, what other kinds of people were buying one, and so on. Now I want one. I didn't want one before one existed. I didn't want one even after it existed but before I knew anything about it. Furthermore, I didn't want one even after I knew about it until Apple told me more about it. Now I want it. That's how demand is built. Galbraith wrote, "The most important and intrinsically most evident source of consumer demand is the advertising and salesmanship of those providing the product. First you make the good, then you make the market."[180] If you don't create that specific demand, I won't have it. If you don't create or show me new things for me to demand or desire, I will go to other markets that do.

There are some things you will never need to market to get people to demand—food, water, and other basic necessities. Still, the purveyors of those things advertise. "The incredible edible egg." "Pork. The other white meat." "Got milk?" The milk industry doesn't limit itself only to our natural, unstimulated desire for milk. It stimulates greater desire through marketing. It recognizes that, even with a staple, in the absence of marketing people will buy other nonessential substitutes (sodas, flavored waters, etc.) or simply spend more money on nonbeverage items. Yes, people will buy milk even if you don't market it. But they will buy more milk if you do. Same with charity. People will give money to charity. They will give more if you market to them. The ceiling for that giving is unknown. It is an uncharted sea of potential.

Go beyond the category of basic necessities and you will find that most of our demands have been created by manufacturers and marketers, at our request. They create demands for two reasons: because they can make a living and a profit and, ironically, because we want, or think we want, new things and new categories of things—that is, the biggest thing we demand is that the market create new demands.

The Mechanics of the Present Discrimination

There may be categories that equal, but no category that surpasses, marketing in proving the validity of the adage "It takes money to make money." As I said earlier, in general, businesses apply the following rule to their advertising expenditures: continue to spend up until the *incremental* benefit of the last dollar is zero. In charity, by contrast, the rule that gets applied is radically different: don't pay attention to *incremental* dollars, and, in order to meet the 65 percent watchdog standards for "efficiency," spend only when you know the benefit of the *average* dollar *will be* sixty-five cents (which you have to guess at ahead of time because you are trying to predict the future, which you have to do because you cannot make a mistake). Small wonder that little money is spent to make money, on marketing or anything else.

Let me offer an example. Say that I have a for-profit company that makes and sells widgets. I advertise my widgets in the newspaper. An ad costs $35. First, because I am a for-profit business, I can advertise without fear of moral judgment, even if the result fails to meet expectations. Second, because I am a for-profit business, I can continue to run the ad so long as I make one penny after all my costs. In this way I saturate the market and take advantage of all the value to be had. In charity, by contrast, paid advertising is discouraged to begin with. There is not much more to say. Even if there were, if I want to challenge that sacred cow, I have to predict, with no data, that the ad will generate $100 in contributions and $65 in "profit" for the cause ($100 minus $35 for the ad = $65 = 65 percent return) in order to meet watchdog standards. If it does, this should be a no-brainer. The matter deserves no more discussion than that. (Even so, charities are still routinely afraid to spend the money, and are forced to discuss it ad nauseum instead of actually doing it.) But what if it doesn't? If it generates only $90, I must discontinue running the ad, and discontinue taking in the $55 net that could have gone to my cause. I leave tremendous value on the table. *The for-profit sector comes in and scoops it up. Indeed, it has been. Individual giving as a percentage of personal consumption expenditures, excluding food and energy, dropped from 3.8 percent in 1965 to 2.8 percent in 2005.*[181] *What's more, Generation X—those born between 1964 and 1981—are giving a lower share of their income to charity than the preceding generation did at the same age.*[182]

Interestingly, a ninety-two-page supplement to *Time* magazine in 2008 entitled *Luxury for the Next Generation*—packed with ads for Gucci, Louis Vuitton, Tiffany & Co., and Prada—studies the luxury habits of "millenials"—those born between 1980 and 2000. Ninety-two percent said they love to look at ads for luxury goods. Ninety-six percent said they love wearing designer clothing, jewelry, and watches. It says that, "Their income is lower than that of most [baby] boomers, yet core luxury millenials are much more psychologically engaged in luxury than their parents' generation."[183] Is it any wonder why?

With respect to the example above, this is not the worst of it. This is the restriction I have to deal with when I can *directly* measure the sales from an ad. If I want to do something as bold as build long-term interest in my charitable brand, with no short-term result in mind, by means of an ad whose productivity is far more difficult to measure, my entry into the market is strictly prohibited. This long-term brand building is by far the most powerful form of advertising. What do I mean by this? There is a world of difference between an ad that says, "Call this number now to order a ticket to this concert," and an ad that simply says, "Coca-Cola." The Coca-Cola ad has no short-term result in mind. Its ambition is much greater than that. It aims to indoctrinate you for life. If it takes ten years to do that, so be it. It will all be worth it in the end. Charity is afforded no such luxury. As a result, the long-term imaginations of the public have been captured by the mega–consumer brands.

Thomas Merton, a Trappist monk and one of the most influential Catholic writers in modern times, observed:

> Businesses are, in reality, quasi-religious sects. When you go to work in one you embrace a new faith. And if they are really big businesses, you progress from faith to a kind of mystique. Belief in the product, preaching the product, in the end the product becomes the focus of a transcendental experience. Through "the product" one communes with the vast forces of life, nature, and history that are expressed in business. Why not face it? Advertising treats all products with the reverence and seriousness due to sacraments. . . . Compare our monastery and the General Electric plant in Louisville. Which one is

the more serious and the more "religious" institution? One might be tempted to say "the monastery" out of sheer habit. But, in fact, the religious seriousness of the monastery is like sandlot baseball compared with the big-league seriousness of General Electric. It may in fact occur to many, including the monks, to *doubt* the monastery and what it represents. Who doubts G.E.?[184]

Imagine what would happen if a charity embarked on a branding campaign that didn't produce short-term—in fact, immediate—results. We don't need to hypothesize about it. Bono's "Red" campaign has been touted by some as a sign of a new convergence of charity and capitalism. It may well be. But society has not yet given its permission for such a convergence. So, predictably, Bono slammed into a wall that he didn't see coming. A 2007 *Advertising Age* article on the campaign begins with the headline "Costly Red Campaign Reaps Meager $18 Million: Bono & Co. Spend up to $100 Million on Marketing, Incur Watchdogs' Wrath." Given that the ad campaign was big, the article asks the question, "So you'd expect the money raised to be, well, big, right? Maybe $50 million or even $100 million. Try again: The tally raised worldwide is $18 million."[185] The demand is for an immediate result. The article goes on, "The disproportionate ratio between the marketing outlay and the money raised is drawing concern among nonprofit watchdogs. . . . It threatens to spur a backlash . . . contributions don't seem to be living up to the hype."[186]

What watchdog is going to get involved if Coca-Cola spends $100 million on long-term brand development that doesn't produce an immediate $100 million bump in sales? What's remarkable is that these were not even charitable dollars spent on the advertising—the money was all put up by the likes of the Gap, Apple, and Motorola. But it doesn't matter where the money came from. To nonprofit ideology, charity and advertising are oil and water.

This ideological segregation creates the most crippling kind of economic discrimination. Galbraith, again, although writing about the provision of government services to meet needs, nonetheless makes the point:

> By failing to exploit the opportunity to expand public [services], we are missing opportunities for enjoyment which otherwise we might have. Presumably a community can be as well rewarded by buying better schools or parks as by buying more expensive automobiles. By concentrating on the latter rather than the former, it is failing to maximize its satisfactions. . . . It is scarcely sensible that we should satisfy our wants in private goods with reckless abundance, while in the case of public [services] . . . we practice extreme

self-denial. . . . The conventional wisdom holds that the community, large or small, makes a decision as to how much it will devote to its public services. . . . But . . . given that consumer wants are created by the process by which they are satisfied—the consumer makes no such choice. He or she is subject to the forces of advertising and emulation by which production creates its own demand. Advertising operates exclusively . . . on behalf of privately produced goods and services. Since management of demand . . . [operates] on behalf of private production, public services will have an inherent tendency to lag behind. Automobile demand which is expensively synthesized will inevitably have a much larger claim on income than parks or public health . . . where no such influence operates. The engines of mass communication, in their highest state of development, assail the eyes and ears of the community on behalf of more beverages but not of more schools. Even in the conventional wisdom it will scarcely be contended that this leads to an equal choice between the two.[187]

Galbraith continues, "The economy is geared to the least urgent set of human values. It would be far more secure if it were based on the whole range of need."[188] Our nonprofit belief system is in no small part the reason the economy is geared this way.

Application to Charity

There is an adage about fundraising that the more you ask the more you will raise, and the less you ask the less you will raise. This is the first thing that everyone in the fundraising profession learns. If they ever sold Girl Scout cookies or Little League raffle tickets, they learned it long before they ever got into fundraising. The sector already recognizes the correlation between awareness and revenue. It is simple common sense. More advertising and marketing are essentially the equivalent of asking more people to give more often. What more is there to discuss?

The tsunami that struck Asia in 2004 generated $3.16 billion in contributions for relief efforts. The Center on Philanthropy at Indiana University reported, "The overwhelming majority of disaster-relief giving came not from million-dollar corporate or foundation gifts, but from the combined gifts of individuals nationwide." Twenty-five percent of all American households gave, with an average donation of $135.[189]

Before the tsunami, the cause didn't exist. It had zero contributions. This sudden outpouring of compassion is not explained by the fact that

people suffered. Millions of people suffer every day under equally devastating conditions without any equivalent display of support. It was
not because people were left homeless. God knows homelessness is a
persistent condition in most American cities and we don't see billions
contributed to its alleviation in any given month. It wasn't because people died. People die unjustly every day. It was because people throughout the world were exposed to the suffering, the homelessness, and the
death, over and over and over again, in newspapers, on television, on
radio, on the Internet, during prime time. Hundreds of millions of
dollars of media equivalents went into the fundraising campaign. It was
advertised. It was marketed. People gave because demand was created,
or stimulated, by the massive engines of the national media. Reuters reported that "the Indian Ocean tsunami got more media attention in the
first six weeks after it struck than all of the world's top 10 'forgotten'
emergencies combined have received in the past year."[190] In two
months, the tsunami received thirteen times as much media attention as
HIV/AIDS. Three hundred thousand people died in the tsunami. In a
year, approximately 3 million people die of AIDS.[191] For a brief moment, a great cause enjoyed the kind of attention that beer gets every
day and raised $3 billion as a result.[192]

Massive displays of compassion are always connected to massive
media attention. Only the most obstinate observer would deny the correlation. Giving USA noted, "The year 2005 had some of the most intense disasters ever, which led to an unusually large amount of charitable giving for rescue and relief work."[193] They went on to say, "The
media played an important role, not only in communicating the details
of the tragedies, but also in expressing the compelling need and taking
the case for support to the American people."[194]

Hurricane Katrina generated similarly remarkable giving—more
than $3.5 billion from American individuals, corporations, and founda-
tions.[195] Again, the suffering was no different from that which persists
on a day-to-day basis already. Thousands of people live in filth on skid
row in Los Angeles, without water, electricity, sanitation, or a roof over
their heads. A 2005 Department of Agriculture study revealed that 11.9
percent of American households reported not having enough food at
some point in 2004 because they had insufficient funds.[196] The Giving
USA annual report for 2007 reveals that "food pantries now provide food
for about 12 percent of U.S. adults."[197] The National Alliance to End
Homelessness estimated in January 2005, months before Katrina hit, that
more than three-quarters of a million Americans were homeless, and

nearly half of them were unsheltered. Nearly a hundred thousand homeless families were counted.[198] This report is buried deep in the Internet. By contrast, the media machine was turned on full steam for Katrina. We were made aware of the situation, repeatedly, throughout the day, for many days on end. The ongoing transmission of the images of twelve thousand temporary refugees living in squalor at the New Orleans Superdome was all it took to arouse the American spirit of compassion. The thousands of homeless living on skid row in Los Angeles enjoy no such attention, or the billions of dollars that come with it.

If there were no correlation between advertising and compassion, why would the Jerry Lewis telethon not last just an hour? In fact, why does it air at all? It stays on for twenty-four hours because it raises something on the order of twenty-four times more than it would if it stayed on for only one. Why do public television and radio stations stage media campaigns on a regular basis to raise their annual budgets? Why do they air the campaigns for weeks on end? Why do charities even attempt to get advertising donated?

Moreover, while traditional fundraising efforts are distinct from advertising, they are derivative of it. They represent the use of resources to reach out, as opposed to the expectation that donations will simply flow in unelicited. They work. According to Dan Tinkelman, professor of accounting at Hofstra University, "Every academic study that has looked at the average impact of fundraising efforts on donations has found that fundraising efforts work for charities—they bring in more dollars to charities than they cost." Giving USA reported on a 2001 study of 1,540 organizations that documented the correlation, finding that on average, twenty-four cents spent on fundraising brought in one dollar of donations.[199]

The correlation is similarly noted in Giving USA's annual report for 2007, which quoted findings from Arthur Brooks, a professor of public administration at Syracuse University, who argues that "people who attend worship services regularly (once per week) give more to religion and give more to secular causes than do people who attend less often."[200] Religious services are a form of advertising. What else would you call being held captive by a one-hour message repeated on a weekly basis? Here is a staggering fact: of the $295 billion given to charity in 2006, one-third of it, or $96.82 billion, was given to religious institutions. Ironically, Brooks concludes that "religious conservatives donate far more money than secular liberals to charity."[201] No wonder. They are advertised to far more.

Table 7

Return on Investment in Advertising for Select First-Year Pallotta TeamWorks Events

Event	Marketing Expense ($)	Revenue ($)	Net ($)	ROI (%)
AIDSRide, Los Angeles, 1994	37,333	1,540,000	1,013,000	4,125
AIDSRide, San Francisco, 1995	154,333	2,264,000	1,256,000	1,470
AIDSRide, New York, 1995	160,000	3,404,000	2,146,000	2,127
AIDS Vaccine Ride, Alaska, 2000	721,000	8,558,000	4,163,000	1,187
Out of the Darkness, Washington, D.C., 2002	637,466	4,206,153	1,291,289	660
Breast Cancer 3-Day, Los Angeles, 1998	387,000	7,205,000	4,222,000	1,862
Breast Cancer 3-Day, Chicago, 1999	496,000	7,544,000	4,797,000	1,520
Breast Cancer 3-Day, San Francisco, 2000	453,000	10,178,000	6,958,000	2,247
Breast Cancer 3-Day, Seattle, 2001	653,000	8,745,000	4,952,000	1,340
Breast Cancer 3-Day, San Diego, 2002	767,035	10,450,157	6,667,539	1,362

SOURCE: Pallotta TeamWorks, "Record of Impact 1994–2002" (Los Angeles, 2006). Marketing expenses for AIDSRides in Los Angeles, San Francisco, and New York calculated by applying the Breast Cancer 3-Day 2:1 "Administration" to "Marketing" ratio to "Marketing/AIDS Awareness/Administration" expenses.

The historic success of our AIDSRides and Breast Cancer 3-Day events had its basis in one strategy: we advertised them. That the events we were advertising entailed a difficult physical challenge, and not a sought-after consumer item, and that they were so successful, only adds to the case that advertising stimulates giving. Table 7 lists the approximate marketing expenditures and the resulting gross and net revenues for a few of our first-year events—in other words, events that had no previous market and by which demand was built through paid advertising and marketing efforts alone.

After the first year of an event, word of mouth added to second-year demand, as did second-year advertising. In total, over the course of our nine years of production, we spent approximately $48.9 million on advertising and marketing and generated $556 million in total revenues, for a gross return on investment of 1,137 percent.[202]

What about the question of destructive competition, of cannibalization? Will massive increases in advertising by one cause take donations away from a different cause? First, we should worry about the fact that massive advertising by the manufacturers of entertainment and fast foods takes donations away from *all* causes, every day. That's the real competition. Second, this is the kind of question that comes to bear when the limits of demand have been reached. Given that charity has not even attempted to explore the demand it might be able to build, we are a long way from needing to ask it. Furthermore, this fear is the equivalent of the mercantilists' concerns. Their theories predated Adam Smith. They called for severe trade sanctions on the assumption that the economic potential of the world was fixed and that the only way to increase one nation's wealth was by taking it away from another; the only way to protect one's wealth was to defend it against another—it was a zero-sum game. We can extrapolate from the failure of those ideas—it turned out that economic potential was not a zero-sum proposition. The productivity of the global economy grows to meet demand. Where once there were only huts and horses, now there is much more.

Many in the nonprofit sector might say that same-cause competition for donor dollars is already fierce. Will massive increases in advertising by one organization take away donations from another organization working on the same cause? Not unless the two groups are intentionally cannibalistic. Competition is fierce in large part because everyone is fighting over the same pie—appealing to the same foundations and donors. By investing in marketing, we can increase the size of the pie. New marketing efforts designed to reach new potential constituents and new market segments that would not otherwise give to the cause would do that. For instance, the AIDSRides brought new dollars to the cause without damaging the AIDS walk-a-thons because the two events appealed to people with two different psychographic profiles. The AIDSRides appealed to a small market segment interested in something extremely physically demanding with a four-figure fundraising requirement. The AIDS walk-a-thons appealed to a larger market segment interested in a single-day event without a high mandatory fundraising requirement.

Competition is also fierce because more and more organizations are created every day to try to get a piece of the pie. Giving USA has shown that *ninety-seven new nonprofit organizations are created in the United States every day—around 35,000 a year*.[203] This says nothing about our ability to build new demand. It is only a comment on our ability to build new nonprofits. It speaks to a need for supplier consolidation. We can achieve tremendous economies of scale by joining forces. We don't need hundreds of fragmented approaches to the same problems. We don't need fragmented and redundant fundraising models. In business, we get mergers and acquisitions so that organizations reach optimal size. There is a mergers and acquisitions market. Nonprofit ideology hasn't considered this. There is no economic incentive. Furthermore, a nonprofit merger smacks of commercialism or grandiosity, and it seems to infringe on the rights of an unlimited number of people to make a benevolent gesture by creating and maintaining new nonprofits. But so long as mergers and acquisitions inside the sector are undertaken with an eye to the morality of the outcomes, they should be encouraged and pursued. Building new demand is likely to create the conditions within a given cause that will stimulate this.

Imagine for a moment a reciprocal of the world with which I opened this section. Imagine if the *Los Angeles Times* this morning has eight full-page, ten half-page, and twenty quarter-page advertisements. Not one of them is for a consumer product. They are all for charity. "End hunger." "Make your day by making a contribution now to a child with leukemia." The *New York Times* has ten full-page ads. Not one for a consumer product. The Super Bowl runs fifty-one ads. All for charity. I go to the mall. There are high-style retail stores for Oxfam America, the American Cancer Society, Amnesty International, the Make-a-Wish Foundation. Not one for a consumer product. Is there any doubt that consumer spending on charity would skyrocket?

What we need is a just balance, where both consumer products and charity are advertised and marketed, a world where the odds are not made lopsided and unjust—by moral regulations, of all things—that favor the less moral outcome. Moreover, this is not a zero-sum game. If, through advertising and marketing, people can begin to imagine a world where they can have their flat-screen televisions and a world free of hunger, it stands to reason that productivity will increase to provide both.

Productivity expands with demand. This is widely known. We have transitioned from a world just four hundred years ago where poverty and suffering were the norm for all people to a world today where they are not. This we have accomplished by our ambition and increased productivity. Productivity was only ever increased by a vision of a better life. People need something to work for that they believe is worth working for. Up to now, all we have offered people are visions of better products. Consumers have increased their productivity in order to earn the money to acquire them, but in horribly unequal balance to the money that has gone to the needy. We don't know how people will react to the possibility of a world of abundance for everyone if the case is adequately made. The demand for that world has not been generated. It has been kept, by and large, in the closet. Empirical evidence suggests that it is limited only by its own obscurity.

These issues aside, there is an additional asset to be built that goes far beyond new revenues from consumers. Building consumer demand with respect to social issues has political implications. Once a demand is built, consumers will not arbitrarily limit their demonstration of it to their pocketbooks. They will also demonstrate it with their votes. A world in which the consumer is educated about great social issues by repeated exposure to them is one in which civil conversation and concern about those issues will be multiplied across every feature of the democracy. This effect will spill over into political discussion and political behavior, from the candidates for whom consumers cast their votes, to the actions voters expect from them once they are elected. Our consciousness of the issues will be elevated. Elevated consciousness affects behavior. It has far-reaching implications.

I will close this section with an unexpected reflection by Franklin Roosevelt, a man who believed in the unlimited potential of America and who indeed, by way of vision, helped to make manifest a period of historic abundance and prosperity. He was a marketer too. He marketed the possibility of a world made better and more just by the people who inhabit it:

> If I were starting life over again, I am inclined to think I would go into the advertising business in preference to almost any other. . . . The general raising of the standards of modern civilization among all groups of people during the past half century would have been impossible without the spreading of the knowledge of higher standards by means of advertising. Advertising nourishes the consuming power of men. It sets up before a man the goal of a better home, better clothing, better food for himself and his family. It spurs individual exertion and greater production.[204]

Surely advertising can set up before men and women the goal of a better world as well, and it can be just as successful in realizing it.

The Fifth Error—Prohibition on Investment Return: The Limits of No Return, and a Stock Market for Charity

Where will charity get the surplus capital to build this demand? It can't take $80 billion a year out of the $295 billion philanthropic pie to spend on marketing without having an equivalent negative impact on present-day services. Where will it get the surplus capital to hire more expensive leaders or to build organizational infrastructures, or to take new chances?

Adam Smith wrote, "In some countries, the interest of money has been prohibited by law." The nonprofit sector is such a country. He continued, "But as something can every-where be made by the use of money, something ought every-where to be paid for the use of it."[205] Even St. Thomas Aquinas "accepted the legitimacy of profiting from a loan *if* the lender bore some of the risk."[206] We turn now to the investment, and human implications of, the three-letter prefix to the "nonprofit" sector's name. Where there is no philosophical permission to reap financial profits, there can be no payment for the use of money, that is, no return to investors. Where there is no return, there will be no investors. Conversely, where there is a return, there *will* be investors. There is a revolutionary idea at our disposal.

Just as there is a limit to what our desire to help others can do in the labor market, so too there is a limit to what it can do in the capital market. If I have $1 million in discretionary funds, I may be willing to donate $100,000 to charity altruistically. I am not likely to donate the other $900,000. That, I will put into stocks, bonds, and other financial assets that offer me a financial return. I cannot earn a financial return off my money in charity (now). It is prohibited on moral grounds, there is no organized market for it, and there are legal barriers to creating one. The moral objections here are identical to the moral objections in the labor market: those who want to make money from charity are obscene, and so on. There is no need to discuss them further. The real question is, What could be the benefit to the needy of opening charity to the possibility of investment with a *financial* return to the investor? What if charity could get a chunk of that $900,000 that would otherwise go into for-profit sector investments? Equally important, what is the impact of prohibiting charity from doing so?

Charities took in $295 billion in donations in 2006.[207] Donations represent pretty much the only source from which charities can hope to obtain any surplus capital. Banks offer financing but rarely for anything other than collateralized real estate acquisitions or upgrades, mostly in the form of a charity's facilities. Not many banks will fund new, uncollateralized ideas for generating more revenue. The government provides tens of billions of dollars to charity annually, but these funds must typically be used to deliver contracted services at cost. Nonprofit organizations also take in hundreds of billions more annually in fees for services, but I discount these as a source of capital for eradicating society's most urgent suffering and need for at least two reasons.[208] First, fees for services (for example, the $150 an opera-goer pays for a front-row ticket to see Placido Domingo at a nonprofit opera) go disproportionately to the arts, colleges, religious institutions, and well-funded hospitals. Very little of it comes into the local homeless shelter, AIDS clinic, overseas hunger-relief organization, or even the small multiple sclerosis research lab. The poor and the indigent have no money with which to pay for services. Opera-goers, on the other hand, do. Second, to the extent that fees do go to charities addressing more urgent social needs, the indigence of their clients mandates that they charge no more than what the service costs them to provide, and even at that price it puts the services out of reach of hundreds of millions of people. Social service charities can hardly mark up the price of their services to the indigent to amass surplus capital for long-term visions. It would be asking people who are starving to capitalize the end of starvation. So, for the charities serving humanity's most vulnerable citizens, donations represent pretty much the lone opportunity to eke out any surplus capital for long-term solutions.

But where is it written that the only way to help a charity is by making a donation? It is an extreme example of our philosophical discrimination against charity that we have not even considered that it might also be advanced by investment that pays a return. In an economic world fed by a smorgasbord of financial instruments, charity doth live by bread alone.

Limiting charity to revenue by donation doesn't limit only revenue. Donations come with severe philosophical restrictions. Given that we expect donations to be spent immediately and cautiously to help the needy, there is no capital available to test new revenue models, to execute long-term vision, or to build organizational capacity. If charity is to be liberated from the ideology that forbids it to use the tools of capitalism, one axiom must be recognized above all others: *if you don't have capital, you don't have capitalism*. According to the Morino Institute:

> Nonprofits are chronically undercapitalized. For the most part they find themselves limited to just one financial instrument—the charitable donation—and most of what they do is financed on a pay-as-you-go basis. This is in direct contrast to the way virtually everything else of value gets built. No one buys or builds a home without financing it. Almost every business, large and small, at least attempts to make judicious use of debt and equity. But nonprofits are risk-averse and often unaware of the broader range of financial tools that may be available. . . . Because nonprofits are chronically undercapitalized, they rarely achieve their objectives, which in turn makes it less likely they will receive the resources they need. And so the cycle continues.[209]

With no mechanism for offering a return on investment capital, all the investment capital goes into the for-profit sector. As of 2004, Americans held about $37 trillion in household financial assets.[210] Thirty-four percent of all Americans own some sort of financial risk asset, such as stocks, bonds, or mutual funds.[211] The median investor is forty-seven years old, earns an annual income of $62,500, and owns financial assets worth $100,000, half of which are invested in equities (stocks, mutual funds, etc.).[212] All of this is invested in the for-profit sector. What if we were to open a market for social change that would provide a *financial* return on investment to this market of financial investors?

This question is fundamentally different from the question asked by the recent social venture capital trend. The return that venture philanthropy provides the "investor" is strictly an *altruistic* one. Venture philanthropy offers no incentive to the investor seeking a *financial* return. Therefore, it cannot attract such an investor. It is simply another form of charitable contribution, with the difference being that it seeks to fund more maverick, less traditional approaches to problem solving. In other words, investors, as the venture philanthropy trend calls them, might *donate* $100,000 to the development of an innovative approach to helping at-risk youth (which really makes them donors, not investors), hoping that it will pay a dividend in the form of fewer youth at risk. While admirable, such an approach is subject to all the same limits of altruism as the market for making contributions. No financial return is offered. The few models that have been set up are novel, but they don't stimulate, or even address, new markets for their own funding. They will simply claim a slice of the existing, never-expanding pie. Some might say this is not so, that the new venture philanthropists are also bringing in new money. We cannot say that for certain. They simply have a claim on that piece of the national wealth that would otherwise go to more traditional forms of philanthropy if it were to remain in the hands of a more traditionally minded donor. There is no evidence that venture philanthropists are giving a larger *percentage* of their wealth to charity. So, essentially, the more new social ventures are funded, the less traditional program needs will be funded. They are part of an essentially zero-sum game.

A market for investment capital, on the other hand, could increase the size of the pie. In doing so, it could provide the capital for investment critical for progress at a variety of institutional levels. Ralph Smith, senior vice president of the Annie E. Casey Foundation, wrote the following comment with respect to new social venture funds, but he could just as easily have been discussing the much larger idea being discussed here:

A rational capital market for the social sector would attract and match willing investors to the capital needs of at least three types of social purpose enterprises: start-ups, scale-ups, and mature, successful organizations. Start-ups need venture funding to develop new products or services. Scale-ups are proven performers needing an infusion of capital to replicate and expand successful efforts. Mature, successful organizations produce good results and function at appropriate scale, but still need to close the gap between expenditures and . . . income.[213]

An obvious question arises. For-profit businesses produce products and services that the public buys. They earn a profit from those products and services. Charity provides a service to the needy. There is no profit. How could it offer a return?

Charity offers more than a service to the needy. It offers a service to the donor, as I have discussed. It is from that service that it derives revenue. It is from that revenue that it can derive a profit or fund investor returns. A breast cancer research charity is a broker for research, offering the donor a chance to purchase two things: the social good of the eradication of breast cancer, or progress toward the same, and the personal good feeling that comes with it (and, in many cases, valuable name recognition). A homeless shelter is a broker for the creation of a more decent community in which the donor can live, a more productive community in which the homeless are lifted up and become contributors to community good, and an outlet for the satisfaction of altruistic desire. By prohibiting it from trading a portion of future revenues to investors who help enlarge those revenues, we are doing only one thing—keeping capital out of the market, limiting the market to what naturally comes in as a result of donations, limiting a multitrillion-dollar annual need to $295 billion in annual funding.

We don't mind a portion of the dollar we spend on our high-definition television going to the investor who provided the capital that made its development and manufacture possible. Indeed, we recognize it as essential. Why would we object to a portion of our donation going to the investor who made it possible for us to give it in the first place, perhaps by jump-starting a new charitable program or a new fundraising event about which we may never have known in the absence of the advertising that the investor helped to fund?

The moral purist will at this point cry heresy. But it would be heresy only if we continue to allow people to suffer needlessly. Here we have to challenge all that we hold sacred, for the simple reason that it is an obstacle to progress. This feeling of heresy comes from seeing in our minds only the payment of a dividend, or the realization of a profit to the investor (who might be a retiree or a schoolchild or a single mom or you), and not the benefit of the investment going to the charity. The investor does not receive a dividend or earn a profit for nothing. He receives it in return for putting his own money at risk.

Here is a simple example. A homeless charity has a $4 million annual budget. It has a new fundraising event idea. It needs $500,000 to get the event off the ground. The charity estimates that it could net $20 million over five years. It doesn't have the money to launch the event, so it makes an investment offering — 1 percent return on the net revenues from the event. Five investors each put up $100,000, and each gets a 1 percent share of the net in return. Their investments are unsecured. If the charity nets nothing, they get nothing. If the charity loses $500,000, they all lose their investments. The charity stages the event and it is a success. It grosses $8 million and nets $4 million in the first year, after all expenses (including repayment of the $500,000 investment). The charity pays the investors the 1 percent dividend promised — $40,000 each, or $200,000 total — and $3,800,000 is left for the cause, nearly doubling the organization's budget. The investors have made a 40 percent return on their money in one year. How is this a bad thing? How is it anything but an amazing thing? Would we prefer that the $500,000 in investment funds had gone instead to Exxon to finance a new oil rig?

By expanding this thinking, we can imagine an open market for shares in the unsecured future revenues of tens of thousands of charities, whereby the rights to all of them can be transferred and thus traded. This is a futures market for charity.

Along with the development of such a market, brokerages for the shares will develop. Brokerages will assess risk. Investors will buy mixtures of shares with a variety of risk levels.

Capital makes all the difference. With it, miraculous things can happen. Without it, miraculous things are sacrificed. It was with six- and seven-figure capital that Pallotta TeamWorks' events were created and launched on a massive scale relative to the launch of other charitable events. In 2000, 2001, and 2002, we used bank financing to implement new ideas. But for the lack of more financing, we could have achieved much more. Sadly, during the expansion of the AIDSRides, we saw many smaller charities that, lacking any capital, were unable to make the investments that larger charities were capable of, and were therefore excluded from the revenues the events could have generated for them. Ironically, even larger charities face the same problem, except on a different scale. Here we have a way to alleviate the problem for both.

Some obvious questions arise. Why should the investor get a return when the donor doesn't? Simply because the investor wouldn't make the investment if he didn't get a return. It is essential for the creation of the market. The donor, on the other hand, *will* make a donation without a return. Donors and investors seek different things. They are in two different markets, one of which involves business transactions and the other, acts of charity. The business transaction comes with less altruistic satisfaction (certainly no name recognition) than acts of charity do. It is probable, if not predictable, that both donors and investors will participate in both markets. A given individual will make charitable contributions to and investments in charitable institutions at the same time. These two markets exist right now. Banks can make loans to charity, and do. Shareholders earn a profit from the interest the bank charges on the loan. The shareholders for the bank also make donations to charity.

What if the donors stop giving and instead start investing all of their dollars with the expectation of a return? This assumes that the presence of economic incentive is fatal to our desire to help others. We know this is not the case, because donors have that option right now and individual donating to charity survives at the rate of $222 billion a year.[214] They could take the $100 they are giving to a homeless shelter and instead invest it in the Dow Jones. They don't because, to some degree, they are charitable. Charity is personal. It does not depend on the behavior of others. The market for it doesn't vanish because of the presence of other markets. Consumers don't now withhold their money from a charity simply because others are investing their money in stocks or in buying a new car. Why would they in the face of one more investment market?

How will donors decide in which charities to invest? Through the equivalent of a stock market that buys and sells their futures. Such an exchange will develop naturally out of the opportunities of the larger market, just as it does for the for-profit sector. The modern stock market started with one opportunity—the ability to buy shares in the Dutch East India Trading Company in 1609, which allowed for the recruitment of more capital than any single individual was willing to put up.[215] Trading was voluminous, and an exchange developed a year later.[216]

In the later part of the seventeenth century these "'Dutch' techniques of finance spread to England" and a stock market developed there.[217] B. Mark Smith, in his *History of the Global Stock Market,* observes:

> A new generation of "moneyed men," who spurned the old theological critiques of profit and interest, came to prominence in London. The new liberal ideology replaced feudal beliefs, making what had formerly been seen as vices (. . . profit, money lending, and consumption) into attributes. Anticipating Adam Smith's writings of nearly a century later, the new creed held that the active pursuit of personal profit actually benefited, not harmed, society.[218]

The London market began with a handful of joint stock companies around 1690. By 1695 the handful had grown to 150 such companies.[219] Just twenty-five years later, "the total capitalization of the London market was over £500 million, roughly one hundred times the amount of 1695."[220] Smith writes that John Houghton, in his biweekly paper of the day, *A Collection for the Improvement of Husbandry and Trade*:

> . . . correctly identified a crucial advantage of joint-stock companies: shares that could be easily bought and sold. A ready market for these shares meant that joint-stock company investors were not locked into long-term, illiquid investments, like real estate or unwieldy forms of government debt. This was extremely important, because it made investors much more willing to buy joint-stock company shares, and pay higher prices for those shares. This in turn meant that entrepreneurs could now raise significant quantities of new capital at attractive terms through joint-stock ventures, making modern capitalism feasible.[221]

Our nonprofit belief system has frozen charity in a time before the Dutch East India Trading Company ever existed. For four hundred years the for-profit sector has been racing ahead.

Will there not be a tendency for investors to limit their investments to larger charities that are less risky than smaller ones? There will be, in the same way that investors tend now to invest more money in blue chips than in smaller propositions. But they invest in all. Investment may be disproportionate, but it will exist, where it now doesn't, and it will exist for all. If the worst thing that comes of this is that a popular cause like breast cancer raises enough capital to cure that disease first, there will be little cause for disappointment.

In addition to the effect of the new capital itself, there is the circular effect of more capital for organizational capacity and infrastructure development. Investors want a return on their dollar. Donors want the highest possible percentage of their dollar to go toward alleviating need. There is a positive correlation between charitable spending on infrastructure (hiring top-tier leaders, investing in staff training, long-term planning, advertising, etc.) and building a more robust organization, as we will see later in the discussion on "efficiency" measures. There is, furthermore, a positive correlation between robust organization and revenue. Investors will want to put money into capacity development, which donors tend not to want to fund (although I hope those who read this book will want to much more). Capacity building will help to generate more revenues. This will allow for greater returns to investors. The larger the organizations get, the better able they will be to take advantage of economies of scale and provide services more efficiently. This will increase donations. This will increase investment returns yet again. The approach should appeal perfectly to the interests of each market.

Also, because investors want the highest possible return on their investment, they will tend to fund new ideas for generating revenues, funding for which charities now lack almost completely. From these new revenues, charities will have an excess of capital to devote to even greater efforts at revenue generation, activating yet another circular effect.

Would current tax laws allow this, or would tax laws have to change? Current tax laws certainly permit banks to make loans and charge interest to charities, but there is a statutory obstacle to a futures market. For an organization to be eligible for charitable tax-exempt status, "no part of the net earnings of the organization may inure to the benefit of any private shareholder or individual."[222] Benefits to private individuals must have the primary effect of furthering the organization's charitable purposes. Certainly capital investment would have that effect. Nonetheless, it is likely that this statutory regulation would have to be removed or significantly changed.

Alternatively, there is the possibility that for-profit corporations could provide the same kinds of charitable services traditionally limited to non-profit organizations. They would face no such statutory restriction. Where is it written that only a nonprofit organization can provide charitable services? That question in and of itself opens up a world of possibility.

In any event, it is beyond the scope of this discussion to tackle the legal obstacles to such an idea. The law will make room for new ideas if we make new ideas our priority. The need for capital is fundamental. We must change whatever laws we must to make it flow.

American charitable giving hovers at around 2.1 percent of gross domestic product. Over the past thirty-five years, it has not fluctuated a great deal. At its lowest, around the end of the 1970s, it was at 1.7 percent, and at its highest, near the end of the tech boom, it reached 2.3 percent. But it was at 2.1 percent in 1969, was still at 2.1 percent thirty-six years later, in 2005, and came in virtually unchanged, at 2.2 percent in 2006.[223] This share of the national wealth has proved to be woefully inadequate for eradicating the great problems that confront us. Where will additional funds come from?

It is clear that they will not come from maintaining the status quo. They can come from building demand, as we just discussed. But they needn't come from building demand alone. They can come also, and faster, from the same place they come from in the for-profit sector. They can come from a market for investment. Such a market will bring to charity the kind of enthusiasm for new projects and new vision that it has brought to every other community to which it has been introduced over time. The *Times* of London wrote in 1825 of the new investment opportunities in Latin America, "A new day seldom passes without the arriving at maturity of some great project, requiring a large amount of capital."[224] It is time for charity to dream of its great projects, to dream its great dreams, and to have the capital to finance them too. The implications of such a market are beyond immediate comprehension. What is certain is that its doors will open the moment we stop equating charity with self-deprivation, the moment we stop calling profit bad and self-interest a sin. It is a phenomenon waiting to happen. All we have to do is stop prohibiting it.

Conclusion

This chapter has been an effort to deconstruct the fundamental errors of the nonprofit ideology that directs charity in America today. These errors mirror the fundamental error of Puritan doctrine: that the self is depraved and, therefore, that self-interest is sinful. While the rest of the economic universe has moved on from the Puritan vision, nonprofit ideology has constructed an imaginary world for its protection. It is a world made of "shoulds." People *should* work for charity without regard for their self-interest. People *should* be at their maximum readiness to give without the need for prompting through expensive advertising. All money *should* go directly and immediately to the needy. The ideology does not concern itself with whether people *will* do these things or not or whether any of this works. It is not concerned about outcomes. Its greatest concern is the maintenance of the ideological edifice. To quote Galbraith, "It is far, far better and much safer to have a firm anchor in nonsense than to put out on the troubled seas of thought."[225]

As it turns out, people *will not* do the things that nonprofit ideology demands in sufficient numbers to eradicate suffering in the world. They *will not* migrate to an employment market that fails to recognize their true value. They *will not* invest money they could invest elsewhere *for* a return for *no* return. In a sea of for-profit consumer brand advertising, they *will not* remember to give in amounts adequate to address the real needs without external prompting from competitive advertising for charity. Furthermore, the natural laws of the universe refuse to conform to the artificial laws of nonprofit ideology. The natural law *will not* allow people and organizations to learn without making mistakes. It *will not* allow people to create long-term value without long-term financial investment. It *will not* allow dreams to come true unless people take a chance on making their dreams come true and accept the risk that goes with it.

But never mind. The belief system imposes itself anyway. Incapable of imagining human decency through any means other than mandate and strict regulation, it imposes on charity an oppressive set of commandments that keep it petrified in exile from its potential. The very doctrine we entrust with the transfiguration of suffering in the world instead institutionalizes it. It does this by acting as a regulatory mechanism on the natural world and on the natural tendencies of human beings to identify and solve the problems in their world, motivated by a combination of self-interest and self-interested interest in others.

The best way to measure the impact of these prejudices is to imagine a world without them. Without a prohibition on value-based compensation, many top business school graduates would have moved into leadership roles in initiatives to combat suffering. Without a prohibition on profit, billions of investment dollars would have flowed to these initiatives to capitalize grand projects. Without a prohibition on paid advertising, billions of dollars would have been spent on building demand for solving the complex social problems that face us, creating massive increases in revenues, with all of the ensuing snowball effects. Without a need for immediate gratification, long-term goals could be pursued, and charity would have its own versions of "Amazon.com" for curing disease, tackling poverty, and the other things. Without a prohibition on making mistakes, charity would be light-years ahead of where it now stands in terms of institutional know-how. Without a prohibition on failure, charity could dream.

Everywhere the for-profit sector needs a yes, it has a yes, for no other reason than that there is no ideology imposing a restriction on nature. Capitalism is not a contrivance. Adam Smith did not write a fantasy of a wrathful God with a litmus test for predestined salvation. He simply codified his observations about the natural tendencies of human beings and extrapolated from them. The title of his work was *An Inquiry into the Nature and Causes of the Wealth of Nations*. He did not fill it with warnings about God's wrath if capitalism were not strictly observed. In five books, totaling some 1,028 pages, there is not a single direct reference to God. By contrast, John Winthrop's "Modell of Christian Charity," at just five pages, has eleven, not to mention all his references to "the Lord."[226] Winthrop did not observe nature. He condemned it. His "Modell" is more than a contrivance. It is a religion. We don't use religion as the basis for building cars or manufacturing refrigerators. Why would we use it to eradicate breast cancer or end homelessness?

So the prescription becomes obvious—begin paying people according to their value, begin investing in the long term, begin experimenting with new projects and dreams, begin marketing to build demand, and begin raising the capital to finance it by offering a return. Once this happens, the old world will fade into the past. A new vision will come into focus.

The self is not depraved. Once this error is removed, so too fall away all the errors that flow from it.

CHAPTER 3

Stop Asking This Question

Not everything that counts can be counted, and not everything
that can be counted counts.
—A SIGN THAT REPORTEDLY HUNG IN
ALBERT EINSTEIN'S OFFICE AT PRINCETON

Efficiency Measures—The Puritan Guard

The U.S. Supreme Court issued the following decision in May
2003 in support of an earlier decision made by the Illinois Supreme Court:

The Illinois Supreme Court in the instant case correctly observed that "the
percentage of [fundraising] proceeds turned over to a charity is not an accurate measure of the amount of funds used 'for' a charitable purpose."[1]

More than thirty years ago, Steven Smallwood and Wilson Levis,
writing in the *Philanthropy Monthly* warned:

The summary bottom-line percentage figure in most instances fails to accurately measure fund-raising cost levels and effectiveness, can be misleading, is
subject to manipulation, is not a reliable guide to the efficiency or worthiness
of an organization, and is likely to be counterproductive to the general need
for effective public understanding of the practices of fundraising for charity.[2]

Nevertheless, the entirety of nonprofit ideology is guarded by this
simple question—it has staggering power: "What percentage of my donation goes to the cause?" This is the question we have been trained to
ask. We do not even think to ask a different question. We wouldn't
begin to know what other questions are available to us. Similarly, we

have been taught that the answer to this question is the absolute measure of the real charity being done.

Virtually any violation of the ideology will trigger a fall in percentage returns. Pay a new executive director a higher salary, and the percentage will fall. Invest in long-term image advertising, and the percentage will fall. Try something new and fail, and the percentage will fall. Invest in long-term organizational improvements, and the short-term percentage will fall. Low percentage returns will trigger outcries of immorality. Petrified of this, charities are careful not to do anything that will precipitate a fall in the percentage return below watchdog standards. The question of what percentage of one's donation goes to the cause functions as a kind of coercive, authoritative, life-sucking state that reigns over the whole of nonprofit endeavor.

Evolution

How did it come to be the only question we ask? By far the most powerful explanation is that it enforces our underlying ideology. Second, although its simplicity is what makes it dangerous, we are addicted to simplicity. In an age of information overload and overwhelm, we want simple dividing lines for deciding right from wrong, and this one seems to fit the bill. However, Richard Steinberg, writing in the *Case Western Law Review* nearly twenty years ago, noted that the measure "has little to commend itself *besides* simplicity" (emphasis added).[3]

Third, we are very interested in weeding out fraud, and this measure would seem on its surface to be an easy way to detect it. Theoretically, if you were going to pocket funds solicited from the public, this measure would expose that. There are two problems with this. The first is that anyone committing fraud would most likely cover her tracks, in which case the measure would not expose the fraud. In restating its 1984 decision in the *Munson* case, in which a professional fundraiser challenged a Maryland statute that prohibited a charitable organization from paying expenses of more than 25 percent of the amount raised in connection with any fundraising activity, the Supreme Court said that, if a percentage-based test "actually prevented fraud in some cases it would be 'little more than fortuitous.'"[4] The second problem is the fact that if fraud produces a lower percentage return, that does not in turn mean that a low percentage return is evidence of fraud. In the *Munson* case, the Supreme Court wrote that the statute "operates on a fundamentally mistaken premise that high solicitation costs are an accurate measure of fraud."[5] It said that the *Munson* decision demonstrated "that there is no nexus between the percentage of funds retained by the fundraiser and the likelihood that the solicitation is fraudulent."[6] Far worse than the fact that the measure is not a reliable indicator of fraud is the fact that it can make a good charity look suspect. This is exactly the kind of injustice we are trying to avoid. This is fraud in and of itself.

As early as the mid-1800s, Americans were suspicious of philanthropists. They felt that philanthropy was just a way for the wealthy to "atone" for their wealth and that it was little more than pretense.[7] Henry David Thoreau "scorned 'a charity which dispenses the crumbs that fall from its overload tables, which are left after its feasts!'"[8] As the wealthy established huge foundations for giving away a portion of their wealth, suspicions grew that they were trying to evade taxes and that they were not really furthering the causes of the poor or the needy. Unlike Bill Gates, John D. Rockefeller and his peers were not highly thought of. President Taft was opposed to the effort to incorporate the Rockefeller Foundation in 1913. The late 1800s showed the first signs of concern about imposters and con artists in retail solicitations, as well as disorganization in the distribution of aid as the scope and scale of charity grew. "Charity organization" societies began to spring up, not to aid the poor, but to monitor the aid that was being given and to uncover fraud. A 1961 congressional investigation into the misuses of foundation tax laws resulted, seven years later, in stricter regulations. The new laws were enacted under the assumption "that charitable organizations dependent upon the public for support were less suspect and less in need of supervision than private foundations endowed by a single individual or family."[9]

In the 1970s, public concern about "questionable uses of funds" and excessive fundraising and administrative costs in traditional nonprofits gathered momentum.[10] By the end of the decade, "twenty states and numerous county and local governments had adopted laws or ordinances limiting charity solicitations to organizations that could prove a sizeable proportion of the collection went for charitable purposes rather than for salaries and administrative costs."[11] This was the first evidence of the institutionalization of the belief that the percentage question was an important measure of charitable effectiveness.

Furthermore, the percentage of funds going to charitable programs is a very cheap and easy number to produce. All one has to do is divide what's left after overhead by revenue. The data for that simple calculation are easily acquired from the IRS Form 990 that many charities are required to file. The number of charities in America has exploded in the past fifty years, from about forty-five thousand registered nonprofit organizations in 1960 to over 1 million today.[12] With so many types of causes and so many types of needs and so many different possible methods for measuring progress, this simple measure is an infinitely easier and less expensive number to come up with than some measurement for actual charitable impact—a measure that still eludes the sector today.

None of this, of course, means that the measure is any good. There is no evidence that people began using it because they thought it was. It was just easy.

In a vicious circle, the nonprofit sector, anxious to please the donating public or face its wrath, has adopted and promoted this measure, giving it even more legitimacy. Lester Salamon, in *The State of Nonprofit America*, writes:

> A serious fault line seems to have opened in the foundation of public trust on which the entire nonprofit edifice rests. This may be due in part to the unrealistic expectations that the public has of these institutions, expectations that the charitable sector ironically counts on and encourages.[13]

As a result, a $295 billion piece of the economy—and that's just by measure of annual donations—relies almost entirely on the answer to a question whose usefulness the public has not investigated.[14] Under the light of examination, it turns out to be a dangerous question with often meaningless or misleading answers. Smallwood and Levis, in addition to warning about its shortcomings, warned in the 1970s of its oncoming influence:

> The focus on fund-raising costs has become so intense that many well-intentioned evaluators (including potential contributors) of charitable organizations are tending to view the level of such costs as the principal or perhaps the only characteristic to take into account in estimating the "worthiness" or legitimacy of the organizations.[15]

Watchdogs, the Media, and Circular Reinforcement

It's hard to overstate how heavily we rely on this measure. If we're thinking of giving to a breast cancer research charity, we want to know what percentage of our dollar will actually go to breast cancer research. If we donate to a soup kitchen, we want to know what percentage actually goes to soup. If 95 percent of donations to the soup kitchen go to soup, we think that's a good charity. If only 50 percent of donations to the soup kitchen go to soup, we think it's a bad charity.

Who is teaching us to think this way? Watchdog agencies, the media, government, and charities themselves. It is a testament to the sector's own oppression that it has not taken serious issue with the barbaric and violent image of a "watchdog" aimed at its throat.

According to the Better Business Bureau (BBB) Wise Giving Alliance standard, a charity should "spend at least 65% of its total expenses on program activities."[16] The *Chronicle of Philanthropy* announced this new guideline in 2002: "The nation's major charity watchdog group, the BBB Wise Giving Alliance, this week is releasing proposed guidelines that call on non-profit groups to devote at least 65 percent of their total expenditures to charitable programs."[17] Their standard used to be 60 percent. The economics of fundraising hasn't changed. Why are organizations that used to be approved of suddenly disapproved of?

In its list of charitable accountability standards, the first criterion included under finance on the BBB Wise Giving Alliance website in 2008 is that the charity shall "spend at least 65% of its total expenses on program activities."[18]

At the top of the BBB Wise Giving Alliance website is its new slogan, "Start with Trust." Implicit in this is the notion that you can trust, at least at some level, the criteria embodied in the standards. The visually dominant measure used in each charity profile gauges the percentage of donations that went to the cause. Although the alliance has twenty accountability standards for charities, the profiles on the site have just one large graphic—the only graphic in the profile—a large pie chart that reveals values as you run your cursor over it.[19] It tells you what percentage of the charity's revenues went to charitable programs versus fundraising and administration. It is the only interactive graphic feature in the profile.[20] Everything about it says that this is important information to examine.

The American Institute of Philanthropy is another watchdog.[21] As of 2008 the first headline—large and red—in the "criteria" section of its website says, "PERCENT SPENT ON CHARITABLE PURPOSE." The institute states, "In AIP's view, 60% or greater is reasonable for most charities."[22] So what's reasonable to one watchdog is less reasonable to another. The first sentence on the "Top-Rated Charities" page reads, "The mission categories below list charities which get *high grades* from AIP for putting 75% or more towards program cost while generally spending $25 or less to raise $100."[23]

Charity Navigator promotes itself as "Your Guide to Intelligent Giving."[24] Implicit in this is the idea that the measures this watchdog uses are intelligent. At the top of the page on "Methodology," a headline asks, "How Do We Rate Charities?" The first area is "organizational efficiency": "Our ratings show givers how efficiently we believe a charity will use their support today. . . . Analyzing a charity's efficiency reveals how well it functions day to day. Charities that are efficient spend less money to raise more."[25] Charity profiles begin with their "organizational efficiency" rating, and for each profile there is a pie chart similar to that presented by the BBB Wise Giving Alliance showing what percentage of expenses goes to programs versus fundraising and administration.[26] The Charity Navigator website states, "We believe that those spending less than a third of their budget on program expenses are simply not living up to their missions. Charities demonstrating such gross inefficiency receive zero points for their overall organizational efficiency score."[27]

The American Institute of Philanthropy tells you that it "encourages each donor to consider these factors and others, which you may feel are more significant, when making charitable giving decisions. AIP provides this information to help you make your own decision concerning which charity to support."[28] The advice seems weak considering that the institute has already passed judgment on the percentage-to-programs question, implying that it is one of the most important things you can ask by making it such a priority on the website and by telling you what the answer should be.

As for the Better Business Bureau, a qualification in the *Chronicle of Philanthropy*'s "Watchdog Watch" section said, "The alliance does not approve or disapprove of charities, and urges donors to evaluate the importance of variations from the standards."[29] Come on now. When the Better Business Bureau tells us that a charity has or has not met its most prominent standards, doesn't that cause us to approve or disapprove? Disclaimers don't balance the weight of the Better Business Bureau's name and seal. In testimony to Congress in 2004, Art Taylor, president and CEO of the BBB Wise Giving Alliance, stated plainly, "Our association with the Better Business Bureau, a name familiar to virtually the entire public, lends it high credibility."[30]

Beyond that, the qualification seems weak when you consider that the BBB Wise Giving Alliance licenses its "National Charity Seal" for a fee ranging from $1,000 to $15,000 to charities that have met its standards, but not to those that haven't.[31] (Approximately two hundred charities were on its list of participants as of 2008.)[32] While it may caution donors not to judge a charity by the numbers alone, the numbers alone can disqualify a charity from getting a seal. It must consider the numbers pretty important. In 2008, the alliance's website contained the following description:

> The BBB Wise Giving Alliance is committed to protecting the integrity of the charity seal. Seal holder organizations will be monitored for adherence to the program's requirements, and national charities that no longer qualify for participation will be required to cease display of the seal.[33]

Amazingly, our Breast Cancer 3-Day program, which netted $194.4 million in five years, would not qualify for an alliance seal because our historic average donor dollar return to charity was 60 percent and not 65 percent.

The very fact that watchdogs set a standard threshold for the measure means that they vouch for the fundamental validity of the measure itself, even though the Supreme Court did not. *When someone vouches for a gauge's threshold, the validity of the thing being gauged is conceded.* The FDA wouldn't give you a recommended daily allowance for vitamin C if it didn't think vitamin C was important.

Whether the watchdogs qualify their standards or not, and whether they have more than one standard, the fact is the media places extremely heavy and often exclusive emphasis on the "percentage to the cause" or "efficiency" measure. If that measure makes no sense, or indeed does damage, the watchdogs have to take a serious look at whether they should promote it in any manner or, indeed, whether they should actively discourage its use.

It is little wonder that these organizations rely on measures and information that are simple to calculate and acquire. They don't have the resources to do much more. In 2006, BBB Wise Giving Alliance tax forms show that it took in $1.8 million in revenues and spent $1.6 million on operations, yet it was reporting on complex charities with annual budgets in the tens of millions of dollars.[34] As of 2008, the alliance's website indicated it had a staff of nine employees, of whom just three were research analysts.[35] As of 2006, they offered reports on a thousand national charities.[36]

Dan Prives, a consultant to nonprofit organizations in Baltimore, writing for the *Chronicle of Philanthropy* in an article entitled "Charity Standards Proposed by Watchdog Group Are Deeply Flawed," made the following observation:

With for-profit businesses, the Better Business Bureau provides a consumer service of informing the public about complaints by other consumers. The organization does not attempt to tell the consumer which firms are managed better than others. No evidence exists that the BBB Wise Giving Alliance can effectively perform such an evaluation for tens of thousands of charities nationwide.[37]

On whether the Better Business Bureau is even up to the task, he continued, "The alliance is trying to cover too much ground with too few resources to be effective and fair. In the long run, charities will suffer."[38]

The other watchdog agencies do not have significantly greater resources. Charity Navigator's website lists eleven staff members as of 2008.[39] They were evaluating 5,300 of the nation's 700,000 active charities.[40] The group's tax returns show total operating and administrative expenses of $1 million for 2005.[41] The American Institute of Philanthropy in 2002 had four staff members.[42] Its website in 2006 said, "Over 500 charities rated in AIP's Charity Rating Guide & Watchdog Report."[43] Its 2006 Form 990 shows functional expenses of about $372,000.[44] Paul Nelson, writing for the *Philanthropy Roundtable*, made the interesting additional point that "the financial stability of charity oversight groups is probably more precarious than many charities they monitor."[45]

The media takes over where the watchdogs leave off, not only promoting the standards they set, but promoting the percentage question and pointing you directly to the watchdog websites, where the question gets reinforced.

A 2007 *Los Angeles Times* pre-Christmas story advising readers on holiday giving paraphrases an expert saying that "donors should expect the vast majority of revenue be spent on 'programs'; the cause the charity purports to support. Any group that spends more than 25% of its budget on marketing and administration is not providing much bang for your buck."[46]

In a November 2006 story in *Time* magazine on giving to smaller charities, the very first thing they said about analyzing a charity was, "One way to vet nonprofits is by looking for charities with low operating costs. Ask a nonprofit what percentage of the budget covers overhead and how much the CEO takes as salary."[47]

A 2004 front-page web story on "Forbes.com" begins with the headline "Special Report: America's Most (and Least) Efficient Charities." It states, "Charitable commitment shows how much of total expenses went for the charitable purpose, excluding management, overhead and fundraising."[48] "Charitable commitment?" The lower the number is, the less committed the charity is? The story then gives you "5 Smart Ways to Give." Tip number 2 is, "Watch the Fundraising Cost. . . . We calculate fundraising efficiency as the amount of contributions left after subtracting fundraising costs. Anything below 70% is in our judgment very questionable. The average on our list was 89%." Tip number 1 is "Do Your Due Diligence. . . . If it's a national charity, the Better Business Bureau maintains detailed reports at www.give.org."[49]

Money magazine did a story in 2004 that advises you to evaluate charity yourself, "or you can rely on watchdog groups to do the analysis for you," and points you to "Charitywatch.org," "Charitynavigator.org," and the Better Business Bureau Wise Giving Alliance.[50]

The media's involvement has a circular effect, sending more and more people to the watchdog websites. Charity Navigator's website in 2008 says, "Last year alone, more than four million donors used the site that *Time* magazine called 'One of America's 50 Coolest Websites for 2006.' . . . Additionally, the site . . . was selected by *Reader's Digest* as one of the '100 Best Things About America.'"[51] In 2004, the BBB Wise Giving Alliance reported that charity reports were "accessed more than 2.3 million times" and that they had an "unusually large volume of hits after the December 26th tsunami tragedy when the public sought information about charities involved with relief efforts."[52]

From there, even government agencies promote not only the standards, but the watchdogs themselves. The city of Los Angeles requires that all solicitations include an information card. That card contains three pieces of data: how much the event raised last year, how much went to the charity, and, you guessed it, what percentage went to expenses (the reciprocal of the percentage that went to the cause).[53] Even the California attorney general's website lists the BBB Wise Giving Alliance as an "additional resource for wise charitable giving."[54]

Charities themselves then cement the importance of the measure, often including the watchdog logos and approvals on the homepage of their websites and in their promotional materials. This begins with some of the largest and best-known charities in America and trickles down. As of 2008, the United Way, the American Lung Association, and the American Cancer Society websites all featured the BBB Wise Giving Alliance logo on the *main page* of their websites. *Ironically, even Grameen Foundation, considered a vanguard of new thinking about charity, features the Better Business Bureau "Accredited Charity" seal on the main page of its website.*[55] The Hunger Project, founded by Werner Erhard, an iconoclast if ever there was one, has the Better Business Bureau seal and the Charity Navigator "Four Star" seal on the front page of its website. The Charity Navigator seal is bigger than the Hunger Project logo itself.[56] The American Red Cross features the Charity Navigator "Four Star Charity" seal on its donations page. Indeed, the Red Cross issued a 2006 press release headlined, "American Red Cross Receives Four Stars from Charity Navigator: For the Fifth Consecutive Year, the American Red Cross Receives Highest Rating from Charity Watchdog."[57] The American Diabetes Association features on its donations page the Wise Giving Alliance seal, along with a brightly colored pie chart showing what percentage of donations goes to programs versus fundraising and management.[58] The list goes on and on.

Effects

The indoctrination works. Studies show that we want answers—not to the questions that are most important, but to the question we have been trained to think is important, to the exclusion of things that we might objectively realize are far more important.

A study by the Princeton Survey Research Associates conducted for the BBB Wise Giving Alliance found:

> A series of closed-end questions asked of all adults—not just self-identified information seekers—also shows finances at the top of the list of what the public needs to make an informed decision about giving. . . . More than three-fourths (79%) of adults say it's very important to know what percent of a charity's spending goes toward charitable programs.[59]

The following statistic is amazing. Only 6 percent of respondents to this survey cited "Genuine needs / Makes a difference" as the thing they most want to know when deciding whether to give to a charity.[60] We have been systematically trained not to ask whether our gifts will make a difference, but rather to ask what percentage of the gift goes to the cause—probably because we assume the two questions are the same. We would all concede with a moment's thought that the most important question we could ask is, How much of a difference is being made? The fact that we ask a different question shows that we think it will give us the same answer. We just think we're asking it in a different way. As the next section illustrates, that could not be further from the truth.

The Real Question

We have come to believe that the answer to "What percentage of my donation goes to the cause?" tells us pretty much everything we need to know about a charity. With that little piece of information in hand, we believe that we know if the charity is a good one or a bad one, how it compares to other charities, how much we can trust it, and whether or not we should donate to it. This is odd when we consider the multitude of questions we ask before making other important decisions in our lives. If we are buying a new car, there are a dozen things we want to know, from the mileage it gets to all the subtleties of the warranty. We spend two years watching our presidential candidates answer a thousand questions before we cast a single vote. We ask more questions about the ingredients in an Oreo cookie than we ask about our most important charities. *But we act as if we know everything we need to know about our charities, simply because we asked what percentage of our donation went to the cause.*

If the efficiency measure were the panacea society has made it out to be, none of this would be a problem. The question we turn to now is whether or not it is and whether or not it deserves the extraordinary power we have given to it.

Efficiency Measures Miss the Point

The way the system calculates the percentage of a donation that goes to the cause is by measuring the percentage it thinks does not. The things that fall into the latter category include fundraising and administrative costs, collectively called, ignominiously, "overhead." In an amicus brief in the Supreme Court's 2003 *Madigan v. Telemarketing Associates* case, 176 nonprofit organizations joined in making the following statement: "Cost of fundraising measures, however calculated, are of marginal, if any, utility to the potential donor attempting to ascertain the actual efficacy or accomplishments of a charity soliciting donations."[61] Bill Shore, the founder of Share Our Strength, wrote in his *Revolution of the Heart*: "An organization can have administrative expenses lower than all the other organizations in the field, but if it's not accomplishing much, then what good is it?"[62]

Probably the most important question one can ask about a charity is, How effectively does it use the money left over *after* overhead? When I ask only, "What percentage *went* to overhead?" I am told nothing about how intelligently it spent the remainder.

Here is a simple example. Soup Kitchen A says it sends 90 percent of my donation to the cause—the cause being soup. Soup Kitchen B says it sends only 60 percent to the cause. Conventional wisdom would tell me to choose A. But what if A spends its 90 percent on lukewarm, watered-down broth, served in a filthy space by a burned-out staff, and B spends its 60 percent on hot, nutritional soup made from a fresh protein source and vegetables served with a warm roll by a friendly staff in a bright, clean facility? Now which soup kitchen would it make more sense to give to? And how would I know Soup Kitchen B is the better of the two if I only asked "What percentage of my donation actually goes to soup?" Wouldn't it be better to ask, "How much of my money goes to *good nutritional* soup?" In that case, the answer is 0 percent for Soup Kitchen A, and 60 percent for Soup Kitchen B. A completely different reality. And yet Soup Kitchen A can get a seal of approval and Soup Kitchen B cannot.

The question that is completely overlooked, of course, concerns the charity's effectiveness in achieving its mission—in other words, how good is it at doing what it's supposed to be good at? With the money it has for the needy, how well does it serve them? How effective is its approach? The issue that is of paramount importance is the issue that is ignored. Charity Navigator's website, for example, says, "At this time, evaluating the effectiveness of a charity's programs is out of our scope."[63]

Judging a charity by its overhead percentage alone is like concluding that someone who is 6 feet tall and weighs 250 pounds is fat without ever meeting him. He might be fat. But on the other hand, he might be a Hercules with 0 percent body fat. The weight might be all muscle. No one can tell by looking only at numbers.

The Ford, Charles Stewart Mott, David and Lucille Packard Foundations, along with the Atlantic Philanthropies, funded a research initiative entitled *Nonprofit Overhead Cost Project*. The study was conducted in three phases, including an analysis of IRS Form 990 tax returns of 250,000 charities, survey results from 1,500 of those, and in-depth case studies of 9 of those. An August 2004 brief concluded:

> Absent good, comparative information about program or mission effectiveness, donors and charity watchdogs often place excessive reliance on financial indicators. Of particular concern to us is the use of overhead cost and fundraising cost ratios as stand-ins for measures of program effectiveness. No

organization in our study was an extravagant spender on fundraising and administration. Yet contrary to the popular idea that spending less in these areas is a virtue, our cases suggest that nonprofits that spend too little on infrastructure have more limited effectiveness than those that spend more reasonably.[64]

According to Paul Nelson, the General Accounting Office agrees: "The GAO also urges caution about relying too heavily on ratios and spending efficiency; it adds that how well a charity accomplishes its mission is an important aspect of its worthiness."[65] That's an understatement, but at least it's stated.

Charities typically have three major categories of operation—fundraising, administration, and program operations—the third being the part of the organization that operates the *charitable programs* that serve the need. All three are important components of the overall operation. Typically, most of the money goes, or at least is reported as going, to charitable programs. But the efficiency of the fundraising and administrative operations is where we put all the emphasis. This isn't logical. The fact that a charity has an efficient fundraising operation does not necessarily mean that it has a good program operation. Conversely, the fact that its fundraising operation may be less efficient than another charity's does not mean that it doesn't have effective charitable programs.

The system hurts all good charities because it forces them to keep reported overhead low, even if that might harm the program side of the operation. Bright people are forced to make choices that aren't in the interest of the greatest good. Of equal concern is the fact that we have no good way of weeding out those charities that are ineffective at running their programs, because their ineffectiveness is obscured by what appear to be "good," that is, low, overhead percentages.

Believe it or not, there is no national apparatus in America for evaluating the worthiness of charitable programs, which is the only reason that charities exist.

What we should want to know is, How good is an AIDS service charity at providing effective AIDS services? How good is an adoption home at getting the kids adopted? How good is a suicide prevention hotline at picking up the phone on the first ring? Yet these questions are never asked. Mark Hager and Janet Greenlee, in "How Important Is a Nonprofit's Bottom Line? The Uses and Abuses of Financial Data," wrote of the watchdogs' evaluation methods:

> None is based principally on program effectiveness. All are primarily based on financial information that nonprofits provide to the IRS each year. . . .

Possibly the most important criticism of financial analysis of nonprofits is that it takes the place of trying to determine whether the organization is doing a good job of fulfilling its mission or not.[66]

Consider two diabetes research charities, Charity A and Charity B. Each took in $10 million in donations last year. Charity A reports that 90 percent of every dollar donated goes directly to diabetes research and only 10 percent to overhead. Its website prides itself on this percentage. The charity looks impressive on paper. Donors are likely to admire the lean way it seems to run its operation. It is likely to do well in the market for donations.

Charity B, on the other hand, gets some negative publicity: "Critics complain that of the $10 million Charity B raised last year, only $7 million went to diabetes researchers. Unbelievably, more than $3 million of donor contributions went to overhead costs. One activist urged an investigation by the attorney general." Three million dollars spent on overhead sounds inefficient. Donors will have no difficulty considering the organization wasteful. It is likely to have a hard time in the market for donations.

Behind the scenes there is a different picture. Most of Charity A's $1 million overhead goes to salaries and rent for its executive staff and offices. It spends only $100,000 on a full-time person who makes decisions about which researchers will get the $9 million it gives away every year. This person is not a medical researcher, but a former sales executive. He decides to give $3 million back to the government [the National Institute of Diabetes and Digestive and Kidney Diseases (NIDDK)], which already gets money from your taxes. He gives another $3 million to a university that the charity has been giving money to for ten years. He doesn't really investigate what the university does with the money. He gives the remaining $3 million to three other universities, all in the vicinity of Charity A's headquarters. None of these are among the top ten research units in the country.

Charity B, on the other hand, spends $3 million on overhead, as the newspapers told us. Of this, $500,000 is spent on executive salaries and rent. The other $2.5 million is spent on a full-time staff of fifteen program officers, all highly trained former medical researchers themselves, who spend their year visiting research facilities and immunobiologists, reviewing and re-reviewing sophisticated grant proposals from all applicants. They have $7 million to give away ($2 million less than Charity A). After a year of painstaking work, they give away 140 grants of

$50,000 each to some of America's most creative and promising re-searchers at the finest universities in the country.

Charity B's investment in overhead and its commitment to its mission has made for a much more intelligent, effective expenditure of donations. It is more likely to find a cure for diabetes. It is more effective at funding research, even though it appears to be less effective at keeping overhead low.

Now which charity seems more worthy? How could anyone have ever known that if they only asked about overhead percentages? The better question would be, How effective is the charity at funding good diabetes researchers? But that question never gets asked.

According to the *Nonprofit Overhead Cost Project*:

> Arbitrarily limiting a nonprofit in how much it can spend to raise its needed operating revenues is counterproductive and unfair. . . . Nonprofit organizations can provide highly effective programs and at the same time have a comparatively high cost of administration and higher than average cost of fundraising. Indeed, an organization may be effective in service delivery precisely because of its spending on administration and costly investments in raising donations![67]

Just because a lot of my donation goes to the cause doesn't mean it does a lot of good. And just because less of it goes to the cause doesn't mean that it is doing less good. This is the opposite of what the system teaches us. "Efficiency" measures measure overhead. And even that they don't do well. They *don't* measure charity.

Efficiency Measures Don't Measure Efficiency

Efficiency measures fail at measuring even efficiency in at least five critical ways: they overlook (1) real dollars, (2) incremental effects, (3) intangibles, (4) the future value of a dollar, and (5) the economic value of the result produced.

Real Dollars

The question What *percentage* of money goes to the cause? ignores the question, What *amount* of money goes to the cause? Percentages are not cash. They cannot be tendered in return for anything or transferred. I cannot buy a homeless person a bowl of soup with a percentage.

Consider the example of two fundraising events—a bake sale that sends 95 percent of every donation directly to the cause and a marathon that sends "only" 60 percent of every donation to the cause. The bake sale is the better event, if judged just on the basis of these percentages. But what if the bake sale raises a total of ten *thousand* dollars and the marathon raises ten *million*? The bake sale sends $9,500 to the cause, and the marathon sends $6 million to the cause. The percentage measure ignores this reality. It tells us to think less of an effort that is doing much greater good.

An article in *POZ* magazine used efficiency measures to criticize our AIDSRides. By the year the story appeared, an average of 57.9 percent of every donor contribution went to the cause. They compared us unfavorably with another cycling event that achieved a cost of fundraising of less than 25 percent. The article stated:

> Pro Events International in Minneapolis has produced cycling events such as the Habitat 500 that achieve a COF [Cost of Fundraising] of 10 percent to 25 percent. "With the AIDS Rides, less than half of the money raised goes to charities," says Pro Events president Tom Sullivan. "That's just not right."[68]

The statement that "less than half the money raised goes to charities" was false. Moreover, the article didn't mention the vastly different scale of the events. Our AIDSRides, by the time the article was published, had netted more than $50 million. According to its website, the Habitat 500 raised $225,000 in 2002.[69] Our average event had *netted* $2.9 million by the time this article appeared—over twelve times as much as the 2002 Habitat 500 *raised*.

When the scales of the two endeavors are so vastly different, it is no longer even efficiency that is being measured. To compare the efficiency of two operations is to compare the resources they use to achieve the same outcome. If the two outcomes are different, there is no longer a basis for measurement.

Moreover, it is necessarily less expensive, on both a dollar and a percentage basis, to do things on a very small scale than to do them on a very large scale. In 1983, when thirty-nine of my college classmates and I rode our bikes across America to raise money to fight world hunger, we stayed in high school gyms and church basements that cost us nothing. People made us casseroles for dinner and pancakes for breakfast that cost us nothing. That can be done with thirty-nine college cyclists, and percentage costs can be kept low as a result—in part it is because you don't think to report the cost of the casserole. But it is not tenable for three thousand cyclists to sleep in a church basement or for a small town to make them all pancakes. Money has to be spent on professional services to accommodate participants on that scale. But inordinately more money can be raised. The thirty-nine of us raised about $80,000. An AIDSRide with three thousand cyclists would net about $5 million. There is no evidence to suggest that if Pro Events had wanted to net $50 million as the AIDSRides did, it could have kept its costs at 25 percent. The only way to measure true comparative efficiency would be to see how much it would have cost Pro Events to net $50 million as well.

Incremental Effects

Incremental effects are perhaps the most fascinating and overlooked phenomena in all of charity. Efficiency standards overlook them entirely. The phenomenon is this: the effect of the dollar I give may be vastly different than the effect of dollars given before me. The percentage of the dollar that goes to charitable programs for *one donor* is very different from the average for *all donors*.

For example, Adam and Zach have each set up a lemonade stand to raise money for the homeless. They each charge a dollar for a glass of lemonade. They each sell 100 glasses and each raise a total of $100. Adam spent $45 to build his lemonade stand, and Zach spent $25 to build his. It costs Adam 5¢ to make a glass of lemonade. It costs Zach more—10¢ per glass. The accounting is shown in table 8.

Assuming everything else is equal, including the quality of the homeless programs, logic would tell me I should give to Zach, because more of my money will go to the cause, correct? Not necessarily.

If I am the forty-ninth customer to buy a glass of Adam's lemonade, he's already sold $48 worth of lemonade and covered the $45 cost of his stand and the cost of 48 glasses of lemonade. The only expense he has when he sells me a glass of lemonade is 5¢. So my decision to buy a $1 glass of lemonade from him means 95¢ cents will go to the homeless. The incremental effect of my donation is not 50 percent, as the average states. It is 95 percent. On the other hand, if I am the twenty-ninth or later customer for Zach, he's already covered the $25 cost of his stand and the cost of 28 glasses of lemonade. But only 90¢ of my dollar will go to the homeless, because my glass of lemonade costs him 10¢ to make. The average percentage measure would send me to the wrong lemonade stand.

In short, once a charity has covered its expenses in any given year, 100 percent of every incremental donation beyond that can go directly to charitable programs, regardless of the *average* percentage. My decision

Table 8

	Adam	*Zach*
Total Raised	$100	$100
Expenses		
Lemonade Stand	$45	$25
Lemonade (100 glasses each)	$5	$10
Amount Left for Programs	$50	$65
Percentage Return	50%	65%

to give or not to give $100 has a *$100* impact on the needy. To slap a "monotone" average percentage on the impact of donations through-out the year does a tremendous disservice to the ability to solicit dona-tions.[70] If people knew at some point that the incremental effect of their giving would be 100 percent, this would dramatically affect donat-ing behavior. Why would I care that the average donation going to, say, breast cancer research is 60 percent if the percentage of mine that will go is 100? Steinberg wrote:

> The average fundraising percentage contains little information of value to in-dividual donors . . . the average-share statistic contains no information about the value of incremental donations. While society may care about the average return to donations, individuals can only control their increment to the dona-tive pool. Thus, it is rational that they should care only about incremental re-turns from their individual donations. . . . Incremental returns do not depend on the average fundraising percentage.[71]

An average is an abstraction. Incremental action, on the other hand, is real. It is the only kind of action I can take. But because efficiency measures are based on average economic activity, they do not measure its efficiency or its impact.

Intangibles

Efficiency standards overlook valuable intangibles. Thus, they do not measure true overall impact and cannot therefore lay claim to measuring efficiency. "Efficiency" is measured by dividing net value by total in-come. If it doesn't include the entire value, it cannot possibly be meas-uring efficiency.

It is easy to account accurately for expenses because they are incurred with cash and cash can be counted. It is easy to account for cash donations for the same reason. But what about value that comes to the cause in some form other than money? That doesn't get counted. Generally accepted accounting practices aren't very good at allowing us to count the value of new awareness to a cause or the value of inspiring people. This doesn't mean these intangible values don't exist.

Charity, in particular, is in the business of inspiration, so it is particularly problematic for charity that the value of inspiration is not measured and not given any benefit, even if only in our thinking. For example, many of the people who did our AIDSRides were HIV positive. For them, the events were a reaffirmation of life. They gave them hope, tremendous support, motivation to get into the best physical shape they could, and a vitally new positive outlook. A huge number of participants in the Breast Cancer 3-Days were breast cancer survivors—some in the midst of treatment. The events had far-ranging positive effects on their lives too. Some might say that if no other benefit came from the events, they would have been worth it for the difference they made in these people's lives alone, but none of this gets measured. As far as overhead measures are concerned, it never happened.

In addition, by about the third year of the AIDSRides, a majority of the riders were heterosexual. The rides provided a rare environment for mutual understanding between gay people and straight people. The rides brought people into the cause who otherwise would never have had reason to do something significant about AIDS. This, too, had lasting value that was never measured.

After the events, many of the participants did amazing things to help society that, in their own words, they say they would not have done had they not participated in the events. They began taking part in similar events for other causes, and raising money for and awareness of those causes. They began volunteering at adoption homes and AIDS charities. One started a charity that takes inner-city kids on bike rides in the country to reduce inner-city violence. One began an Internet chat room to promote human kindness. There are hundreds of stories like this.

When we fail to account for all the value accrued, we get a skewed picture of the cost, and otherwise wonderful, valuable efforts get mislabeled, by otherwise very intelligent people, as bad instead of good. We are not actually measuring efficiency.

The Future Value of a Dollar

Efficiency measures overlook the fact that money changes in value over time. If I receive a dollar bill ten years from now, it's less valuable than if I receive it today. If I put a dollar bill in the bank today at 3 percent annually compounded interest, in ten years it will be worth $1.34, not $1. Conversely, if I receive a dollar in ten years, with an interest rate of 3 percent, it is really worth about $0.70 to me right now. Efficiency measures don't recognize this.

On a larger scale, consider a charity dinner with 30 percent overhead and a charity concert with 40 percent overhead. If the dinner nets $1 million a year over the next ten years, that's considerably less valuable than the concert, which nets $10 million right now. In fact, if interest rates stay at 3 percent, the present value of the dinner's eventual $10 million is a little less than $8.6 million. If interest rates were 5 percent, the present value of the dinner's $10 million would drop to $7.8 million. This changes the present-day efficiency picture considerably. But the current so-called efficiency measures don't take that into account, so they're not measuring efficiency.

The Economic Value of the Result—Questions of Life and Death

Is not a dollar that saves lives more valuable than a dollar that doesn't? The value of future savings in health care costs—let alone the future economic productivity of the people whose lives have been saved—would seem to indicate that it is. The percentage question applies one standard to all causes and no value to the future economic benefit of the present-day endeavor. But we may well value progress on one cause more highly than progress on another. If we give added weight to a less "efficiently" raised dollar because it saves lives, it becomes less "inefficient." Once again, "efficiency" loses its meaning.

Suppose, for instance, that Jonas Salk's lab was "inefficient" at raising money. Of every dollar given to him, on average, only fifty cents went to the cause. Imagine, by contrast, that a polio clinic taking care of the afflicted raised money very efficiently—ten cents on the dollar. If you adhered to contemporary thinking, you would give to the clinic rather than to Jonas Salk. But fifty years later, tens of millions of lives had been saved by his work. The economic benefit is inestimable—many billions of dollars. We cannot go back in time; these data were not apparent to the people donating to Salk because they were never measured. Moreover, in our example, Salk's lab was compared with another institution whose output had significantly less economic value. The system discourages us from investing in this kind of long-term economic windfall simply because the short-term efficiency on a few million dollars of research money is below an arbitrary standard, or lower than it might be for another charity. *Polio has been cured, but the system by which we measure the value of different causes has not.* Future benefit is as obscure to us today as it was in the 1950s. The value of saving lives is not captured in our accounting. A system that does not take into account the value of saving lives is not a system that will save human lives on a great scale.

There is another facet to this, and that is the value of velocity. It costs more to do things quickly. There is a saying that "you can have it fast, you can have it cheap, or you can have it good. Pick two." To raise a million dollars in a month will cost more than to do it in a year. But the eleven months could mean the difference between life and death.

If a massive amount of money is being raised right now, it may be of significantly more economic value to the people in need, even if the percentage of overhead is higher, than a much smaller amount raised more "efficiently." If I need $100,000 for a heart transplant now, that money has a lot more value than $100,000 that comes to me after I'm dead, at which point it has none. Velocity has social value, but we don't measure it.

Consider a great famine somewhere. An emergency fundraising operation is put in place to get $50 million to the cause very quickly at 50 percent overhead—higher than it might otherwise be because it is expensive to raise the funds quickly. A phone center has to be set up, television ads have to be purchased, premiums and rush charges have to be paid, and so on. It is much faster to pay for these things than to try to get them donated. If we wait to get them donated, the death toll will be extreme. Would we say the campaign should never be attempted, simply because it doesn't meet the watchdog standards? And what about breast cancer, which kills forty thousand women each year in America? If we could raise a lot of money very quickly to help keep those women from dying, wouldn't it be logical to say that, so long as the costs are legitimate, I don't care what the percentage is, get as much money to that cause as you can? Is not that the more moral strategy?

As mentioned earlier, the Supreme Court weighed in on this in the 1988 *Riley* case, stating that the use of a percentage measure does not necessarily protect a charity:

There are several legitimate reasons why a charity might reject the State's overarching measure of a fundraising drive's legitimacy—the percentage of gross receipts remitted to the charity. For example, a charity might choose a particular type of fundraising drive or a particular solicitor, expecting to receive a large sum as measured by total dollars . . . rather than the percentage of dollars remitted. . . . [Or it] may choose to engage in the advocacy or dissemination of information during solicitation, or may seek the introduction of the charity's officers to the philanthropic community during a special event.[72]

I am not advocating that we should accept low percentage returns no matter what. Nor am I advocating anything less than maximizing efficiency. But it has to be efficiency we are truly measuring. If costs are legitimate—if people are doing their best, working hard, and still incurring a high percentage of overhead—it is not at all necessarily bad, and it is not necessarily "inefficient." Here again, if the calculation is made without regard to the economic benefit of the outcome, it is not efficiency that is really being measured. The data are not "decision-useful."

Efficiency Measures Are Unjust

Efficiency measures are unjust for at least five reasons: (1) they reward comparatively aggressive program accounting, (2) they discriminate against less popular causes, (3) they hurt charities during hard times, (4) they create the illusion of free resources, and (5) the standards associated with them are flawed.

Rewarding Comparatively Aggressive Program Accounting

If one charity says the donation money it spent on an advertisement was money that went to the cause, and another charity says of the same amount spent on advertising that it was not, the first charity will show a higher percentage of donations going to the cause, regardless of the fact that both charities did the same thing. What a conservative charity might call a fundraising expense a less conservative charity might call a program expense, and this makes all the difference. By a simple accounting maneuver, percentages can be dramatically altered. If I take in a million dollars in donations, spend 50 percent of it on fundraising and 50 percent of it on charitable programs, but decide to call my fundraising expense a program expense, I will show 100 percent of all donations going to programs. Another charity that does not do this will only show 50 percent. To say that one is more efficient than the other, without knowing anything about their accounting practices, is upside down.

Does this happen in the real world? Do some charities say that a fundraising expense is really a program expense and vice versa? The *Nonprofit Overhead Cost Project* studied the Forms 990 of 126,956 charities.[73] The following findings are remarkable:

- Nearly half of the charities studied reported zero fundraising expenses. Of the larger charities with annual revenues between $1 million and $5 million, one-quarter reported zero fundraising expenses.[74]
- Twenty-seven percent classified some or all accounting fees as program expenses, despite the fact that the 990 instructions give accounting fees as an example of what is meant by "management and general" expenses.[75]
- Only 25 percent of nonprofits receiving foundation grants properly account for those proposal-writing expenses as fundraising costs.[76]
- Just 17 percent of nonprofits receiving government grants properly account for those proposal-writing expenses as fundraising costs.[77]

In addition, in a working paper for the study entitled "Understanding Management and General Expenses in Nonprofits," Thomas Pollak, Patrick Rooney, and Mark Hager found that 13 percent of the 160,000 Forms 990 they studied reported zero "management and general" expenses:

> Our review of organizations' Forms 990 reporting no [management and general] expenses found very few that appeared plausible. Most reported at least one item on the form itself or in the "other expenses" attachments that would typically have an M&G component. Examples include accounting and legal fees, bank charges, salaries (one expects at least some of the chief staff person's time to be spent on overall organizational management), and insurance.[78]

The rules on the IRS 990 reporting forms and generally accepted accounting practices leave so much room for practical application as to be practically ineffectual. The organizations in the *Madigan* amicus brief made the following observation:

As the GAO [Government Accounting Office] recently acknowledged, charities have considerable discretion in determining how to allocate expenses among the program services, management, and fundraising categories, differences that can affect comparisons across charities. Neither the IRS nor professional accounting accrediting bodies require or prohibit particular allocation methods, so long as they are reasonable and consistently applied.[79]

With respect to the roles and responsibilities of auditors, only a few states have laws that require that charities be audited, and there can be inconsistencies even when those audits are conducted.[80] According to the *Overhead Cost Project*:

Auditors, hired by the organization, wish to retain the organization's business. Thus, they, too, have an incentive to accept their client organization's "reasonable" allocations of expenses, even if they do not fully endorse a client's practices.[81]

Hager explains the opportunities for multiple interpretations of charitable expenses:

Nonprofit cost accounting practices invite organizations to place or divide expenditures among three functional categories . . . program expenses, . . . fundraising expenses, . . . and management and general expenses. . . . The job of tagging and tallying functional expenses is complicated by the fact that some items and tasks span two or all three categories. For example, an organization may have one total for the paper, toner, electricity, and repairs associated with the copying machine. However, because the copying machine is probably used for program, administrative, and fundraising purposes, the copier costs should be divided in some reasonable way among these three functions. Another example is staff time for people who wear multiple hats.[82]

The *Nonprofit Overhead Cost Project* observed how this tagging process often plays out in practical application. In the in-depth case studies that followed the examination of tax returns, the project found:

For most nonprofits, salaries are the largest single cost, yet our study revealed that *functional expense* tracking of personnel time is a low priority, due to the low perceived benefit of the practice. Only three of our nine sites had a paper or automated tracking system that could serve as the basis of functional expense classification, and only one of those used it for that purpose. However, even in that case, the development officer charged grantwriting time to the [charitable] program for which the money was raised rather than properly accounting for the expense as fundraising. This nullified the purpose of tracking functional expenses. The other sites had no plans to begin time tracking. The people we interviewed saw little value to themselves or their organization in this particular accounting activity. At most sites, one or two staff members make a retrospective judgment once per year about how everyone spent their time.[83]

If one charity's retrospective judgment on an expense is different from that of another charity, any comparative measure of efficiency is fatally undermined. As a result, the use of the measurement is unjust.

The biggest problem is that, by artificially lowering the percentage of donations reported as spent on overhead, the nonprofit sector reinforces the public belief that these low rates of overhead are actually achievable and that the lowered reported overhead expenditures represent what is adequate for organizational optimization. The *Nonprofit Overhead Cost Project* wrote in its recommendations:

> That virtually all the errors our study uncovered in functional expense reporting had the effect of understating the organizations' administrative and fundraising cost is no coincidence. Nonprofits are clearly responding to pressure from public and private sector funders to keep real and reported overhead costs low. In addition, nonprofits may be adapting to funder policies against funding adequate levels of overhead costs by classifying some such costs as program costs.[84]

Wing, Pollak, and Rooney, in their 2004 paper, "Toward a Theory of Organizational Fragility in the Nonprofit Sector," comment on the effects of that dynamic:

> Underreporting of infrastructure costs by [nonprofit organizations] suggests they need even less than they actually spend now. The errors that we found on 990s and in audited financials tended to result in nonprofits reporting less spending on administration and fundraising than was in fact the case. This could lead users of this financial information, such as major funders, charity watchdogs and others, to believe that nonprofits need less than they are getting now.[85]

In another article, they write, "Many nonprofits are sacrificing organizational infrastructure needs to tell foundations what they want to hear about overhead costs."[86] They add:

> Unfortunately, many individual donors have unrealistic ideas about nonprofit overhead. . . . The media urges people to channel their donations to low-overhead charities. Fundraising appeals by some nonprofits claim "100

percent goes to charity" or show a pie chart with an unrealistic claim that 4 percent to 5 percent goes to overhead. . . . The nonprofit sector desperately needs to deal with this problem.[87]

They conclude that "common nonprofit weaknesses stem from systemic factors, such as the effect of underreporting overhead costs and the ways in which this misleads funders about how much overhead is enough."[88]

The implication is jarring. Much of what the public believes about how much it costs to deliver charitable services is most likely inaccurate, and significantly so. The public's education comes directly from the nonprofit sector. Charities vouch for the efficiency standards by either displaying on their websites the seals of the watchdogs that set them or stating on their websites that they meet the standards. Then by using accounting methods that understate fundraising costs, they give the false impression that the watchdog standards are achievable. They are given a moral Hobson's choice—find an accounting method to validate a flawed set of standards, go without important overhead in order to meet those standards, or face the judgment of the watchdogs, the media, foundations, government funders, and the donating public, all of which will put your very survival at risk. In this illusion of choice lies the ultimate injustice of this system. There *is* no good moral choice.

Discrimination Against Less Popular Causes

In the 1988 *Riley* case, the Supreme Court wrote of the statute in question that "the Act is impermissibly insensitive to the realities faced by small or unpopular charities, which must often pay more than 35% of gross receipts collected to the fundraiser due to the difficulty of attracting donors."[89] A charity whose cause is less popular than another will necessarily have to spend more money raising money. It is less expensive to raise large dollar amounts for a cause with which the wealthy sympathize than for one with which they don't. A newly established charity will have all kinds of fundraising expenses that an established one won't. Since efficiency measures are based in large part on fundraising costs, they inherently discriminate against less popular causes, causes with a less affluent constituency, and new charities.

Consider causes that have some stigma associated with them—suicide prevention or substance abuse, for instance. That stigma makes it harder for organizations working in these arenas to attract constituents and donors. Every October, major consumer brands like General Motors and Yoplait rally around the cause of breast cancer. How many corporations do we see making major sponsorships around issues like Native American substance abuse? How many large-scale, corporate-sponsored metropolitan walk-a-thons are devoted to obscure issues?

When a cause is less popular than others, every aspect of fundraising becomes more expensive. Instead of money flowing into the charity's mailbox unsolicited and without any expense, as it can with a popular cause, organizations have to use a paid professional fundraising staff to go out and get it. They have to speak to donors more frequently and for a longer period of time. They have to spend more money on materials to educate potential donors about the cause, on research to find them, and a host of other things.

Consider a cause like breast cancer versus the cause of AIDS in Africa. Every year, about 180,000 American women are diagnosed with breast cancer, and about 40,000 women die. If every woman diagnosed with breast cancer has at least ten friends and family members in her closest circle, 1.8 million new Americans are intimately affected by the disease each year. If each of those people also has at least ten close friends and family members, that's 18 million new Americans who know someone intimately affected each year. Add up ten years and you get 180 million Americans in that category—more than half the population. Add to this the fact that one in nine American women will be diagnosed with breast cancer in her lifetime, and there is almost no one who is not intimately affected. Many of us know someone who has died of breast cancer. This means it is much less difficult to get people to donate to breast cancer research than to some other, more obscure cause. How many of us know someone with AIDS in Africa?

Unknowingly, we conducted an important controlled experiment on this in 2001. That year we produced a series of breast cancer events *and* a series of AIDS Vaccine Rides. A $100,000 radio campaign for the Breast Cancer 3-Days in Los Angeles brought in about 1,400 phone calls. The same $100,000 spent on the Vaccine Rides brought in only 261 phone calls.[90] A $1 million marketing campaign for the 3-Days would bring in close to seven thousand walkers. For the Vaccine Rides, the same amount brought in only about two thousand riders—more than three times poorer performance.[91] For every $1,000 spent on advertising for the Breast Cancer 3-Days, we recruited participants who generated around $16,000 for the cause. On the AIDS Vaccine Rides it only generated about $4,000 for the cause. The return on investment in advertising for the Breast Cancer 3-Days was four times better than the return for the Vaccine Rides.[92] This made our overhead much higher for the AIDS vaccine events than the breast cancer events. In 2001, our return to charitable services for the breast cancer events was 60.34 percent—about $5.6 million per event. Our return on the AIDS vaccine events was 21.37 percent—about $1.3 million per event.[93] The advertising was about four times more expensive for the AIDS vaccine events, and the percentage return to charity was about three times less. We used the same staff and the same approach for both events. It was not lower "efficiency" that produced these numbers. It was a lower level of public interest.

Consider also the issue of free publicity. A cause like relief for the victims of the tsunami disaster in 2004 is popularized on television for free on a massive scale, as discussed. Billions of dollars of free media equivalents are, in effect, "donated." Every television outlet on the planet is heightening awareness of the disaster and, in many cases, actually putting up the phone numbers of the charities to which we should donate. Consequently, money pours in at virtually zero cost to the charity. It is unfair, then, to compare the percentage costs of that charity with those of one that will never be mentioned by CNN or CBS, and call the former more "efficient."

A 2005 press release from Oxfam America, the international development agency, makes the point: "For emergencies like the current Asia Earthquake Fund appeal, Oxfam America spends relatively little on overhead. . . . Oxfam's general fund-raising costs are higher than its emergency fund-raising costs. . . . It costs more to raise funds for less 'imminent' needs."[94]

The fact that major emergencies stir people's emotions and inspire them to act and that they also get massive free publicity creates a double diminishing impact on fundraising costs. First, there is the free publicity; second, there is a cause to which people are already prepared to give. Oxfam's press release adds, significantly, "In years with major emergencies, the overhead is less."[95] It would be unfair to compare Oxfam's fundraising costs in a year in which a disaster occurred with those in a year in which one did not, and call it less "efficient." Similarly, it would be unjust to compare an organization that does no disaster relief with one that does it all the time, and use their percentages of overhead to compare their "efficiency." Yet this is exactly what the current system encourages.

These issues of fairness extend to charities that are less established. If I start a charity this year, I have expenses for basic infrastructure that a long-established charity does not. My overhead is necessarily going to be higher. This doesn't mean that I work less "efficiently." On this issue, Bruce R. Hopkins writes in *The Law of Fundraising*:

> An institution such as a university or hospital, for example, is likely to have an established donor base and a wide range of fundraising options and, accordingly, a relatively low fundraising cost ratio. By contrast, newer organizations undertaking costly campaigns to increase their donor base are likely to have relatively high fundraising cost percentages, such as 80 or 90 percent, or even in excess of 100 percent.[96]

On top of this, there are significant variations in the cost of the fundraising tools available to charities. Unfortunately, charities that do not have access to wealthy benefactors have to use the more expensive methods.

A Giving USA study found that a dollar spent to solicit major gifts (gifts from wealthy donors) produced $24—the highest performance on their list of methods. Direct mail, the solicitations we get in our mailboxes, produced only $10. Special events produced just $3.20.[97] The less access a charity has to major donors, the less it can employ the very efficient method of soliciting funds from them. This is why so many community-based organizations rely heavily on special events— walks and bake sales and casino nights, as well as direct mail efforts. Consequently, their percentage costs are much higher. The question "What percentage of my donation goes to the cause?" punishes them for that. But they have few other options.

Lack of access to wealthy donors means lack of access to the most "efficient" fundraising practices. The game is stacked against charities created in poor communities and those with less affluent constituencies. The rich get richer, in the very game that's supposed to counteract that dynamic. The poorer the charity, the less celebrated its cause, the more likely it is to be slapped with a label of "inefficiency" and have its problems compounded by negative publicity.

Hard Times

"Efficiency" measures hurt charities when they most need help. The percentage of donations that goes to the cause is arrived at by a simple calculation:

$$\frac{\text{Total Used for the Cause (Total Not Spent on Overhead)}}{\text{Total Donations}}$$

If a charity raised $10 million, spent $3.5 million on overhead, and used the remaining $6.5 million for charitable programs, it would say that 65 percent of donations went to the cause:

$$\frac{\$6.5 \text{ Million Used for the Cause (Total Not Spent on Overhead)}}{\$10 \text{ Million in Donations}}$$
$$= 65\% \text{ of Donations Goes to the Cause}$$

Obviously, the more a charity spends on overhead the worse its percentage will be. But the percentage can also decline if the donations go down, even if the overhead expense stays the same. Using the same example, say that a year later, because of a bad economy, the same charity took in only $7 million in donations. It didn't spend any more on overhead—that stayed constant at $3.5 million—but only $3.5 million was left to go to the cause. This is what happens to the charity's percentage:

$$\frac{\$3.5 \text{ Million Used for the Cause (Total Not Spent on Overhead)}}{\$7 \text{ Million in Donations}}$$
$$= 50\% \text{ of Donations Goes to the Cause}$$

Now its hard times have just become harder, because it has to worry about bad publicity. That will make matters even worse.

In the example, the charity hasn't done anything to try to cut its expenses to keep pace with the downturn in donations. Consider if it had cut its overhead by half a million dollars, down to $3 million, leaving $4 million for charitable programs:

$$\frac{\$4 \text{ Million Used for the Cause (Not Spent on Overhead)}}{\$7 \text{ Million in Donations}}$$
$$= 57\% \text{ of Donations Goes to the Cause}$$

Even with cuts in the overhead, the percentage to the cause fell from 65 to 57 percent. In actuality, it would be very hard for the charity to cut its overhead during the economic downturn. Economic downturns don't become apparent until after they've happened. Moreover, if the charity could see it coming, the responsible thing to do would be to spend more money on fundraising (overhead) to try to overcome it. It might also spend money on new methods to overcome it. Some of those methods might fail, raising overhead instead of lowering it.

Without knowing this, donors conclude that since the percentage going to the cause fell, the charity spent *more* on overhead. After all, it is called an "efficiency" measure. After September 11, for instance, charities across the nation saw their incomes fall. A *Chronicle of Philanthropy* report entitled "Charitable Giving Slides" stated, "American individuals, corporations, and foundations contributed $212-billion to charity last year, or 2.3 percent less than in 2000 when inflation is taken into account," adding:

> The figures released last week provided the first official nationwide, comprehensive look at the effects that the recession and the September 11 terrorist attacks have had on donations from private sources. The numbers confirmed what many fund raisers say they have witnessed in the past 12 to 18 months: Raising a dollar takes at least twice as much effort as it did when the economy was booming—and often takes experimenting with new approaches to appeals.[98]

Didn't donations to charity go up in the wake of September 11? They did for charities helping the victims of the attacks, like the Red Cross, which created the opposite effect. Because the media was promoting them heavily, for free, donations poured in, at virtually no cost to the charities, so their overhead percentages went down. But they were not any more efficient than the charities who saw their overhead go up. One group of charities were benefactors of circumstances beyond their control, and the others were victims.

The problem becomes worse for smaller charities that cannot cut their costs. What is a charity with a small office and one full-time employee to do? There *is* nothing to cut. Once again, the system discriminates on an economic basis.

The Illusion of Free Resources

My neighbor and I are each building a home. His bricks are donated, and I pay for mine. When it comes time to show what it cost to build our homes, I include the cost of the bricks and he does not. He was not a more "efficient" builder. His expense for the bricks simply went on someone else's books. Efficiency measures have conditioned us to believe that a charity that gets part of its expense donated in kind is more efficient than one that does not. This is a fallacy. Someone is paying for the effort. The fact that it is not the charity doesn't have any bearing on it efficiency.

Consider two charities that each put on a black-tie chicken dinner. Charity A raises $100,000 and Charity B raises $125,000. Charity A gets $25,000 worth of chicken donated. Charity B pays for the chicken with $25,000 in cash. When it comes time to report the results, Charity A says 100 percent of all donations went to the cause, and Charity B says that 80 percent of all donations went to the cause ($125,000 minus the $25,000 for chicken). But this is not true. Someone donated $25,000 worth of chicken to Charity A. Zero percent of that donation went to the cause. It is inaccurate for Charity A to report that 100 percent of average donations went to the cause. It is not including the donor of the chicken in the average. If it did, the percentage of *all* donations that went to the cause would be 80 percent—the same as for Charity B.

Any charity campaign that has obvious expenses but says that 100 percent of donations go to the cause is not including in the average the value of the donated goods and services that did not. Therefore, its efficiency cannot be compared with that of another charity that may have paid for those goods and services with cash. The former is essentially carrying the expense on someone else's books. This doesn't apply just to a charity claiming 100 percent efficiency, but to any organization that does not include in-kind services on its books. Again, it is not efficiency that is being measured.

Watchdog Standards Are Flawed

In addition to implying, by their very use, that efficiency measures are important, the watchdogs, and some media, make the additional leap of setting standards for the measures, as discussed. Not insignificantly, they each set a different one. The American Institute of Philanthropy uses 60 percent.[99] It gives its highest grade to those who meet a 75 percent standard.[100] The BBB Wise Giving Alliance uses 65 percent.[101] "Forbes.com" used a figure of 70 percent.[102] The *Los Angeles Times* used 75 percent.[103]

Nonprofit consultant Dan Prives, writing in the *Chronicle of Philanthropy*, notes that the BBB Wise Giving Alliance's efficiency measure is based in part on a survey it conducted asking people what percentage of their contributions they *thought* should go to the cause:

> The [Better Business Bureau's Wise Giving] alliance sponsored a consumer survey that found public support for a program-spending test. The survey asked the rather leading question, "In general, what percent of a charity's

total spending do you think should go toward charitable programs, as opposed to fund-raising or administrative costs?" Survey participants were asked to choose among five percentages, from 50 percent to more than 80 percent. "Don't know" was not offered as a choice. Forced to choose among a range of percentages, respondents, not surprisingly, tended to pick the highest figure for programs (more than 80 percent) and the lowest for fund raising (less than 10 percent).[104]

According to Art Taylor, chief executive officer of the BBB Wise Giving Alliance, "'The donating public, according to our survey, wanted to see 85 percent of the money spent on programs.'"[105]

This is like asking the public how long it thinks the average heart transplant surgery should take and then using the answers to develop a standard for surgeons. Without any expertise in the realities of what it costs to raise a dollar, what the public thinks is immaterial. There are data on this subject. If the public's opinion were accurate, it should be the exclusive basis for determining standards. Unfortunately, as we have seen, it is not accurate. This leaves us with little basis for a standard. Whether there is a data basis or not, there should be no tolerance for the use of uneducated guesses, or wants or desires, in determining a standard in a domain as important as this.

Prives wrote of the alliance's standard:

Large numbers of organizations would fail the new test. Here are some examples, based on an analysis of current Forms 990 obtained from GuideStar, an Internet database of nonprofit groups: More than two out of five art and history museums fall below the proposed 65-percent guideline for program spending. One in four of the fund-raising arms of hospitals and other health institutions, one in five Christian groups, one in six fund-raising arms of educational institutions, and one in 10 centers for the elderly also would fail to meet the [BBB Wise Giving] alliance's standard.[106]

He added:

In a recent study by the Center for Effective Philanthropy, in Boston, the chief executives of foundations expressed nearly unanimous concern about using measures of administrative costs to evaluate performance. . . . First, a single numerical standard for program expenditures is not appropriate. Second, stating that 65 percent of total expenses should be spent on programs will unfairly stigmatize many legitimate charities. And third, the Wise Giving Alliance's fixed standard would push many nonprofit groups to divert attention from management to accounting concerns. Just as with for-profit businesses, the pressure to "make the numbers" would become a distraction from the mission of the organizations.[107]

Finally, he wrote that it "will be confusing to the public and potentially damaging to charities."[108]

Tinkelman and Bhattacharya obtained an extract of Form 990 data from the NCCS Guidestar database for fiscal year 2001. After eliminating religious organizations, higher-education institutions, and what are called mutual benefit organizations, they were left with 441,416 organizations. Of these, they found:

- Seventy-five percent, or 329,522 charities, reported either zero management and general expenses or zero fundraising expenses.
- Of the remaining 111,894 organizations that reported positive fundraising or management and general expenses, 30 percent—approximately 33,000 charities—did not meet the Better Business Bureau Wise Giving Alliance 65 percent standard.
- Of the 111,894, 20 percent (19,294 organizations) of human service organizations did not meet the standard, 40 percent (15,979 organizations) of arts, culture and humanities organizations did not meet it, and 32 percent (17,197 organizations) of education organizations did not meet it.

Of the 45,348 organizations reporting revenues from special events—again, a popular tool among less affluent organizations—20 percent of these, or 9,069 organizations, were unable to meet the standard.[109]

So, even among organizations that report fundraising as well as management and general expenses, tens of thousands of charities are unable to meet the watchdog standards. Tens of thousands more would be unable to meet Charity Navigator's highest standard of 75 percent. It is impossible to say how many other charities would fail these tests if all accurately accounted for fundraising as well as management and general expenses.

It can hardly be the case that one out of every three charities in America, honest enough to report fundraising as well as management and general expenses, are undeserving of our support. This is a pass–fail system. Falling 1 percent below the standard is not a B+. It is an F, a failure to meet the standard. Any standard eliminating a third of the population is by its nature unreasonable. The equivalent would be to tolerate an elementary-school grading system that failed one-third of the students who we knew for certain had no advantage when taking their tests. When we then consider that there are hundreds of thousands of charities we can't legitimately put to the test, the standard becomes useless.

No wonder charities get the cynical rap that "none of my money ever gets to the people who need it." What kind of reputation would any profession have if it were judged by a standard it was inherently and chronically unable to meet?

The following example is sobering. In 1995, Physicians for Human Rights had revenues of approximately $1.3 million. They spent approximately $750,000, or 58 percent of revenues, on programs.[110] Today it would fail all of the watchdog standards for "efficiency." It would not be eligible for a seal of approval. The Nobel Peace Prize committee felt differently. Physicians for Human Rights won the Nobel Prize in 1997 for its work as a founding member of the International Campaign to Ban Landmines.

Overhead Is a Fiction

The very thing we are trying to measure is a phantom. We are taught to think of overhead as the enemy of all good causes. Its evil is supernatural. But there is no such thing as overhead—not as we have been taught to think about it, as something separate and distinct from the cause itself.

The definition of a cynic has been said to be a person who knows the cost of everything and the value of nothing. The issue of nonprofit overhead ratios is a cynic's paradise. When we ask, "What percentage of my donation goes to the cause?" we are asking about overhead, and we give rise to this illusion of something *other* than the cause—something that has little or no value to the cause. We create a sharp dividing line between one kind of expense and another kind of expense, *both of which are going to help the cause* but one of which we are told is not. The word "overhead" explicitly encourages us to create a distinction about expenses that has no basis in reality. Not only is what we call overhead *not* bad, it's not *not* going to the cause. In fact, it is. The distinction is a distortion.

One hundred percent of the money we donate to charity goes to charity, unless some kind of fraud is going on or some kind of ineptitude. And if there is fraud or ineptitude, asking what percentage of donations goes to the cause is hardly likely to reveal it. People who commit fraud don't report it in line-item detail. People who are inept are as inept at reporting their overhead percentages as they are at performing good works. *Absent these problems,* we should assume that every cent out of every dollar we give to charity is going in good faith to serve some kind of charitable purpose, as the charity best sees fit to serve that purpose. The boldness of this statement is not lost on me. But it is far less bold than what we have been taught.

What we have been taught is that things like the salary for the receptionist at our favorite charity has little or nothing to do with the cause and that she *herself* has little or nothing to do with the cause. She is stigmatized as "overhead." Her employment reduces the number of stars the charity gets on its efficiency scorecard and, we are told, should reduce our confidence in its efficiency. But tell the scientist doing cancer research that he has to start running to the reception desk to pick up the phone fifty times a day and we will soon stop saying the receptionist has nothing to do with the cause. At least the scientist will.

The effect of what we have been taught is troubling. The Chronicle of Philanthropy reported in 2008 that "$4 out of every $5 that foundations give are earmarked for a charity's programs, which means they cannot be used to pay for basic operating costs like utilities, rent, supplies, and clerical help."[111] The Ellison Research study released in 2008 showed that 62 percent of Americans "believe the typical non-profit spends more than what is reasonable on overhead expenses."[112] Ellison's president, Ron Sellers, noted that "'We've spoken to tens of thousands of donors over the years, and the one thing that is consistent is that most people really don't know much about how non-profits operate . . . But even when people are misinformed, their perceptions still influence how they make giving decisions.'"[113] These misperceptions are dangerous. Sellers noted that, even when people are lacking information on a specific charity, "they'll tend to judge it by how they see charities in general. The people who believe non-profits are spending too much on overhead will tend to make that assumption about any non-profit they come across. It's almost as if organizations are automatically under suspicion until they prove themselves innocent."[114]

But this whole notion of overhead—the idea that some part of our donation goes to the cause and another doesn't—falls apart under the most rudimentary consideration. All we have to do is consider the things that overhead expenses buy. For instance, most charities have a development director who oversees all of its fundraising. This person's salary is typically allocated to overhead, or should be, under current rules. But all day long that person talks to potential donors about the cause, relays statistics about the cause, and tries to motivate people and their friends to give to the cause. This work is essential to the advancement of the cause. If it were not done, no money would get raised, no research would get done, no soup would get served. It is inextricably linked with the cause. In fact, I would argue that it *is* the cause as much as the soup is. If the soup doesn't exist without it, how can it be *other?*

If we are speaking about a new cause that has little name recognition and the charity has 100 percent "overhead" because it is trying to educate people about the cause, those dollars are being spent on the only *conceivable* thing that *could* help the cause at this stage in its development. Creating awareness is the most important work that one could *possibly* do for that cause, right now, at this formative point in its evolution. It becomes a choice between doing that or doing nothing. *To say that it is a bad expense is like saying that the launch pad is a bad expense, because it is really the rocket in which we are interested.* It becomes nonsensical.

The Supreme Court saw the light in the *Riley* case. The opinion refers to the use of a professional fundraiser, but the point is dead on:

> The State presumes that the charity derives no benefit from funds collected but not turned over to it. Yet this is not necessarily so. For example . . . where the solicitation is combined with the advocacy and dissemination of information, the charity reaps a substantial benefit from the act of solicitation itself. . . . Thus, a significant portion of the fundraiser's "fee" may well go toward achieving the charity's objectives even though it is not remitted to the charity in cash.[115]

Most charities have an executive director. Much of that person's salary is called overhead. But all day, that person is out talking to potential donors, soliciting foundations, and educating them about the charity and the cause. She is spreading information. That has tremendous value to the cause, but she is told not to record any of that value on the "cause" side of the charity's books. Any rational stakeholders in the cause would be neutral on the question of whether their donations should go to her salary or to the cause because they would not draw a distinction between the two.

Charities themselves feel the same way. Pollak, Rooney, and Hager wrote:

> From the perspective of nonprofit executives, management and general expenses are real costs, necessary to the lifeblood of their organizations. Nonetheless, institutional funders, individual donors, and the media often act as if they believe these expenses are unworthy of public support.[116]

Is there anything a charity does that is not related to the cause? The people who work for Save the Children are all trying to save children, in one way or another. They are either saving the children or raising money to save the children or managing the staff that will save the children or printing the brochures that will save the children. In the end, everything they do is an effort to save children. They are certainly not trying to hurt the children. They are certainly not ignoring the children.

It is simply not intuitive to draw this distinction, anymore than I would look at some of my household expenses as going to the "cause" of my family and some of them as going to "overhead." They're all going to my family, whether they are something as visible as the shoes on my children's feet or something more hidden from view, like my home insurance payment. If there were a fire in the house, God forbid, I would certainly look at the investment in insurance as a direct benefit to my family.

Professionals in charity do not construct their organizations along these lines either, except when they are forced to do so at reporting time. The *Nonprofit Overhead Cost Project* wrote that the study "raises questions about the wisdom of distinguishing between program and overhead costs. No nonprofit studied made this distinction in managing the organization."[117]

Nevertheless, the nonprofit sector once again validates a concept that acts against its own interests. The following example is remarkable. In 2007, the *Stanford Social Innovation Review* reported on a new approach to overhead being applied by the United Way of Central New Mexico. The program is called Corporate Cornerstones. The report says that the charity

> entices area businesses to foot the bill for its annual administrative expenses. It can then tell individual donors that every penny of their donations goes directly to their chosen causes. The result is that contributions from both corporations and individuals have soared. . . . Promising individual donors that their entire pledge will go toward assisting needy people proved to be an attractive selling point.[118]

The idea for the project originated in 1997 with a fact-finding project that uncovered two reasons donors might not give to charity, one of which was that "nonprofits might use part of the gift to cover administrative costs."[119]

Not only does this kind of approach artificially reinforce in the public's mind the notion that charities can operate with o percent

spending on administration or "overhead," it gives the charity a potentially unfair advantage. It is not the case that 100 percent of *all* donations are going to the cause (and, to be clear, the charity never said it
was). It is only true that 100 percent of the *individual's* donations are
going to the cause. But if donors miss that small but crucial point, they
will believe the organization is fundamentally more "efficient" than another charity with a lower percentage that does not have its administrative expenses covered by corporate donations. But of course it is not.

Why, if a charity can make the case to businesses, apparently with
great success, that overhead is important, does it not attempt to do the
same with the public? One of the corporate underwriters explained,
"it's easier for the business community to understand the importance
of administrative costs than it is for average givers, who just want to
know that their dollar is going into helping their community."[120] So in
the interest of short-term benefit, the public is told what it wants to
hear, what it has always wanted to hear, what it has always been told,
and the critical long-term objective of getting the public to understand
reality is sidestepped.

Another striking example of internal reinforcement involves the
Combined Federal Campaign created in 1961 by President Kennedy. It
is the federal government's annual charity appeal to federal employees—
"the world's largest and most successful annual workplace charity campaign."[121] In 2005, it donated $268 million to charities.[122] In 2006, the
U.S. Office of Personnel Management, to its credit, decided "to drop
its requirement that charities must spend no more than 25 percent of
their total revenue on administration and fundraising expenses."[123] Remarkably, the Community Health Charities of America campaigned
against the change. Its president said that the requirement was a "distinguishing feature" of the campaign and "'gives federal donors confidence that their gifts will be used for services, not overhead,'" adding
that the proposed removal "'will also bring into the program thousands
of additional charities that are currently ineligible because they do not
meet basic requirements that ensure donations go to services.'"[124]

The result of this demonization is that charities spend fewer critical
dollars on building organizational strength. We penalize charities for
investing in organizational infrastructure because it is labeled "overhead." We tell them that it is better to do without. If a charity wants to
hire a better, more seasoned executive director, it is penalized for spending more on overhead. If it wants to invest in new donor-tracking software, it is penalized for an increase in overhead. In their 2004 working

paper, Wing, Pollak, and Rooney asked, "Why do funders who want grantee organizations to be successful fail to fund their administrative or infrastructure costs at levels that would permit them to be effective?"[125]
The *Nonprofit Overhead Cost Project* observed:

> Nonprofits in the arts, community development, and human services describe how their development efforts were hindered by inappropriate donor database software. One site described the unproductive downtime and frequent maintenance associated with "free" but mismatched, outdated computers. In agencies where key positions such as development director either did not exist or were filled with inexperienced staff, the CEO had to fill that role, thereby neglecting parts of the leadership role. Sites without experienced finance staff had only rudimentary financial reporting and had limited ability to involve program mangers in financial management, perform more sophisticated analysis or identify financial issues for board and senior management. Backup for key roles was nonexistent, leaving basic functions like payroll, benefits, and network support dependent on a single person in even the largest nonprofits with which we spoke.[126]

The report concluded:

> Based on our research, [nonprofit organizations] are clearly struggling with inadequate administrative and fundraising infrastructure and it is having an impact on their organizational effectiveness. [Nonprofit organizations] clearly implicate the fundraising preferences of their major funders as part of the causal mix. . . . If our model is close to correct, then [the] nonprofit sector is facing a very troubling situation, in which the level of infrastructure spending preferred by major funders is a key driver of [nonprofit] effectiveness, but the particular level preferred is not set with reference to a level of desired effectiveness, but through a fundraising dynamic where [nonprofits] in effect compete on price for funding by having low infrastructure costs, and exacerbate the problem by reporting even less than the minimal amounts they actually spend.[127]

Thus, any notion that nonprofit overhead expenditures are not going to the cause is quickly dismissed by the fact that organizational effectiveness at impacting the cause diminishes when overhead spending is reduced. Moreover, if there is no correlation between overhead and impact, why allow charities to spend money on overhead at all? Why a 35 percent threshold? Clearly even the watchdogs recognize the correlation. Where then are the data indicating that the correlation ends at 35 percent?

If there is any doubt about this issue, here is another sobering example:

Another case concerned a hotline that could not afford to upgrade its phone system—an expense that was considered part of overhead—because of its restricted funding. Without this upgrade, a suicidal caller could get a busy signal, even though some hotline extensions were not busy. It is hard to imagine a better example of sacrificing the mission on the altar of low overhead. As these cases suggest, foundations would be wiser to focus less on what is called "program" and what is called "overhead" and more on whether the nonprofit organizations have what they need for mission effectiveness.[128]

Summary

The concept of overhead and the efficiency measures used to monitor it are the guardians of nonprofit ideology and the enforcers of the economic apartheid the ideology creates. There is no equivalent in business. We do not ask about General Motor's administrative overhead. We do not have efficiency measures for Heineken. We measure business by its bottom line. The bottom line for charity is effectiveness. It is more difficult to measure than corporate profits. It does not lend itself easily to numeric translation, and certainly not to a single metric. But this is no reason to use a measure that does.

The fact that efficiency measures ignore the all-important question of program effectiveness is but the beginning of the problem. They do not take into account the volume of good being done. They do not take into account the future value of the dollars being raised. They do not take into account the economic value of the end result. They do not take into account the incremental effect of a donation. They do not consider extreme variations in the way different charities account for program expenses. They do not take into account the relative popularity of the cause. They do not factor in hard times. They favor charities that do not account for in-kind contributions. On top of all this, the standards by which we have been taught to separate the wheat from the chaff are fundamentally flawed. All of this converges to create extreme irrationality and injustice.

In this chapter, I have examined each factor in isolation. But they do not occur in isolation. More often than not, three or four factors are compounded to multiply the injustice that occurs with only one. For instance, on one hand, we have a charity that properly allocates all its expenses, has a harder time raising money than others do because it supports a less popular cause, and has superior programs. On the other, we have a charity that does not properly allocate its expenses, raises money cheaply because it has a popular cause, and has incredibly shoddy programs. For each of these, the efficiency measures penalize the better charity and reward the lesser one. Add in four or five more factors, and the experience is hallucinatory.

Then there are the effects of the enforcement of nonprofit ideology. Efficiency measures prevent charities from investing adequately in infrastructure, discourage them from hiring the talent they need, penalize them for courage and reward them for timidity, prevent them from pursuing long-term vision, discourage them from investing in advertising to build demand, and, if given the chance, penalize them for paying a return on investment capital. In all these ways, they methodically institutionalize the very suffering we want to eradicate.

Moreover, we have thrust upon our charities the weight of society's most challenging problems. They are asked to solve them in a complex world of millions of living colors. To have their work reduced to black and white, to good and bad, by the use of a single simplistic measure, simply because it's cheap and because it's the only measure we have, is at best irresponsible. To then ask charities to sacrifice their founding missions on its altar is morally backward.

It is time to stop using this measure altogether and to campaign aggressively toward that end. Critics will call for a moderated approach. This is how they keep the status quo in place—by making the problem the subject of ongoing discussion and debate, thereby reinforcing their position as the answer. But how does one moderate a disaster? By making it moderately less disastrous?

I am aware of the unorthodox nature of what I am arguing. The concept of overhead is the underpinning of nonprofit ideology. This is precisely why we must get rid of it. The ideology is rotten. Yet it strikes me that the admonition to do away with this mere tactical feature of the ideological edifice will be of more radical import than the call to eradicate the ideology itself. Imagine a world without efficiency measures. It sends a shiver up the spine. This is because it is the place where abstraction intersects reality. Eradicating the ideology is an abstraction. Firing the guard that stands watch over it is real. To stop asking a question we have asked all our lives, which we have used for moral comfort, which we have been taught by our forebears, is to stand naked in front of the terrifying possibility of a new future constructed by our own design. It is the difference between talking about an adventure and buying the plane ticket.[129]

We know intuitively that this question is the linchpin in the belief system. We understand that once it goes away, the ideology will begin to go with it. So the issue puts our courage to the test. Do we want things to change, or do we want them to stay the same? Do we want the status quo, masquerading behind meaningless modifications, or do we want the world of our dreams? Are we fighting on the side of our causes and the needy for whom they are intended, or are we fighting on the side of the system?

New Questions and a Very Large Assessment Apparatus

What is the solution to all of this? To begin with, we must withdraw our support, as Rand said, for the efficiency measure. This should happen today. Never has more meaning been assigned to something more meaningless.

We must internalize this simple truth: when we are told what percentage of donations a charity spends on programs, we have a useless piece of information. To continue using it is like using a broken thermometer to take your child's temperature. It is dangerous. Better to admit you don't know your child's temperature than to believe it is five degrees lower than it actually is. Bad information leads to bad outcomes.

With what measure will we replace this question on which we rely so heavily? The answer is that no single measure will suffice. We need multiple measures and an apparatus of very large scale to collect, read, and communicate them.

New Questions

The single greatest flaw of the "efficiency" measure may well be that it only asks one question. A study by the Henry Bloch School of Business and Public Administration at the University of Missouri concluded: "Nonprofit organizational effectiveness is multi-dimensional. Nonprofit organization effectiveness cannot be assessed with a single indicator."[130] We have seen in the preceding sections that many more questions deserve to be asked. We must refuse to be content to ask only one or to have only one asked about us. We must demand that all get a hearing. These issues extend far beyond fundraising efficiency:

   1. How effective are the charity's programs and how is efficacy being measured?

2. What is the quality of the organization's program staff?
3. How do the organization's clients rate its efforts?
4. What is the scale of the achievement, and are comparisons being made with achievements of equal scale?
5. What is the incremental effect of a donation in the present moment?
6. How new is the charity?
7. How well known is the cause to the public, and does the charity face greater difficulty than its peers in raising funds?
8. How have economic conditions affected the charity?
9. Are comparisons being made between charities that account for program expenses in an identical manner?
10. Are intangible benefits being accounted for?
11. Is the future value being accounted for?
12. Is the value of the outcome being accounted for?
13. Is the organization attempting any bold initiatives that might affect the dollars going to programs?
14. What is the organization's long-term vision and what is it doing to achieve it?
15. How is long-term investment affecting the short-term financial picture?
16. Does the organization have adequate infrastructure?

We don't need to wait to begin asking these questions. We can begin asking them now. At the very least, in the absence of answers, we can refuse to be persuaded by "efficiency" numbers.

A Very Large National Assessment Apparatus

We must reject the notion that the present measuring apparatus is the best we can do. We must create a dramatic new solution to provide us with the answers to these questions in a systematic way. Simple measures provide simple distinctions. In the interest of simplicity, the "efficiency" measure allows for two possibilities—good or bad. Its methodology for making that distinction is flawed. Our assessments of charity need to make room for far more subtlety and must be far more accurate.

There has been a minor debate about the problems with efficiency measures inside the nonprofit sector. It has never risen to more than a whisper in the public consciousness because no one has found a suitable substitute measure. We have failed to find the measure we are looking for until now because of *what* the sector has been looking for. It has been looking to re-place one simplistic measure with another, searching for a single indicator that can be produced inexpensively, easily, and at a distance. We will get what we pay for. Only when we understand that what we need is a rich array of information, produced by human beings as well as calculators, and that it will be neither simple nor inexpensive to obtain, will we be looking in the right direction. We need better measures, we need to mea-sure more important things, we need rich narrative as well as metrics, and we need several *billion* dollars in resources with which to do it. We must transform our whole conception of what it means to evaluate charity.

Such a conception must look beyond the language of numbers. It must use words. Beyond numbers, there is vision, intention, commitment, and challenge. There are the people who benefit from a charity's programs, the people who work for the charity, the community in which the charity op-erates, and the donors and board members that serve it. Their assessment deserves a voice as well. There are the charity's hopes and dreams and its dedication to them. These are not captured by numbers.

This conception must also move beyond suspicion. It must abandon the image of a "watchdog" and embrace the idea of watching good. It must be motivated by humility, respect, and a spirit of cooperation and mutual education. Madeline Lee, former president of the New York Foundation, wrote:

> Humility does not come naturally to me, but my work as a foundation execu-tive has given me such humility as I have. I have learned to keep my thoughts to myself in order to hear the thoughts of the people who work much harder than I ever have, who risk much more than I have ever risked, who face lives far harder than mine, who, if you listen, will share their lives and their dreams in the most open and courageous way.[131]

A state-of-the-art assessment apparatus has to be built on a mission statement with these kinds of values.

With hundreds of thousands of charities, how can we make thorough assessments like this and keep those assessments up to date and readily available to the public? We deserve to have and will have to build something magnificent. We will have to build an army of excep-tional people with exceptional technology and leadership—an organiza-tion situated across the nation, where our charities actually operate. It will require that professionals visit our charities each year, in teams of specialists, to perform a many-faceted audit. *We will have to make the pro-cess a human one—face to face and person to person.*

The following is just a rough sketch, but it gives a sense of how feasible it would be to construct a solution. The idea is to build a powerful national surveying apparatus funded at the level of approximately half of one percent of charitable donations annually to provide in-depth program, organizational, and financial information in numeric and narrative formats, updated annually, for every active charity in America. By no means do I think this is the only way to address the need. This is one idea. I do believe we need something on this scale. Once we come face to face with the hard reality that the system we have is woefully inadequate to the task, a real conversation can begin that will give rise to all kinds of creative and intelligent approaches. But they cannot be simple and they cannot be small.

The approach I am suggesting here would involve teams of data-gathering analysts. They would conduct face-to-face meetings, tours of facilities, surveys of clients, surveys of donors, surveys of financial information, analyses of long-term plans, infrastructure planning, and conversations about dreams and needs. They would compile their information according to consistent formats that could be easily sorted and perused online with extremely user friendly interfaces. A user could flip online through a variety of client testimonials, candid staff comments, comments from other donors, and financial metrics and information ranging over a period of years, not months.

The approach would include measures that would help us understand the challenges and successes related to the effectiveness of a charity's programs. Tinkelman suggests a brand new way of looking at this:

> To judge effectiveness, we need to consider how much high quality output is produced, and to judge efficiency, we really want to examine the number of units of high quality charitable outputs per dollar donated to the cause. For example, a literacy program's effectiveness depends on the number of new readers it produces, and its efficiency should be judged in terms of new readers per dollar contributed. There are two consequences to this goal. The first is that we have to confine our comparisons to charities with similar outputs. We can't compare an overseas hunger relief organization to a literacy program. The second is we need to disaggregate the goal . . . to more closely examine performance. . . . So, if we are comparing two literacy programs, we might consider: 1) how many people enroll for lessons, . . . 2) how many actually learn to read . . . of the ones who enroll, 3) how many people the organization can enroll per dollar of spending on teachers, and 4) how many dollars the organization can spend on teachers out of each dollar raised.[132]

Even with such measures, we would have to be careful to understand program effectiveness and efficiency within a larger definition of what constitutes the cause. This would include awareness, the building of a base of support, and other intangibles. Causes would have to be defined broadly.

How would we fund such an apparatus? One-half of 1 percent of the $295 billion donated to charities each year (as of 2006) is $1.475 billion.[133] Assuming a management and general rate of 30 percent off of that total, $1.03 billion would be left for assessment. This figure suits itself to meaningful investigations. If the examining agency's analysts were paid $65,000 annualized ($1,250 weekly, or $31.25 hourly), and assuming 700,000 active charities in the nation, the funds would provide enough resources for about forty-seven hours, or about six days, of investigation and summary for each charity per year. Assessment of larger charities might take a week or two more, that of smaller charities a few days less.

As for the gathering of these funds, it could be achieved by the market. A national for-profit or nonprofit organization could be established to contract with charities to provide the service. The more the public demanded the information, the greater the incentive for charities to participate. The existing watchdogs could play an important role in the organization's development and could even collaborate to create it. Ultimately, the cost would be paid for by increases in donations that would come from fewer public misperceptions and negative opinions and greater public confidence. It would also be paid for by new ideas that would spring from charities' better understanding of themselves. A new approach would have the additional advantage of replacing disparate information currently gathered by attorneys general throughout the country and by the tens of thousands of foundations that have to do their own assessments before making large gifts to charity. It could be funded in part by reduced costs to charities that otherwise have to spend significant resources on redundant reporting to multiple entities. The government could also be petitioned to provide funding.

This is consistent with the funding of for-profit sector business evaluation. The Public Company Accounting Oversight Board, created by Sarbanes-Oxley, is supported by fees paid by public companies. Tinkelman writes:

> The issue underlying public concern over charitable organization's spending
> is asymmetrical information between potential donors and the charities. In
> other words, donors are worried because they can't be sure they know what

charities do with their donations. . . . Buyers and sellers must have common ground for a market to work, and it's in both parties' interest to make sure buyers can trust sellers. In the public sector, we see a number of institutions that are funded to reduce information asymmetry. The government supports the funding of the Securities and Exchange Commission. Companies that want their bonds rated by Moody's or Standard & Poor's must pay a fee. A sophisticated rating agency for charities would fill exactly the same economic role, of reducing reasons for donors to distrust charities. The increase in trust should increase donations, more than paying for the costs of the rating agency.[134]

Cynics will claim that this apparatus is far too big and too expensive. If $1.5 billion is more than we can gather to measure the way we make progress, then all hope is lost. If this proposal is beyond the limit of our potential, we might as well forget about ending world hunger and be honest about it. There is no real use in measuring anything, for we would be resigned to being forever distant from the financial resources we would need to actually eradicate the underlying problems. But it is *not* the limit of our potential. Far from it. We shouldn't be looking to cynics to figure out how to build a new world or even to measure it. What is their alternative? To continue to fund assessment with chicken feed and never mind the inaccuracy and injustice? "Our doubts about the feasibility of such a project should be tempered by an understanding of its necessity."[135]

The three major watchdog agencies have somewhere in the area of thirty combined staff. Their combined annual operating expenses are around $2.97 million—equal to what the head of Dell Computer makes every two weeks.[136] This is what we spend to inform the public about the impact of $295 billion in annual giving. This figure of $2.97 million is 0.001 percent of $295 billion, or statistically *zero*. According to the *Chronicle of Philanthropy*, in a discussion document prepared in 2004 by aides to the Senate Finance Committee, a proposal was made to have the federal government allocate a whopping $10 million to help the IRS oversee a nationwide charitable accreditation program[137]—about $14 for each of the active and $10 for each of the registered charities in America. *For a society and a sector that up until now have spent maybe a few million dollars a year on watchdog organizations, a billion and a half dollars might well sound insane. In reality, it is lunacy for us to give away $295 billion a year without spending one-half of 1 percent of that to make sure all of the giving is intelligent.*

An apparatus even remotely similar to what I am proposing would create a transformation in information. Instead of a magic number about finances, we would have numbers about programs, and a thorough and objective narrative. We would also have a comprehensive assessment of the entire field, not just of a few thousand charities. Furthermore, there would be an almost instant transformation in public confidence and understanding. Imagine having meaningful data at our fingertips that would allow us to compare charitable programs. Imagine knowing what impact our dollars are having.

This does not need to take forever to create. If we were able to put a Starbucks on every corner of America within ten years, surely we can accomplish this project in the same amount of time. This is a small step of affirmation to ourselves and all those in need that we are more committed to possibility than to resignation, to hope over despair, to progress over inertia, to life over death. This is a $1.5 billion project we can use to see, as a first step, if we are really up to the larger task that lies ahead.

CHAPTER 4

Courage

When a resolute young fellow steps up to the great bully, the world, and takes him boldly by the beard, he is often surprised to find it comes off in his hand, and that it was only tied on to scare away the timid adventurers.
— RALPH WALDO EMERSON

Buckminster Fuller said that "a problem well stated is a problem well on its way to being solved." My objective here has been twofold: first, to identify the right problem and, second, to state it clearly. I have tried to undertake this within the largest possible context—not from inside the existing framework, but outside of it; not to see how we can score better on the grading system imposed upon us, or even to find a better grading system, but to see how we might transform the whole of the society in which we live. Problems are vulnerable to thought. Once a problem can be seen for what it really is, the solution is not far behind. The pace of our progress is limited only by the pace of our thinking and by the courage we supply to support it.

The problem began a long time ago. The early Puritan settlers in America were naturally self-interested. They came to New England to create God's new Israel and to separate themselves from a church they saw as too closely allied with Rome. They also came to pursue new economic opportunities. They believed that wealth was a sign of divine approval. They were the early builders of American capitalism. They were also Calvinists and believed in Calvin's view of human depravity. This made their natural self-interest psychologically problematic. They therefore compartmentalized it. Self-interest could only be pursued in the interest of others or in the interest of set-asides for future charity or the pretense of the same. Therefore, charity became another world— an economic sanctuary of morality and an ameliorative influence on self-interest. In this way charity and self-deprivation became synonymous. Self-depriving charity gave them psychological permission to pursue their natural self-interest elsewhere. Charity became a mechanism for regulating self-interest, profit making, and, therefore, capitalism. Capitalism, profit making, and self-interest were necessarily banished from the sanctuary itself.

This is problematic. Capitalism produces economic wealth. It produces a wealth of labor, leadership, capital, demand, productivity, ideas, and progress and a wealth of surplus that has a multiplier effect on all of these. Nonprofit ideology, on the other hand, produces economic poverty. It produces a poverty of leadership, capital, demand, and ideas and leaves no surplus at the end of the day, thereby forcing the sector to live from paycheck to paycheck. It discourages compensation based on value, paid advertising, experimentation, long-term investment, and the payment of a financial return on capital investment. Capitalism, it is alleged, produces inequity in society. The nonprofit sector, along with government, is assigned the task of restoring balance to the situation. Yet it is asked to create this balance without the tools of capitalism. Thus, the imbalance widens. This we call charity.

Because it would be impossible to police every clandestine violation of nonprofit ideology in the sector, a simple detection mechanism has been established to ensure compliance with it. This is called the "efficiency" measure. It polices wages, the use of paid advertising, experimentation, the use of donor funds for anything other than short-term relief or set-asides for a rainy day, and a prohibition on financial return on investment. This we call the *measure* of charity.

Such a system will never produce the change we seek. It wasn't designed to. It was designed to compensate for depravity. It never had a larger objective in mind. The sobering reality is this: if *we* do not have a larger objective in mind, there is no need to take issue with the existing ideology in the first place. We might just as well abide by it. It serves us perfectly well for keeping things the same. But if we *do* have a larger objective in mind, we must summon the courage to state it. We must fashion the ideology around that objective, and not the other way around.

A Cold World?

This notion of marrying charity and capitalism will be controversial. I fear it will be controversial more because it doesn't *feel* right than because it is not sound or will not work. I have seen it work. Even so, these ideas often don't *feel* right even to me. Here I have written a book on self-interested charity, and yet I find a few lines about materialism and selflessness from Thomas Merton unsettling. A Trappist monk himself, he talks about why people become Trappists:

> What is the use of living for things that you cannot hold on to, values that crumble in your hand as soon as you possess them, pleasures that turn sour before you have begun to taste them . . .? Men have not become Trappists merely out of a hope for peace in the next world: something has told them . . . that heaven can be theirs now . . . if they give their lives to the one activity which is the beatitude of heaven. That activity is love: the clean, unselfish love that does not live on what it gets but on what it gives; a love that increases by pouring itself out for others, that grows by self-sacrifice and becomes mighty by throwing itself away.[1]

By contrast, I seem to have painted a picture of a cold, materialistic world, where no one helps the poor unless there is something in it for himself. Isn't Thomas Merton's world a far more beautiful one? Shouldn't we try to get everyone to be selfless?

First, Thomas Merton's is not a selfless world. It is quite the opposite. The monks give themselves to others because of the joy they receive in return. Indeed, in the same book Merton writes, "A monk is a man who has given up everything in order to possess everything. He . . . has abandoned desire in order to achieve the highest fulfillment of all desire."[2] If giving to others brought the monks nothing in return, it wouldn't be long before they were out looking for something that did. We confuse everyone and everything by use of this word "selfless" to describe something that is actually self-fulfilling. The monks may be smarter or more enlightened than the rest of us, but they aren't more selfless. They are as interested in themselves as the next guy. They've just figured out that doing for others delivers a better rate of return to self than a Maserati. They have found a way to do for others and self at the same time. To go around asking the rest of us to be selfless is to ask us to live up to an impossible standard, which even the monks themselves don't attempt to meet.

Second, Merton paints a picture of a highly spiritually evolved world. We don't live in that kind of world, at least not yet. We will not get to it by lamenting its absence or sitting around wishing for it. If we want a world where people are at their maximum potential for giving to others, we had better start promoting the idea on a massive scale. People aren't going to get interested in it by osmosis. We had better start proactively competing with the world that pummels them with messages about golf clubs and Botox. Thomas Merton may have lived in a cloister and wore a robe, but in his heart he was an advertising man. He had a message, and if his message never got to me I would never have been moved by it. I bought his book from a for-profit bookseller. It was printed on paper made at a for-profit mill. It was delivered on a truck made in a for-profit factory financed by a stock market that allowed it to raise capital. *Thomas Merton's message about the joys of helping others were delivered to me by capitalism.*

No matter how you slice it, the only way you get to a world that has more love and less materialism is through the system that sells the world on materialism. What is the other option? Just ask people to be more loving? By what means? You are immediately faced with the fact that to mount a campaign to convert 6 billion people to love—which is essentially the *role* of charity—takes a lot of money. The most efficient system for asking 6 billion people to be more loving and more giving is capitalism. Raise the capital to promote the idea by offering a return on investment, hire the best people to manage the effort, and run the advertising to spread the word. You beat capitalism at its own game. And it is entirely willing to allow you to do it. Capitalism didn't stop the truck that delivered Merton's book. It created it. It is indifferent about its end products. It is just as happy to produce charity as it is to produce video games. All you have to do is ask.

One thing is certain: we're not going to finance a global love campaign by selling monk-made cheese from a nonprofit monastery via mail-order catalogues. Thomas Merton's abbey at Gethsemani sells cheese, and in the 160 years since it was founded it has grown from forty-four monks to precisely sixty-five.[3]

In a world where we free the nonprofit sector to use the tools of capitalism, we won't get more materialism, we'll get more giving. We won't get a colder world. We'll get a warmer world. And a smarter world to boot.

All of this should serve as a warning to us about relying too much on what we feel. What we feel often comes from what we are taught. Garbage in, garbage out. If I am told an innocent man is guilty, I will despise him. I might even execute him. Centuries of conditioning have made us feel that the right thing is actually the wrong thing. We can't trust our feelings to help us do the right thing. For that we must apply our rational minds. We must seek the truth. If we do, in the end we will have more to feel good about than we ever thought possible. Knowing that, we can feel good about it right now. What is there to feel good about in a world sentenced to staying the same?

Strategic Plan

What is the strategic plan for changing things? What is the solution? My purpose here has been to try and state as clearly as I can that we have a problem—a problem we are not talking about and not dealing with. That problem is the denial to charity of cetain rights that are enjoyed without restraint by the rest of the economic world. My purpose has also been to suggest that the answer to this problem is simply to stop denying charity these rights. The solutions already exist in the tools of the free market. They are available to us if we refrain from prohibiting their use. So it is not a matter so much of what we must *do* as what we must *stop doing*. Toward that end, we confront a simple but profound philosophical challenge, not a complex organizational problem. We are not developing a national health insurance plan. This is about changing our thinking and behavior. Each of us has the power to do that right now. We need not wait for a government program. Even the assessment apparatus I have suggested is not a prerequisite for us to stop relying on efficiency measures. We can stop relying on those right now too, simply of our own volition.

Some readers might expect that in this final chapter I would suggest some dramatic statutory re-engineering—the end of the entire not-for-profit tax-exempt classification or something on that scale. But that is to put the cart before the horse. Even sweeping and fundamental statutory revisions are of secondary importance to changing the way we think about charity. Legislative changes would serve no purpose if we were still convinced of the validity of these old ideas. We must address ourselves to the nonprofit ethos before we start looking at the nonprofit tax code. We can achieve transcendent progress even in the absence of structural changes if we stop equating charity with self-deprivation and stop looking down our noses at self-interest, risk-reward incentives, and the other drivers of capitalism.

No law has to change for us to give charity permission to compensate people based on the value they can produce, or to give it the freedom to spend donor dollars on advertising to build demand, on long-term problem-solving, or on experiments with new revenue models. No law has to change for us to stop evaluating charity by efficiency measures, or to develop new methods of measurement. As I said earlier, we would probably have to make statutory changes in order to allow for a stock market for charity, and that is perhaps the largest opportunity of all. Those changes are easy enough to explore. But they too are of secondary importance to the *idea* of a stock market for charity itself—of the rejection of the notion that it is some violation of morality to pay people a financial return for investing in charity even if it produces massive additional capital.

Moreover, the energy required to enact statutory changes could never be mustered even if they were advisable without a rejection on a mass level of the old paradigm. The Civil Rights Act came as a result of and after the civil rights movement, not the other way around. We need to develop an organized opposition to these old ideas, and then whatever statutory changes are required will become apparent and can become enacted. In fact, systemic changes in our thinking must be achieved on a large scale before we will even be able to see fully the possibilities ahead of us or any of the statutory accommodations we would need to make room for them. We have to clear away the underbrush of this obsolete thinking first. Then we will know and can work toward whatever needs to be done on a structural level. But again, structural changes will avail us of nothing in the absence of philosophical changes.

What we need now more than anything is courage. Obsolete ideas are vulnerable to courage. Nevertheless, it is an understandable consistency of human nature that when asked to gather courage we instead start assembling PowerPoint presentations and working on messaging. But these are a distraction. We must stop giving sanction to ideas that make no sense. We need no strategic plan for that. We must disrupt the inertia that keeps them in place. We must stop trading the dreams we have for our communities for the approval we want from our regulators. This takes courage. New ideas are not won easily. One must suffer the moral judgment of the establishment. One must endure the pain of being misunderstood. But this, it seems to me, is the ultimate expression of charity. There is no charity in silent acquiescence to a charity that doesn't work. It is easy to be a crusader for feeding the hungry. One has the whole world on one's side. But to point out that *the way* we seek to feed them is what *keeps* them hungry—to challenge the sacred edifice of "selfless" charity itself and the unmerited sanctimony that goes with it—this is real heroism. In the absence of that, no strategic plan will suffice.

There is no scarcity of opportunity. Whether it is to stop placing watchdog seals of approval on our websites if we don't believe in the validity of their measures or to hire a new director who can quadruple our results, even if he wants quadruple the salary ever paid to anyone in the position, the need for bravery is everywhere.

Reclaiming Our Dreams

Our courage must be addressed to the dreams we have abandoned and the dreams we have been afraid to dream, either because they are too breathtaking or because it has been too difficult to imagine how they could possibly be realized inside our existing confinement. The following story appeared in the *Los Angeles Times* on January 31, 2004:

> San Diego—Long before her death, Joan Kroc had begun building her legacy. In the mid 1990s, her representatives approached the Salvation Army with an idea for erecting a community center in a rundown neighborhood here. Officials from the group penciled out several rough budgets. Kroc, who died in October at age 75, rejected them all. "Think big," she exhorted, "bigger than you've ever thought before." Two weeks ago, the world discovered just how big Kroc had been thinking. Her estate announced a bequest of more than $1.5 billion to the Salvation Army—one of the largest charitable gifts in the nation's history—to build 25 to 30 community centers across the United States in hopes of transforming blighted neighborhoods.[4]

No wonder. Joan Kroc's dreams were nurtured and encouraged by a free-market capitalist tradition. Her true self was acknowledged instead of annihilated. Her aspirations were supported instead of denied. She came from another world. It is to that same world that we must give ourselves permission to travel, for the sake of our own souls and all those we hope to serve.

To allow all our time, energy, and enthusiasm to be consumed by issues of overhead is to forfeit our very existence. To spend our days appeasing every donor with assurances that we are properly self-sacrificing is to deny our dreams and all they could bring to the world. To allow our passion to be beaten down by limitation and its entourage of minutiae is to abandon our true selves and all those counting on us. We do the poor no favors by bowing to a system that would sentence us to live twenty thousand leagues below our potential. According to Emmett Carson:

By whatever name is used: the nonprofit sector, the independent sector, the third sector, the nongovernmental sector, the social sector, or public benefit corporations, our sector is starting to lose touch with the American people. The fact that we can't agree on what to call ourselves underscores a larger problem that we aren't sure what we stand for and as a result no one else knows what we stand for. The questions that loom before us as a sector are, Who are we and what do we stand for?[5]

It is time for us to define ourselves by the dreams we have been afraid to dream, time to stop settling for a system incapable of setting its sights on anything more exciting than a seal of approval. Where before we thought of opening a homeless shelter, we need now to ask what it would take to end homelessness in our city. Where before we thought of how we could raise a million dollars, we must think now about how to raise a hundred million. Let us challenge our cancer charities to band together and set a goal for the eradication of cancer within the next ten years. Let our AIDS charities converge and commit themselves to an impossible goal for the eradication of AIDS. And let us stand behind them as they attempt it, defend them against their detractors as they experiment, and praise them when they stumble. By its very nature this kind of thinking will force a confrontation with the existing ideology.

Moreover, the declaration of a great dream to end some vexing social problem within a limited time frame transforms the discussion. It brings a new world to life. It gives rise to new questions, more rigorous discourse, infinitely greater urgency, and a catalogue of the impossible things that would need to happen if we were even to come close to achieving our goal. It reveals operational requirements never before considered. It produces the engineering plans for a new reality.

In the final analysis, we don't need to concern ourselves with dismantling an ideology. We don't need to concern ourselves with a strategic plan. We need to reclaim our forgotten hopes and dreams. They are the only reason for engaging in this discussion in the first place. Again, if we want social change to progress at the pace of molasses, then the system works fine as it is. But if we want dramatic improvement on the great social issues of our time, then we need dramatic changes to the paradigm that orders our efforts. If we are happy with the persistence of poverty and the lack of any end in sight, then we don't have to take any issue with our rules for compensation in the nonprofit sector. But if we hope to leave this earth with that problem behind us, then the nonprofit sector needs the same freedoms we give to business. If we are content for AIDS orphans and millions of preventable AIDS deaths to form a cultural backdrop for humanity until God-knows-when, then we should continue to prohibit charities from spending serious money on advertising. But if we want to see the end of AIDS on a dramatic timeline, then charities need unlimited freedom to create demand for the end of AIDS on that timeline. If we are content to accept the notion that every great achievement has to be fifty or seventy-five years off in the distance, then we have a perfectly suitable system for painstakingly long, drawn-out progress. But if we would like to see problems solved at a pace we never before imagined, then we also need economic freedoms we never before imagined.

But ultimately, these freedoms and the system that denies them are secondary matters. We can't challenge the system for no reason. We must lead with our dreams. They carry our moral authority, and without them, we have none. So we must imagine the marvelous world we could create together on the far side of caution—the real influence charity could have in building a new society. If we have the courage to articulate that vision and the constitution to fight for it, we will find ourselves de facto achieving the economic liberation of charity, because none of our dreams can be realized without it. Put another way, if we have the courage to be true to our most daring ideas, the ideology will have to surrender to their magnificence and our determination to make them real.

To get involved and meet others interested in these issues, visit: www.uncharitable.net.

ACKNOWLEDGMENTS

My thanks to Ellen Wicklum, Sarah Welsch, Elizabeth Rawitsch, and everyone at University Press of New England and John Schneider and everyone at Tufts for their belief in this project. I would also like to thank my friends and family for their love and support, especially Peter Anton, Clive Davis, Peter Diamandis, Arielle Ford, Freeman Frank, Herb Hamsher, Paul Horne, Rick Jacobs, Cecil Jones, Kris Kepp, Judith Light, Debbie Luican, Chris Markl, Neil McCarthy, George O'Har, Barbara Osborn, Torie Osborn, Anthony and Patricia Pallotta, Mark Pick, Paul Salamanca, Joe Short, Sara Smirin, Jimmy Smith, Gary Stewart, Randy Sturges, Stephanie Tade, Lois Walden, Irv Warner, Paiwei Wei, Bob Weiss, and Glenn Whitehead. Thanks to Chris Allegaert, Richard Neff, and Darryl Cluster for their assistance. Special thanks to Dan Tinkelman for his research and constructive criticism and to George O'Har for his tremendous assistance with editing. Thanks to Crew Creative for shooting the cover art. Thanks to Dana LaRue for running to Kinko's every ten minutes and to Ali M. Meghdadi for all of his help with the endnotes and bibliography. I would also like to thank all of the academics on whose rich and important work I have drawn. Last, I wish to thank all of the amazing people who participated in the Pallotta TeamWorks events over the years and all of the staff who worked so hard on them. None of this would have been possible without you.

CASE STUDY—
PALLOTTA TEAMWORKS

Security is mostly a superstition. It does not exist in nature, nor do
the children of men as a whole experience it. Avoiding danger
is no safer in the long run than outright exposure. Life is either
a daring adventure or it is nothing at all.

— HELEN KELLER

Centuries after the Puritans arrived in New England, I found myself
trapped by their beliefs, caught between my desire to do good and my desire to build an economic future for myself. I grew up in Malden, Massachusetts, settled by Puritans in 1640 on land purchased, in 1629, from the
Pawtucket Indians.[1] I was one of those few lucky human beings whose
first years on the planet coincided with the primes of Martin Luther
King, John and Robert Kennedy, Neil Armstrong, and with the landing
of the *Eagle* on the Sea of Tranquility, all at pretty much the same time.
The spirits of these individuals animated my imagination and left me
hungry to do something to make a difference. Their words gave rise to
new possibilities for the kind of world we could all create together. They
stood in sharp contrast to the dreary images of bloodied Vietnam soldiers
I saw on Walter Cronkite's news—images that I didn't understand, but
that depressed me and spoke of an indifferent world where things
dragged on, nothing ever changed, and all life was resignation.

Years later, while I was still in college, I had an opportunity. From
1979 to 1982, I was the chair of the undergraduate Harvard Hunger Action Committee, and I was frustrated by the puny fundraisers we did to
bring in a thousand dollars here and there through largely symbolic one-
meal fasts on campus. The summer before my senior year, an idea came
to me on the radio; I heard about two guys bicycling across America for
cancer research. I knew instantly that was the kind of scale I had been
seeking. The next summer, thirty-nine of us spent nine and a half weeks

bicycling 4,256 miles from Seattle to Boston to raise money to combat and heighten awareness of world hunger. We raised about $80,000, and when we rode back into Boston at the end of our long journey, I think we all felt we had exhausted the full measure of our potential.

Pallotta TeamWorks began in the early 1990s with a single event that was a response to the AIDS epidemic and the loss of many of my friends.[2] At the time, the epidemic was nearing its height in the United States. Close to fifty thousand Americans were dying every year. I was meeting the parents of my young friends for the first time at their sons' memorial services in the Hollywood hills homes of their surviving friends. It was the age before protease inhibitors. A friend would tell you he'd just found out he was HIV positive. Three weeks later he'd have symptoms of AIDS, and five months later he'd be dead. And there was nothing the average person could do that could match the scale of their grief.

By 1993, I had been mulling over the idea of a bike ride from San Francisco to Los Angeles for a few years, and I finally decided to refine it. We called it California AIDSRide. We brought the idea to the Los Angeles Gay & Lesbian Community Services Center, which provided seed funding, among other things, and served as beneficiary.[3]

We didn't market the event to cyclists. We marketed it to average people from all walks of life who had it in them to do something epic and extraordinary. Each registrant had to agree to ride for seven days, rain or shine, sleep in a tent, and raise a minimum of $2,000 for the privilege. Our later ads said, "I'm not an athlete, I'm not a cyclist, but I'd climb Mount Everest to make a difference in the fight against AIDS." Most of the riders hadn't been on a bike in years. Most didn't even own one.

In the years that followed, we would expand the events around the nation, with rides from Boston to New York, Minneapolis to Chicago, Austin to Dallas, and more, benefiting a variety of AIDS charities across the country. A few years later, we applied the same model to the issue of breast cancer. We created a series of events we called the Breast Cancer 3-Days. We asked ourselves why walk-a-thons had to be short— why were they always five or ten kilometers? Why couldn't they cover long distances and last for days? The Breast Cancer 3-Days did exactly that, asking people to walk for three days, twenty miles a day, for the loved ones they'd lost to breast cancer, and to raise a minimum of $1,200 in order to participate. We then created a series of even more challenging events in more remote and more difficult terrain to raise money for AIDS vaccine research. We also created a twenty-six-mile walk through the night for suicide prevention.

In nine years of producing these events, we raised more than half a billion dollars and netted 305 million dollars for the broad array of charities that were the beneficiaries of the events and for the clients they served.

Harvard Business School's interest in social entrepreneurship led them to commission a case study on our methods in 2002. On a functional level, the events broke with tradition in three ways. They lasted days instead of hours; they required participants to raise a mandatory minimum of contributions that ranged from $1,000 to $10,000, depending on the event; and they were marketed to a mass audience using funding levels and methods that previously were largely the domain of big consumer brands. On an emotional and philosophical level, the events asked people to do the most they could do, instead of the least. Tens of thousands of people responded. It was like a coming out for their humanity.

Here are a few of the company's employees', volunteers', and participants' top-line achievements from 1994 to 2002:

- Our events raised $556 million in total donor contributions.[4]
- We netted $305 million, after all expenses, for direct charitable service (breast cancer research, AIDS services, etc.)
- The company produced seventy-nine large-scale multiday events, each with an average of 2,279 walkers or riders, each traveling anywhere from sixty miles on foot to six hundred miles by bicycle.[5]
- A total of 180,043 people rode or walked.[6]
- Tens of thousands of people volunteered for days on end as crew members on the roads and campsites of the events.
- Approximately 7.4 million individual donations were made to the events.[7]
- The average participant raised $3,039 from his or her friends and family.[8]

The $305 million we netted was in addition to tens of millions of dollars raised and used to heighten awareness of the various causes we supported. Also, this $305 million was unrestricted—the most valuable kind of funding a charity can get and the most difficult to raise. Dollars received from foundations and the government almost always come with significant restrictions. Nonprofit organizations in America get 30 percent of their funding from the government.[9] By contrast, the dollars we netted came with only one caveat—they had to be spent on the cause for which they were raised. Beyond that, charities had complete freedom to use the money as they saw fit.

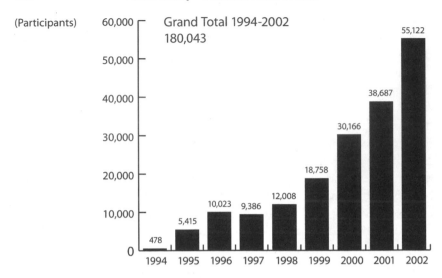

(Participants)

Grand Total 1994-2002
180,043

Figure 1. Pallotta TeamWorks: Total Participants, 1994–2002
SOURCE: Pallotta TeamWorks, "Record of Impact 1994–2002" (Los Angeles, 2006).

In 2002 alone, our events netted $81.9 million in unrestricted funds. This was more than the annual giving of the Exxon Mobil and General Motors Foundations combined for the previous year and more than half the annual giving of the Rockefeller Foundation.[10] It was more than the 2003 cash giving of Anheuser-Busch, AT&T, Boeing, Chevron-Texaco, Hewlett-Packard, IBM, Merrill Lynch, Microsoft, Pepsico, Motorola, Procter & Gamble, Sara Lee, Sears, UPS, the Walt Disney Company, or Xerox Corporation.[11] Of the seventy thousand foundations in America listed in the 2006 Foundation Directory, including the likes of Gates, Ford, Pew, and MacArthur, only fifty gave away more money than the net income from our 2002 events.[12]

The AIDSRides netted $99 million for AIDS service agencies to provide critical case management, HIV testing, medical care, hot meals, subsidized medicines, and prevention education services to people throughout the United States. In addition, the AIDSRides spent an estimated $13.5 million on marketing that heightened awareness of the cause.[13]

The Breast Cancer 3-Days netted $194.4 million in five years—quadruple the fundraising rate of the AIDSRides—for a wide array of services for women with breast cancer and for breast cancer research. In addition, the 3-Days spent $23 million on marketing that heightened awareness of the cause.[14]

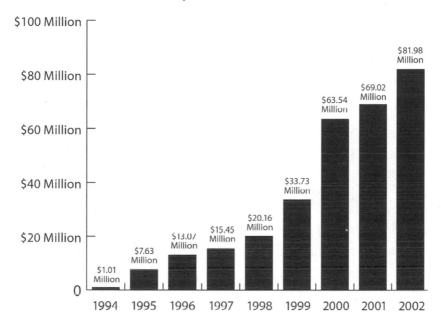

Figure 2. Pallotta TeamWorks, 1994–2002: Annual Net Dollars Available for Direct Charitable Service, All Causes Combined
SOURCE: Pallotta TeamWorks, "Record of Impact 1994–2002" (Los Angeles, 2006).

Our AIDS Vaccine events netted $8.7 million for AIDS vaccine research at the UCLA AIDS Institute, the Emory Vaccine Center, and the Aaron Diamond Center.[15] These funds made critical AIDS vaccine trials possible.

In addition, we launched the nation's first mass event for suicide prevention—a twenty-six-mile walk through the night with more than twelve hundred walkers, netting more than $1,291,000 in unrestricted funds for the American Foundation for Suicide Prevention.[16] We also produced the largest cross-country bike ride in American history for the American Lung Association; 730 people bicycled approximately three thousand miles from Seattle to Washington, D.C., to net $1.1 million.[17]

Beyond this, we provided full-time employment to over 350 people in 2002 alone, and probably to more than 600 people for various amounts of time over the course of our history. The company's events generated, arguably, several billion dollars in economic activity, including purchases of bicycles and gear, camping gear and walking shoes, hotel room rentals, airline tickets, meals, fitness center memberships, and much more. Figures 1, 2, and 3 chart our results.

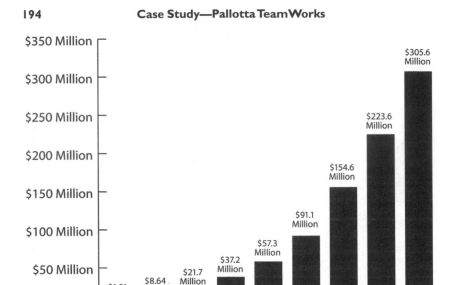

Figure 3. Pallotta TeamWorks, 1994–2002: Cumulative Net Dollars Available for Direct Charitable Service, All Causes Combined
SOURCE: Pallotta TeamWorks, "Record of Impact 1994–2002" (Los Angeles, 2006).

This is the financial and statistical side of the story. The stories of heroism and personal conquest, by average citizens, people with AIDS and HIV, breast cancer survivors, suicide survivors, and their friends and families, could fill volumes. They struggled up hills, endured mile after mile of blisters, bicycled over the Alaska Range in the snow, crossed the Continental Divide in the scorching Montana summer heat, trekked through the hills of South Africa, and pedaled through rain and sleet and against the wind. They did something unparalleled in the history of organized charity and compassion.

In addition, the AIDSRides and the 3-Days brought educational prevention messages outside of liberal urban centers to hundreds of remote and rural small towns across America, live and in person, offering thousands of average Americans and their children the chance to learn more about AIDS and breast cancer and to meet real American heroes, face to face, who were doing something about it. And, unexpectedly, the AIDSRides brought opportunities for gay and lesbian people to mix with straight people who were doing the rides for friends they had lost, fostering new levels of understanding and mutual admiration.

You had to see these events to believe them—thousands of people, some gay, some straight, some HIV positive, some breast cancer survivors, all shapes, sizes, ages, and colors, some wealthy and some not, in all kinds of ragtag outfits, their knees wrapped in Ace bandages, their feet full of blisters, sometimes draped in trash bags and Mylar if it was raining—walking, pedaling, and sometimes limping—down all manner of roads and highways all over America for days on end—all of them having raised an amount of money they didn't think they were capable of raising. The closing ceremonies for these events were festivals of tears—of joy, sorrow, beauty, and possibility—with thousands of the riders' and walkers' friends, families, and loved ones gathered to see them arrive en masse like a battalion of returning heroes.

The events also built community. One of our messages was "Human. Kind. Be Both." During the orientation video shown before each event, we asked people to experiment rigorously with kindness—to stop and help other riders with a flat tire, even though the shower line might get longer by the time they got into camp, or to help set up a walker's tent, just to surprise them, even though the dinner line might get longer. People responded with tremendous enthusiasm. The events became sanctuaries of kindness. At the end of each day, the participants would amass around the entry to camp—hundreds of people would gather—to cheer on the last rider or walker of the day often the oldest or most fragile participant. The emotion of those moments was extraordinary.

Each of the events involved complex logistics that included the creation and movement of a mobile city that the participants called home each night. Dozens of tractor-trailer trucks, fuel trucks, service trucks, circus tents, and a complex array of other infrastructure made up the city, providing hot meals and hot showers, sinks and chemical toilets, stages for scientists, breast cancer survivors, and those with AIDS to speak to the participants at night, a general store, lighting, a massive range of signage, command and communications centers, medical, massage, and chiropractic facilities, and much more. All of this infrastructure had to be moved every day as the riders and walkers trekked to the next campsite for the night. Hundreds of volunteers helped to break down and reassemble the city. On the road were fleets of cargo trucks to transport luggage, dozens of roving passenger vans to pick up people unable to finish their day's walk or ride, water and nutrition stops along each day's route, and hundreds of chemical toilets placed methodically along the roads and moved each day.

Despite the fact that "efficiency" measures are a useless gauge of value for all the critical information they omit, they must be mentioned here simply because they were pretty much the sole measure by which our company and all of its good people were being judged. Total expenses (staff, rent, advertising, printing, meals, shower tucks, other logistics expenses, etc.) averaged 45 percent of donor contributions for all eighty-three events we undertook (including those that performed poorly and four that were canceled). Forty-five percent was five percentage points away from the forty percent overhead guideline recommended by the Better Business Bureau Wise Giving Alliance at the time. The AIDSRides' average was 47 percent. The Breast Cancer 3-Days' was 40 percent. *Our historic mean was 43 percent, and the average for our top fifty campaigns was just 36 percent.*[18]

The employees at Pallotta TeamWorks worked harder than any group of people I have ever known to get these numbers to these levels. I watched each of them give from parts of themselves they didn't even know existed to achieve these numbers. I reject with all of my being any charge that any of these people or their efforts were anything less than models of efficiency and conscientiousness. I challenge anyone else to match what they accomplished. I watched them work until late in the evenings at cold campsites in the pouring rain. I watched them give up their weekends to drive to a rider or walker's house party to give a fundraising pitch. I watched them volunteer to lead training rides and walks, and much more—all the while having to read stories in the media about the "inefficiency" of their efforts. It was remarkable that they were able to get the numbers anywhere near the "watchdog" guidelines for the measure, let alone often exceed them, given the extreme logistical complexity of the events, the added value of the experience being provided to participants, the massive awareness being raised for the causes by media coverage and paid advertising, the velocity of our fundraising, and the unprecedented hundreds of millions of unrestricted dollars we netted for the causes after all expenses, none of which was reflected in any of these percentages. *More remarkable than anything is the fact that they achieved these numbers even with the conservative accounting methodology we used to calculate them, as I will discuss later.*

It is important to note that 100 percent of the funds donated to our events were deposited directly into the accounts of our charitable beneficiaries. By stipulation of most of our own written agreements, the charities were required to open lock box accounts to take in all donations. Donations were *not* made payable to Pallotta TeamWorks. Therefore, figures like the 60 percent referred to above simply reflect the charities' funds remaining after they paid our production fee and reimbursed us for the expenses we incurred on their behalf.

Except for our first event in 1994, which had a simple bonus structure, Pallotta TeamWorks charged a flat fee for its services that was agreed upon in advance by contract with all of the charities. In most cases, those agreements were submitted to the various states' attorneys general, registrars of charitable trusts, and other state regulatory agencies. The company's fees were never based on a percentage of donations raised. Our fees ranged from $140,000 to $450,000 per event.[19] Statements of all of our fees were available online on our website, so that the public could make informed decisions about participation. By hindsight calculation, our fees as a percentage of gross dollars raised decreased as the years went on and the success grew. In 1994, our fees for California AIDSRide represented 9.09 percent of gross income. By 2002, our historical average for the AIDSRides was 5.3 percent. For the Breast Cancer 3-Days, fees from 1998 through 2002 represented 3 percent of gross income.[20] By contrast, the 2004 California Attorney General's report on commercial fundraisers states that historical figures show that, on average, commercial fundraisers retain more than 50 percent of contributions as a fundraising fee.[21]

Methods and Controversy

The AIDSRides, the Breast Cancer 3-Days, and Pallotta TeamWorks' philosophies in general challenged sacred cows. We didn't set out to do this. We simply set out to do what we believed would raise the most money for charity.

For-Profit Structure, For-Profit Sector Compensation Philosophy

We were a for-profit company raising money for nonprofit causes. We were not the first for-profit entity ever to do business with a charity. For-profit transactions with nonprofit organizations are ubiquitous, from the telephone company selling a charity phone service at a profit, to a building contractor earning a profit constructing a new homeless shelter. We were unique, however, in that we were the primary interface with the customer. This created a lightning rod effect that made us the center of debate on the for-profit versus nonprofit issue on an unprecedented level. In addition, we paid our employees salaries that were market based. In at least several cases, including my own, these salaries were in excess of $200,000 a year.

Even though we were a for-profit company, it wasn't about the money for us. But it must also be said that it wasn't *not* about the money; that is, it wasn't about self-denial on behalf of others. It was as much about idealism and a dream as anything else, if not more so, but the money wasn't unimportant to us, or at least to me. This conflicted emphatically with traditional ideology.

Related Criticism

A representative *New York Times* story reported, "Critics argue that there is something wrong about a venture that does so well by doing good."[22] An ad run in 2001 by a group called the "AIDS Community Donor Action" stated, "Pallotta TeamWorks continues to profiteer by promoting AIDS 'fundraising events' that in reality provide little benefit to AIDS charities."[23] At the time this ad ran, we had netted in excess of $100 million for AIDS charities. *POZ* magazine quoted an activist calling me "the biggest AIDS profiteer since Burroughs Wellcome."[24] Later *POZ* described me as "the queen of AIDS profiteering."[25] Another activist was quoted as saying, "I see Pallotta TeamWorks as a parasite, really looting the community of resources that should have gone to AIDS groups and AIDS services."[26] These demonizations were typical of our most vocal critics. While they represented an extreme minority, the incendiary language allowed them to disproportionately animate the debate.

Ironically, for an average event our advertising payments to the media—the very institutions broadcasting the criticism—were at least as large as the production fee we were being paid by the charity. It is safe to say that the media earned at least as much, if not more, profit than we did as a direct result of our existence. For example, our advertising budget for the 2002 San Diego Breast Cancer 3-Day was $500,000.[27] Our production fee was $370,000. This was fairly typical. Over the course of our nine years, we paid, conservatively, $19.75 million for advertising that went to for-profit entities like the *New York Times,* CNN, the *Washington Post, Oprah, Time* magazine, and hundreds of other radio stations, television channels, newspapers, and other media.[28]

A story in "Salon.com" commented on the tension between profit and piety. It could easily have been written by a historian observing the Puritans:

> Almost from the beginning, riders have had a love–hate relationship with the company. Pallotta delivers fun, smooth-running events that some even describe as "visionary," but the fact that he does it as a business bothers riders who worry about corporate taint . . . they balk at the fact that part of every donation collected goes to Pallotta TeamWorks.[29]

While it is not true that part of every donation went to Pallotta TeamWorks (our fees were not tied to donations), we *were* being paid by charities *out of* donations, and we were a for-profit entity; we were earning a profit in a charitable setting.

The Most You Can Do

Instead of asking people to do the *least* they could do, our events asked people to do the *most* they could do. This included bicycling or walking up to 105 miles a day on some of the AIDSRides and up to 22 miles a day on the 3-Days, for days on end. Also, you had to sign up for the whole event—you could not sign up for just one or two days—and you had to raise a mandatory minimum of $1,000 to $10,000. If you didn't raise the minimum, you couldn't participate in the event. The traditional standard allowed you to take part in a charity event no matter how much you raised, even if it was less than what it cost the charity to accommodate you. This was not logical to us. If the charity had expenses associated with each participant, it had a right to set a minimum fundraising requirement.

Individual and group empowerment was a by-product of the scale of the events, and a marketing message as well. We were trying to show people that their potential was beyond what they may have imagined. One of our slogans was "I'mpossible." This kind of approach had never been applied in a systematic way on any grand scale in a charitable context. The *New York Times* called our achievement "a breakthrough in the history of American enterprise: the first successful marketing of pain."[30]

Related Criticism

Critics took issue with the idea of individual empowerment and construed our logistics expenses as an inefficient related cost. In truth, the long distances gave rise to the need to spend money on things like food, showers, and chemical toilets. The large volume of donations to riders and walkers was a direct result of the fact that they could tell their friends they were traveling these long distances. If participants were empowered, it was merely a by-product of traveling the long distances on which the fundraising model depended. It was not achieved by spending dollars on "empowerment." *We needed to feed and shower people whether they were being empowered or not.*

One story on the front page of the *Washington Post* in 2001 stated that our events "Stress 'Human Potential' at Cost to Charities, Some Say."[31] In addition to misconstruing the economics, the *Post* story all but exemplifies the Puritan prohibition on self-regard, in this case, the notion that people shouldn't empower themselves with charitable dollars. This take misrepresents the new dollars being raised by these *empowered* participants *for* the cause as a "cost" to the charities. We ourselves even fell into the trap of devaluing the empowering charac- teristics of the events—we never allocated any of the expense that went into empowerment or raising awareness as money going "to the cause," even though generally accepted accounting practices allow it.

One activist, conflating personal transformation with charitable det- riment, complained, " 'That's telling people the way to fight AIDS is to take a prepackaged transformative vacation.' "[32] One story said, "This focus on the participant and his or her experience has 'engendered scru- tiny and criticism,' " and quoted an ACT-UP activist saying of the *riders themselves* that "they're greedy. They have their friends and relatives pay for a four-day bike journey with food, showers and massage. It's a glo- rified vacation."[33] The notion that riding a bike for seven days and six hundred miles while surviving on Gatorade and bananas is a vacation can be maintained only by someone who has never attempted it.

A spokesperson for one of our charities, after they decided to stage their own ride, said of their new venture, "Riders will not hear, 'This is about you, this will change your life,' because the event isn't about changing riders' lives—it's about raising money for HIV and AIDS."[34] This exorcism of self-interest didn't survive. Their lead headline on their website in 2007 didn't address itself to AIDS, but focused squarely on the consumer's self-interest, asking, "How many experi- ences do you remember for a lifetime?"[35] Four centuries later charities find themselves caught in the Puritans' double bind, eschewing and promoting self-interest in the same breath.[36]

Paid, Professional Advertising and Marketing

We challenged the idea that charities should not pay for advertising—that they should use only what they can get donated. We took our cues from the successful consumer brands and for-profit direct-response industries—from Disneyland to Madonna concerts, from Geico to Target. We knew that money had to be invested in building demand—that the more money invested in it, the more demand would grow and the more money we would raise for the cause. This is consistent with the way every consumer products company perceives the world. Apple builds demand for its iPod with substantial paid advertising and expensive retail stores. It doesn't depend merely on people's love of music. While that will build some sales, it won't allow them to exploit the full potential for sales. But we expect charity to operate under a different set of rules and still demand that it be successful.

We rejected this prohibition on paid advertising. We developed detailed paid-marketing plans that integrated a variety of media with very strategic intent. We created marketing plans for each event that called for specific ads to run at specific times in synch with others. We paid for the ads so we could get them when we wanted them, where we wanted them. Imagine if Coca-Cola were told it was at the mercy of donated advertising to execute its marketing plans. The opportunity cost of missing key advertising windows could be higher than the cost of the ad itself. Our goals were significant, and most times we met or exceeded them. For instance, our combined contract budgets with Avon for the Breast Cancer 3-Days projected a total of 87,428 walkers. We actually had 106,352. Our net income projections totaled $136.4 million. We actually netted $194.4 million.[37] Our events often had half-million-dollar advertising and marketing budgets—sometimes even more—for a single event.

Brochures and other printed materials were always professionally designed according to exacting visual standards and featured a visual aesthetic that was uncommonly refined for a charitable special event. Our logic was that we needed to appear every bit as professional as the premium consumer brands if we expected people to trust us to accommodate them safely and professionally on these extremely demanding journeys. On paper, we looked like Lexus. This was intentional.

Related Criticism

None of these practices fit the romantic view of charity as small, understated, and mimeographed. In an environment where people think a donated ad is more efficient, or more frugal, than a paid ad, our methods made us appear to some to be unconcerned with frugality. Our logic was that the spirit of frugality, or efficiency, is the maximization of revenue, not the maximization of savings. Our purpose was not to save as much money as we could, but to raise as much money as we could.

PlanetOut.com described us as "the increasingly controversial Pallotta TeamWorks, often criticized for its expensive and slick marketing."[38] Ironically, if our marketing was "expensive," it was only because of the rates charged by the very newspapers and magazine reporting that it was. Furthermore, "expensive" is a relative term. An ad that costs $50,000 but raises $500,000 might, in many circles, be considered cheap. In charity, however, the fact that something is paid for rather than donated is viewed with suspicion. The newspaper ads we bought were running alongside ads that Bloomingdale's, CitiBank, and Cingular were buying every day. Why are the former criticized as "expensive," while the latter are considered simply normal business expense? Why is it any more moral for Cingular to pay for ads to help sell phones than for a breast cancer charity to pay for ads to help end breast cancer?

Furthermore, in the for-profit sector, one would not characterize advertising as "slick" simply because it is professional. The *Berkeley Daily Planet* was typical in referring to our "slickly produced books, glossy brochures and signs."[39]

We aren't sensitive about gloss when we are in an auto showroom. But we are in a charitable context. Again, the dividing line appears. This gives rise to the irrational notion that we should use the best printing processes available to bring out the detail of a fine car interior in the interest of selling it, but we should not use the same process to bring out the detail of the sorrow on the face of a starving child in sub-Saharan Africa to bring it home to a potential donor.

Brand Building

We wanted to build our own brand. This in and of itself challenged the idea that profit in charity is bad. It challenged the idea that a for-profit event producer should remain hidden in the background—that only the charity should be known to the consumer. Again, these traditional ideas were not logical to us. We wanted to build relationships with all of our riders and walkers nationwide, across all of our causes. We wanted them to know who we were, *as well as* who the charities were. We wanted to do this so that people would talk to their friends about Pallotta Team-Works—so that they could make a mental connection between an event we were producing in Los Angeles and one in Boston in the hope that, because of their good experience with us in Los Angeles, they might do our Boston event as well or tell their friends in Boston about us. This would help both the Los Angeles and the Boston charity.

Our overall strategy was consistent with the methods every business in America uses to build a brand, scale, customers, and results. We wanted to build the first for-profit brand that would have a relationship of mutual trust and affection with its consumers, for the benefit of everyone. We wanted to build the Disney of meaning. That was our master plan.

Related Criticism

Building brand equity was a smart way to raise more money for charity. It was also a smart way to build Pallotta TeamWorks. Critics were uncomfortable with a win–win situation in which one of the winners was a for-profit firm. In building our own brand equity, we were satisfying a self-interest *and* a charitable interest at the same time. Even though the two were directly correlated—that is, the more we grew, the more dollars to charity grew—we offended the traditional construction.

Criticism focused on self-interest. A story in the *Los Angeles Times* quoted a typical AIDS activist saying that "these AIDS rides are not about raising money at all. They are all about building Dan Pallotta's empire."[40] This was at odds with the fact that our AIDS Rides and AIDS Vaccine events *netted* $108 million for people with AIDS and for AIDS research. The presence of self-interest is blinding. Other critics used similar characterizations like "grandiose," "lavish self-promotion," and "shameless self-promotion."[41] The implication is that if, like the Puritans, we had been properly ashamed of ourselves, it would have made up for everything else.

The multiday events that have followed in our footsteps, many of them produced by our former employees, eliminate any mention of the for-profit production companies that operate or assist in the day-to-day operations of the events. They are hidden from view. Few of them, if any, are trying to build relationships with the event participants independent of the charities. This represents a tremendous lost opportunity for fundraising through cross-promotion.

Desegregation of Causes

We confronted the notion that causes should be segregated from one another, that you don't talk about AIDS at a breast cancer event or about breast cancer at an AIDS event. We were looking beyond a single disease to a world where our common compassion elevated action against all diseases. In 2002, we began cross-marketing causes and events. We did this in four ways: by consolidating the various event brochures into a single catalogue, by promoting our *entire* calendar of charity events in the safety video played at *each* event, by talking about the *entire* calendar of events one night at camp during *each* event, and by bringing a marketing trailer to *each* event that advertised the *entire* calendar of events and causes.

The consolidated-event catalogue was a critical element of our strategy. It was the principal printed piece for the official registration of participants for all events. Previously, each of our events had had its own brochure. The new strategy was motivated by a commonsense idea for raising all boats: in 2002, more than half a million people wanted information on one of our events, but only forty thousand inquired specifically, for example, about California AIDSRide. Why send them only a brochure on California AIDSRide when we could send them a brochure about all twenty events? And why not send every one of our half-million information seekers that same catalogue showing them all twenty of our events? That way, half a million people, instead of forty thousand, would get to read about California AIDSRide, as well as all the other events—a dramatic twelve-fold increase in exposure for each event and each cause.

The catalogue included events for AIDS, breast cancer, suicide prevention, urban poverty, and child adoption. It was large—a foot high and about a foot and a half wide. The purpose was to give it enough stopping power so people would want to open it, to make the type and images large enough to envelope people in the spirit of the events, and to make it a coffee table and conversation piece that would be shared with friends.

Pallotta TeamWorks became the unifying parent brand on the piece, similar to the way Toyota, for instance, is the unifying brand for its subsidiary products—Camry, Scion, Prius, and so on. Our logo alone was placed diminutively on the bottom of the cover. The collection of different causes featured inside gave rise to the need for a unifying cover message as well, one that would be relevant to all of the causes. Since there were not just AIDS or just breast cancer or just suicide prevention events inside, we couldn't put just an AIDS or breast cancer or suicide prevention message on the cover. We chose the common denominator—

people's desire to improve their world. The cover began with the words "We the people, in order to form a more beautiful world . . ." and the inside cover continued with

> do hereby commit our time on earth and place in history to the here and now, to open the floodgates of our hearts onto the parched deserts of the underserved and overburdened, so that no soul be denied the dignity of our full attention, so that no heart be held in contempt of its dreams, so that every darkness may be enlightened, so that a sea change may be effected on our planet, and kindness be an island no more.[42]

The first page introduced this new concept—a kind of Yellow Pages of compassion—with the following words:

> Inside this document we describe 24 events we have created for 2002. On each, you have the opportunity to create a new predictor of your own potential and contribute to the alleviation of others' suffering and despair. The events address the issues of AIDS, breast cancer, suicide prevention, and adoptions for children who do not have a safe place to call home. What matters is not which cause you choose, but that you choose at least one, and in so doing, choose the greatest cause of all—the cause of action in the service of humanity.[43]

Large panels inside the piece were dedicated to specific statistics on each cause.

We also cross-marketed the various events at the events themselves. In 2001, the safety and orientation video we showed before each event pitched all of the 2002 events—all of the causes—at every event. The tactic was modeled fairly routinely on the movie trailers that preview upcoming films before the feature.

On top of that, there was a large custom trailer at each event—a fun mobile diner with a kind of lunch counter where participants could sit down, flip through the new catalogues, and register for an upcoming event. Everyone on the AIDSRides learned about our breast cancer efforts and all of our Breast Cancer 3-Day participants learned about our AIDSRides, etc. Finally, we gave an overview of the entire roster of 2002 events one night at camp—all causes at each event.

Related Criticism

Critics said that we had lost focus on the specific causes, that we had abandoned our commitment to the real issues, and that we were becoming commercial or corporate.

One story claimed that the events "no longer focused on a community touched by AIDS, but instead reinforced Pallotta's ubiquitous messages of human kindness and personal transformation" and referred to "complaints about Pallotta's focus on self-promotion rather than AIDS and HIV issues."[44]

Another story commenting on our California AIDSRide charities said that they "complained about heavy marketing and cross-promotion . . . of other Pallotta-planned events, such as the Avon Breast Cancer 3-Day walk."[45] The *Los Angeles Times* wrote about "too much 'cross-promotion' of breast cancer walks and other company events."[46] Yet others cited *not enough* focus on breast cancer: "The breast cancer message during the 3DAY was also increasingly diluted by the focus on personal transformation and empowerment, and by PTW's cross-marketing of its other events on behalf of other causes."[47] It is a phenomenon unique to charity. We don't complain about the cross-marketing of a new Disney children's movie inside a McDonald's, but react negatively to the presence of a breast cancer message at an AIDS event. We don't complain about having to watch previews for upcoming films before viewing the one we came to see, but critics bristle at the mention of a suicide prevention event at an AIDS fundraiser.

An article in the *Advocate* similarly referred to "what appeared to be a shift in focus from AIDS prevention to the cross-promotion of TeamWorks' growing list of other events."[48] Another reported, "The cause had always been at the center of every event. But in 2001 that focus began to change. PTW began cross-marketing events for other new events and causes to existing participants using slick brochures, kiosks, and infomercials disguised as safety videos. . . . To event participants the PTW brand smacked of commercialism."[49] In this construction, commercialism—as in commerce—is necessarily negative. From 2001 to 2002, our net proceeds to charity rose from $69 million to $81 million. The commercial things we were doing were working.

Taking Risks

We launched events in remote places like Africa, Alaska, and across the Continental Divide in Montana, not knowing with 100 percent certainty whether they would be popular with the public. We launched events for new causes, also not knowing with certainty whether they would resonate with the public. We launched events in smaller cities for causes we had already succeeded with in the top-tier urban cities in

America. We followed the example of every great commercial enter-prise by pursuing new markets and bold new endeavors. Some of the new things we tried surpassed all expectations and some were disap-pointing. Of the eighty-three events we attempted, four were canceled for lack of interest. Of the remaining seventy-nine events, sixty-seven had net returns to charity of greater than $1 million. Of the twelve that did not, three lost money. Of those, only one lost money for the charity. Of the seventy-nine events that were produced, the average amount netted for charitable services from each was $3,868,611, for a total of $305 million after all expenses.[50]

Related Criticism

It was on this front that the company took the greatest criticism by far—directly when an event had *percentage* returns that dipped below the standards set by watchdog agencies, and indirectly when those low-performing events brought down the hindsight *percentage average* of all the events. The criticism was whipped up according to two standard sleights of hand. First, critics would focus only on the "failures," and second, they would focus only on percentages. By excluding data about *actual dollars* and excluding stories about the successes that represented the vast majority of our events, they were able to build controversy. Furthermore, by entirely ignoring the research and prevention educa-tion services being made possible by the millions of actual dollars being raised, the media was able to build lopsided narratives that seduced peo-ple into believing no good was being done. This is how we get trained to ask one question and one question only: "What percentage of my donation went to the cause?" This is the system that got us where we are today, with a world of suffering we seem incapable of addressing and an opinion on the part of most of the public that the money given to charity never gets to the people it is intended for.

A 1997 *U.S. News & World Report* headline asked, "Do Some AIDS Events Take Donors for a Ride?"[51] with a subheadline that read, "Ex-penses at Dan Pallotta's Bikeathons Leave Less Money for the Char-ities." Less money than what? By this time, we had been in business for just three years and had already netted $22 million for AIDS charities. Within three months after the story came out, we would add another $15.4 million to that, bringing the total dollars netted for charity to more than $37 million.[52] Using "efficiency" measures to justify the headline, the story itself said, "The National Charities Information

Bureau recommends that fund-raising costs not be more than 35 cents on the dollar. According to numbers provided by Pallotta TeamWorks, 43 cents of every dollar donated goes to administration or to ride expenses."[53] Four paragraphs into the story, and in much smaller type, there is mention of how much money we raised. By this time we had produced campaigns in fourteen cities. Twelve had returns above 50 percent. Six had returns above 60 percent. Three had returns above 70 percent. The story cites the specific percentage returns, in fact focuses on the returns, for only two events—the two that had returns below 50 percent—ignoring the twelve successes. And even those two netted $769,000 for AIDS services.[54] The people who got the money might think that was a success.

The story goes on to compare our events with the American Lung Association's two-day bike-a-thons that have cost ratios of twenty-five to forty cents on the dollar, according to the article.[55] It doesn't mention the scale of those events. The American Lung Association's Washington ride, for instance, as late as 2006, planned for total fundraising of $200,000 and three hundred riders, nearly eight times fewer riders than took part in our 1997 California AIDSRide.[56] And at $200,000 a year, *it would take forty-four years to raise the $8.98 million that California AIDSRide raised in 1997.*[57] Another American Lung Association event called the Pacific Coast Ride planned for thirty-nine riders and had fundraising that "exceeded $100,000."[58] Percentage returns are not contained in the press releases. Our average event had 2,279 walkers or riders and grossed $7.04 million.[59] Is it fair to compare events that different in scale?

A study by Giving USA of 1,540 organizations found that they varied widely in how much they needed to spend to raise money through special events, and events not nearly as complex as ours. While the top 25 percent were able to hold fundraising spending to under 16 percent of donations, the bottom 25 percent found they needed to spend 50 percent or more on fundraising. The median was 31 percent.[60] The average of 40 percent that we spent on fundraising through 1996, while higher than the median, was very much in the mainstream, without considering our extraordinary dollar volumes, which were far above the mainstream. Accusing us of "taking donors for a ride" would have been a cheap shot even if what we were doing was a normal, run-of-the mill special event like organizing a big annual chicken dinner.

Why did our percentage returns fluctuate above and below the standards? The majority of operating costs for our events were fixed.

Newspapers don't charge less for an ad that brings in fewer riders. The landlord for the recruitment office doesn't lower the rent. Rider and walker numbers mattered. If enough people didn't sign up, fixed costs would eat us alive. If we had fixed costs of $1 million for an event, and enough walkers signed up to raise $3 million, the fixed costs would only be 33 percent. But if only half that number of walkers signed up, the fixed costs would double to 66 percent.

We were trying something new. There were no data to support that it was humanly possible to achieve the volume we were achieving, at the speed we were achieving it, on the scale we were doing it, for the number of causes we were supporting, along with the intangible benefits we were generating, and meet a 35 percent cost threshold, particularly with the conservative accounting methods we used to calculate our percentages.

By conservative accounting methods, I refer to the issues in the previous discussion about how "efficiency" measures reward certain accounting methods and penalize others. *Zero percent of our expenses were characterized as expenditures for the cause in calculating our percentage return to the cause.* In other words, every penny spent to produce the events was ultimately accounted for as an event expense, whether it was an advertisement, a brochure, or a chemical toilet. If we spent $2 million to produce an event that raised $4 million in donations, our accounting recorded $2 million in expenses and $2 million in donations going to the cause, and reported that 50 percent of donations went to the cause.

This might sound like a confusing statement of the obvious. How else would you account for the event expenses? What charity tells the public that money that went to an event-related expense was money that went to the cause? "The cause" means things like medical research and food for the hungry, right? It doesn't mean event brochures and newspaper advertisements for a fundraising event, right?

As discussed previously, this is actually not right. Many charities legitimately account for some of the money they spend on events—say, for things like a newspaper ad that talks about the cause while at the same time asks you to walk or to ride—as money spent, at least in part, on the cause. *Change the definition of the cause, and you can change the definition of how much money went to the cause.* The more liberal an organization is in defining the cause, the higher the percentage of your dollar it will be able to tell you goes to the cause. As I have made clear, I believe in a liberal definition of the cause, but it is unfair to compare financial results between different fundraising efforts without knowing the differences in their accounting.

Using the earlier $4 million example, if $1 million of our $2 million in expenses was for advertising, and we changed our definition of the cause to include advertising for the cause; that $1 million is no longer an expense—it is now $1 million extra that we can say went to the cause. *What was a liability becomes an asset.* Instead of saying $2 million went to the cause, we can say $3 million went to the cause, and our percentage immediately changes from 50 to 75 percent, well above most watchdog standards.

According to Tinkelman, one of the national event series that followed in our footsteps—the Avon Walks for Breast Cancer—characterized 43 to 51 percent of their annual event-related expenses as expenditures for breast cancer programs.[61] With respect to advertising Tinkelman notes, "In 2003, Avon allocated $5,423,601, or 99.9% of total advertising spending of $5,428,487, to the Breast Cancer Crusade program, classifying only $4,886 (0.1%) as fund raising";[62] as a result of this accounting, "reported fundraising costs were . . . 38% of public donations."[63] This comes close to the Better Business Bureau's 35 percent cost guideline. However, if the allocated expenses were put back into the fundraising category, fundraising *costs* would rise to 67 percent of the funds raised from the public, 32 percentage points higher than the Better Business Bureau 35 percent cost guideline.[64]

If Pallotta TeamWorks had taken 99.1 percent of its $23.3 million in Breast Cancer 3-Day marketing expenses and reported them as going to the cause instead of as fundraising expenses, our historic return of 60 percent of every donor's dollar going to the cause would have immediately risen to 67.4 percent. If we had taken 50 percent of all our expenses for all our events[65] and said they went to the cause, our returns would have jumped to 80 percent, simply as a result of redefining the cause. We would have been the poster child for "efficiency," met every watchdog standard ever set, and inoculated ourselves against any criticism about percentages.[66] Figure 4 shows how simple accounting changes could have dramatically improved the percentage of donor dollars we reported as going to the cause.

All of the percentage returns cited in this book for Pallotta TeamWorks' events were calculated with 0 percent of event-related costs allocated to the cause.

The focus on percentages is misleading even absent asymmetric accounting practice, because it ignores differences in scale, as discussed earlier. The following story appeared in the *Boston Globe* on September 14, 2003, about a year after we went out of business:

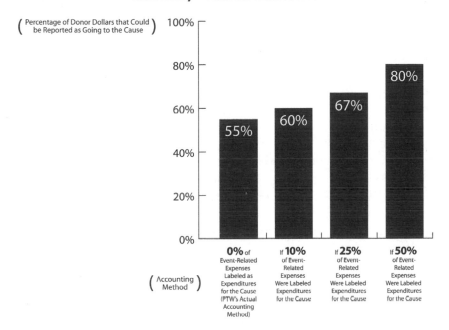

Figure 4. Pallotta TeamWorks, 1994–2002: Percentage of Donor Dollars That Could Be Reported as Going to the Cause with Varying Accounting Methods
(Based on total expenses of $275,650,170 and net income of $305,620,303 with no event-related expenses allocated to the cause.)

Pallotta TeamWorks, a Los Angeles fund-raising company, came under fire when critics complained that only a small percentage of fund-raising proceeds actually went toward AIDS and cancer research while the rest went to high overhead costs. . . . Because [Pallotta TeamWorks'] popular Boston-to-New York bike ride for AIDS shut down in a swirl of controversy last year, about 60 cyclists came out yesterday for a new ride, one that they say will prove the fund-raiser can be done right. The [new] AIDS ride began at 6 a.m. in front of the popular South End hangout Club Cafe and ended 125 miles later in Provincetown. So far, the cyclists have raised $125,000 for AIDS/HIV research and outreach.[67]

By contrast, our AIDSRide from Boston to New York had an average of 2,626 riders each year, and an average of $3.11 million went to charity each year for a total of $24.87 million after all expenses.[68] If we compare firsts, the first year of our event had 3,556 riders, netted $4.38 million for charity, and had a return of 67.7 percent of every donation going back to the cause.[69] What we *netted* was thirty-five times what this other event *grossed*.

The media teaches us that it's better to raise $125,000 for the needy instead of tens of millions of dollars if you have a better *percentage* — that is, it's better to send a high percentage of a small amount of money to charity than to send a lower percentage of a very large amount of money to charity. This is what they call proving that a "fund-raiser can be done right."

Thoughtful people who have considered the problems of raising funds for charitable causes realize there are legitimate reasons to prefer a large amount of money over meeting artificial percentage measurements. As Justice William J. Brennan, writing for the U.S. Supreme Court in the 1988 *Riley* case, noted, "A charity might choose a particular type of fundraising drive, or a particular solicitor, expecting to receive a large sum as measured by total dollars rather than the percentage of dollars remitted."[70] Yet this percentage measurement is the one we are taught to revere.

1995–1996

Controversy about "efficiency" ratios began almost with our first success. In our first two years of producing the events, we netted a total of $8.6 million for charity. Percentage returns were 73 percent in 1994, and 67 percent in 1995.[71] Then, in 1996, we did an event in Philadelphia that was plagued by controversy about racism, and our percentage returns were low. We were subsequently fined by the Pennsylvania attorney general because the *percentage* returns fell below what they claimed we had said they would be. We had produced only three events up until that year, and none of them had performed poorly. We had not been in the habit of guaranteeing any particular percentage return, but thereafter made it explicit on all donation forms that we made no guarantees about percentage returns. In the settlement we admitted no wrongdoing.

1998

In 1998, we launched the Breast Cancer 3-Days, and they met with tremendous success, netting more than $20 million in their first two years.[72] I was the focus of a cover story in the *Los Angeles Times Magazine* in May 1998 headlined "Rider in the Storm . . . 'Dan Pallotta's Fundraisers Have Made Millions for AIDS Charities. So Why Are People Mad at Him?' "[73] Although the story was positive, a sensational narrative was gathering momentum.

2000

By the beginning of 2000, we had netted a total of $91.07 million. The AIDSRides had an average return of 55 percent, the Breast Cancer 3-Days, 59 percent. In addition to twelve other events, that year we launched the Alaska AIDS Vaccine Ride specifically to raise money for AIDS vaccine research (as opposed to our other AIDSRides, which raised funds for local services). Our aim was to liberate researchers from the distraction of writing grants instead of performing critical research. We borrowed money from our bank to finance the event and shielded the charity from any losses in case the event was not successful. I put my home up as collateral. The event was successful: 1,494 of us bicycled for a week across Alaska—one day in the snow with temperatures below freezing—and netted $4.1 million for vaccine research at three of the leading AIDS research institutions in America.[74]

A year later, at the end of 2000, we had netted a total of $154.61 million for charity. Our average percentage return across all events for all years was 60 percent.[75] At the time, this was exactly what the Better Business Bureau recommended as a threshold return. Still, the media would write about our expense ratios, often dredging up the Philadelphia experience and some lone ACT-UP activist's scathing opinion about us.

2001

On the basis of the significant success of our inaugural Alaska event the year before, and in addition to thirteen other AIDS and breast cancer events we had planned for 2001, we unveiled an ambitious trio of AIDS Vaccine Rides (Alaska, again, one across Montana, and another across the Canadian border). Once again, we borrowed the financing from our bank so the charities did not have to put up any money, and we shielded them from any financial liability. But the market wasn't ready for three AIDS vaccine events, and we couldn't attract enough riders to match the *percentage* results of the year before. Still, we netted another $4 million for charity. But our *percentage* returns on those three rides were significantly below standards set by the Better Business Bureau and others. Of every donor dollar contributed, 21.37 percent ($4.01 million total) remained for charitable service.[76]

This led to a highly publicized lawsuit by a rider who claimed that we did not meet a certain threshold for percentage return to charity on the

Vaccine Rides. The Vaccine Rides had netted more than $8 million by this point.[77] These funds were making critical AIDS vaccine trials possible—trials that had no other source of funding.

Nonetheless, the disappointing *percentage* return inflamed critics. While all the attention was focused on the percentage returns of these three bike rides, the other thirteen events we produced netted a total of $65.01 million for AIDS and breast cancer *in the year 2001 alone,* bringing our eight-year total amount netted for charity to $223.63 million. Our average percentage return on all events was 57 percent, just three points below the Better Business Bureau's recommendation.[78]

The high-profile nature of these disappointments gave critics and the media powerful ammunition. Judgments were made in moral terms. One group ran an ad against us that said, "Pallotta TeamWorks' high-profile, low-benefit events betray participants" and asked, "Can we afford to have our charity donations squandered by a private company pursuing profit over purpose?"[79] In other communication materials, they wrote:

> Pallotta's actions, in our view, have reached such a pinnacle of disrepute that they threaten not only the AIDS organizations that are still bound by contracts with Pallotta TeamWorks, but indeed threaten the credibility of the AIDS movement itself. Negative publicity regarding Pallotta TeamWorks and its tactics is now garnering front-page attention.[80]

Experimentation was creating controversy, and the controversy itself was creating more controversy.

Another story around the same time conflated low percentage returns with the fact that we were a for-profit company, quoting a critic saying, "'Shame on Pallotta,' . . . for us to have to witness his greed and unabashed profiteering off the good intentions of others. People with AIDS do not need his services. We can learn from Hawaii's Paradise Ride, a grass roots organization that donates directly to AIDS organizations themselves."[81] The 2004 annual report of the Paradise Ride's charity states, "Nearly 43 riders came together to pedal across O'ahu, Maui, Moloka'I . . . raising more than $100,000 for Life Foundation."[82] Our 2001 AIDS Vaccine Rides *netted* forty times more. The report doesn't give the percentage returns. On the subject of greed, my 2001 salary was $394,500, or about *three-tenths of 1 percent* of the $133.05 million donated to our events that year.[83]

Bill O'Reilly similarly took the opportunity to distort a good-faith disappointment that netted $4 million for AIDS and present it as a scam, judging all of our events and results on the basis of one event that hadn't done as well as the others:

> What we have here is the people who run the Pallotta TeamWorks organization—and again, you may not know the name out there ladies and gentlemen, but if you've been pitched to walk or ride for AIDS or breast cancer, chances are it's—the executives of this company are getting very wealthy off this. If they're keeping $20 million out of $28 million. That's a lot of jack. . . . Basically Pallotta is selling Americans, hey, you go out, you raise the money. For every mile you walk, you know, people give you money. You give it to us. We give it to AIDS and breast cancer. However, they're not giving it. They're only giving 30 percent of it.[84]

My salary for the three Vaccine Rides in question totaled approximately $73,968. Bill O'Reilly's salary, on the other hand, for criticizing our efforts and making it harder to raise money for AIDS on top of it, was reported in 2004 to be $20 million. On the *Tonight Show*, he said that "his wealth doesn't define him, it only serves to provide security for his family."[85] Perhaps so. But he certainly uses the notion of wealth to define others, however erroneously. Our fee for producing the three events was *not* $20 million. It was $1.02 million.[86] Ironically, the amount we spent on marketing and advertising to motivate people on the issue, much of it on the kind of television advertising that generates Mr. O'Reilly's salary, was $7.8 million.[87] The media's profit had to have far exceeded any that we earned.

If the ultimate consequence of large-scale charitable experimentation is to crucify anyone who fails, how will we ever have anything more than forty people on bicycles trying to end the AIDS epidemic? If we only measure charitable initiatives by percentages and not results, how will we ever produce great results? If we forever conflate efficiency with impact, how will we ever have a tremendous impact?

Summary

In all of these ways we challenged conventions. Our methods worked. Yet every new practice that worked met with new criticism. Criticism on any one of these fronts would have been debilitating. Criticism on all of them at the same time created a perfect storm of controversy. It was ultimately more than a small company, or its charitable beneficiaries, could withstand. If what works best at raising money to alleviate suffering is not allowed to work because it offends a construction of morality, then something is wrong with our construction of morality.

Collapse of the Company

Around the time in 2001 that controversy was reaching a fever pitch, a board member of the Los Angeles Gay & Lesbian Center told us the center was considering discontinuing having us produce the extremely successful California AIDSRide on its behalf. It was considering this, it was said, in large part because expenses were over budget, and because, after seven years with returns above 60 percent, 2001 returns had fallen to almost 50 percent.[88] The director of one of the charities was quoted as saying that "Pallotta TeamWorks exceeded the expense budget dramatically and it appears the cost of fund-raising will come in at 50 cents on the dollar."[89] The *Advocate* reminded everyone about efficiency standards: "The Better Business Bureau's Wise Giving Alliance recommends fund-raising costs not exceed 35 cents for every dollar of related contributions."[90] We disagreed about whether we were actually over budget, but percentage expenses were high in part because we had invested in new infrastructure to improve the safety and quality of the production, as I mentioned earlier, which caused a one-year spike in expenses, and in part because we had halted rider registration too soon, believing we would be short on campsite space, which artificially reduced revenues for the year. Still, the 2001 ride netted more than $5.9 million for AIDS services after all expenses.[91]

We were told that some major donors to one of the charities were threatening to stop giving because of the elevated expenses of the ride. One critic was quoted as saying that "she was 'appalled' that only 50 cents for every dollar went to charity."[92] California AIDSRide had netted $41.6 million after all expenses for this charity's services and those of the San Francisco AIDS Foundation in the eight years since it began—an average of about $5 million per year.[93] Were the donors and critics who were pressuring the board and the charity to cut ties with Pallotta TeamWorks prepared to match the dollars that might be lost if their notion that it could be done better proved to be inaccurate?

The *Berkeley Daily Planet* wrote that the two charities "say . . . Pallotta TeamWorks . . . has mismanaged the event and increased its overhead so much that they're better off running it themselves."[94] There was no evidence or data to support that they could. However, the pressure charities are under to conform to these percentage standards is so intense that they often feel they have no choice.

These charities were not alone. The *Nonprofit Overhead Cost Project* found:

Nonprofits are responding to perceived and explicit pressure to keep real and reported administrative and fundraising costs low. One agency was planning to change its functional expense allocation method because reported administrative and fundraising costs were higher than those reported by peer agencies. Another had been threatened with having its funding cut off by one funder because its overall administrative and fundraising cost ratio was too high. A third reported that maintaining a lean, low-cost administrative cost structure was important in maintaining ongoing funding support. Other sites noted that low overhead is a factor in winning public sector funding and that funders and donors are even more sensitive to the level of fundraising costs than they are to the level of administrative costs.[95]

The two charities went forward with plans to produce their own version of the ride. A spokesperson for one of the charities said, "'We really have no choice. . . . California AIDSRide has generated a quarter of our budget for years. . . . We need [the new ride] in order to provide essential services to our clients.'"[96]

That was just the tip of the iceberg. Around the time of the charities' decision, but unknown to us, the Avon Products Foundation, beneficiary of the Breast Cancer 3-Days, was considering parting ways with us as well. It was coming on 2002, which would be our most successful year, with $81.98 million netted for charity, bringing our nine-year total net to charity to $305.62 million.[97]

By this time our company had grown significantly: we had 350 full-time employees and had just moved into a new 50,000-square-foot headquarters, after years in segregated, cramped, and mostly un-air-conditioned quarters. The new space was an empty tilt-up warehouse, and we had just put $2 million into outfitting it for our operation—pretty much everything we had. This was not to lay down marble floors. We used raw exposed lumber on the walls and shipping containers for executive offices.

We had spent the past two years centralizing our operations. The business was no longer modular—it was all connected. The Breast Cancer 3-Day program was by far the largest event series we had. It was slated to be more than 75 percent of our 2003 business. If for any reason it was damaged, our business would not be able to survive. It would be like McDonald's losing the hamburger. As in the previous two years, we had borrowed funds to launch new events for new causes in 2002. This time, for the first time in our history, several events lost money, some because of the impact of September 11, which occurred the week we were to begin promoting the new events, and some because the causes were not popular. We were indebted to our bank for about $6 million. While this was a huge setback, it wasn't enough to put us out of business. The Breast Cancer 3-Day program was robust; we were profitable enough to be able to pay off the bank debt in two to three years, and our bank was prepared to allow us to do so.

Then the unthinkable happened. The Avon Products Foundation appropriated our Breast Cancer 3-Day event concept, in violation of one of our many contracts with them. That led to the cancellation of plans to continue the Breast Cancer 3-Days in 2003 with another charity.[98] Within days we were out of business. We were not in a position to scale down.

One of Avon's principal explanations was that it was concerned about rising costs and our loss of focus on the cause. This in a year when we netted $77.5 million for the breast cancer cause, $26 million more than we had netted for them the year before, and $13 million more than we had projected to net for them for the year in our contracts.[99] Avon also expressed concern about the Better Business Bureau raising its standard of the minimum percentage that should go to the cause from 60 to 65 percent. Like our AIDSRide charities, Avon was also suffering from battle fatigue as a result of the criticism being leveled at us.

Despite this, we simply had not adequately imagined that a charity committed to the breast cancer cause would walk away from a $77.5 million annual net revenue stream for breast cancer research.

It was April 2002 when Avon told us they wanted to part ways with us. We had already begun planning for the 2003 events. We were caught off guard, without any time to find a replacement charity for the program. Somehow, though, within a week we found another interested charity and began a four-month due-diligence process, with the goal of launching fifteen Breast Cancer 3-Days in 2003. For the next four months, hard-eyed consultants for our bank and accountants from one of the Big Five accounting firms engaged in an intense due-diligence process, which we passed. The bank was ready to restructure our loan, and the charity was all set to sign our new deal for the Breast Cancer 3-Days. It was the first week of August.

Then, on August 11, 2002, Avon announced to the world, in full-page newspaper ads, that they would themselves be staging multiday breast cancer walks in 2003. As an arbitrator later found, Avon's events were the same in material respects as the 3-Days.[100] They were also planned for some of our most successful cities on dates very close to the traditional dates our events were held. Once again, we were caught off guard. We learned about Avon's events from a telephone call the day before the rest of the world heard about them.

Within days of the ads running, our new partner told us they had to call off the deal. They felt the Avon events were the same as the 3-Days and that they would jeopardize the 3-Days' ability to meet revenue projections and drive percentage costs up. There was no time to find a replacement. The 3-Days required about $10 to 12 million in annual financing. We couldn't find a new $12 million funding source overnight all over again, and there were employees to be paid and lights to be kept on that week.

On August 23, we laid off all 350 of our employees, including myself and the entire executive team, both at our headquarters in California and at some sixteen field offices around the United States. It was a horrible day. It was a death in every respect. A company that had taken ten years of sweat equity to build, that was producing the most remarkable benefits for people with AIDS and breast cancer, that was breaking fundraising records all over the United States closed its doors.

Shortly thereafter, we sued Avon for breach of contract. In the contract on which we sued, Avon had guaranteed that it would not use our event concept. Specifically, the contract stated:

> The multi-city . . . walkathon event with a 4-figure minimum pledge required of participants, as well as the marketing and fund-raising tools used to make the event successful, are original concepts of TeamWorks and Avon guarantees that they shall not be used, by Avon regardless of the termination of this Agreement, without the express written consent of TeamWorks.[101]

No one at Avon ever asked for our consent, written or otherwise.

A David versus Goliath battle ensued. Weeks after we filed the lawsuit, Avon filed a countersuit, in part demanding an accounting for the five years of the 3-Day program and, eventually, claiming that it was owed some $20 million.[102]

In July 2005, three years after the suit was filed, and after sixty-six full days of hearing and testimony that lasted over one year and generated a 22,000-page record, an independent arbitrator ruled in Pallotta TeamWorks' favor on our breach of contract claim. He acknowledged that Avon "entered into multiple contracts containing idea protection provisions over the course of four years."[103] He stated that the contract on which we sued "precludes Avon's unauthorized use of the 3Day event and/or event concept and certain fundraising and marketing tools."[104] He further stated, "PTW has also shown by a preponderance of the evidence that the two events are the same in material respects. The nature of the events is the same . . . The structure of the events is the same in material respects . . . In addition, certain other important features are the same."[105] He also stated that, "The Arbitrator finds that the Avon Walk is the same as the 3Day in material respects and, therefore, that Avon has made an unauthorized use of a protected idea."[106] He found that Pallotta TeamWorks' former senior vice president's "memo referring to the '2-Day walk concept' is 'basically the 3-Day concept shortened to 2 days'" "supports the PTW contention that Avon appropriated the 3Day event."[107]

He also found that "PTW has proven with the requisite certainty that Avon's breach of Section IB.7.2 is the actual and direct cause of PTW's loss of the [charity] opportunity," referring to the loss of the new charitable partner we were going to do the events with in 2003, and that "absent the breach, [charity] would have entered into a contract with PTW and the contract would have become effective."[108]

As for Avon's $20 million counterclaim, after an exhaustive review the arbitrator denied all but $474,361 of it, about half of which was related to a dispute over which of us owned the giant dining tents used for the events.[109] We argued that we did.

With respect to Avon's $8.4 million claim related to the method by which we allocated costs to all our events, the arbitrator found that "PTW did not violate the Contract," that "PTW did not violate its fiduciary duty to Avon," and that "Avon has not shown that PTW violated the Contract with respect to any of the charges allocated to Avon in 2002."[110] With respect to our cost allocations, he further stated:

> PTW sent to Avon very detailed invoices and other documentation that reflected the precise percentages charged to Avon for a particular cost under the fairness split. As a sophisticated entity, Avon had the capacity to understand what it was being charged . . . PTW fulfilled whatever fiduciary obligation may have existed to make full disclosure of the relevant facts.[111]

He also stated that "PTW did not act improperly."[112]

Avon claimed it was owed $9.3 million related to invoices, expense documentation, and final reports that we never provided to them.[113] We argued that we could not provide the invoices in large part because of the disruption Avon had caused in our business.[114] The arbitrator found that the "documents that Avon sought should have been provided." He wrote that "The Arbitrator further finds that PTW's explanations may excuse a late provision of the invoices and reports, but cannot excuse a total failure to provide this documentation."[115] However, the arbitrator concluded, "while Avon was entitled to an accounting of the $9,310,923 for which no invoices had been filed, PTW provided such an accounting at the Arbitration Hearing. Avon is not entitled to any further relief with respect to this claim."[116]

Impact on Organizations' AIDS and Breast Cancer Fundraising

Charities' AIDS Fundraising

"AIDS Lifecycle" was the name the charities decided on for the event that copied our California AIDSRide concept. A spokesperson for one of the charities said:

> We broke away believing we had to protect the people we're here to serve, people living with HIV and AIDS, to protect our ability to provide the services they need. . . . We believe we made the right decision.[117]

What resulted was a drop in net returns to charity from $6.0 million to $1.6 million.[118] *Percentage* returns, using a "Traditional Calculation," fell from 51.8 to 34 percent.[119] These figures compare the 2001 California AIDSRide we produced for the charities with the 2002 AIDS Lifecycle they produced on their own. The figures come from an independent group called the Care Exchange, made up of riders from the events and not affiliated with the charities or Pallotta TeamWorks.[120]

Shortly after the AIDS Lifecycle event, the executive director of the Los Angeles Gay & Lesbian Center at the time resigned.[121] Within days of the event the *San Francisco Examiner* reported that the San Francisco AIDS Foundation would lay off twenty-eight of its one hundred workers "in the wake of falling federal aid and poorly performing fund-raising events," and the *San Francisco Chronicle* reported that the organization would cut its budget to $20.7 million, down from $24 million.[122] Gay.com/PlanetOut.com reported that the Los Angeles Gay & Lesbian Center "eliminated 55 jobs, or 20 percent of its work force."[123]

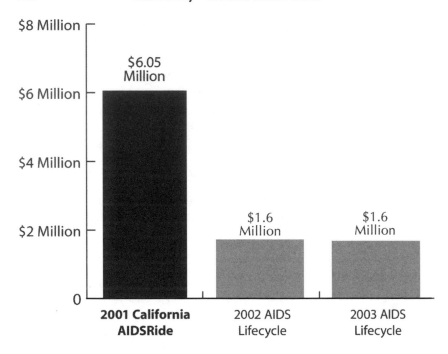

Figure 5. Dollar Return to Charities, 2001–2003
SOURCE: Care Exchange.

In the second year of AIDS Lifecycle, 2003, ridership increased, but the charities' net results were similar. The Care Exchange reported a $1.6 million total return to the charities from AIDS Lifecycle, compared with $6.0 million for the 2001 California AIDSRide we produced for them.[124] Care Exchange calculated the 2003 AIDS Lifecycle percentage return at 37 percent, slightly higher than the year before, but 14 percentage points lower than the 51.8 percent for the 2001 California AIDS-Ride.[125] Figures 5 and 6 show the Care Exchange data.

To the charities' great credit, the AIDS Lifecycle results improved in subsequent years, but it took the charities six years (until 2007) to get fundraising back up to the level, in unadjusted dollars, California AIDSRide was already achieving for them in 2001. California AIDS-Ride raised $11.58 million in 2001, the year the charities parted ways with us.[126] Income and rider numbers had grown slightly from 2000 to 2001. It is difficult to say how much it would have been raising by 2007 if the decision to launch AIDS Lifecycle had never been made,

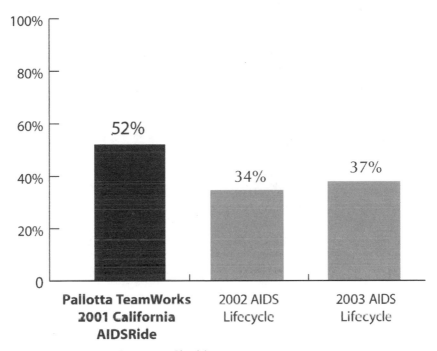

Figure 6. Percentage Return to Charities, 2001–2003
SOURCE: Care Exchange.

but we had the advantage of a national database of more than 65,000 AIDS riders, another 120,000 people who had participated in other events, and hundreds of thousands of information seekers, as well as a national field office operation and national advertising. But even if one starts with the assumption that California AIDSRide would not have grown at all from 2002 to 2007, the cumulative negative variance in gross income it might have raised for the charities over what they raised with AIDS Lifecycle for the same period totals approximately $29 million.[127]

After we went out of business, with the exception of California, there were no AIDS cycling events that replaced what we had been doing on anywhere close to the same scale as our most successful events. The events that sprang up were independent of one another. They netted hundreds of thousands of dollars where once there were millions. The media's spin on one of these was, "Charities Cut the Fat."[128] Typically missing the point, they failed to ask what happened to the muscle.

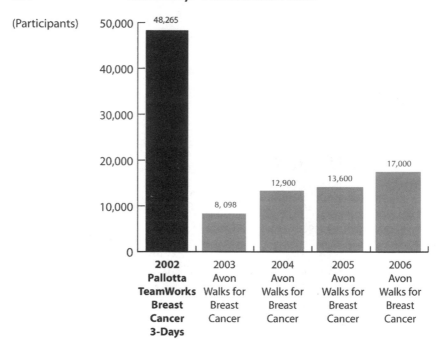

Figure 7. Total Walkers/Participants

SOURCE: The data for this figure were derived from the following sources: Avon Foundation, "News on the Avon Walk for Breast Cancer 2003 and 2004." "Avon Foundation" website, 2004, http://walk.avonfoundation.org, accessed January 26, 2005; The Avon Foundation, "Avon Walk for Breast Cancer: Summary of Results and Funding Grants Announced at Each Closing Ceremony," "Avon Foundation" website, 2004, http://walk.avonfoundation.org, accessed January 26, 2005; "Local and National Communities Receive $3 Million to Fight Breast Cancer," Avon Foundation press release, New York, October 2, 2005; "Local Communities Receive More Than $1 Million to Fight Breast Cancer," Avon Foundation press release, Denver, June 26, 2005; "Local Communities Receive More Than $1.4 Million to Fight Breast Cancer," Avon Foundation press release, Los Angeles, September 18, 2005; "Local Communities Receive More Than $2 Million to Fight Breast Cancer," Avon Foundation press release, San Francisco, July 10, 2005; "Local Communities Receive More Than $2,150,000 to Fight Breast Cancer," Avon Foundation press release, Chicago, June 5, 2005; "Local Communities Receive More Than $2,250,000 to Fight Breast Cancer," Avon Foundation press release, Boston, May 15, 2005; "Local Communities Receive More Than $2.7 Million to Fight Breast Cancer," Avon Foundation press release, Washington, D.C., May 1, 2005; "Local Communities Receive More Than $500,000 to Fight Breast Cancer," Avon Foundation press release, Charlotte, NC, April 17, 2005; "Avon Walk for Breast Cancer Boston Raises $6.3 Million," Avon Foundation press release, Boston, May 21, 2006; "Avon Walk for Breast Cancer Chicago 2006 Raises $8.2 Million—Sets Record for Annual Event," Avon Foundation press release, Chicago, June 25, 2006; "Avon Walk for Breast Cancer Denver 2006 Raises over $2 Million," Avon Foundation press release, Denver, June 25, 2006; "Avon Walk for Breast Cancer Los Angeles Raises over $3.6 Million," Avon Foundation press

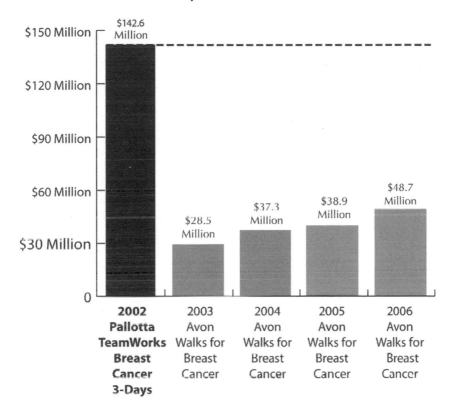

Figure 8. Total Raised

Avon Walks' Breast Cancer Fundraising

Unfortunately, this pales in comparison with what happened to Avon's breast cancer fundraising when Avon replaced the Breast Cancer 3-Days with their own multiday walks called the "Avon Walks for Breast Cancer." Walker numbers fell from 48,265 to 8,098.[129] The total raised fell from $142.6 million to $28.5 million.[130] (These figures compare our

release, Long Beach, CA, September 17, 2006; "Avon Walk for Breast Cancer New York Breaks Records, Raises $9.7 Million," Avon Foundation press release, New York, October 8, 2006; "Avon Walk for Breast Cancer San Francisco Raises over $5.4 Million," Avon Foundation press release, San Francisco, July 9, 2006; "Avon Walk for Breast Cancer Washington, D.C. Raises $5.8 Million," Avon Foundation press release, Washington, D.C., April 30, 2006.

Some of the Avon Walk for Breast Cancer figures may include volunteer crew members.

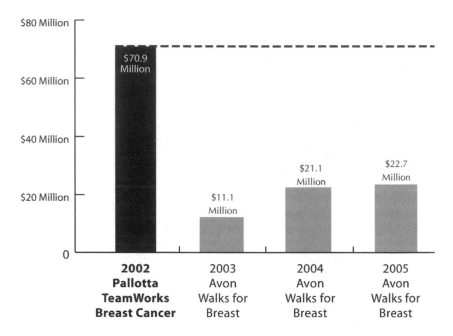

Figure 9. Estimated Net Income Available for Grant Making After Expenses

2002 Breast Cancer 3-Day results with the 2003 results of the events Avon produced on their own.)

Worse, estimates indicate that net income available for making grants dropped from $70.9 million to $11.1 million, a $59.8 million negative variance over what our events had achieved the year before.[131]

On a per-event basis, our 2002 Breast Cancer 3-Days raised an average of $11 million. That figure fell to $3.6 million on the 2003 Avon walks.[132]

A year later, Avon saw similar differences. Their 2004 walks raised $37.3 million.[133] This compares with $142.6 million on our 2002 events—a $105.3 million negative variance. The total amounts Avon raised for 2005 and 2006 were $38.9 million and $48.7 million, respectively, annual negative variances of about $104 million and $94 million below what they had been raising with us in 2002.[134] The combined gross variance for Avon over the four-year period, comparing what they might have raised with us and what they actually raised, using our 2002 results as a baseline and assuming the Pallotta TeamWorks events would not have grown (in fact, they were growing and were going to expand to new cities), totals $417 million just through 2006—approaching half a *billion* dollars.[135]

Net dollars available for making grants seem to have followed the same pattern. Compared with the 3-Days in 2002, estimates using Avon's financial statements indicate a $49.8 million negative variance in 2004 and a $48.3 million negative variance in 2005.[136] Added to the estimated $59.8 million 2003 variance, this totals $157 million in just three years.

In terms of percentage costs, Tinkelman writes, "If one compares the total of Avon's fund-raising costs and joint costs it allocated to programs to the gross receipts from the public, the resulting event cost ratios for the four years 2003 through 2006 are 67%, 46%, 46% and 52%."[137] He notes that all four years would have failed to meet the Better Business Bureau 35 percent guidelines. He further notes that Avon's percentage results compare "unfavorably" with the results for the Breast Cancer 3-Day events we produced for them, "which had average event cost ratios of around 41% through 2001."[138]

Figures 7, 8, and 9 show before and after data pertaining to the events Pallotta TeamWorks produced for Avon compared with the events Avon produced on their own.

This is the sum and substance of what happened. This is the cost of what we have been taught to value. This is one example of the stakes in the conversation. A company that might have functioned as a model for a new paradigm instead became an example of what happens when old ways are challenged. Nobody gained here. Not Pallotta Teamworks, and not the people it tried to serve. Good people with good intentions were placed at odds with one another. Fundraising scales that took years to achieve were sent back in time. The future became a victim of the past.

I have presented this case study for two reasons. First, to dispel any notion that those who operate in the nonprofit sector have the same freedom we give to business to use the tools of the free market and capitalism. Every time Pallotta TeamWorks attempted to use those tools in their fullest expression, whether that was with massive paid advertising campaigns, stunning printed materials, compensation that acknowledged self-interest, cross-promotion of causes, taking a long-term view, taking calculated chances, or placing the value of a dollar above the value of a percentage, we found ourselves caught in the Puritan stranglehold on our contemporary values. Let this be a warning to those who venture down the same path. Until we change the fundamental way we think about charity, they will face a fundamentally similar fate.

Second, my purpose has been to use a very large scale social experiment to quantify and chart the social disruption caused by society's insistence on loyalty to an ideology that is fundamentally flawed, in the hope that people might see that the case for its future no longer exists.

NOTES

Introduction (pages xi–xv)

1. Pallotta TeamWorks, "Record of Impact 1994–2002," summary of fund-raising results (Los Angeles, 2006).
2. Allen Grossman and Liz Kind, "Pallotta TeamWorks," Harvard Business School paper no. N1-302-089, April 12, 2002.
3. Pallotta TeamWorks, "Record of Impact 1994–2002" (Los Angeles, 2006); with respect to Pallotta TeamWorks' events, all references to "net income" or funds available for charitable purposes "after all expenses" or "net income available for grant making after expenses" or similar phrases exclude donation processing and/or service charges charitable beneficiaries may have paid their financial institutions.

Chapter 1: The Morality of Outcomes (pages 1–34)

1. Francis J. Bremer, *John Winthrop: America's Forgotten Founding Father* (Oxford: Oxford University Press, 2003), pp. 180, 188. John Winthrop, *The Journal of John Winthrop, 1630–1649,* ed. Richard S. Dunn et al. (Cambridge: Belknap Press of Harvard University Press, 1996), p. xix.
2. Perry Miller and Thomas H. Johnson, *The Puritans: A Sourcebook of Their Writings, Two Volumes Bound as One* (Mineola, NY: Dover Publications, Inc., 2001), p. 195.
3. Ibid., p. 198.
4. Ibid., p. 199.
5. John Calvin, *Calvin: Institutes of the Christian Religion,* 2 vols., ed. John T. McNeill, trans. Ford Lewis Battles (Louisville, KY: Westminister John Knox Press, 1960), pp. 251–252.
6. David E. Parks, "Calvin: The Man and His Doctrine," "Waterford Church of Christ" website, http://www.wcofc.org/deep/calvin%20the%20source%20of%20his%20doctrin.htm, accessed December 13, 2006.
7. Ellison Research, "Most Americans Believe Non-Profits Spend Too Much on Overhead," Ellison Research website, http://www.ellisonresearch.com/releases/20080213.htm, accessed March 5, 2008, p. 1.

8. Penelope Wang, "Making Your Generosity Pay," *Money* online, December 2004, via Lexis-Nexis, http://web.lexis-nexis.com, accessed June 30, 2006.
9. Suzanne Perry, "Public Confidence in Nonprofit Groups Slides Back New Survey Finds," *Chronicle of Philanthropy,* April 3, 2008. p. 12.
10. Center on Philanthropy at Indiana University, *Giving USA 2007: The Annual Report on Philanthropy for the Year 2006* (Bloomington, IN: Giving USA Foundation, 2007), p. 12.
11. Ibid., p. 8.
12. Harvy Lipman, "Americans Give Bigger Share to Charity Than Residents of Other Countries," *Chronicle of Philanthropy: The Newspaper of the Nonprofit World* online, November 22, 2006, http://philanthropy.com/free/update/2006/11/2006112202.htm, accessed November 27, 2006.
13. National Center for Charitable Statistics 2007, "The Nonprofit Sector in Brief: Facts and Figures from the *Nonprofit Almanac 2007*" (Washington, DC: Urban Institute Press, 2007), p. 4.
14. Ibid., pp. 1, 3.
15. Ibid., p. 3.
16. Alexis De Tocqueville, *"Democracy in America" and Two Essays on America,* trans. Gerald E. Bevan (London: Penguin Books, 2003), p. xxxv.
17. Center on Philanthropy at Indiana University, *Giving USA 2007: The Annual Report on Philanthropy for the Year 2006* (Bloomington, IN: Giving USA Foundation, 2007).
18. Grameen Foundation, "2006 Annual Report" (Washington, DC: Grameen Foundation, 2006).
19. Ibid., p. 10.
20. Steve Lohr, "A Capitalist Jolt for Charity," *New York Times,* February 24, 2008, http://www.nytimes.com/2008/02/24/business/24social.html, accessed February 25, 2008, p. 1.
21. Ibid., p. 3.
22. Jonathan Rauch, "'This Is Not Charity,'" *Atlantic Monthly* 300, no. 3 (October 2007).
23. Hernando De Soto, *The Mystery of Capital: Why Capitalism Triumphs in the West and Fails Everywhere Else* (New York: Basic Books, 2000), p. 1.
24. Center on Philanthropy at Indiana University, *Giving USA 2007: The Annual Report on Philanthropy for the Year 2006* (Bloomington, IN: Giving USA Foundation, 2007), p. 45.
25. John Kenneth Galbraith, *The Affluent Society* (Boston: Houghton Mifflin Company, 1958), p. 7.
26. Stephen Innes, *Creating the Commonwealth: The Economic Culture of Puritan New England* (New York: W.W. Norton & Company, 1995), p. 101.
27. Amanda Porterfield, "Protestant Missionaries: Pioneers of American Philanthropy," in *Charity, Philanthropy, and Civility in American History,* ed. Lawrence J. Friedman and Mark D. McGarvie (Cambridge: Cambridge University Press, 2003), pp. 49, 51.
28. Ibid., p. 52.

29. Stephen Innes, *Creating the Commonwealth: The Economic Culture of Puritan New England* (New York: W.W. Norton & Company, 1995), p. 12.

30. Perry Miller and Thomas H. Johnson, *The Puritans: A Sourcebook of Their Writings, Two Volumes Bound as One* (Mineola, NY: Dover Publications, Inc., 2001), p. 1.

31. Ibid., p. 1.

32. Stephen Innes, *Creating the Commonwealth: The Economic Culture of Puritan New England* (New York: W.W. Norton & Company, 1995), p. 34.

33. Francis J. Bremer, *John Winthrop: America's Forgotten Founding Father* (Oxford: Oxford University Press, 2003), p. 184.

34. Ibid.

35. Perry Miller and Thomas H. Johnson, *The Puritans: A Sourcebook of Their Writings, Two Volumes Bound as One* (Mineola, NY: Dover Publications, Inc., 2001), p. 199.

36. Stephen Innes, *Creating the Commonwealth: The Economic Culture of Puritan New England* (New York: W.W. Norton & Company, 1995), p. 92.

37. John Winthrop, "A Model of Christian Charity" (1630), http://religious freedom.lib.virginia.edu/sacred/charity.html, accessed November 14, 2006.

38. Stephen Innes, *Creating the Commonwealth: The Economic Culture of Puritan New England* (New York: W.W. Norton & Company, 1995), pp. 97 98.

39. Ibid., p. 56.

40. Ibid., p. 61.

41. Ibid., p. 9.

42. Ibid., p. 5.

43. Ibid., p. 9.

44. Ibid., p. 121.

45. Ibid.

46. Perry Miller, *The New England Mind: The Seventeenth Century* (Cambridge: Belknap Press of Harvard University Press, 1939), p. 474.

47. Ibid., p. 477.

48. Max Weber, *"The Protestant Ethic and the 'Spirit' of Capitalism" and Other Writings,* ed. and trans. Peter Baehr and Gordon C. Wells (New York: Penguin Books, 2002), pp. 184–185.

49. Ibid., p. 110.

50. Stephen Innes, *Creating the Commonwealth: The Economic Culture of Puritan New England* (New York: W.W. Norton & Company, 1995), p. 188.

51. Ibid., p. 122.

52. Ibid., p. 123.

53. Ibid., p. 310.

54. Ibid., p. 125.

55. Perry Miller, *The New England Mind: The Seventeenth Century* (Cambridge: Belknap Press of Harvard University Press, 1939), p. 43.

56. Stephen Innes, *Creating the Commonwealth: The Economic Culture of Puritan New England* (New York: W.W. Norton & Company, 1995), p. 97.

57. Perry Miller, quoted in Stephen Innes, *Creating the Commonwealth: The Economic Culture of Puritan New England* (New York: W.W. Norton & Company, 1995), p. 12.

58. Max Weber, *"The Protestant Ethic and the 'Spirit' of Capitalism" and Other Writings,* ed. and trans. Peter Baehr and Gordon C. Wells (New York: Penguin Books, 2002), p. 110.

59. Stephen Innes, *Creating the Commonwealth: The Economic Culture of Puritan New England* (New York: W.W. Norton & Company, 1995), p. 25.

60. Perry Miller, quoted in Stephen Innes, *Creating the Commonwealth: The Economic Culture of Puritan New England* (New York: W.W. Norton & Company, 1995), p. 27.

61. Stephen Innes, *Creating the Commonwealth: The Economic Culture of Puritan New England* (New York: W.W. Norton & Company, 1995), p. 27.

62. Perry Miller, quoted in Stephen Innes, *Creating the Commonwealth: The Economic Culture of Puritan New England* (New York: W.W. Norton & Company, 1995), p. 28.

63. Stephen Innes, *Creating the Commonwealth: The Economic Culture of Puritan New England* (New York: W.W. Norton & Company, 1995), p. 25.

64. Ibid., p. 7.

65. Ibid., p. 310.

66. Ibid., p. 312.

67. Ibid., p. 98.

68. Ibid., p. 310.

69. Ibid.

70. Perry Miller, quoted in ibid., p. 27.

71. Hernando De Soto, *The Mystery of Capital: Why Capitalism Triumphs in the West and Fails Everywhere Else* (New York: Basic Books, 2000), p. 1.

72. Perry Miller and Thomas H. Johnson, *The Puritans: A Sourcebook of Their Writings, Two Volumes Bound as One* (Mineola, NY: Dover Publications, Inc., 2001), pp. 195, 196.

73. Richard Gross, "Giving in America: From Charity to Philanthropy," in *Charity, Philanthropy, and Civility in American History,* ed. Lawrence J. Friedman and Mark D. McGarvie (Cambridge: Cambridge University Press, 2003), p. 33.

74. Francis J. Bremer, *John Winthrop: America's Forgotten Founding Father* (Oxford: Oxford University Press, 2003), p. 174.

75. Stephen Innes, *Creating the Commonwealth: The Economic Culture of Puritan New England* (New York: W.W. Norton & Company, 1995), pp. 102–103.

76. Perry Miller and Thomas H. Johnson, *The Puritans: A Sourcebook of Their Writings, Two Volumes Bound as One* (Mineola, NY: Dover Publications, Inc., 2001), p. 195.

77. Stephen Innes, *Creating the Commonwealth: The Economic Culture of Puritan New England* (New York: W.W. Norton & Company, 1995), p. 312.

78. Ibid., p. 313.

79. Ibid., p. 36.

80. Amanda Porterfield, "Protestant Missionaries: Pioneers of American Philanthropy," in *Charity, Philanthropy, and Civility in American History,* ed. Lawrence J. Friedman and Mark D. McGarvie (Cambridge: Cambridge University Press, 2003), p. 64.

81. Lawrence J. Friedman and Mark D. McGarvie, eds., *Charity, Philanthropy, and Civility in American History* (Cambridge: Cambridge University Press. 2003), p. 24.

82. Stephen Innes, *Creating the Commonwealth: The Economic Culture of Puritan New England* (New York: W.W. Norton & Company, 1995), p. 136.

83. Max Weber, *"The Protestant Ethic and the 'Spirit' of Capitalism" and Other Writings,* ed. and trans. Peter Baehr and Gordon C. Wells (New York: Penguin Books, 2002), p. 9.

84. Stephen Innes, *Creating the Commonwealth: The Economic Culture of Puritan New England* (New York: W.W. Norton & Company, 1995), p. 136.

85. Ibid., p. 137.

86. Howard Zinn, *A People's History of the United States: 1492–Present* (New York: Harper Collins, 1980), p. 21.

87. Stephen Innes, *Creating the Commonwealth: The Economic Culture of Puritan New England* (New York: W.W. Norton & Company, 1995), p. 31.

88. Ibid., p. 32.

89. Amanda Porterfield, "Protestant Missionaries: Pioneers of American Philanthropy," in *Charity, Philanthropy, and Civility in American History,* ed. Lawrence J. Friedman and Mark D. McGarvie (Cambridge: Cambridge University Press, 2003), p. 60.

90. Stephen Innes, *Creating the Commonwealth: The Economic Culture of Puritan New England* (New York: W.W. Norton & Company, 1995), p. 32.

91. Jennifer Davis McDaid, review of *Women's Struggle for Equality,* by Jean V. Matthews, H-Women@msu.edu, May 1998, http://www.holysmoke .org/fem/fem0592.htm, accessed January 23, 2007.

92. Kathleen D. McCarthy, "Women and Political Culture," in *Charity, Philanthropy, and Civility in American History,* ed. Lawrence J. Friedman and Mark D. McGarvie (Cambridge: Cambridge University Press, 2003), p. 182.

93. Ibid., p. 183.

94. Lawrence J. Friedman and Mark D. McGarvie, eds., *Charity, Philanthropy, and Civility in American History* (Cambridge: Cambridge University Press, 2003).

95. "The Nonprofit World: Financial and Employment Trends," *Chronicle of Philanthropy: The Newspaper of the Nonprofit World* online, March 21, 2002, http://philanthropy.com/premium/articles/v14/i11/11003201.htm, accessed January 23, 2007.

96. *Merriam-Webster Dictionary,* s.v. "chastity."

97. John Calvin, *Calvin: Institutes of the Christian Religion,* 2 vols., ed. John T. McNeill, trans. Ford Lewis Battles (Louisville, KY: Westminister John Knox Press, 1960), p. 931.

98. Stephen Innes, *Creating the Commonwealth: The Economic Culture of Puritan New England* (New York: W.W. Norton & Company, 1995), p. 130.

99. Ibid., p. 116.

100. Amanda Porterfield, "Protestant Missionaries: Pioneers of American Philanthropy," in *Charity, Philanthropy, and Civility in American History*, ed. Lawrence J. Friedman and Mark D. McGarvie (Cambridge: Cambridge University Press, 2003), p. 53.

101. Robert Sobel, *The Big Board: A History of the New York Stock Market* (Washington, D.C.: Beard Books, 1965), p. 5.

102. Amanda Porterfield, "Protestant Missionaries: Pioneers of American Philanthropy," in *Charity, Philanthropy, and Civility in American History*, ed. Lawrence J. Friedman and Mark D. McGarvie (Cambridge: Cambridge University Press, 2003), p. 59.

103. Robert H. Bremner, *American Philanthropy*, 2nd ed., ed. Daniel J. Boorstin (Chicago: University of Chicago Press, 1960), pp. 11, 12.

104. DL, "Cotton Mather," "About.com" website, http://womenshistory.about.com/gi/dynamic/offsite.htm?zi=1/XJ/Ya&sdn=womenshistory&cdn=education&tm=2&f=00&tt=14&bt=0&bts=0&zu=http%3A//www.law.umkc.edu/faculty/projects/ftrials/salem/SAL_BMAT.HTM, accessed November 27, 2006.

105. Perry Miller and Thomas H. Johnson, *The Puritans: A Sourcebook of Their Writings, Two Volumes Bound as One* (Mineola, NY: Dover Publications, Inc., 2001), pp. 195, 199.

106. Howard Zinn, *A People's History of the United States: 1492–Present* (New York: Harper Collins, 1980), p. 13.

107. Ibid., p. 14.

108. Francis J. Bremer, *John Winthrop: America's Forgotten Founding Father* (Oxford: Oxford University Press, 2003), p. 314.

109. Howard Zinn, *A People's History of the United States: 1492–Present* (New York: Harper Collins, 1980), p. 15.

110. Amanda Porterfield, "Protestant Missionaries: Pioneers of American Philanthropy," in *Charity, Philanthropy, and Civility in American History*, ed. Lawrence J. Friedman and Mark D. McGarvie (Cambridge: Cambridge University Press, 2003), p. 68.

111. Ibid., pp. 68, 69.

112. John Kenneth Galbraith, *The Affluent Society* (Boston: Houghton Mifflin Company, 1958), pp. 2, 4–5.

113. Ibid., p. 3.

114. Ibid., p. 20.

Chapter 2: The Foundations of Our Misconstruction (pp. 35–127)

1. Adam Smith, *The Wealth of Nations* (New York: Modern Library, 2000), p. 15.

2. William H. Shore, *Revolution of the Heart: A New Strategy for Creating Wealth and Meaningful Change* (New York: Riverhead Books, 1995), p. 88.

3. Adam Smith, *The Theory of Moral Sentiments* (Amherst, MA: Prometheus Books, 2000), p. 3.

4. Community Wealth Ventures, Inc., "Venture Philanthropy: Landscape and Expectations," (Reston, VA: The Morino Institute, 2000).

5. Ayn Rand, *The Virtue of Selfishness: A New Concept of Egoism* (New York: Signet Books, 1961), pp. 49–51.

6. Helen Briggs, "Altruism 'in-Built' in Humans," *BBC News* online, March 3, 2006, http://news.bbc.co.uk/1/hi/sci/tech/4766490.stm, accessed October 29, 2007.

7. Ayn Rand, *The Virtue of Selfishness: A New Concept of Egoism* (New York: Signet Books, 1961), p. ix.

8. Matthew Fox, ed. *Meditations with Meister Eckhart* (Santa Fe: Bear & Company, 1983).

9. Paul Krugman, "In Praise of Cheap Labor: Bad Jobs at Bad Wages Are Better Than No Jobs at All," "Slate.com" website, March 21, 1997, http://www.slate.com/id/1918, accessed February 9, 2007.

10. Elizabeth Schwinn and Ian Wilhelm, "Nonprofit CEO's See Salaries Rise," *Chronicle of Philanthropy: The Newspaper of the Nonprofit World* on line, October 2, 2003, http://philanthropy.com/premium/articles/v15/i24/24002701.htm, accessed April 19, 2004.

11. "Beckham: Can He Save U.S. Soccer?" *Week* online, January 19, 2007, http://www.theweekmagazine.com/news/articles/news.aspx?Article ID=1896, accessed January 24, 2007.

12. Adam Smith, *The Wealth of Nations* (New York: Modern Library, 2000), p. 93.

13. Elizabeth Schwinn, "Rooting Out Errors on Charity Tax Forms," *Chronicle of Philanthropy: The Newspaper of the Nonprofit World* online, March 22, 2007, http://www.philanthropy.com/premium/articles/v19/i11/11003301.htm, accessed March 20, 2007.

14. *Randolph Riley, etc., et al. v. National Federation of the Blind of North Carolina, Inc., et al.,* no. 87–328, Supreme Court of the United States, June 29, 1988.

15. James Irvine Foundation, "About Irvine: Assets & Financial Information: Total Grantmaking," "James Irvine Foundation" website, http://www.irvine.org/about_irvine/assets/total.shtml, accessed January 27, 2008.

16. Stephen G. Greene, "Former Irvine Foundation CEO and His Wife Repay Fund for Benefits That Raised Questions," *Chronicle of Philanthropy: The Newspaper of the Nonprofit World* online, January 8, 2004, http://philanthropy.com/premium/articles/v16/i06/06004302.htm, accessed March 18, 2004; James Irvine Foundation, "About Irvine: History: Timeline," "James Irvine Foundation" website, http://www.irvine.org/about_irvine/timeline.shtml, accessed January 27, 2008.

17. James Irvine Foundation, "About Irvine: Assets & Financial Information: Asset Size and Allocation," "James Irvine Foundation" website, http://www.irvine.org/about_irvine/assets/size.shtml, accessed January 27, 2008.

18. Eric Nalder, "CEO's Rewards at Non-Profit," *San Jose Mercury News* online, April 27, 2003, http://www.bayarea.com/mld/mercurynews/news/special_packages/5278417.htm, accessed October 27, 2003.

19. Stephen G. Greene, "Former Irvine Foundation CEO and His Wife Repay Fund for Benefits That Raised Questions," *Chronicle of Philanthropy: The Newspaper of the Nonprofit World* online, January 8, 2004, http://philanthropy.com/premium/articles/v16/i06/06004302.htm, accessed March 18, 2004.

20. Eric Nalder, "CEO's Rewards at Non-Profit," *San Jose Mercury News* online, April 27, 2003, http://www.bayarea.com/mld/mercurynews/news/special_packages/5278417.htm, accessed October 27, 2003.

21. Ibid.

22. Ibid.

23. Ibid.

24. Ibid.

25. Community Wealth Ventures, Inc., "Venture Philanthropy: Landscape and Expectations," *Morino Institute Youth Social Ventures* (Reston, VA: The Morino Institute, 2000).

26. Mal Warwick, "Guess Who's Socially Responsible? Nonprofits Aren't as Nice to Their Employees as You Might Think," *Stanford Social Innovation Review* online, January 22, 2007, http://www.ssireview.org/articles/entry/guess_whos_socially_irresponsible/, accessed January 30, 2007.

27. Eric Nalder, "CEO's Rewards at Non-Profit," *San Jose Mercury News* online, April 27, 2003, http://www.bayarea.com/mld/mercurynews/news/special_packages/5278417.htm, accessed October 27, 2003.

28. Families USA, "Private Health Plans that Service Medicare Provide Lavish Compensation to Executives," "FamiliesUSA.org: The Voice for Health Care Consumers" website, June 24, 2003, http://www.familiesusa.org/resources/newsroom/press-releases/2003-press-releases/press-release-private-health-plans-that-service-medicare.html, accessed April 19, 2004.

29. Stephen G. Greene, "Former Irvine Foundation CEO and His Wife Repay Fund for Benefits That Raised Questions," *Chronicle of Philanthropy: The Newspaper of the Nonprofit World* online, January 8, 2004, http://philanthropy.com/premium/articles/v16/i06/06004302.htm, accessed March 18, 2004.

30. Brad Wolverton, "Rethinking Charity Rules," *Chronicle of Philanthropy: The Newspaper of the Nonprofit World,* July 22, 2004.

31. Harvy Lipman, "Charity Executives' Median Pay Is $42,000, Report Says," *Chronicle of Philanthropy: The Newspaper of the Nonprofit World* online, January 10, 2002, http://philanthropy.com/premium/articles/v14/i07/06004902.htm, accessed March 18, 2004.

32. Harvy Lipman and Elizabeth Schwinn, "52 Top Executives Are Paid at Least $1-Million," *Chronicle of Philanthropy: The Newspaper of the Nonprofit World* online, June 24, 2004, http://philanthropy.com, accessed August 5, 2004.

33. CNN Money, "Millionaire Has-Beens," "CNNMoney.com" website, June 12, 2003, http://money.cnn.com/2003/06/11/pf/millionaire/millionaires/, accessed May 1, 2004.

34. Mercer, "Mercer Issues Annual Study of CEO Compensation at Large US Firms: CEO Pay, Company Performance Show Close Alignment for 2004," "Mercer" website, April 11, 2005, http://www.mercerhr.com/summary.jhtml?idContent=1176860, accessed January 22, 2007.

35. Blair Tindall, "The Plight of the White-Tie Worker," *New York Times* online, January 27, 2008, http://query.nytimes.com/gst/fullpage.html?res=9F0CE5D91238F937A35754C0A9629C8B63, accessed January 27, 2008.

36. Joe Drape, "Coaches Receive Both Big Salaries and Big Questions," *New York Times* online, January 1, 2004, http://www.nytimes.com/2004/01/01/sports/ncaafootball/01SALA.html?ex=1388293200&cn-8a434e3c0518b2c6&ei=5007&partner=USERLAND, accessed June 27, 2006.

37. Harvy Lipman and Elizabeth Schwinn, "52 Top Executives Are Paid at Least $1-Million," *Chronicle of Philanthropy: The Newspaper of the Nonprofit World* online, June 24, 2004, http://philanthropy.com, accessed August 5, 2004.

38. Scott DeCarlo, "Big Paychecks," "Forbes.com" website, May 3, 2007, http://www.forbes.com/2007/05/03/ceo-executive-compensation-lead-07ceo-cx_sd_0503ceocompensationintro.html, accessed February 2, 2008.

39. Noelle Barton, Maria Di Mento, and Alvin P. Sanoff, "Top Nonprofit Executives See Healthy Pay Raises," *Chronicle of Philanthropy: The Newspaper of the Nonprofit World* online, September 28, 2006, http://philanthropy.com/premium/articles/v18/i24/24003901.htm, accessed January 28, 2007.

40. Ibid.

41. Ibid.; Mercer, "Mercer Issues Annual Study of CEO Compensation at Large US Firms: CEO Pay, Company Performance Show Close Alignment for 2004," "Mercer" website, April 11, 2005, http://www.mercerhr.com/summary.jhtml?idContent=1176860, accessed January 22, 2007.

42. "Cot's Baseball Contracts: New York Yankees," http://mlbcontracts.blogspot.com/2005/01/new-york-yankees_111398168678860040.html (accessed January 27, 2008).

43. Elizabeth Schwinn and Ian Wilhelm, "Nonprofit CEO's See Salaries Rise," *Chronicle of Philanthropy: The Newspaper of the Nonprofit World* online, October 2, 2003, http://philanthropy.com/premium/articles/v15/i24/24002701.htm, accessed April 19, 2004.

44. Sara Kugler, "Bill Clinton to Write New Book," *USA Today* online, May 17, 2006, http://www.usatoday.com/life/books/news/2006-05-17-clinton-book_x.htm, accessed February 2, 2008.

45. John Solomon and Matthew Mosk, "For Clinton, New Wealth in Speeches: Fees in 6 Years Total Nearly $40 Million," *Washington Post* on-line, February 23, 2007, http://www.washingtonpost.com/wp-dyn/content/article/2007/02/22/AR2007022202189.html, accessed March 3, 2007.

46. Amanda Porterfield, "Protestant Missionaries: Pioneers of American Philanthropy," in *Charity, Philanthropy, and Civility in American History,* ed. Lawrence J. Friedman and Mark D. McGarvie (Cambridge: Cambridge University Press, 2003), p. 60.

47. Ibid., p. 61.

48. CompassPoint Nonprofit Services, "Daring to Lead 2006: A National Study of Nonprofit Executive Leadership" (San Francisco, 2006), p. 2.

49. Ibid., p. 17.

50. Ibid., pp. 17, 19.

51. Paul C. Light, "The Content of Their Character: The State of the Non-profit Workforce," *Nonprofit Quarterly* online, October 2, 2002, http://www.brookings.edu/views/papers/light/20021002.htm, accessed June 29, 2006.

52. Ibid.

53. Peter Grant and Rebecca Buckman, "Fatter Pay Lures University Endowment Chiefs," *Wall Street Journal,* June 27, 2006.

54. Ibid.

55. Thomas J. Tierney, "The Nonprofit Sector's Leadership Deficit, Executive Summary," Bridgespan Group, Inc., March 2006, http://www.bridgespangroup.org/kno_articles_leadershipdeficit.html, p. 2.

56. Emmett D. Carson, "Public Expectations and Nonprofit Sector Realities: A Growing Divide with Disastrous Consequences," *Nonprofit and Voluntary Sector Quarterly* 31, no. 3 (2002), p. 430.

57. Thomas J. Tierney, "The Nonprofit Sector's Leadership Deficit, Executive Summary," Bridgespan Group, Inc., March 2006, http://www.bridgespangroup.org/kno_articles_leadershipdeficit.html, p. 2.

58. Michael Anft, "A Growing Debt to Society," *Chronicle of Philanthropy: The Newspaper of the Nonprofit World* online, March 23, 2006, *http://philanthropy.com/premium/articles/v18/i11/11003101.htm,* accessed January 28, 2007.

59. Louis Lavelle et al., "The Best B-Schools of 2006," *BusinessWeek,* October 23, 2006, pp. 56–57; University of Chicago Graduate School of Business, "Full-Time MBA Costs," "University of Chicago Graduate School of Business" website, http://chicagogsb.edu/fulltime/admissions/costs.aspx, accessed January 28, 2007; Wharton School, University of Pennsylvania, "The Wharton MBA: Cost Summary," "Wharton School, University of Pennsylvania" website, http://www.wharton.upenn.edu/mba/admissions/finance/cost.cfm, accessed January 28, 2007; Harvard Business School MBA Program, "Financial Aid: Cost Summary," "Harvard Business School MBA Program" website, http://www.hbs.edu/mba/admissions/costsummary.html, accessed January 28, 2007.

60. "Chart: In the Money," *Business Week* online, October 23. 2006, http://businessweek.com/magazine/content/06_43/b4006005.htm?chan=bestbs, accessed January 28, 2007; Louis Lavelle et al., "The Best B-Schools of 2006," *BusinessWeek* online, October 23, 2006, pp. 56–57.

61. Yahoo! Education, "Admissions to Business School: Business School Admissions Tips," "Yahoo!" website, http://education.yahoo.com/college/essentials/articles/biz/bschool-admissions.html, accessed January 28, 2007.

62. Harvy Lipman, "Charity Executives' Median Pay Is $42,000, Report Says," *Chronicle of Philanthropy: The Newspaper of the Nonprofit World* online, January 10, 2002, http://philanthropy.com/premium/articles/v14/i07/06004902.htm, accessed March 18, 2004.

63. "How We Conducted the Survey: By Old Fashioned Mail and E-Mail, We Contacted 4,800 of 5,700 MBAs from the Class of '92," *Business Week* online, September 22, 2003, http://businessweek.com/@@fEskoGQQsd7PJyAA/premium/content/03_38/b3850609.htmm, accessed January 28, 2007.

64. "Minding the Medians," *Business Week* online, http://businessweek.com/magazine/content/03_38/photo_essay/mediantable.htm, accessed January 28, 2007.

65. Ibid.

66. Debra E. Blum, "Median Pay for Foundation Chiefs Was $110,000 Last Year, Study Finds," *Chronicle of Philanthropy: The Newspaper of the Nonprofit World* online, February 3, 2005, http://philanthropy.com/premium/articles/v17/i08/08002401.htm, accessed January 28, 2007.

67. Harvy Lipman, "Unbalanced Pay Scales," *Chronicle of Philanthropy: The Newspaper of the Nonprofit World,* May 31, 2001, http://philanthropy.com/premium/articles/v13/i16/16003301.htm, accessed January 28, 2007.

68. Noelle Barton and Peter Panepento, "Executive Pay Rises 4.6," *Chronicle of Philanthropy: The Newspaper of the Nonprofit World* online, September 20, 2007, http://philanthropy.com/premium/articles/v19/i23/23003401.htm, accessed February 20, 2008; Noelle Barton, Maria Di Mento, and Alvin P. Sanoff, "Top Nonprofit Executives See Healthy Pay Raises," *Chronicle of Philanthropy: The Newspaper of the Nonprofit World* online, September 28, 2006, http://philanthropy.com/premium/articles/v18/i24/24003901.htm, accessed January 28, 2007; Mercer, "Mercer Issues Annual Study of CEO Compensation at Large US Firms: CEO Pay, Company Performance Show Close Alignment for 2004," "Mercer" website, April 11, 2005, http://www.mercerhr.com/summary.jhtml?idContent=1176860, accessed January 22, 2007.

69. Gary Strauss and Barbara Hansen, "CEO Pay Soars in 2005 as a Select Group Break the $100 Million Mark," *USA Today* online, April 11, 2006, http://www.usatoday.com/money/companies/management/2006-04-09-ceo-compensation-report_x.htm, accessed January 29, 2007.

70. Noelle Barton, Maria Di Mento, and Alvin P. Sanoff, "Top Nonprofit Executives See Healthy Pay Raises," *Chronicle of Philanthropy: The Newspaper of the Nonprofit World* online, September 28, 2006, http://philanthropy.com/premium/articles/v18/i24/24003901.htm, accessed January 28, 2007.

71. Community Wealth Ventures, Inc., "Venture Philanthropy: Landscape and Expectations," *Morino Institute Youth Social Ventures* (Reston, VA: The Morino Institute, 2000).

72. Warren F. McFarlan, "Working on Nonprofit Boards: Don't Assume the Shoe Fits," *Harvard Business Review,* November 1, 1999, via *Harvard Business Review* archive, http://harvardbusinessonline.hbsp.harvard.edu/b01/en/hbr/hbr_current_issue.jhtml;jsessionid=EWABL3ILJNQY0 AKRGWDR5VQBKE0YIISW, accessed February 10, 2007.

73. Thomas J. Tierney, "The Leadership Deficit," *Stanford Social Innovation Review* online, June 1, 2006, http://www.ssireview.org/articles/entry/the_leadership_deficit/, accessed January 30, 2007.

74. "25 Most Generous Young Americans," *Worth* 11, no. 10 (December 2002).

75. Ibid.

76. "Highest Paid Athletes, 2004: Andre Agassi," "Forbes.com" website, http://www.forbes.com/athletes2004/LIR1YUQ.html?passListId=2& passYear=2004&passListType=Person&uniqueId=1YUQ&datatype= Person, accessed January 29, 2007.

77. "100 Best Charities (and 10 worst)." *Worth* 11, no. 10 (December 2002), p. 83.

78. Dan Neil, "Saleen Machine," *Worth* 11, no. 10 (December 2002), p. 42.

79. Print and online advertisements, February 2007.

80. Infiniti, "Horsepower Is What Sends You Against the Back of Your Seat," print advertisement, February 2007.

81. Lincoln, "There Was a Time When I Couldn't See the Road Ahead," print advertisement, February 2007.

82. Queen Mary 2, "It's Just the Way It Used to Be," print advertisement, February 2007.

83. Holland America Line, "Intrigue Your Senses," print advertisement, February 2007.

84. Landrover USA, "The Range Rover for 2007," online advertisement, http://www.landroverusa.com/us/en/Vehicles/Range_Rover/Overview.htm, accessed January 28, 2007.

85. British Airways, "Because the Shortest Distance Between Two Points Is a Good Night's Sleep," print advertisement, February 2007.

86. Vanessa Summers, "The Sutras of Holistic Wealth: Part One," *Yogi Times,* February 2007, pp. 80–81.

87. Vanessa Summers, "Prosperity NOW; Free Wealth & Success Workshops with Financial Guru Vanessa Summers," print advertisement, February 2007.

88. Hästens Vividus, "How Much Is Great Sleep Worth?" print advertisement, February 2007.

89. Stephen M. Silverman and Susan Mandel, "Oprah Winfrey: Wealth Is 'a Good Thing,'" *People* online, April 11, 2006, http://www.people.com/people/article/0,,1182572,00.html, accessed January 29, 2007.

90. Print and online advertisements, January/February 2007.

91. "Around the World by Private Jet, January 5–27, 2008," UCLA Alumni Association brochure (Los Angeles, 2007).

92. Smith Barney, "I Am Working Wealth," print advertisement, February 2007.

93. John Kenneth Galbraith, *The Affluent Society* (Boston: Houghton Mifflin Company, 1958), p. 235.

94. Ken Kragen, "Kragen & Company Charity," "Kenkragen.com" website, http://www.kenkragen.com/charity_more.html, accessed January 27, 2008.

95. Buck Wolf, "Great Shakes: 'Hands Across America' 20 Years Later: The Day Oprah, President Reagan, Mickey Mouse and 5 Million Other Americans Joined Hands," *ABC News* online, May 23, 2006, http://abcnews.go.com/Entertainment/WolfFiles/story?id=2044810&page–1, accessed August 15, 2006.

96. Richard Stengel, "Joining Hands," *Time* online, http://www.time.com/time/magazine/article/0,9171,1075101,00.html, accessed February 3, 2008.

97. Associated Press, "Hands Across America: Reach Exceeded Grasp," *New York Times,* May 26, 1987, A21, via Lexis-Nexis, http://web.lexis-nexis.com, accessed August 15, 2006.

98. Associated Press, "Around the Nation: Hands Across America Faces Costs and Delay," *New York Times,* August 18, 1986, via Lexis-Nexis, http://web.lexis-nexis.com, accessed February 5, 2007.

99. Ibid.

100. Associated Press, "Costs Eat Up Hands Across America Proceeds," *Associated Press,* August 18, 1986, via Lexis-Nexis, http://web.lexis-nexis.com, accessed February 5, 2007.

101. Dennis McDougal, "Hands Across America: Can Ken Kragen Make It Work?" *Los Angeles Times* online, November 24, 1985, http://pqasb.pq archiver.com/latimes/advancedsearch.html, accessed February 5, 2007.

102. Dennis McDougal, "$11 Million for Poor from 'Hands,'" *Los Angeles Times* online, June 12, 1986, http://pqasb.pqarchiver.com/latimes/advanced search.html, accessed February 5, 2007.

103. Victor Valle and Dennis McDougal, "Hands' Grasp: Mixed Reaction Series—First in a Series of Three Articles Assessing the Continuing Influence of Mega-Events Like Hands Across America on Social Issues," *Los Angeles Times* online, June 17, 1986, http://pqasb.pqarchiver.com/latimes/advancedsearch.html, accessed February 5, 2007.

104. Ibid.

105. Ibid.

106. Ibid.

107. Dennis McDougal, "New Deal: Hands Does a Recount," *Los Angeles Times* online, August 25, 1986, http://pqasb.pqarchiver.com/latimes /advancedsearch.html, accessed February 5, 2007.

108. Ibid.

109. Ibid.

110. John Porretto, "$40 Billion Profit for Exxon," *Beaver County Times & Allegheny Times* online, February 1, 2008, http://www.timesonline.com/ articles/2008/02/01/news/top_stories/doc47a3d4061d24d653846165.txt, accessed February 3, 2008.

111. Dennis McDougal, "New Deal: Hands Does a Recount," *Los Angeles Times* online, August 25, 1986, http://pqasb.pqarchiver.com/latimes/advanced search.html, accessed February 5, 2007.

112. Dennis McDougal, "Hands Across America, May 25, 1986: Hands Bills Paid in Full, but Homeless Still Waiting," *Los Angeles Times* online, November 2, 1986, http://pqasb.pqarchiver.com/latimes/advancedsearch .html, accessed February 5, 2007.

113. Sally J. Sommer, "When Will Hands Across America Touch the Poor?" *Los Angeles Times* online, February 11, 1987, http://pqasb.pqarchiver.com/la times/advancedsearch.html, accessed February 5, 2007.

114. Dennis McDougal and Victor Valle, "Hands Across America's Nonpolitical Status Challenged by Partisan Anti-Hunger Activists Series: Last in a Series Assessing the Continuing Influence of Mega-Events Like Hands Across America on Social Issues," *Los Angeles Times* online, June 19, 1986, http://pqasb.pqarchiver.com/latimes/advancedsearch.html, accessed February 5, 2007.

115. Pallotta TeamWorks, "Record of Impact 1994–2002" (Los Angeles: Pallotta TeamWorks, 2006); throughout, registration fees paid by participants are excluded from income in calculating Pallotta TeamWorks' percentage of "donor dollars" remaining for the cause.

116. Jim Provenzano, "Wheels of Fortune: AIDS Ride 99—Part 1: AIDS Riders Gear Up for Controversy," *Bay Area Reporter* online, 1999, http:// members.trpiod.com/~homeo/wheels1.html, accessed November 22, 2006.

117. "Open Wide, AIDS Ride," *POZ: Health, Life & HIV* online, http://www .poz.com/articles/232_1655.shtml, accessed October 26, 2003.

118. Pallotta TeamWorks, "Record of Impact 1994–2002" (Los Angeles, 2006).

119. Jim Provenzano, "Wheels of Fortune: AIDS Ride 99—Part 1: AIDS Riders Gear Up for Controversy," *Bay Area Reporter* online, 1999, http: //members.trpiod.com/~homeo/wheels1.html, accessed November 22, 2006.

120. Pallotta TeamWorks, "Record of Impact 1994–2002" (Los Angeles, 2006).

121. Ibid.

122. David Ho, email to Dan Pallotta, March 11, 2002.

123. Christine W. Letts, William Ryan, and Allen Grossman, "Virtuous Capital: What Foundations Can Learn from Venture Capitalists," *Harvard Business Review,* March 1997, via *Harvard Business Review* online archive,

http://harvardbusinessonline.hbsp.harvard.edu/b01/en/hbr/hbr_current _issue.jhtml;jsessionid=EWABL3ILJNQY0AKRGWDR5VQBKE0YIISW, accessed January 30, 2007.

124. Community Wealth Ventures, Inc., "Venture Philanthropy: Landscape and Expectations," *Morino Institute Youth Social Ventures* (Reston, VA: The Morino Institute, 2000).

125. Gary A. Tobin, "Getting Megagifts to the Neediest Causes," *Chronicle of Philanthropy: The Newspaper of the Nonprofit World* online, May 1, 2003, http://philanthropy.com/premium/articles/v15/i14/14004901.htm, accessed January 30, 2007.

126. Mark Kramer, "Venture Capital and Philanthropy: A Bad Fit," *Chronicle of Philanthropy: The Newspaper of the Nonprofit World* online, April 22, 1999, http://www.philanthropy.com/premium/articles/v11/i13/13007201.htm, accessed February 4, 2008.

127. Metro-Goldwyn-Mayer, "2002 Annual Report" (Los Angeles, 2003).

128. Community Wealth Ventures, Inc., "Venture Philanthropy: Landscape and Expectations," *Morino Institute Youth Social Ventures* (Reston, VA: The Morino Institute, 2000).

129. Paul C. Light, "Charities Must Make Innovation an Ordinary Act," *Chronicle of Philanthropy: The Newspaper of the Nonprofit World* online, March 12, 1998, http://philanthropy.com/premium/articles/v10/i10/1000 4201.htm, accessed February 9, 2007.

130. Princeton Survey Research Associates, Inc., "BBB Wise Giving Alliance Donor Expectations Survey: Final Report" (Princeton, NJ, 2001), p. 6.

131. Mark Rosenman, "McKinsey Study Shows Stunning Lapse in Logic," *Chronicle of Philanthropy: The Newspaper of the Nonprofit World* online, May 29, 2003, http://philanthropy.com/premium/articles/v15/i16/16003401 .htm, accessed February 10, 2007.

132. Stephanie Strom, "A Nation Challenged: Charities—Narrowly Drawn Rules Freeze Out Tens of Thousands of Indirect Victims, Report Says," *New York Times,* April 23, 2002, via Lexis-Nexis, http://web.lexis-nexis .com, accessed August 15, 2006.

133. Diego Ibarguen, "Some Money Raised for Red Cross' Liberty Fund to Go to Long-Term Plans," *Associated Press State & Local Wire,* October 30, 2001, via Lexis-Nexis, http://web.lexis-nexis.com, accessed August 15, 2006.

134. Susan Edelman, "Red Cross Prez Quits: Dispute over $500M in WTC Donations," *New York Post,* October 27, 2001, via Lexis-Nexis, http://web .lexis-nexis.com, accessed August 15, 2006.

135. Susan Saulny, "Red Cross Announces Plans for Rest of Disaster Funds," *New York Times,* February 1, 2002, via Lexis-Nexis, http://web.lexis-nexis .com, accessed August 15, 2006.

136. Diego Ibarguen, "Some Money Raised for Red Cross' Liberty Fund to Go to Long-Term Plans," *Associated Press State & Local Wire,* October 30, 2001, via Lexis-Nexis, http://web.lexis-nexis.com, accessed August 15, 2006.

137. Ibid.

138. Susan Saulny, "Red Cross Announces Plans for Rest of Disaster Funds," *New York Times,* February 1, 2002, via Lexis-Nexis, http://web.lexis-nexis.com, accessed August 15, 2006.

139. Shannon McCaffrey, "Watchdog Faults Red Cross on Sept. 11 Fund-Raising," *Associated Press State & Local Wire,* August 15, 2002, via Lexis-Nexis, http://web.lexis-nexis.com, accessed August 15, 2006.

140. Stephen Innes, *Creating the Commonwealth: The Economic Culture of Puritan New England* (New York: W.W. Norton & Company, 1995), p. 145.

141. Suzanne Perry, "Interim CEO Resigns from Red Cross," *Chronicle of Philanthropy: The Newspaper of the Nonprofit World,* May 31, 2007, p. 50.

142. Thomas J. Tierney, "The Leadership Deficit," *Stanford Social Innovation Review* online, June 1, 2006, http://www.ssireview.org/articles/entry/the_leadership_deficit, accessed February 10, 2007.

143. Les Silverman and Lynn Taliento, "What Business Execs Don't Know—but Should—About Nonprofits," *Stanford Social Innovation Review* online, January 22, 2007, http://www.ssireview.org/articles/entry/what_business_execs_dont_know_but_should_about_nonprofits, accessed February 10, 2007.

144. Ibid.

145. Pallotta TeamWorks, "Record of Impact 1994–2002" (Los Angeles, 2006).

146. "Amazon.com," "Information Headquarters" website, http://www.informationheadquarters.com/Amazon.shtml, accessed March 18, 2004.

147. Larry Dignan, "Amazon Posts Its First Net Profit," "CNET News.com" website, January 22, 2002, http://news.com.com/2100-1017-819688.html, accessed March 18, 2004; Christine Frey and John Cook, "How Amazon.com Survived, Thrived, and Turned a Profit: E-tailer Defied Predictions It Would Do None of These," *Seattle Post Intelligencer* online, January 28, 2004, http://seattlepi.nwsource.com/business/158315_amazon 28.html, accessed March 18, 2004.

148. Wikipedia, "Amazon.com," "Wikipedia: The Free Encyclopedia" website, http://en.wikipedia.org/wiki/Amazon.com, accessed November 14, 2006.

149. Christine Frey and John Cook, "How Amazon.com Survived, Thrived, and Turned a Profit: E-tailer Defied Predictions It Would Do None of These," *Seattle Post Intelligencer* online, January 28, 2004, http://seattlepi.nwsource.com/business/158315_amazon28.html, accessed March 18, 2004.

150. "Super Bowl Ad Cost through the Years: Business of Super Bowl," *MSNBC* online, http://www.msnbc.msn.com/id/16874732/, accessed February 14, 2007.

151. YouTube, "Supervote: The Super Bowl Commercials Ranked Your Way," "YouTube.com" website, 2007, http://www.youtube.com/superbowl, accessed February 13, 2007.

152. "Top U.S. Advertisers by Revenue per Ad Dollar," *Advertising Age* online, 2008, http://adage.com/datacenter/datapopup.php?article_id=118677, accessed January 27, 2008.

153. Brad Wolverton, "Community Foundations Plan to Spend More on Advertising," *Chronicle of Philanthropy: The Newspaper of the Nonprofit World* online, February 6, 2003, http://philanthropy.com/premium/articles/v15/i08/08003002.htm, accessed February 14, 2007.

154. Jennifer Moore and Grant Williams, "Cultivating Clout," *Chronicle of Philanthropy: The Newspaper of the Nonprofit World* online, June 18, 1998, http://philanthropy.com/premium/articles/v10/i17/1704101.htm, accessed February 14, 2007.

155. Federal Trade Commission, "Cigarette Report for 1999," "Federal Trade Commission" website, March 13, 2001, http://www.ftc.gov/opa/2001/03/cigarette.htm, accessed February 13, 2007.

156. Beth Snyder Bulik, "Apple Plan: Lead Consumers into Temptation—and Away from Vista," *Advertising Age,* February 12, 2007, pp. 1, 28.

157. Rebecca Barr, "Microsoft Ads Aim to Erase 'Huge' Image: Software Marker's Campaign to Cost $120 Million," *Seattle Post Intelligencer* online, January 21, 2006, http://seattlepi.nwsource.com/business/256523_msftads21.html, accessed February 14, 2007.

158. "Special Report: 100 Leading National Advertisers Supplement," *Advertising Age,* June 26, 2008, pp. 1–9.

159. Department of the Treasury, Internal Revenue Service, "Form 990: Return of Organization Exempt from Income Tax," filing organization: Save the Children Federation, Inc., Westport, CT, filing year: 2004.

160. Department of the Treasury, Internal Revenue Service, "Form 990: Return of Organization Exempt from Income Tax," filing organization: Foundation for AIDS Research (DBA amfAR, AIDS Research Foundation), New York, filing year: 2005.

161. Department of the Treasury, Internal Revenue Service, "Form 990: Return of Organization Exempt from Income Tax," filing organization: United Way of America, Alexandria, VA, filing year: 2005.

162. Department of the Treasury, Internal Revenue Service, "Form 990: Return of Organization Exempt from Income Tax," filing organization: The Leukemia & Lymphoma Society, Inc., White Plains, NY, filing year: 2004.

163. Department of the Treasury, Internal Revenue Service, "Form 990: Return of Organization Exempt from Income Tax," filing organization: Amnesty International USA, Inc., New York, NY. Filing year: 2005; 2005 Form 990 says the expense is for "Advertising,pubs&subsc."

164. Maia Szalavitz, "No Market for Marketing," *Stanford Social Innovation Review* online, December 1, 2005, http://www.ssireview.org/articles/entry/no_market_for_marketing/, accessed January 30, 2007.

165. Ibid.

166. Ibid.

167. "Deposition," *Pallotta TeamWorks v. Avon Products Foundation, Inc.,* no. 1420011424, Judicial Arbitration and Mediation Services (Los Angeles, May 28, 2003), pp. 10–11.

168. *Jack Myers Media Business Report* (New York City: Myers Publishing, 2005).

169. Center on Philanthropy at Indiana University, *Giving USA 2007: The Annual Report on Philanthropy for the Year 2006* (Bloomington, IN: Giving USA Foundation, 2007), p. 16.

170. *Jack Myers Media Business Report* (New York City: Myers Publishing, 2005); Center on Philanthropy at Indiana University, *Giving USA 2007: The Annual Report on Philanthropy for the Year 2006* (Bloomington, IN: Giving USA Foundation, 2007), p. 16.

171. Tom Watson, "Consumer Philanthropy: Nonprofits Spend Billions to Reach Consumers," *On Philanthropy* online, December 13, 2006, http://www.onphilanthropy.com/site/News2?page=NewsArticle&id=6863, accessed January 4, 2008.

172. John Kenneth Galbraith, *The Affluent Society* (Boston: Houghton Mifflin Company, 1958), p. 112.

173. Center on Philanthropy at Indiana University, *Giving USA 2007: The Annual Report on Philanthropy for the Year 2006* (Bloomington, IN: Giving USA Foundation, 2007), p. 12.

174. *Jack Myers Media Business Report* (New York City: Myers Publishing, 2005).

175. Sam Kean, "Charity Ads Are Broadcast During Key Times, Study Finds," *Chronicle of Philanthropy: The Newspaper of the Nonprofit World,* May 31, 2007, p. 51.

176. Matthew Creamer, "Marketers Can't Grade Shops but Fail Them Anyway," *Advertising Age,* February 26, 2007, p. 41.

177. John Kenneth Galbraith, *The Affluent Society* (Boston: Houghton Mifflin Company, 1958), p. 127.

178. David Ogilvy, *Confessions of an Advertising Man* (London: Southbank Publishing, 2004), p. 185.

179. David Ogilvy, *Ogilvy on Advertising* (New York: Vintage Books, 1983), p. 118.

180. John Kenneth Galbraith, *The Affluent Society* (Boston: Houghton Mifflin Company, 1958), p. ix.

181. Center on Philanthropy at Indiana University, *Giving USA 2006: The Annual Report on Philanthropy for the Year 2005* (Bloomington, IN: Giving USA Foundation, 2006), p. 39.

182. Center on Philanthropy at Indiana University, *Giving USA 2007: The Annual Report on Philanthropy for the Year 2006* (Bloomington, IN: Giving USA Foundation, 2007), p. 66.

183. "The Luxury Survey: An In-depth Report on how U.S. Millennials Look at Luxury," *Time Style & Design* (Spring 2008), pp. 58–59.

184. Thomas Merton, *Seeds,* ed. Robert Inchausti (Boston: Shambhala, 2002), pp. 37–38.

185. Mya Frazier, "Costly Red Campaign Reaps Meager $18 Million," *Advertising Age* online, March 5, 2007, http://adage.com/article?article_id=115287, accessed March 12, 2007.

186. Ibid.

187. John Kenneth Galbraith, *The Affluent Society* (Boston: Houghton Mifflin Company, 1958), pp. 193–194.

188. Ibid., pp. 223–224.

189. Suzanne Perry, "Donations to Victims of 2004 Asian Tsunamis Topped $3-Billion," *Chronicle of Philanthropy: The Newspaper of the Nonprofit World* online, January 11, 2007, http://philanthropy.com/premium/articles/v19/i06/06002801.htm, accessed February 28, 2007.

190. Mark Jones, "Tsunami Coverage Dwarfs 'Forgotten' Crises-Research," *Reuters Foundation Alertnet* online, March 10, 2005, http://www.alertnet.org/thefacts/reliefresources/111044767025.htm, accessed February 28, 2007.

191. Carole J. L. Collins, "World's Worst Disasters Overlook: Survey Identifies Biggest 'Forgotten' Crises," *FAIR* online, February 28, 2007, http://www.fair.org/index.php?page=2537, accessed February 28, 2007.

192. Suzanne Perry, "Donations to Victims of 2004 Asian Tsunamis Topped $3-Billion," *Chronicle of Philanthropy: The Newspaper of the Nonprofit World* online, January 11, 2007, http://philanthropy.com/premium/articles/v19/i06/06002801.htm, accessed February 28, 2007.

193. Center on Philanthropy at Indiana University, *Giving USA 2006: The Annual Report on Philanthropy for the Year 2005* (Bloomington, IN: Giving USA Foundation, 2006), p. 57.

194. Ibid., p. 64.

195. Center on Philanthropy at Indiana University, "Gulf Coast Hurricane Relief Donations," "Center on Philanthropy at Indiana University" website, http://www.philanthropy.iupui.edu/Research/Giving/Hurricane_Katrina.aspx, accessed February 28, 2007.

196. The Center on Philanthropy at Indiana University, *Giving USA 2006: The Annual Report on Philanthropy for the Year 2005* (Bloomington, IN: Giving USA Foundation, 2006), p. 7.

197. Center on Philanthropy at Indiana University, *Giving USA 2007: The Annual Report on Philanthropy for the Year 2006* (Bloomington, IN: Giving USA Foundation, 2007), p. 136.

198. National Alliance to End Homelessness, "Homelessness Counts," "National Alliance to End Homelessness" website, January 10, 2007, http://www.endhomelessness.org/content/general/detail/1440, accessed March 2, 2007.

199. Center on Philanthropy at Indiana University, "Sources of Contributions: Giving by Individuals," *American Association of Fundraising Counsel Trust for Philanthropy* (Bloomington, IN: 2003).

200. Center on Philanthropy at Indiana University, *Giving USA 2007: The Annual Report on Philanthropy for the Year 2006* (Bloomington, IN: Giving USA Foundation, 2007), p. 65.

201. Ibid., p. 106.

202. Pallotta TeamWorks, Record of Impact 1994–2002" (Los Angeles, 2006). $32,415,254 in "Marketing/Cause Awareness" expenses for all events except the AIDSRides. AIDSRide "Marketing/Cause Awareness" expenses

of $16,506,962 were calculated using the Breast Cancer 3-Day 2:1 "Administration to Marketing" ratio.

203. Center on Philanthropy at Indiana University, *Giving USA 2006: The Annual Report on Philanthropy for the Year 2005* (Bloomington, IN: Giving USA Foundation, 2006), p. 55.

204. David Ogilvy, *Confessions of an Advertising Man* (London: Southbank Publishing, 2004), pp. 179–180.

205. Adam Smith, *The Wealth of Nations* (New York: Modern Library, 2000), p. 387.

206. Stephen Innes, *Creating the Commonwealth: The Economic Culture of Puritan New England* (New York: W.W. Norton & Company, 1995), p. 169.

207. Center on Philanthropy at Indiana University, *Giving USA 2007: The Annual Report on Philanthropy for the Year 2006* (Bloomington, IN: Giving USA Foundation, 2007), p. 12.

208. National Center for Charitable Statistics 2007, "The Nonprofit Sector in Brief: Facts and Figures from the *Nonprofit Almanac 2007*" (Washington, DC: Urban Institute Press, 2007), p. 4.

209. Community Wealth Ventures, Inc., "Venture Philanthropy: Landscape and Expectations," *Morino Institute Youth Social Ventures* (Reston, VA: The Morino Institute, 2000).

210. Akira Yasuoka, *Evolution of the US Retail Securities Market (Volume 1): Financial Institutions Prepare for Retiring Baby Boomers* (New York City: Nomura Research Institute, 2006), p. 3.

211. Ibid., p. 4.

212. Ibid., p. 5.

213. Ralph Smith, "Many Happy Returns," *Worth* online, August 2, 2004, http://www.worth.com/Editorial/Money-Meaning/Philanthropy/Opportunities-Exposures-Many-Happy-Returns.asp?ht=many%20happy%20returns%20many%20happy%20returns, accessed June 30, 2006.

214. Center on Philanthropy at Indiana University, *Giving USA 2007: The Annual Report on Philanthropy for the Year 2006* (Bloomington, IN: Giving USA Foundation, 2007), p. 12.

215. B. Mark Smith, *A History of the Global Stock Market: From Ancient Rome to Silicon Valley* (Chicago: University of Chicago Press, 2003), p. 16.

216. Ibid., p. 17.

217. Ibid., p. 18.

218. Ibid.

219. Ibid., p. 21.

220. Ibid., p. 35.

221. Ibid., p. 22.

222. Department of Treasury, Internal Revenue Service, "Standards for Recognition of Tax-Exempt Status of Private Benefit Exists if an Applicable Tax-Exempt Organization Has Engaged in Excess Benefit Transaction(s)," *Federal Register* 70, no. 174 (September 9, 2005).

223. Christopher Farrell, "The Booming Economy Is Greasing Charitable Giving," *Business Week* online, September 15, 2000, http://www.business week.com/bwdaily/dnflash/sep2000/nf20000915_565.htm, accessed March 12, 2007; "Disasters Help Boost American Charitable Giving to Near All-Time High," *Fox News* online, June 19, 2006. http://www.foxnews.com/story/0,2933,200065,00.html, accessed March 12, 2007; The Center on Philanthropy at Indiana University, *Giving USA 2007: The Annual Report on Philanthropy for the Year 2006* (Bloomington, IN: Giving USA Foundation, 2007), p. 218; Center on Philanthropy at Indiana University, *Giving USA 2006: The Annual Report on Philanthropy for the Year 2005* (Bloomington, IN: Giving USA Foundation, 2006), p. 37.
224. B. Mark Smith, *A History of the Global Stock Market: From Ancient Rome to Silicon Valley* (Chicago: University of Chicago Press, 2003), p. 55.
225. John Kenneth Galbraith, *The Affluent Society* (Boston: Houghton Mifflin Company, 1958), p. 131.
226. Perry Miller and Thomas H. Johnson, *The Puritans: A Sourcebook of Their Writings, Two Volumes Bound as One* (Mineola, NY: Dover Publications, Inc., 2001), pp. 195–199.

Chapter 3: Stop Asking This Question (pp. 128–176)

1. *Illinois ex rel. Madigan, Attorney General of Illinois v. Telemarketing Associates, Inc., et al.,* no. 01–1806, Supreme Court of the United States, May 5, 2003, p. 18.
2. Stephen J. Smallwood and Wilson C. Levis, "The Realities of Fund-Raising Costs and Accountability," "Philanthropy Monthly" website, September 1977, http://nccsdataweb.urban.org/PubApps/levis/realities.html, accessed August 25, 2006, p. 8.
3. Richard Steinberg, "Economic Perspectives on Regulation of Charitable Solicitation," *Case Western Law Review,* 1989, via Lexis-Nexis, http://web.lexis-nexis.com, accessed June 22, 2003.
4. *Randolph Riley, etc., et al. v. National Federation of the Blind of North Carolina, Inc., et al.,* no. 87–328, Supreme Court of the United States, June 29, 1988.
5. *Secretary of State of Maryland v. Joseph H. Munson Co., Inc.,* no. 82–766, Supreme Court of the United States, June 26, 1984, via Lexis-Nexis, http://web.lexis-nexis.com, accessed June 30, 2006.
6. *Randolph Riley, etc., et al. v. National Federation of the Blind of North Carolina, Inc., et al.,* no. 87–328, Supreme Court of the United States, June 29, 1988.
7. Robert H Bremner, *American Philanthropy,* 2nd ed., ed. Daniel J. Boorstin (Chicago: University of Chicago Press, 1960), p. 42.
8. Ibid., p. 56.
9. Ibid., p. 182.

10. Ibid., p. 190.

11. Ibid.

12. Ibid., p. 180; Center on Philanthropy at Indiana University, *Giving USA 2007: The Annual Report on Philanthropy for the Year 2006* (Bloomington, IN: Giving USA Foundation, 2007), p. 45.

13. Lester M. Salamon, ed., *The State of Nonprofit America* (Washington, D. C.: Brookings Institution Press, 2002), p. 19.

14. Center on Philanthropy at Indiana University, *Giving USA 2007: The Annual Report on Philanthropy for the Year 2006* (Bloomington, IN: Giving USA Foundation, 2007), p. 18.

15. Stephen J. Smallwood and Wilson C. Levis, "The Realities of Fund-Raising Costs and Accountability," "Philanthropy Monthly" website, September 1977, http://nccsdataweb.urban.org/PubApps/levis/realities.html, accessed August 25, 2006.

16. BBB Wise Giving Alliance, "Standards for Charity Accountability," "Give.org: BBB Wise Giving Alliance" website, http://www.give.org/standards/newcbbbstds.asp, accessed March 16, 2004.

17. Grant Williams, "Watchdog Group Proposes Changes in Evaluating Charity Operations," *Chronicle of Philanthropy: The Newspaper of the Nonprofit World* online, January 24, 2002, http://philanthropy.com/premium/articles/v14/i07/07002401.htm, accessed March 17, 2004.

18. BBB Wise Giving Alliance, "Standards for Charity Accountability," "BBB Wise Giving Alliance" website, http://us.bbb.org/WWWRoot/SitePage.aspx?site=113&id=4dd040fd-08af-4dd2-aaa0-dcd66c1a17fc, accessed January 26, 2008.

19. BBB Wise Giving Alliance, "Welcome to Give.org," "Give.org: BBB Wise Giving Alliance" website, http://www.give.org/, accessed March 17, 2004.

20. BBB Wise Giving Alliance, "Report: AARP," "BBB Wise Giving Alliance" website, http://charityreports.bbb.org/public/Report.aspx?CharityID=3261&bureauID=9999, accessed January 27, 2008.

21. American Institute of Philanthropy, "Welcome," "American Institute of Philanthropy: Helping You Give Wisely to Charity" website, http://www.charitywatch.org/, accessed November 1, 2006.

22. American Institute of Philanthropy, "How American Institute of Philanthropy Rates Charities," "American Institute of Philanthropy: Helping You Give Wisely to Charity" website, http://www.charitywatch.org/criteria.html, accessed October 31, 2006.

23. American Institute of Philanthropy, "Top-Rated Charities," "American Institute of Philanthropy: Helping You Give Wisely to Charity" website, http://www.charitywatch.org/toprated.html, accessed November 1, 2006.

24. Charity Navigator, "Methodology: Our Ratings Tables," "Charity Navigator: Your Guide to Intelligent Giving" website, http://www.charitynavigator.org/index.cfm/bay/content.view/cpid/48.htm, accessed January 26, 2008.

25. Charity Navigator, "Methodology: How Do We Rate Charities?" "Charity Navigator: Your Guide to Intelligent Giving" website, http://charity navigator.org/index.cfm?bay=content.view&cpid=35, accessed March 16, 2004.

26. Charity Navigator, "Charity Rating: American Diabetes Association," "Charity Navigator: Your Guide to Intelligent Giving" website, http://www.charitynavigator.org/index.cfm?bay=search.summary&orgid=3251, accessed February 1, 2008.

27. Charity Navigator, "Methodology: Our Ratings Tables," "Charity Navigator: Your Guide to Intelligent Giving" website, http://www.charity navigator.org/index.cfm/bay/content.view/cpid/48.htm, accessed January 26, 2008.

28. American Institute of Philanthropy, "Top-Rated Charities," "American Institute of Philanthropy: Helping You Give Wisely to Charity" website. http://www.charitywatch.org/toprated.html, accessed November 1, 2006.

29. "Watchdog Watch," *Chronicle of Philanthropy: The Newspaper of the Nonprofit World*, August 19, 2004, p. 30.

30. U.S. Congress, Senate, Committee on Finance, "Charity Oversight and Reform: Keeping Bad Things from Happening to Good Charities," testimony of H. Art Taylor, president and CEO of BBB Wise Giving Alliance (Arlington, VA, June 22, 2004).

31. BBB Wise Giving Alliance, "Charity Seal Program," "BBB Wise Giving Alliance" website, http://www.us.bbb.org/WWWRoot/SitePage.aspx?site=113&id=6a21a739-e081-4e1a-9e51-a6983b8a4587, accessed January 26, 2008.

32. BBB Wise Giving Alliance, "National Charity Seal Program," "BBB Wise Giving Alliance" website, http://charityreports.bbb.org/public/participants.asp, accessed January 26, 2008.

33. Ibid.

34. Department of the Treasury, Internal Revenue Service, "Form 990: Return of Organization Exempt from Income Tax," Filing organization: BBB Wise Giving Alliance, Arlington, VA, filing year: 2006.

35. They added that, in addition, staff members from the affiliated Council of Better Business Bureaus, Inc., provide administrative personnel, media, accounting, information technology, legal, and office services to the BBB Wise Giving Alliance. U.S. National BBB.org, "U.S. National BBB.org: Staff," "U.S. National BBB.org" website, http://www.us.bbb.org/WWW Root/SitePage.aspx?site=113&id=41018df4-9a11 4ed1-a767-29776 5eed bf6, accessed January 26, 2008.

36. BBB Wise Giving Alliance, "U.S. National BBB.org: 2006 Annual Report," "BBB Wise Giving Alliance" website, http://us.bbb.org/WWW Root/SitePage.aspx?site=113&id=a727ed2e-dd7d-44a8-bca8-d424495 ded83, accessed January 26, 2008.

37. Dan Prives, "Charity Standards Proposed by Watchdog Group Are Deeply Flawed," *Chronicle of Philanthropy: The Newspaper of the Nonprofit*

World online, March 17, 2004, http://philanthropy.com/premium/articles /v14/i13/13006501.htm, accessed March 17, 2004.

38. Ibid.

39. Charity Navigator, "Board and Staff," "Charity Navigator: Your Guide to Intelligent Giving" website, http://charitynavigator.org/index.cfm?bay =content.view&cpid=19, accessed January 26, 2008.

40. Charity Navigator, "Charity Navigator Homepage," "Charity Navigator: Your Guide to Intelligent Giving" website, http://charitynavigator.org/, accessed January 26, 2008.

41. Department of the Treasury, Internal Revenue Service, "Form 990: Return of Organization Exempt from Income Tax," filing organization: Charity Navigator, Mahwah, NJ, filing year: 2005.

42. "The Nation's Major Charity-Watchdog Groups: At a Glance," *Chronicle of Philanthropy: Newspaper of the Nonprofit the World* online, November 28, 2002, http://philanthropy.com/premium/articles/v15/i04/04002501.htm, accessed March 17, 2004.

43. American Institute of Philanthropy, "Welcome," "American Institute of Philanthropy: Helping You Give Wisely to Charity" website, http://www .charitywatch.org/, accessed November 1, 2006.

44. Department of the Treasury, Internal Revenue Service, "Form 990: Return of Organization Exempt from Income Tax," filing organization: American Institute of Philanthropy, Chicago, filing year: 2006.

   Guidestar is a data-gathering organization that deserves mention. It doesn't fall into the "watchdog" category. As its website states, "GuideStar does not judge nonprofits; it is not a watchdog organization" (GuideStar Philanthropic Research, Inc., "Frequently Asked Questions," "GuideStar.org" website, http://www.guidestar.org/help/faq.jsp, accessed January 27, 2008). According to the site, Guidestar's database has 1.7 million organizations and contains 3.1 million IRS form 990 images (GuideStar Philanthropic Research, Inc., "About GuideStar and Philanthropic Research, Inc.," "GuideStar.org" website, http://www.guidestar .org/about/index.jsp?source=dnabout, accessed January 27, 2008). In 2006 it had expenses of approximately $6 million (GuideStar Philanthropic Research, Inc., "Financial Statements for the Years Ended December 31, 2006 and 2005" [GuideStar Philanthropic Research, Inc., Washington D.C., March 9, 2007]).

45. Paul D. Nelson, "Useful, but Limited: What Donors Need to Know about Rating Services," *Philanthropy* online, 18, no. 1 (January/February 2004), http://www.philanthropyroundtable.org/magazines/2004/january /Rating%20Services.htm, accessed August 20, 2004.

46. Kathy M. Kristof, "Charity Takes Lots of Clarity," *Los Angeles Times* online, December 2, 2007, http://www.latimes.com/business/la-fi-charity2 deco2,1,6214425.story?coll=la-headlines-business, accessed December 4, 2007.

47. Daniel Kadlec, "How to Give to the Little Guys," *Time,* November 6, 2006, p. 97.
48. William P. Barrett, "America's Most (and Least) Efficient Charities," "Forbes.com" website, November 24, 2004, http://www.forbes.com/2004/11/23/04charityland.html, accessed December 6, 2004.
49. Ibid.
50. Penelope Wang, "Charitable Giving: The Right Match," *Money,* December 22, 2004, *CNNMoney.com,* http://money.cnn.com/2004/12/22/pf/poverty_giving3_0412/index.htm, accessed June 30, 2006.
51. Charity Navigator, "Overview," "Charity Navigator: Your Guide to Intelligent Giving" website, http://www.charitynavigator.org/index.cfm?bay=content.view&cpid=628, accessed February 1, 2008.
52. BBB Wise Giving Alliance, "BBB Wise giving Alliance 2004 Annual Report," "Give.org: BBB Wise Giving Alliance" website, http://www.give.org/about/2004annualrpt.asp, accessed October 31, 2006.
53. City of Los Angeles, Information card no. A1590, Los Angeles Police Commission Charitable Services Section, Issued to AIDS Action Foundation, Washington, D.C., for "Dinner and Spring Fashion Show on May 6, 2004 at Neiman Marcus Beverly Hills."
54. California Department of Justice, Office of the Attorney General, "Using Your Heart to Give Wisely—Giving Wisely," "California Department of Justice, Office of the Attorney General" website, http://ag.ca.gov/charities/charit_giving.php, accessed February 1, 2008.
55. Grameen Foundation, "Latest News," "Grameen Foundation" website, http://www.grameenfoundation.org/?gclid+CPL4yfv9JECFQo6awodX23nxA (accessed March 4, 2008).
56. Ibid.
57. Katie Lawson, "American Red Cross Receives Four Stars from Charity Navigator," "American Red Cross" website, December 5, 2006, http://www.redcross.org/article/0,1072,0_312_5824,00.html, accessed March 12, 2007.
58. United Way, "United Way Homepage," "United Way" website, http://www.unitedway.org/, accessed January 26, 2008; American Cancer Society, "American Cancer Society Homepage," "American Cancer Society" website, http://www.cancer.org/docroot/home/index.asp, accessed January 26, 2008; American Lung Association, "American Lung Association Homepage," "American Lung Association" website, http://www.lungusa.org/site/pp.asp?c=dvLUK9O0E&b=22542, accessed January 26, 2008; American Red Cross, "American Red Cross Homepage," "American Red Cross" website, http://american.redcross.org/site/PageServer?pagename=ntld_main, accessed January 26, 2008; American Diabetes Association, "Donate—Support the Cause—American Diabetes Association," "American Diabetes Association" website, http://diabetes.org/support-the-cause/make-a-donation.jsp?WTLPromo=HEADER_donate&vms=254789525884, accessed January 26, 2008.

59. Princeton Survey Research Associates, Inc., "BBB Wise Giving Alliance Donor Expectations Survey: Final Report" (Princeton, NJ, 2001), pp. 20–21.

60. Ibid., p. 47.

61. "Brief of Amici Curiae Public Citizen, Inc., American Charities for Reasonable Fundraising Regulation, Inc., and 174 Other Nonprofit Organizations in Support of Respondents," *The People of the State of Illinois ex rel. James E. Ryan, Attorney General of the state of Illinois v. Telemarketing Associates, Inc., Richard Troia and Armet, Inc.*, no. 01–1806, Supreme Court of the United States, January 2003, p. 11.

62. William H. Shore, *Revolution of the Heart: A New Strategy for Creating Wealth and Meaningful Change* (New York: Riverhead Books, 1995), p. 137.

63. Charity Navigator, "FAQ for Donors," "Charity Navigator: Your Guide to Intelligent Giving" website, http://charitynavigator.org/index.cfm?bay=content.view&cpid=484#14, accessed January 26, 2008.

64. Center on Nonprofits and Philanthropy, Urban Institute at the Center on Philanthropy at Indiana University, "Getting What We Pay For: Low Overhead Limits Nonprofit Effectiveness," *Nonprofit Overhead Cost Project: Facts and Perspectives*, brief no. 3 (August 2004), p. 3.

65. Paul D. Nelson, "Useful, but Limited: What Donors Need to Know about Rating Services," *Philanthropy* online, 18, no. 1 (January/February 2004), http: //www.philanthropyroundtable.org/magazines/2004/january/Rating %20Services.htm, accessed August 20, 2004.

66. Mark Hager and Janet Greenlee, "How Important Is a Nonprofit's Bottom Line? The Uses and Abuses of Financial Data," in *In Search of the Nonprofit Sector*, ed. P. Frumkin and J.B. Imber (New Brunswick, NJ: Transaction Publishers, 2004), pp. 88, 93.

67. Center on Nonprofits and Philanthropy, Urban Institute at the Center on Philanthropy at Indiana University, "The Pros and Cons of Financial Efficiency Standards," *Nonprofit Overhead Cost Project: Facts and Perspectives*, brief no. 5 (August 2004), p. 3.

68. "Open Wide, AIDS Ride," *POZ: Health, Life & HIV* online, http://www.poz.com/articles/232_1655.shtml, accessed October 26, 2003.

69. Habitat 500, "History of the Habitat 500," "Habitat 500" website, http://www.habitat500.org/habitat500/Habitat500/history.html, accessed January 26, 2008.

70. Richard Steinberg, "Should Donors Care About Fundraising?" in *The Economics of Nonprofit Institutions*, ed. S. Rose-Ackerman (New York: Oxford University Press, 1986).

71. Richard Steinberg, "Economic Perspectives on Regulation of Charitable Solicitation," *Case Western Law Review*, 1989, via Lexis-Nexis, http://web.lexis-nexis.com, accessed June 22, 2003.

72. *Randolph Riley, etc., et al. v. National Federation of the Blind of North Carolina, Inc., et al.*, no. 87–328, Supreme Court of the United States, June 29, 1988.

73. Center on Nonprofits and Philanthropy, Urban Institute at the Center on Philanthropy at Indiana University, "What We Know About Overhead Costs in the Nonprofit Sector," *Nonprofit Overhead Cost Project: Facts and Perspectives,* brief no. 1 (February 2004), p. 1.

74. Ibid.

75. Kennard Wing, Mark Hager, Thomas Pollak, and Patrick Rooney, "Paying for Not Paying for Overhead," *Foundation News and Commentary* 46, no. 3 (May/June 2005), http://www.foundationnews.org/CME/article.cfm?ID=3313, accessed June 29, 2006.

76. Ibid.

77. Ibid.

78. Thomas H. Pollak, Patrick Rooney, and Mark A. Hager, "Understanding Management and General Expenses in Nonprofits," Overhead Cost Study working paper presented at the Annual Meeting of the Association for Research on Nonprofit Organizations and Voluntary Action, New Orleans, 2001, p. 10.

79. "Brief of Amici Curiae Public Citizen, Inc., American Charities for Reasonable Fundraising Regulation, Inc., and 174 Other Nonprofit Organizations in Support of Respondents," *The People of the State of Illinois ex rel. James E. Ryan, Attorney General of the state of Illinois v. Telemarketing Associates, Inc., Richard Troia and Armet, Inc.,* no. 01-1806, Supreme Court of the United States, January 2003, p. 10.

80. Thomas H. Pollak, Patrick Rooney, and Mark A. Hager, "Understanding Management and General Expenses in Nonprofits," Overhead Cost Study working paper presented at the Annual Meeting of the Association for Research on Nonprofit Organizations and Voluntary Action, New Orleans, 2001.

81. Ibid., p. 6.

82. Mark A. Hager, "Current Practices in Allocation of Fundraising Expenditures," *New Direction for Philanthropic Fundraising* 41 (Fall 2003).

83. Center on Nonprofits and Philanthropy, Urban Institute at the Center on Philanthropy at Indiana University, "The Quality of Financial Reporting by Nonprofits: Findings and Implications," *Nonprofit Overhead Cost Project: Facts and Perspectives,* brief no. 4 (August 2004), p. 1.

84. Ibid., p. 4.

85. Kennard Wing, Thomas Pollak, and Patrick Rooney, "Toward a Theory of Organizational Fragility in the Nonprofit Sector," Overhead Cost Study working paper presented at the International Conference on Systems Thinking in Management, Philadelphia, PA, 2004, p. 7.

86. Kennard Wing, Mark Hager, Thomas Pollak, and Patrick Rooney, "Paying for Not Paying for Overhead," *Foundation News and Commentary* online, 46, no. 3 (May/June 2005), http://www.foundationnews.org/CME/article.cfm?ID=3313, accessed June 29, 2006.

87. Ibid.

88. Ibid.

89. *Randolph Riley, etc., et al. v. National Federation of the Blind of North Carolina, Inc., et al.,* no. 87–328, Supreme Court of the United States, June 29, 1988.

90. Pallotta TeamWorks, Email to riders, crew, and supporters of the vaccine rides, February 5, 2002.

91. Pallotta TeamWorks, "Record of Impact 1994–2002" (Los Angeles, 2006).

92. Pallotta TeamWorks, Email to riders, crew, and supporters of the vaccine rides, February 5, 2002.

93. Pallotta TeamWorks, "Record of Impact 1994–2002" (Los Angeles, 2006).

94. "A Closer Look at Charity Efficiency Ratings," Oxfam America press release, Boston, January 9, 2005.

95. Ibid.

96. Bruce R. Hopkins, "The Law of Fundraising," in "Brief of Amici Curiae Public Citizen, Inc., American Charities for Reasonable Fundraising Regulation, Inc., and 174 Other Nonprofit Organizations in Support of Respondents," *The People of the State of Illinois ex rel. James E. Ryan, Attorney General of the state of Illinois v. Telemarketing Associates, Inc., Richard Troia and Armet, Inc.,* no. 01–1806, Supreme Court of the United States, January 2003, p. 9.

97. Center on Philanthropy at Indiana University, "Sources of Contributions: Giving by Individuals," *American Association of Fundraising Counsel Trust for Philanthropy* (Bloomington, IN, 2003).

98. Nicole Lewis, "Charitable Giving Slides: Overall Donations Fall 2.3%, but Some Groups See Big Gains," *Chronicle of Philanthropy: The Newspaper of the Nonprofit World* online, June 27, 2002, http://philanthropy.com/free/articles/v14/i18/18002701.htm, accessed November 11, 2006.

99. American Institute of Philanthropy, "How American Institute of Philanthropy Rates Charities," "American Institute of Philanthropy: Helping You Give Wisely to Charity" website, http://www.charitywatch.org/criteria.html, accessed October 31, 2006.

100. American Institute of Philanthropy, "Top-Rated Charities," "American Institute of Philanthropy: Helping You Give Wisely to Charity" website, http://www.charitywatch.org/toprated.html, accessed November 1, 2006.

101. BBB Wise Giving Alliance, "Standards for Charity Accountability," "BBB Wise Giving Alliance" website, http://us.bbb.org/WWWRoot/SitePage.aspx?site=113&id=4dd04ofd-08af-4dd2-aaao-dcd66c1a17fc, accessed January 26, 2008.

102. William P. Barrett, "America's Most (and Least) Efficient Charities," "Forbes.com" website, November 24, 2004, http://www.forbes.com/2004/11/23/04charityland.html, accessed December 6, 2004.

103. Kathy M. Kristof, "Charity Takes Lots of Clarity," *Los Angeles Times,* December 2, 2007, http://www.latimes,com/business/la-fi-charity2dec 02.16214425.story?coll=la-headlines-business, accessed December 4, 2007.

104. Dan Prives, "Charity Standards Proposed by Watchdog Group Are Deeply Flawed," *Chronicle of Philanthropy: The Newspaper of the Nonprofit*

World online, April 2002, http://philanthropy.com/premium/articles/v14/i13/13006501.htm, accessed March 17, 2004.

105. Grant Williams, "Watchdog Group Proposes Changes in Evaluating Charity Operations," *Chronicle of Philanthropy: The Newspaper of the Nonprofit World* online, January 24, 2002; http://philanthropy.com/premium/articles/v14/i07/07002401.htm, accessed March 17, 2004.

106. Dan Prives, "Charity Standards Proposed by Watchdog Group Are Deeply Flawed," *Chronicle of Philanthropy: The Newspaper of the Nonprofit World* online, April 2002, http://philanthropy.com/premium/articles/v14/i13/13006501.htm, accessed March 17, 2004.

107. Ibid.

108. Ibid.

109. Rinku Bhattacharya and Daniel Tinkelman, "How Tough Are Better Business Bureau/Wise Giving Alliance Financial Standards?" *Nonprofit and Voluntary Sector Quarterly,* forthcoming.

110. Dan Tinkelman, memorandum to Dan Pallotta, August 22, 2006.

111. Elizabeth Schwinn, "Back to Basics: More Charities are Seeking—and Getting—Operating Support," *Chronicle of Philanthropy,* May 1, 2008, p. 21.

112. Ellison Research, "Most Americans Believe Non-Profits Spend Too Much on Overhead," Ellison Research website, http://www.ellisonresearch.com/releases/20080213.htm (accessed March 5, 2008), p. 2.

113. Ibid., p. 1.

114. Ibid., p. 2.

115. *Randolph Riley, etc., et al. v. National Federation of the Blind of North Carolina, Inc., et al.,* no. 87-328, Supreme Court of the United States, June 29, 1988.

116. Thomas H. Pollak, Patrick Rooney, and Mark A. Hager, "Understanding Management and General Expenses in Nonprofits," Overhead Cost Study working paper presented at the Annual Meeting of the Association for Research on Nonprofit Organizations and Voluntary Action, New Orleans, 2001, p. 2.

117. Kennard Wing, Mark Hager, Thomas Pollak, and Patrick Rooney, "Paying for Not Paying for Overhead," *Foundation News and Commentary* 46, no. 3 (May/June 2005), http://www.foundationnews.org/CME/article/cfm?ID=3313, accessed June 29, 2006.

118. Dan Gordon, "Giving Donors Control," *Stanford Social Innovation Review* online, April 1, 2006, http://www.ssireview.org/articles/entry/giving_donors_control/, accessed February 10, 2007.

119. Ibid.

120. Ibid.

121. U.S. Office of Personnel Management, "Welcome to the Official One-Stop Source for Information About the Combined Federal Campaign," "U.S. Office of Personnel Management" website, http://www.opm.gov/cfc/, accessed March 26, 2007.

122. Grant Williams, "Nonprofit Groups Seek Congress's Help in Opposing Change to the Federal Charity Drive," *Chronicle of Philanthropy: The Newspaper*

of the Nonprofit World online, February 7, 2007, http://www.philanthropy
.com/free/update/2007/02/2007020701.htm, accessed February 10, 2007.

123. Ibid.

124. Ibid.

125. Kennard Wing, Thomas Pollak, and Patrick Rooney, "Toward a Theory of
Organizational Fragility in the Nonprofit Sector," Overhead Cost Study
working paper presented at the International Conference on Systems
Thinking in Management, 2004.

126. Center on Nonprofits and Philanthropy, Urban Institute at the Center on
Philanthropy at Indiana University, "Getting What We Pay For: Low
Overhead Limits Nonprofit Effectiveness," *Nonprofit Overhead Cost Proj-
ect: Facts and Perspectives,* brief no. 3 (August 2004): pp. 1–2.

127. Kennard Wing, Thomas Pollak, and Patrick Rooney, "Toward a Theory of
Organizational Fragility in the Nonprofit Sector," Overhead Cost Study
working paper presented at *The International Conference on Systems Thinking in Management,* 2004, p. 10.

128. Kennard Wing, Mark Hager, Thomas Pollak, and Patrick Rooney, "Paying
for Not Paying for Overhead," *Foundation News and Commentary* 46, no. 3
(May/June 2005), http://www.foundationnews.org/CME/article.cfm
?ID=3313, accessed June 29, 2006.

129. William H. Murray, "Quotes by W. H. Murray: Until one is committed
there is hesitancy. . . ," "Gaia Community" website, http://www.gaia
.com/quotes/WH_Murray, accessed January 28, 2008.

130. Robert D. Herman and David O. Renz, "Nonprofit Organizational Effectiveness: Practical Implications of Research on an Elusive Concept," Midwest Center for Nonprofit Leadership; L. P. Cookingham Institute of
Public Affairs; Henry W. Bloch School of Business & Public Administration; (University of Missouri—Kansas City, 2002), p. 3.

131. Madeline Lee, "Foundations Should Listen to Charities," *Chronicle of Philanthropy: The Newspaper of the Nonprofit World,* March 4, 2004, pp. 37–38.

132. B. Donabedian and Dan Tinkelman, "Street Lamps, Alleys, Ratio Analysis
and Nonprofit Organizations," *Nonprofit Management and Leadership* 18,
no. 1 (2007), pp. 5–18.

133. The Center on Philanthropy at Indiana University, *Giving USA 2007: The
Annual Report on Philanthropy for the Year 2006* (Bloomington, IN: Giving USA Foundation, 2007), p. 12.

134. B. Donabedian and Dan Tinkelman, "Street Lamps, Alleys, Ratio Analysis
and Nonprofit Organizations," *Nonprofit Management and Leadership* 18,
no. 1 (2007), pp. 5–18.

135. Sam Harris, *The End of Faith* (New York: W.W. Norton & Company,
2004), p. 224.

136. "2003 CEO Compensation," "Forbes.com" website, October 20, 2003,
http://www. Forbes.com, accessed March 18, 2004.

137. Brad Wolverton, "Rethinking Charity Rules," *Chronicle of Philanthropy:
The Newspaper of the Nonprofit World,* July 22, 2004, pp. 31, 33.

Chapter 4: Courage (pp. 177–185)

1. Thomas Merton, *The Waters of Siloe* (San Diego, CA: Harvest Books, 1949), p. xviii.
2. Ibid., p. 3.
3. Monks.org, "Expansion & Renewal—Gethsemani—History—The Abbey of Gethsemani," "Monks.org" website, http://www.monks.org/hist_gethsemani3.html, accessed January 21, 2008.
4. Tony Perry, "Philanthropy That Was Deeply Personal," *Los Angeles Times,* January 31, 2004.
5. Emmett D. Carson, "Public Expectations and Nonprofit Sector Realities: A Growing Divide with Disastrous Consequences," *Nonprofit and Voluntary Sector Quarterly* 31, No. 3 (2002), p. 432.

Case Study—Pallotta TeamWorks (pages 189–228)

1. City of Malden, Massachusetts, "About Malden; History of Malden," City of Malden, Massachusetts, website, http://www.ci.malden.ma.us/index.asp?LI=about&L2=history, accessed February 20, 2008.
2. The company was named "Pallotta & Associates" at the time of our first events.
3. The San Francisco AIDS Foundation became a beneficiary of the event as well, beginning in 1995.
4. Pallotta TeamWorks, "Record of Impact 1994–2002" (Los Angeles, 2006).
5. Ibid.
6. Ibid.
7. Based on $556 million in donor contributions with an estimated average of $75 per donation; number of unique donors not estimated.
8. Pallotta TeamWorks, "Record of Impact 1994–2002" (Los Angeles, 2006).
9. Suzanne Perry, "Courting the New Congress," *Chronicle of Philanthropy: The Newspaper of the Nonprofit World,* January 25, 2007, p. 28.
10. "Foundation Center" website, http://foundationcenter.org/, accessed 2003; "General Motors Foundation, Inc.," "The Foundation Directory Online" website, http://fconline.fdncenter.org/gperl/fdonl_dtgm_show.pl?id =GENE006&row1data=general, accessed March 16, 2004.
11. "Charitable Giving at 93 Major Corporations," *Chronicle of Philanthropy: The Newspaper of the Nonprofit World,* August 5, 2004, pp. 10–15.
12. "Foundation Center" website, http://foundationcenter.org/, accessed 2003.
13. Pallotta TeamWorks, "Record of Impact 1994–2002" (Los Angeles, 2006).
14. Ibid.
15. Ibid.
16. State Division of Consumer Affairs, "Final Accounting Report," solicitor: Pallotta TeamWorks, Inc., charity: American Foundation for Suicide

Prevention, solicitation dates: September 1, 2001–August 31, 2002, campaign description: 26-Mile Walk (Richmond, VA, January 24, 2003).

17. Pallotta TeamWorks, "Record of Impact 1994–2002" (Los Angeles, 2006).
18. Pallotta TeamWorks, "Record of Impact 1994–2002" (Los Angeles, 2006).
19. Pallotta TeamWorks, "Record of Impact 1994–2002" (Los Angeles, 2006).
20. Ibid.
21. Office of Bill Lockyer, Attorney General, State of California, "Attorney General's Summary of Results of Charitable Solicitation by Commercial Fundraisers: Year Ending 2004," (California Department of Justice, Sacramento, 2004).
22. Jeff Wise, "Altruism for Fun and Profit," *New York Times Magazine,* September 7, 1997, p. 65.
23. AIDS Community Donor Action, "Ask Pallotta TeamWorks Will Their Upcoming AIDS Vaccine Events Save Anyone's Future, EXCEPT THEIR OWN?" print advertisement, 2002.
24. "Open Wide, AIDS Ride," *POZ: Health, Life & HIV* online, October 1998, http://www.poz.com/articles/232_1655.shtml, accessed October 26, 2003.
25. Tim Murphy and Kevin O'Leary, "The 2002 POZCARDS," *POZ: Health, Life & HIV* online, January 2003, http://www.poz.com/articles/163_2929.shtml, accessed January 11, 2007.
26. Institute of Design at the Illinois Institute of Technology, "Pallotta TeamWorks: How Design Created Economic Value . . . Then Lost It," "Institute of Design at the Illinois Institute of Technology" website, October 10, 2003, http://trex.id.iit.edu/~bschauer/downloads/PTW_casestudy.pdf, accessed January 9, 2007.
27. Pallotta TeamWorks, "Avon Breast Cancer 3-Day: Budget Summary" (Los Angeles, 2002).
28. Based on seventy-nine events with an estimated advertising budget of $250,000 each.
29. Cyril Manning, "Holier Than Thou: A Bitter Battle Between Organizers and Beneficiaries Tears the California AIDS Ride Apart," "Salon.com" website, February 1, 2002, http://dir.salon.com/story/mwt/feature/2002/02/01/aids_ride/index.html?source=search&aim=/mwt/feature, accessed January 9, 2007.
30. Jeff Wise, "Altruism for Fun and Profit," *New York Times Magazine,* September 7, 1997, p. 65.
31. Carol Morello, "Fundraiser with a Marketer's Touch," *Washington Post* online, June 20, 2001, http://pqasb.pqarchiver.com/washingtonpost/access/74252206.html?dids=74252206:74252206&FMT=ABS&FMTS=ABS:FT& fmac=&date=Jun+20%2C+2001&author =Carol+Morello&desc=Fundraiser+With+a+Marketer%27s+Touch, accessed January 29, 2008.
32. "Open Wide, AIDS Ride," *POZ: Health, Life & HIV* online, October 1998, http://www.poz.com/articles/232_1655.shtml, accessed October 26, 2003.

33. Kaiser Network, "Critics Say AIDS Rides Place Participant 'Experience' Above Charities," "Kaisernetwork.org" website, http://www.kaisernet work.org/daily_reports/rep_index.cfm?hint=1&DR_ID=5367, accessed January 28, 2008.

34. Cyril Manning, "Holier Than Thou: A Bitter Battle Between Organizers and Beneficiaries Tears the California AIDS Ride Apart," "Salon.com" website, February 1, 2002, http://dir.salon.com/story/mwt/feature/2002 /02/01/aids_ride/index.html?source=search&aim=/mwt/feature, accessed January 9, 2007.

35. AIDS/LifeCycle, "7-Day 545 Mile Cycling Event to Support HIV/AIDS Services," "AIDS/LifeCycle" website, http://www.aidslifecycle.org/index .html, accessed January 11, 2007.

36. Stephen Innes, *Creating the Commonwealth: The Economic Culture of Puritan New England* (New York: W.W. Norton & Company, 1995).

37. Pallotta TeamWorks, "Comparisons, Graphs, Data and Photographs," trial support documentation for Judicial Arbitration and Mediation Services, case no. 1420011424 (Los Angeles, 2003).

38. Tom Musbach, "Charities Split with AIDS Ride Promoter," "Gay.com/ PlanetOut.com" website, http://www.planetout.com/news/article.html ?2002/05/31/2, accessed January 9, 2007.

39. Kim Curtis, "AIDS Ride Management Dispute Leads to Lawsuit," *Berkeley Daily Planet* online, December 19, 2001, http://www.berkeleydailyplanet .com/article.cfm?archiveDate=12-19-01&storyID=9064, accessed January 12, 2007.

40. Bob Pool, "AIDS Ride Founder Lays Off L.A. Staff," *Los Angeles Times* online, August 27, 2002, http://www.aegis.com/news/lt/2002/LT020804 .html, accessed January 9, 2007.

41. Tyche Hendricks, "AIDS Ride Firm Closes Its Doors: Raised Millions in Bay Area," *San Francisco Chronicle* online, August 25, 2002, http:// www.aegis.org/news/sc/2002/SC020812.html, accessed January 11, 2007; Tim Murphy and Kevin O'Leary, "The 2002 POZCARDS," *POZ: Health, Life & HIV* online, January 2003, http://www.poz.com/articles/163_2929.shtml, accessed January 11, 2007; Cyril Manning, "Holier Than Thou: A Bitter Battle Between Organizers and Beneficiaries Tears the California AIDS Ride Apart," "Salon.com" website, February 1, 2002, http://dir.salon.com/story/mwt/feature/2002/02/01/aids_ride/ index.html? source=search&aim=/mwt/feature, accessed January 9, 2007.

42. Pallotta TeamWorks, "2002 Event Catalogue" (Los Angeles, 2001).

43. Ibid.

44. Cyril Manning, "Holier Than Thou: A Bitter Battle Between Organizers and Beneficiaries Tears the California AIDS Ride Apart," "Salon.com" website, February 1, 2002, http://dir.salon.com/story/mwt/feature/2002/ 02 /01/aids_ride/index.html?source=search&aim=/mwt/feature, accessed January 9, 2007.

45. Kim Curtis, "AIDS Ride Management Dispute Leads to Lawsuit," *Berkeley Daily Planet* online, December 19, 2001, http://www.berkeleydaily planet.com/article.cfm?archiveDate=12-19-01&storyID=9064, accessed January 12, 2007.

46. Bob Pool, "AIDS Ride Founder Lays Off L.A. Staff," *Los Angeles Times* online, August 27, 2002, http://www.aegis.com/news/lt/2002/LT020804 .html, accessed January 9, 2007.

47. "Avon Products Foundation, Inc.'s Post-Hearing Memorandum in Opposition to Pallotta TeamWorks's Contract Claim," *Pallotta TeamWorks v. Avon Products Foundation, Inc.,* no. 1420011424, Judicial Arbitration and Mediation Services (New York: 2001), p. 91.

48. Jon Barrett, "The World According to Dan," *Advocate,* February 19, 2002, p. 39.

49. Institute of Design at the Illinois Institute of Technology, "Pallotta Team-Works: How Design Created Economic Value . . . Then Lost It," "Institute of Design at the Illinois Institute of Technology" website, October 10, 2003, http://trex.id.iit.edu/~bschauer/downloads/PTW_casestudy .pdf, accessed January 9, 2007.

50. Pallotta TeamWorks, "Record of Impact 1994–2002" (Los Angeles, 2006).

51. Julian Barnes, "Do Some AIDS Events Take Donors for a Ride?" *U.S. News & World Report,* June 16, 1997, via Lexis-Nexis, http://web.lexis-nexis.com, accessed April 10, 2004.

52. Pallotta TeamWorks, "Record of Impact 1994–2002" (Los Angeles, 2006).

53. Julian Barnes, "Do Some AIDS Events Take Donors for a Ride?" *U.S. News & World Report,* June 16, 1997, via Lexis-Nexis, http://web.lexis-nexis.com, accessed April 10, 2004.

54. Pallotta TeamWorks, "Record of Impact 1994–2002" (Los Angeles, 2006).

55. Julian Barnes, "Do Some AIDS Events Take Donors for a Ride?" *U.S. News & World Report,* June 16, 1997, via Lexis-Nexis, http://web.lexis-nexis .com, accessed April 10, 2004.

56. "24th Annual Trek Tri-Island Bicycle Ride," American Lung Association of Washington press release, Seattle, 2006.

57. Pallotta TeamWorks, "Record of Impact 1994–2002" (Los Angeles, 2006).

58. "3rd Annual Pacific Coast Bicycle Ride Raises More Than $100,000 for the American Lung Association of Washington: 39 Lung Health Champions Riding 1,000 Miles to Support Lung Research," American Lung Association of Washington press release (Seattle, 2006).

59. Pallotta TeamWorks, "Record of Impact 1994–2002" (Los Angeles, 2006).

60. Center on Philanthropy at Indiana University, "Sources of Contributions: Giving by Individuals," *American Association of Fundraising Counsel Trust for Philanthropy,* 2003, http://nccsdataweb.urban.org/ kbfiles/554/Giving%20USA%202003%20excerpt.pdf, accessed June 29, 2006.

61. Dan Tinkelman, "Breast Cancer Walks: Linking Organizational Stresses and Questionable Accounting Practices," working paper presented at

ARNOVA conference, Philadelphia, PA, November 2007, p. 50. Professor Tinkelman served as Pallotta TeamWorks' accounting expert in litigation against the Avon Products Foundation.

62. Ibid., p. 24.
63. Ibid., p. 18.
64. Ibid., p. 19.
65. Includes expenses for four canceled events.
66. Pallotta TeamWorks, "Record of Impact 1994–2002" (Los Angeles: 2006).
67. Megan Tench, "AIDS Ride Returns on Different Course," *Boston Globe* online, September 14, 2003, http://www.boston.com/dailyglobe2/257/metro/AIDS_ride_returns_on_different_courseP.shtml, accessed September 14, 2003.
68. Pallotta TeamWorks, "Record of Impact 1994–2002" (Los Angeles, 2006).
69. Ibid.
70. Independent Sector, "Before *Madigan:* A Brief History of the United States Supreme Court and Charitable Solicitation Regulation," "Independent Sector" website, 2004, http://www.independentsector.org/programs/gr/Ryanhistory.html, accessed January 5, 2008; *Randolph Riley, etc., et al. v. National Federation of the Blind of North Carolina, Inc., et al.,* no. 87–328, Supreme Court of the United States, June 29, 1988.
71. Pallotta TeamWorks, "Record of Impact 1994–2002" (Los Angeles, 2006).
72. Ibid.
73. Janet Wiscombe, "Leader of the Pack," *Los Angeles Times Magazine*, May 10, 1998.
74. Pallotta TeamWorks, "Record of Impact 1994–2002" (Los Angeles, 2006).
75. Ibid.
76. Ibid.
77. Ibid.
78. Ibid.
79. AIDS Community Donor Action, "Ask Pallotta TeamWorks Will Their Upcoming AIDS Vaccine Events Save Anyone's Future, EXCEPT THEIR OWN?," print advertisement, 2002.
80. AIDS Community Donor Action. "Pallotta TeamWorks and Its Lawsuit—A Threat to Public Trust in AIDS Fundraising: Need to Distinguish Between Events is Greater Than Ever," *AIDS Community Donor Action* website, http://aidscommunitydonoraction.org/email1.htm, accessed January 13, 2007.
81. Wheels of Fortune, "AIDS Vaccine Ride Cancelled," "Wheels of Fortune: AIDS Ride Updates 2001/2002—Lawsuits, Loss and Lifecycle" website, http://members.tripod.com/~homeo/wheels8.html, accessed January 13, 2007.
82. Life Foundation, "2004 Annual Report" (Honolulu, 2004).
83. Pallotta TeamWorks, "Record of Impact 1994–2002" (Los Angeles, 2006).
84. Bill O'Reilly, "Unresolved Problem," O'*Reilly Factor,* May 17, 2002, via Lexis-Nexis, http://web.lexis-nexis.com, accessed May 1, 2004.

85. Amy Horowitz, "O'Reilly Fights Fraud: From Free Press to FOX," *Daily Free Press* online, January 16, 2002, http://media.www.daily free-press.com/media/storage/paper87/news/2002/01/16/Spotlight/Oreilly .Fights.Fraud.From.Free.Press.To.Fox-164581.shtml, accessed May 1, 2004.

86. Pallotta TeamWorks, "Record of Impact 1994–2002" (Los Angeles, 2006).

87. Ibid.

88. Ibid.

89. Jeremy Quittner, "Breaking the Cycle: Two Top California AIDS Groups Fire Pallotta TeamWorks—AIDS Ride," *Advocate* online, November 20, 2001, http://findarticles.com/p/articles/mi_m1589/is_2001_Nov_20/ai_ 80116717, accessed January 6, 2008.

90. Ibid.

91. Pallotta TeamWorks, "Record of Impact 1994–2002" (Los Angeles, 2006).

92. Kim Curtis, "AIDS Ride Management Dispute Leads to Lawsuit," *Berkeley Daily Planet* online, December 19, 2001, http://www.berkeleydailyplanet .com/article.cfm?archiveDate=12-19-01&storyID=9064, accessed January 12, 2007.

93. The San Francisco AIDS Foundation was not a beneficiary of the 1994 event. Pallotta TeamWorks, "Record of Impact 1994–2002" (Los Angeles, 2006).

94. Kim Curtis, "AIDS Ride Management Dispute Leads to Lawsuit," *Berkeley Daily Planet* online, December 19, 2001, http://www.berkeleydailyplanet .com/article.cfm?issue=12-19-01&storyID=9064, accessed January 12, 2007.

95. Center on Nonprofits and Philanthropy, Urban Institute at the Center on Philanthropy at Indiana University, "The Quality of Financial Reporting by Nonprofits: Findings and Implications," *Nonprofit Overhead Cost Project: Facts and Perspectives,* brief no. 4 (August 2004), p. 2.

96. Cyril Manning, "Holier Than Thou: A Bitter Battle Between Organizers and Beneficiaries Tears the California AIDS Ride Apart," "Salon.com" website, February 1, 2002, http://dir.salon.com/story/mwt/feature/2002 /02/01/aids_ride/index.html?source=search&aim=/mwt/feature, accessed January 9, 2007.

97. Pallotta TeamWorks, "Record of Impact 1994–2002" (Los Angeles, 2006).

98. Michael D. Young, Esq., "Partial Final Award and Statement of Reasons," *Pallotta TeamWorks v. Avon Products Foundation, Inc.,* no. 1420011424, Judicial Arbitration and Mediation Services (New York, July 15, 2005), p. 29.

99. Pallotta TeamWorks, "Record of Impact 1994–2002" (Los Angeles, 2006).

100. Michael D. Young, Esq., "Partial Final Award and Statement of Reasons," *Pallotta TeamWorks v. Avon Products Foundation, Inc.,* no. 1420011424, Judicial Arbitration and Mediation Services (New York, July 15, 2005), p. 23.

101. Ibid., p. 8.

102. Ibid., p. 45.

103. Ibid., p. 10.
104. Ibid., p. 12.
105. Ibid., p. 23.
106. Ibid., p. 22.
107. Ibid., p. 24.
108. Ibid., pp. 29, 30.
109. Ibid., pp. 68, 63.
110. Ibid., pp. 56, 57, 56.
111. Ibid., p. 57.
112. Ibid., p. 59.
113. Ibid., p. 49.
114. Ibid., p. 50.
115. Ibid., p. 51.
116. Ibid.
117. Tyche Hendricks, "AIDS Ride Firm Closes Its Doors: Raised Millions in Bay Area," *San Francisco Chronicle,* August 25, 2002, http://www.aegis .org/news/sc/2002/SC020812.html, accessed January 11, 2007.
118. Care Exchange, "California AIDS Ride Statistical Overview: Financial Overview of the 2002 Ride," "Care Exchange" website, http://www. caree.org/stats/carstats.htm, accessed March 16, 2004; Care Exchange calculates "Total Return to Charities" of $1.6 million for the 2002 AIDS Lifecycle by deducting $3.1 million in "Total Expenses" from "Total Revenue" of $4.7 million, including "Total Pledges & Registration Fees" of $3.2 million and "Total Other Revenue" of $1.5 million. "AIDS Lifecycle" website states that "the event raised $3.2 million" (AIDS/Lifecycle, "Press Room: History of AIDS/LifeCycle," "AIDS/Lifecycle" website, http:// www.aidslifecycle.org/press/history.html, accessed January 4, 2008).
119. Care Exchange, "California AIDS Ride Statistical Overview: Financial Overview of the 2002 Ride," Care Exchange website, http://www.caree .org/stats/carstats.htm, accessed March 16, 2004.
120. In 2002, AIDS Lifecycle was competing with our own California AIDS-Ride, which we went ahead with and produced for another Los Angeles charity. The AIDS Lifecycle was scheduled to take place close to the traditional California AIDSRide dates and employed the same seven-day length and the same proposition: bicycle from San Francisco to Los Angeles, and raise a mandatory four-figure minimum of donations. Consequently, the two events were cannibalizing one another. At the same time, a legal dispute was creating negative publicity. Thereafter, however, we discontinued California AIDSRide, and an event that had netted more than $40 million for people with AIDS ceased to exist (Pallotta TeamWorks, "Record of Impact 1994–2002" [Los Angeles, 2006]).

   Our contract for the 2001 event with the Los Angeles Gay & Lesbian Center stated, "8.2. . .The AIDS Ride bike-a-thon event is an original concept of Pallotta and Center shall not use or exploit such concept at anytime, regardless of the termination of this Agreement, without the express written consent of Pallotta." It further stated, "The parties recognize and agree that any violation of Paragraph 8.2 will cause immediate and irreparable damages to Pallotta, and that accordingly any appropriate equitable or injunctive remedy, including preliminary injunctions, restraining orders, and permanent injunctions, may be obtained without the necessary of proving actual damages therewith" (Pallotta Team-Works, "California AIDS Ride 8—Los Angeles Agreement." [Los Angeles, 2000]).

Our contract for the 2001 event with the San Francisco AIDS Foundation stated, "7.2 . . . The AIDS Ride event is an original concept of Pallotta and S.F.A.F. shall not use or exploit the multi-day bike-a-thon concept at anytime, regardless of the termination of this Agreement, without the express written consent of Pallotta." It further stated, "The parties recognize and agree that any violation of Paragraph 7.2 will cause immediate and irreparable damages to Pallotta and that accordingly any appropriate equitable or injunctive remedy, including preliminary injunctions, restraining orders, and permanent injunctions, may be obtained without the necessity of proving actual damages therewith" (Pallotta TeamWorks, "California AIDS Ride 8—San Francisco Agreement" [Los Angeles, 2000]). Because we thought the charities' events violated these provisions, we filed a motion for a preliminary injunction. The court, however, denied our motion.

Of course, the important issue here is not how one bike ride fared against another, or what impact a preliminary injunction motion may have had on either's results. The point is simply to look at the consequences of our belief system. There wouldn't have been any competing bike rides or any preliminary injunction motion in the first place if we didn't ask charity to respond to short-term financial pressures, efficiency standards, and the controversy which that belief system generates. We don't ask the for-profit sector to respond to any of these things.

121. Gay.com/PlanetOut.com, "Los Angeles Gay Center Cuts 55 Jobs," "Gay .com/PlanetOut.com" website, http://www.planetout.com/news/article .html?2002/03/25/2, accessed January 26, 2008.

122. Michael Stoll, "AIDS Group Chops Staff: Top Exec Taking 12 Percent Pay Cut," *San Francisco Examiner,* June 19, 2002; Christopher Heredia, "Layoffs, Pay Cuts Announced at S.F. AIDS Foundation: Nonprofit Blames Post-Sept. 11 Slump, Costs of Charity Ride," *San Francisco Chronicle,* June 19, 2002.

123. Gay.com/PlanetOut.com, "Los Angeles Gay Center Cuts 55 Jobs," "Gay .com/PlanetOut.com" website, http://www.planetout.com/news/article .html?2002/03/25/2, accessed January 26, 2008.

124. Care Exchange, "California AIDS Ride Statistical Overview: Financial Overview of the 2002 Ride," "Care Exchange" website, http://www.caree .org/stats/carstats.htm, accessed March 16, 2004.

125. Ibid.
126. Pallotta TeamWorks, "Record of Impact 1994–2002" (Los Angeles, 2006).
127. Pallotta TeamWorks figure from ibid. "AIDS Lifecycle" website gives the amounts riders or the events raised from 2002 to 2007, respectively, as $3.2 million, $4.3 million, $5 million, $6.8 million, $8 million, and $11 million. (Care Exchange gives $4.7 million for 2002. I have used the $4.7 million figure in calculating the estimate.)
128. Jacqueline L. Salmon, "Charities Cut the Fat from Sports Fundraisers," *Washington Post* online, January 20, 2004, http://www.washingtonpost .com/wp-dyn/articles/A54750-2004Jun19.html, accessed January 30, 2008.
129. Pallotta TeamWorks, "Record of Impact 1994–2002" (Los Angeles, 2006); Avon Foundation, "News on the Avon Walk for Breast Cancer 2003 and 2004." "Avon Foundation" website, 2004, http://walk.avonfoundation .org, accessed January 26, 2005.
130. Pallotta TeamWorks figures from "Record of Impact 1994–2002" (Los Angeles, 2006). The total raised by participants includes $6.2 million in registration fees. Avon figures from Avon financial statements. Those for 2006 are based on $46,723,824 total income, which Avon states was "from the public," plus a $4,007,777 contribution from Avon Products, less $2 million from the Avon Foundation Awards Celebration, which, according to an Avon press release, "raised nearly $2 million." The figures for 2006 may include income from Avon's Need for Speed Relay Against Domestic Violence. Those for 2005 are based on $36,843,908 total income, which Avon states was "from the public," plus a $4,007,779 contribution from Avon Products, less $2 million from the 50th Anniversary Gala. (An Avon press release says, "The event raised $2 million.") The figures for 2004 are based on $36,278,911 total income, which Avon states was "from the public," plus a $3,189,176 contribution from Avon Products less $2.2 million from the Kiss Goodbye to Breast Cancer event per Avon's website. Those for 2003 are based on $26,928,695 in "special events income" plus a $3,600,656 contribution from Avon Products less $2 million for Kiss Goodbye to Breast Cancer, which, PR Newswire said, "is expected to raise $2 million."
131. The $70.9 million figure for the 2002 Pallotta TeamWorks event is based on gross participant income of $145,372,218 (from Avon 2002 financial statements) and subtracts $2 million in proceeds from Kiss Goodbye to Breast Cancer (per Avon press release) for an adjusted gross participant income of $143,372,218. The net figure specified for Pallotta TeamWorks is calculated by subtracting from the adjusted gross participant income the sum of (1) event expenses of $71,852,150 shown as fundraising (from Avon 2002 financial statements), and (2) $596,000 in estimated expenses from Avon's Kiss Goodbye to Breast Cancer event (using a $2 million income figure [from Avon press release] and applying its 30 percent cost ratio from the 2001 Kiss Goodbye event.) The figure does not

include income or expenses for Avon's 2002 Boogie for Breast Cancer event. See note 130 for information on gross income for the 2003 Avon event. The net figure for the Avon 2003 event is calculated by subtracting from the gross income the sum of (1) $10,231,852 in total event expenses shown as fundraising (from Avon 2003 financial statements), and (2) $7,822,416 in joint costs allocated to the Breast Cancer Crusade (also from Avon 2003 financial statements), and adding back $596,000 in already deducted estimated expenses from the Kiss Goodbye to Breast Cancer event (using a $2 million income figure [from PR Newswire] and applying its 30 percent cost ratio from the 2001 Kiss Goodbye event). Joint costs are deducted in order to achieve a fair comparison, as no event-related costs were allocated to programs on the 2002 Pallotta TeamWorks figures.

132. See note 130.
133. See note 130.
134. See note 130.
135. See note 130.
136. See note 131 for the 2002 Pallotta TeamWorks comparison figure. See note 130 for information on Avon's gross income. The 2004 figure is calculated by subtracting from Avon's gross income the sum of (1) $8,303,428 in total event expenses shown as fundraising (from Avon 2004 financial statements), and (2) $8,536,213 in joint costs allocated to the Breast Cancer Crusade (also from Avon 2004 financial statements); and adding back $655,600 in already deducted estimated expenses from the Kiss Goodbye to Breast Cancer event (using a $2.2 million income figure [from the Avon website] and applying its 30 percent cost ratio from the 2001 Kiss Goodbye event). The 2005 figure is calculated by subtracting from the gross income the sum of (1) $8,478,286 in total event expenses shown as fundraising (from Avon 2005 financial statements) and (2) $8,322,589 in joint costs allocated to the Breast Cancer Crusade (also from Avon 2005 financial statements); and adding back $596,000 in already deducted estimated expenses from its 50th Anniversary Gala (using a $2 million income figure [from Avon press release] and applying the 30 percent cost ratio from the 2001 Kiss Goodbye event). Joint costs are deducted in order to achieve a fair comparison, as no event-related costs were allocated to programs on the 2002 Pallotta TeamWorks figures.
137. Daniel Tinkelman, "Breast Cancer Walks: Linking Organizational Stresses and Questionable Accounting Practices," working paper presented at ARNOVA conference, Philadelphia, PA, November 2007, p. 19.
138. Ibid.

BIBLIOGRAPHY

"African AIDS Trek: 150 Ordinary People Take an Extraordinary 7-Day, 75-Mile Trek Through South Africa to Raise Awareness and Money for an AIDS Vaccine." Pallotta TeamWorks press release. Los Angeles, February 27, 2002.

AIDS Community Donor Action. "Ask Pallotta TeamWorks Will Their Upcoming AIDS Vaccine Events Save Anyone's Future, EXCEPT THEIR OWN?" Print advertisement, 2002.

AIDS/Lifecycle. "Press Room: AIDS/LifeCycle Raises a Record $11 Million to Fight AIDS." "AIDS/Lifecycle" website. http://www.aidslifecycle.org/press/alc6_main.html (accessed January 4, 2008).

———. "Press Room: History of AIDS/LifeCycle." "AIDS/Lifecycle" website. http://www.aidslifecycle.org/press/history.html (accessed January 4, 2008).

———. "7-Day 545 Mile Cycling Event to Support HIV/AIDS Services?" "AIDS/LifeCycle" website. http://www.aidslifecycle.org/index.html (accessed January 11, 2007).

"AIDS/LifeCycle Victory! L.A. Gay & Lesbian Center and S.F. AIDS Foundation Prevail." San Francisco AIDS Foundation press release. San Francisco, January 14, 2002.

Allen, Scott. "Critics Blast Slow Progress on Cancer: Say Costly Drugs Do Little to Extend Lives." *Boston Globe* online, December 2, 2007. http://www.boston.com/news/health/articles/2007/12/02/critics_blast_slow_progress_on_cancer/ (accessed December 3, 2007).

Alvarado, Audrey R. "Are There Too Many Nonprofits?: A Loaded Question." Compiled by Heather Peeler. *Foundation News & Commentary,* May–June 2004, pp. 47–48.

"Amazon.com." "Information Headquarters" website. http://www.informationheadquarters.com/Amazon.shtml (accessed March 18, 2004).

American Cancer Society. "American Cancer Society Homepage." "American Cancer Society" website. http://www.cancer.org/docroot/home/index.asp (accessed January 26, 2008).

———. "Information and Resources for Breast, Colon, Lung, Prostate and Other Forms of Cancer." "American Cancer Society" website. http://www.cancer.org/docroot/home/index.asp (accessed March 12, 2007).

American Cancer Society, Inc. and Affiliate Entities. "Combined Statement of Functional Expenses for the Year Ended August 31, 2005." American Cancer Society, Inc. and Affiliate Entities, 2005.

American Diabetes Association. "Donate—Support the Cause—American Diabetes Association." "American Diabetes Association" website. http://diabetes .org/support-the-cause/make-a-donation.jsp?WTLPromo=HEADER_donate&vms=254789525884 (accessed January 26, 2008).

American Institute of Philanthropy. "About AIP." "American Institute of Philanthropy: Helping You Give Wisely to Charity" website. http://www .charitywatch.org/aboutaip.html (accessed November 1, 2006).

———. "Criteria." "American Institute of Philanthropy: Helping You Give Wisely to Charity" website. http://www.charitywatch.org/criteria.html (accessed November 1, 2006).

———. "How American Institute of Philanthropy Rates Charities." "American Institute of Philanthropy: Helping You Give Wisely to Charity" website. http://www.charitywatch.org/criteria.html (accessed October 31, 2006).

———. "Tips for Giving Wisely to Charity." "American Institute of Philanthropy: Helping You Give Wisely to Charity" website. http://www.charity watch.org/tips.html (accessed March 18, 2004).

———. "Top-Rated Charities." "American Institute of Philanthropy: Helping You Give Wisely to Charity" website. http://www.charitywatch.org/toprated .html (accessed August 16, 2006).

———. "Top-Rated Charities." "American Institute of Philanthropy: Helping You Give Wisely to Charity" website. http://www.charitywatch.org/top rated.html (accessed November 1, 2006).

———. "Welcome." "American Institute of Philanthropy: Helping You Give Wisely to Charity" website. http://www.charitywatch.org/ (accessed November 1, 2006).

American Lung Association. "American Lung Association Homepage." "American Lung Association" website. http://www.lungusa.org/site/pp .asp?c=dvLUK9O0E&b=22542 (accessed March 12, 2007).

American Red Cross. "American Red Cross Homepage." "American Red Cross" website. http://american.redcross.org/site/PageServer?pagename =ntld_main (accessed January 26, 2008).

———. "Donate Now." "American Red Cross" website. http://american.redcross .org/donate/donate.html (accessed March 12, 2007).

Anft, Michael. "A Growing Debt to Society." *Chronicle of Philanthropy: The Newspaper of the Nonprofit World* online, March 23, 2006. http://philanthropy .com/premium/articles/v18/i11/11003101.htm (accessed January 28, 2007).

"Around the World by Private Jet, January 5–27, 2008." UCLA Alumni Association brochure. Los Angeles, 2007.

Associated Press. "AIDS Walk Heads into 'Make-or-Break' Weekend." *Associated Press State & Local Wire,* 2001, via Lexis-Nexis, http://web.lexis-nexis .com (accessed March 18, 2004).

——. "Around the Nation: Hands Across America Faces Costs and Delay." *New York Times,* August 18, 1986, via Lexis-Nexis, http://web.lexis-nexis .com (accessed February 5, 2007).

——. "Berkeley Man Sues AIDS Ride Organizer." *Associated Press,* April 25, 2002. "Wheels of Fortune: AIDS Ride Updates 2001/2002—Lawsuits, Loss and Lifecycle" website. http://members.tripod.com/~homeo/wheels8 .html (accessed January 13, 2007).

——. "Costs Eat Up Hands Across America Proceeds." *Associated Press,* August 18, 1986, via Lexis-Nexis, http://web.lexis-nexis.com (accessed February 5, 2007).

——. "Hands Across America: Reach Exceeded Grasp." *New York Times,* May 26, 1987, via Lexis-Nexis, http://web.lexis-nexis.com (accessed August 15, 2006).

Association of Fundraising Professionals. "Code of Ethical Principles and Standards of Professional Practice." "Association of Fundraising Professionals" website. http://www.afpnet.org/ethics/guidelines_code_standards (accessed January 15, 2007).

Avon Breast Cancer Crusade. "Frequently Asked Questions." "Avon Breast Cancer Crusade" website, 2008. http://www.avoncompany.com/women/ avoncrusade/faq/index.html (accessed January 23, 2008).

The Avon Foundation. "Avon Walk for Breast Cancer: Summary of Results and Funding Grants Announced at Each Closing Ceremony." "Avon Foundation" website, 2004. http://walk.avonfoundation.org (accessed January 26, 2005).

——. "News on the Avon Walk for Breast Cancer 2003 and 2004." "Avon Foundation" website, 2004. http://walk.avonfoundation.org (accessed January 26, 2005).

——. "2003 Avon Foundation Audited Results—Topline Overview." Avon Foundation, New York City, 2004.

Avon Products Foundation, Inc. "Financial Statements: December 31, 2004 and 2003." Avon Products Foundation, Inc., New York, February April 7, 2005.

——. "Financial Statements: December 31, 2005 and 2004." Avon Products Foundation, Inc., New York, February 28, 2007.

——. "Financial Statements: December 31, 2006 and 2005." Avon Products Foundation, Inc., New York, March 13, 2007.

——. "Independent Auditor's Report, December 31, 2002." Avon Products Foundation, Inc., New York, July 28, 2003.

——. "Report on Financial Statements: For the Year Ended December 31, 2001 (with Comparative Totals for 2000)." Avon Products Foundation, Inc., New York, June 21, 2002.

——. "Report on Financial Statements: For the Year Ended December 31, 2003 (with Comparative Totals for 2002)." Avon Products Foundation, Inc., New York, April 16, 2004.

"Avon Products Foundation, Inc.'s Post-Hearing Memorandum in Opposition to Pallotta TeamWorks's Contract Claim." *Pallotta TeamWorks v. Avon Products Foundation, Inc.,* no. 1420011424. Judicial Arbitration and Mediation Services, New York.

"Avon Walk for Breast Cancer Boston Raises $6.3 Million." Avon Foundation press release. Boston, May 21, 2006.

"Avon Walk for Breast Cancer Chicago 2006 Raises $8.2 Million—Sets Record for Annual Event." Avon Foundation press release. Chicago, June 25, 2006.

"Avon Walk for Breast Cancer Denver Raises over $2 Million." Avon Foundation press release. Denver, June 25, 2006.

"Avon Walk for Breast Cancer Los Angeles Raises over $3.6 Million." Avon Foundation press release. Long Beach, CA, September 17, 2006.

"Avon Walk for Breast Cancer New York Breaks Records, Raises $9.7 Million." Avon Foundation press release. New York, October 8, 2006.

"Avon Walk for Breast Cancer San Francisco Raises over $5.4 Million." Avon Foundation press release. San Francisco, July 9, 2006.

"Avon Walk for Breast Cancer Washington, DC Raises $5.8 Million." Avon Foundation press release. Washington, D.C., April 30, 2006.

Baber, William R., and Andrea Alston Roberts. "Charitable Organizations' Strategies and Program-Spending Ratios." *Accounting Horizon* 15, no. 4 (December 2001), pp. 329–343.

Balster, Nick. "The Habitat 500." "Minnesota Housing Partnership VISTA program" website, *VISTA Newsletter* 1, no. 3 (2002). http://www.mhpvista.org/MHPVista/VISTANewsletter/V1Issue3/Issue1V#Habitat500.htm (accessed October 26, 2003).

Barnes, Julian. "Do Some AIDS Events Take Donors for a Ride?" *U.S. News & World Report,* June 16, 1997, via Lexis-Nexis, http://web.lexis-nexis.com (accessed April 10, 2004).

Barr, Rebecca. "Microsoft Ads Aim to Erase 'Huge' Image: Software Marker's Campaign to Cost $120 Million." *Seattle Post Intelligencer* online, January 21, 2006. http://seattlepi.nwsource.com/business/256523_msftads21.html (accessed February 14, 2007).

Barrett, Greg. "Charity Donations Soar, with Strings; Katrina: Americans Again Show Their Generosity, but Most Are Specifying That Gifts Be Used for Hurricane Relief." *Baltimore Sun,* September 10, 2005, via Lexis-Nexis, http://web.lexis-nexis.com (accessed June 29, 2006).

Barrett, Jon. "The World According to Dan." *Advocate,* February 19, 2002, pp. 36–40.

Barrett, William P. "America's Most (and Least) Efficient Charities." "Forbes .com" website, November 24, 2004. http://www.forbes.com/2004/11/23/04charityland.html (accessed December 6, 2004).

Barton, Noelle, Maria Di Mento, and Alvin P. Sanoff. "Top Nonprofit Executives See Healthy Pay Raises." *Chronicle of Philanthropy: The Newspaper of the Nonprofit World* online, September 28, 2006. http://philanthropy.com/premium/articles/v18/i24/24003901.htm (accessed January 28, 2007).

Barton, Noelle, Maria Di Mento, Candie Jones, and Sam Kean. "The 2006 Philanthropy 400." *Chronicle of Philanthropy: The Newspaper of the Nonprofit World* online, 2006. http://www.philanthropy.com (accessed February 13, 2007).

Barton, Noelle, and Peter Panepento. "Executive Pay Rises 4.6." *Chronicle of Philanthropy: The Newspaper of the Nonprofit World* online, September 20, 2007. http://philanthropy.com/premium/articles/v19/i23/23003401.htm (accessed February 20, 2008).

BBB Wise Giving Alliance. "American Civil Liberties Union Foundation, Inc." "Give.org: BBB Wise Giving Alliance" website. http://www.give.org/Public /Report.aspx?CharityID=227 (accessed October 31, 2006).

———. "American Foundation for AIDS Research." "Give.org: BBB Wise Giving Alliance" website. http://www.give.org/reports/care_dyn.asp?1220 (accessed March 16, 2004).

———. "American Lung Association." "Give.org: BBB Wise Giving Alliance" website. http://www.give.org/reports/care_dyn.asp?54 (accessed March 17, 2004).

———. "BBB Wise Giving Alliance 2004 Annual Report." "Give.org: BBB Wise Giving Alliance" website. http://www.give.org/about/2004annualrpt.asp (accessed October 31, 2006).

———. "BBB Wise Giving Alliance Staff." "Give.org: BBB Wise Giving Alliance" website. http://www.give.org/about/staff.asp (accessed March 17, 2004).

———. "BBB Wise Giving Alliance Staff." "Give.org: BBB Wise Giving Alliance" website. http://www.give.org/about/staff.asp (accessed October 31, 2006).

———. "BBB Wise Giving Alliance Standards for Charity Accountability." "Give .org: BBB Wise Giving Alliance" website. http://www.give.org/standards/ newcbbbstds.asp (accessed November 1, 2006).

———. "Charity Seal Program." "BBB Wise Giving Alliance" website. http:// www.us.bbb.org/WWWRoot/SitePage.aspx?site=113&id=6a21a739- e081-4e1a-9e51-a6983b8a4587 (accessed January 26, 2008).

———. "National Charity Seal Program." "BBB Wise Giving Alliance" website. http://charityreports.bbb.org/public/participants.asp (accessed January 26, 2008).

———. "National Charity Seal Program." "Give.org: BBB Wise Giving Alliance" website. http://give.org/seal/abouttheseal.asp (accessed August 5, 2004).

———. "Police Protective Fund." "Give.org: BBB Wise Giving Alliance" website, July 2004. http://charityreports.bbb.org/Public/Report.aspx?Charity ID=3722 (accessed August 5, 2004).

———. "Report: AARP." "BBB Wise Giving Alliance" website. http://charity reports.bbb.org/public/Report.aspx?CharityID=3261&bureauID=9999 (accessed January 27, 2008).

———. "Standards for Charity Accountability." "BBB Wise Giving Alliance" website. http://us.bbb.org/WWWRoot/SitePage.aspx?site=113&id=4ddo 40fd-08af-4dd2-aaa0-dcd66c1a17fc (accessed January 26, 2008).

———. "Welcome to Give.org." "Give.org: BBB Wise Giving Alliance" website. http://www.give.org/ (accessed March 17, 2004).

———. "Standards for Charity Accountability." "Give.org: BBB Wise Giving Alliance" website. http://www.give.org/standards/newcbbbstds.asp (accessed March 16, 2004).

———. "U.S. National BBB.org: 2006 Annual Report." "BBB Wise Giving Alliance" website. http://us.bbb.org/WWWRoot/SitePage.aspx?site=113&id =a727ed2e-dd7d-44a8-bca8-d424495ded83 (accessed January 26, 2008).

"Beckham: Can He Save U.S. Soccer?" *The Week* online, January 19, 2007. http://www.theweekmagazine.com/news/articles/news.aspx?ArticleID=1896 (accessed January 24, 2007).

Bendersky, Ari. "Pallotta TeamWorks Warns of Low Returns." "Gay.com" website, June 28, 2002. http://www.gay.com/news/article.html?2002/06/28/1 (accessed July 29, 2006).

———. "Plug Pulled on Heartland AIDS Ride." "Gay.com" website, July 30, 2002. http://www.gay.com/news/article.html?2002/07/30/1 (accessed July 29, 2006).

Berlo, Beth. "1,500 Cyclists Complete Northeast AIDS Ride." *Bay Windows* online, June 27, 2002. http://ww2.aegis.org/news/bayw/2002/BY020605 .html (accessed July 29, 2006).

Bhattacharya, Rinku, and Daniel Tinkelman. "How Tough Are Better Business Bureau/Wise Giving Alliance Financial Standards?" *Nonprofit and Voluntary Sector Quarterly,* forthcoming.

Bill & Melinda Gates Foundation. "2002 Annual Report." (Seattle, WA: Bill & Melinda Gates Foundation, 2002).

Blum, Debra E. "Colleges, Hospitals, and Museums Receive Biggest Share of Large Gifts, Study Finds." *Chronicle of Philanthropy: The Newspaper of the Nonprofit World,* January 10, 2008, p. 17.

———. "Median Pay for Foundation Chiefs Was $110,000 Last Year, Study Finds." *Chronicle of Philanthropy: The Newspaper of the Nonprofit World* online, February 3, 2005. http://philanthropy.com/premium/articles/v17/i08/08002401.htm (accessed January 28, 2007).

Braking the Cycle. "The Event 2004." Online event advertisement, 2004. http://www.brakingthecycle.org (accessed April 19, 2004).

"Braking the Cycle 2004: Chesapeake Bay to Manhattan September 10–12, 2004." Braking the Cycle event brochure. New York, 2004.

Bremer, Francis J. *John Winthrop: America's Forgotten Founding Father.* Oxford: Oxford University Press, 2003.

Bremner, Robert H. *American Philanthropy.* 2nd ed. Edited by Daniel J. Boorstin. Chicago: University of Chicago Press, 1960.

"Brief of Amici Curiae Public Citizen, Inc., American Charities for Reasonable Fundraising Regulation, Inc., and 174 Other Nonprofit Organizations in Support of Respondents." *The People of the State of Illinois ex rel. James E. Ryan, Attorney General of the State of Illinois v. Telemarketing Associates, Inc.,*

Richard Troia and Armet, Inc., no. 01-1806. Supreme Court of the United States, January 2003.

Briggs, Helen. "Altruism 'in-Built' in Humans." *BBC News* online, March 3, 2006. http://news.bbc.co.uk/1/hi/sci/tech/4766490.stm (accessed October 29, 2007).

British Airways. "Because the Shortest Distance Between Two Points Is a Good Night's Sleep." Print advertisement, February 2007.

"Buffett and the Poor." Editorial. *New York Sun* online, June 28, 2006. http://www.nysun.com/article/35221 (accessed August 19, 2006).

Bulik, Beth Snyder. "Apple Plan: Lead Consumers into Temptation—and Away from Vista." *Advertising Age,* February 12, 2007, pp. 1, 28.

"California AIDS Ride Loses Top Beneficiaries." *Advocate,* October 12, 2001. "Wheels of Fortune: AIDS Ride Updates 2001/2002—Lawsuits, Loss and Lifecycle" website. http://members.tripod.com/~homeo/wheels8.html (accessed January 13, 2007).

"California AIDS Ride: Riders Set to Pedal 575 Miles from San Francisco to Los Angeles." AIDS Project Los Angeles press release. Los Angeles, May 29, 2002.

California Department of Justice, Office of the Attorney General. "Using Your Heart to Give Wisely—Charitable Trusts." "California Department of Justice, Office of the Attorney General" website. http://ag.ca.gov/charities/index.php (accessed February 1, 2008).

——. "Using Your Heart to Give Wisely—Giving Wisely." California Department of Justice, Office of the Attorney General" website. http://ag.ca.gov/charities/charit_giving.php (accessed February 1, 2008).

Calvin, John. *Calvin: Institutes of the Christian Religion.* 2 vols. Edited by John T. McNeill. Translated and indexed by Ford Lewis Battles. Louisville, KY: Westminister John Knox Press, 1960.

Care Exchange. "California AIDS Ride Statistical Overview: Financial Overview of the 2002 Ride." "Care Exchange" website. http://www.caree.org/stats/alcstats.htm (accessed March 16, 2004).

Carson, Emmett D. "Public Expectations and Nonprofit Sector Realities: A Growing Divide with Disastrous Consequences." *Nonprofit and Voluntary Sector Quarterly* 31, no. 3 (2002): pp. 429-436.

Catrone, Vince. "Back to Court: Former AIDS Ride Participant Files Class Action Suit Against Pallotta TeamWorks." *Frontiers* 21, no. 2 (May 24, 2002).

Center on Nonprofits and Philanthropy, Urban Institute at the Center on Philanthropy at Indiana University. "Getting What We Pay For: Low Overhead Limits Nonprofit Effectiveness." *Nonprofit Overhead Cost Project: Facts and Perspectives,* brief no. 3 (August 2004), pp. 1-4.

——. "The Pros and Cons of Financial Efficiency Standards." *Nonprofit Overhead Cost Project: Facts and Perspectives,* brief no. 5 (August 2004), pp. 1-4.

——. "The Quality of Financial Reporting by Nonprofits: Findings and Implications." *Nonprofit Overhead Cost Project: Facts and Perspectives,* brief no. 4 (August 2004), pp. 1-4.

———. "What We Know About Overhead Costs in the Nonprofit Sector." *Nonprofit Overhead Cost Project: Facts and Perspectives,* brief no. 1 (February 2004), pp. 1–2.

———. "Who Raises Contributions for America's Nonprofit Organizations?" *Nonprofit Overhead Cost Project: Facts and Perspectives,* brief no. 2 (July 2004), pp. 1–4.

Center on Philanthropy at Indiana University. "Charity Holds Its Own in Tough Times (Giving USA 2003: *The Annual Report on Philanthropy for the Year 2002)."* "American Association of Fundraising Counsel Trust for Philanthropy" website. http://www.aafrc.org/press_releases/trustreleases/charity holds.html (accessed March 17, 2004).

———. *Giving USA 2007: The Annual Report on Philanthropy for the Year 2006.* Bloomington, IN: Giving USA Foundation, 2007.

———. *Giving USA 2006: The Annual Report on Philanthropy for the Year 2005.* Bloomington, IN: Giving USA Foundation, 2006.

———. "Gulf Coast Hurricane Relief Donations." "Center on Philanthropy at Indiana University" website. http://www.philanthropy.iupui.edu/Research /Giving/Hurricane_Katrina.aspx (accessed February 28, 2007).

———. "Sources of Contributions: Giving by Individuals." *American Association of Fundraising Counsel Trust for Philanthropy,* Bloomington, 2003. http:// nccsdataweb.urban.org/kbfiles/554/Giving%20USA%202003%20excerpt .pdf (accessed June 29, 2006).

"Charitable Giving at 93 Major Corporations." *Chronicle of Philanthropy: The Newspaper of the Nonprofit World,* August 5, 2004, pp. 10–15.

Charity Navigator. "Board and Staff." "Charity Navigator: Your Guide to Intelligent Giving" website. http://charitynavigator.org/index.cfm?bay=content .view&cpid=19 (accessed January 26, 2008).

———. "Charity Navigator Homepage." "Charity Navigator: Your Guide to Intelligent Giving" website. http://charitynavigator.org/ (accessed January 26, 2008).

———. "Charity Rating: American Diabetes Association." "Charity Navigator: Your Guide to Intelligent Giving" website. http://www.charitynavigator.org /index.cfm?bay=search.summary&orgid=3251 (accessed February 1, 2008).

———. "FAQ for Donors." "Charity Navigator: Your Guide to Intelligent Giving" website. http://charitynavigator.org/index.cfm?bay=content.view&cpid =484#14 (accessed January 26, 2008).

———. "Leadership." "Charity Navigator: Your Guide to Intelligent Giving" website. http://charitynavigator.org/index.cfm/bay/content.view/cpid/19 .htm (accessed November 1, 2006).

———. "Methodology." "Charity Navigator: Your Guide to Intelligent Giving" website. http://charitynavigator.org/index.cfm?bay=content.view&cpid =33 (accessed November 1, 2006).

———. "Methodology: How Do We Rate Charities?" "Charity Navigator: Your Guide to Intelligent Giving" website. http://charitynavigator.org/index .cfm?bay=content.view&cpid=35 (accessed February 1, 2008).

———. "Methodology: Our Ratings Tables." "Charity Navigator: Your Guide to Intelligent Giving" website. http://charitynavigator.org/index.cfm?bay =content.view&cpid=48 (accessed January 26, 2008).

———. "Overview." "Charity Navigator: Your Guide to Intelligent Giving" website. http://www.charitynavigator.org/index.cfm?bay=content.view& cpid =628 (accessed February 1, 2008).

———. "What Kind of Charities Do We Evaluate?" "Charity Navigator: Your Guide to Intelligent Giving" website. http://charitynavigator.org/index .cfm/bay/content.view/catid/2/cpid/32.htm (accessed November 1, 2006).

———. "10 Highly Paid CEO's at Low-Rated Charities." "Charity Navigator: Your Guide to Intelligent Giving" website. http://charitynavigator.org/ index.cfm?bay=topten.detail&listid=8 (accessed January 26, 2008).

"Chart: In the Money." *Business Week* online, October 23, 2006. http://busi-nessweek.com/magazine/content/06_43/b4006005.htm?chan=bestbs (accessed January 28, 2007).

Chibbaro Jr., Lou. "D.C. AIDS Ride Yields Lowest Return in Seven Years: Net Proceeds of $500,000 Mean Only 14 Cents of Every Dollar Raised to go [*sic*] AIDS Groups." *Washington Blade* online, August 9, 2002. http://www .aegis.com/news/wb/2002/WB020804.html (accessed July 29, 2006).

———. "Low Return Dooms Tour de Friends AIDS Ride." *Washington Blade* online, October 24, 2003. http://www.washblade.com/2003/1024/news/ localnews/tourde.cfm (accessed November 1, 2003).

———. "New Return Plunges in AIDS Vaccine Rides: Figures Show 78.6% of 2001 Money Went to Overhead Costs." *Washington Blade,* March 1, 2002, in "Wheels of Fortune: AIDS Ride Updates 2001/2002—Lawsuits, Loss and Lifecycle" website. http://members.tripod.com/~homeo/wheels8.html (accessed January 13, 2007).

City of Los Angeles. Information Card no. A1590. Los Angeles Police Commission Charitable Services Section. Issued to AIDS Action Foundation, Washington, D.C., for "Dinner and Spring Fashion Show on May 6, 2004 at Neiman Marcus Beverly Hills."

Clolery, Paul. "Nonprofit Paychecks Continue to Climb." *NonProfit Times* online, February 1, 2001. http://www.nptimes.com/Feb01/sr1.html (accessed June 29, 2006).

"A Closer Look at Charity Efficiency Ratings." Oxfam America press release. Boston, January 9, 2005.

Collin, James, and Jerry I. Porras. *Built to Last: Successful Habits of Visionary Companies.* New York: Harper Business, 1994.

Collins, Carole J. L. "World's Worst Disasters Overlook: Survey Identifies Biggest 'Forgotten' Crises." *FAIR* online, February 28, 2007. http://www .fair.og/index.php?page=2537 (accessed February 28, 2007).

Community of Emmitsburg, MD. "My Little Sister's Interesting Facts." "Emmitsburg.net" website. http://www.emmitsburg.net/humor/archives/ interesting _facts/interesting_facts_2.htm (accessed February 10, 2007).

Community Wealth Ventures, Inc. "Venture Philanthropy: Landscape and Expectations." *Morino Institute Youth Social Ventures,* Reston, VA: The Morino Institute, 2000.

CompassPoint Nonprofit Services. "Daring to Lead 2006: A National Study of Nonprofit Executive Leadership." San Francisco: CompassPoint Nonprofit Services, 2006.

Compton, Phil. "A Letter from Cincinnati Rider Phil Compton." *Post: World Wide Web Edition of the Cincinnati Post* online, June 19, 1998. http://www.cicnypost.com/bike/bike061998.html (accessed July 30, 2006).

Coolworks. Untitled document. "Coolworks.com" website, 2002. http://www.coolworks.com/stories/pmcbeavr/default.asp (accessed July 29, 2006).

"Cot's Baseball Contracts: New York Yankees." http://mlbcontracts.blogspot.com/2005/01/new-york-yankees_111398168678860040.html (accessed January 27, 2008).

County of Los Angeles. *Information Card no. 385.* Business License Commission. issued to American Heart Association, Los Angeles, CA, for "General Appeal." Solicitation Dates: 7/1/2007–6/30/2008.

Cox, Mike. "Charities, the Good, the Bad and the Ugly 10/1999." "Michigan Office of the Attorney General" website. http://www.michigan.gov/ag/0,1607,7-164-34739_20942-44609—,00.html (accessed March 17, 2004).

Creamer, Matthew. "Marketers Can't Grade Shops but Fail Them Anyway." *Advertising Age,* February 26, 2007, pp. 1, 41.

Curtis, Kim. "AIDS Ride Management Dispute Leads to Lawsuit." *Berkeley Daily Planet* online, December 19, 2001. http://www.berkeleydailyplanet.com/article.cfm?archiveDate=12-19-01&storyID=9064 (accessed January 12, 2007).

Dawkins, Richard. *The God Delusion.* Boston: Houghton Mifflin Company, 2006.

DeCarlo, Scott. "Big Paychecks." "Forbes.com" website, May 3, 2007. http://www.forbes.com/2007/05/03/ceo-executive-compensation-lead-07ceo-cx_sd_0503ceocompensationintro.html (accessed February 2, 2008).

De Greef, Wulfert. *The Writings of John Calvin.* Translated by Lyle D. Bierma. Grand Rapids, MI: Baker Books, 1989.

Department of the Treasury, Internal Revenue Service. "Form 8868: Application for Extension of Time to File an Exempt Organization Return." Filing organization: National Resources Defense Council, Inc., New York. Filing year: 2005.

———. "Form 8868: Application for Extension of Time to File an Exempt Organization Return." Filing organization: Save the Children Federation, Inc., Westport, CT. Filing year: 2005.

———. "Form 990: Return of Organization Exempt from Income Tax." Filing organization: American Institute of Philanthropy, Chicago, IL. Filing year: 2006.

———. "Form 990: Return of Organization Exempt from Income Tax." Filing organization: American Lung Association, New York. Filing year: 2004.

———. "Form 990: Return of Organization Exempt from Income Tax." Filing organization: Amnesty International USA, Inc., New York. Filing year: 2005.

———. "Form 990: Return of Organization Exempt from Income Tax." Filing organization: BBB Wise Giving Alliance, Arlington, VA. Filing year: 2004.

———. "Form 990: Return of Organization Exempt from Income Tax." Filing organization: BBB Wise Giving Alliance, Arlington, VA. Filing year: 2006.

———. "Form 990: Return of Organization Exempt from Income Tax." Filing organization: Charity Navigator, Mahwah, NJ. Filing year: 2005.

———. "Form 990: Return of Organization Exempt from Income Tax." Filing organization: The Foundation for AIDS Research, New York. Filing year: 2004.

———. "Form 990: Return of Organization Exempt from Income Tax." Filing organization: Foundation for AIDS Research (DBA amfAR, AIDS Research Foundation), New York. Filing year: 2005.

———. "Form 990: Return of Organization Exempt from Income Tax." Filing organization: Leukemia & Lymphoma Society, Inc., White Plains, NY. Filing year: 2004.

———. "Form 990: Return of Organization Exempt from Income Tax." Filing organization: National Resources Defense Council, Inc., New York. Filing year: 2004.

———. "Form 990: Return of Organization Exempt from Income Tax." Filing organization: Save the Children Federation, Inc., Westport, CT. Filing year: 2004.

———. "Form 990: Return of Organization Exempt from Income Tax." Filing organization: Susan G. Komen Breast Cancer Foundation, Inc., Dallas. Filing year: 2005.

———. "Form 990: Return of Organization Exempt from Income Tax." Filing organization: United Way of America, Alexandria, VA. Filing year: 2005.

———. "Standards for Recognition of Tax-Exempt Status of Private Benefit Exists if an Applicable Tax-Exempt Organization Has Engaged in Excess Benefit Transaction(s)." *Federal Register* 70, no. 174 (September 9, 2005).

"Deposition." *Pallotta TeamWorks v. Avon Products Foundation, Inc.,* no. 1420011424. Judicial Arbitration and Mediation Services, Los Angeles. May 28, 2003.

De Soto, Hernando. *The Mystery of Capital: Why Capitalism Triumphs in the West and Fails Everywhere Else.* New York: Basic Books, 2000.

Dignan, Larry. "Amazon Posts Its First Net Profit." "CNET News.com" website, January 22, 2002. http://news.com.com/2100-1017-819688.html (accessed March 18, 2004).

"Disasters Help Boost American Charitable Giving to Near All-Time High." *Fox News* online, June 19, 2006. http://www.foxnews.com/story/0,2933,200065,00.html (accessed March 12, 2007).

DL, "Cotton Mather." "About.com" website. http://womenshistory.about .com/gi/dynamic/offsite.htm?zi=1/XJ/Ya&sdn=womenshistory &cdn=education&tm=2&f=00&tt=14&bt=0&bts=0&zu=http%3A// www.law.umkc.edu/faculty/projects/ftrials/salem/SAL_BMAT.HTM (accessed November 27, 2006).

DoubleCoog. "My Big Ride." Review of the American Lung Association's Big Ride Across America. "Epinions.com" website, March 16, 2000; Updated October 29 2002. http://www.epinions.com/otdr-review-4b41–378F55C-38D17EB8-prod4 (accessed August 14, 2006).

Downing, Emanuel. "Finding Cheap Labor: Excerpt from a Letter Written in 1645." "The Massachusetts Foundation for the Humanities, Mass Moments" website. http://www.massmoments.org/teachers/primedoc.cfm?pid=27 (accessed January 7, 2007).

Drape, Joe. "Coaches Receive Both Big Salaries and Big Questions." *New York Times* online, January 1, 2004. http://www.nytimes.com/2004/01/01/sports/ncaafootball/01SALA.html?ex=1388293200&en=8a434e3c0518b2c6&ei=5007&partner=USERLAND (accessed June 27, 2006).

Edelman, Susan. "Red Cross Prez Quits: Dispute over $500M in WTC Donations." *New York Post,* October 27, 2001, via Lexis-Nexis, http://web.lexis-nexis.com (accessed August 15, 2006).

Editorial on cycling deaths and the AIDS Ride. *SF Weekly,* May 2, 2001. "Wheels of Fortune: AIDS Ride Updates 2001/2002—Lawsuits, Loss and Lifecycle" website. http://members.tripod.com/~homeo/wheels8.html (accessed January 13, 2007).

Edwards, Michael. *Just Another Emperor? The Myths and Realities of Philanthrocapitalism.* New York City: Demos: A Network for Ideas & Action, 2008.

Elazar, Daniel J. "Covenant and the American Founding." In *The Covenant Tradition in Politics,* vol. 3, chap. 1. http://www.jcpa.org/dje/books/ct-vol3-ch1.htm (accessed December 15, 2006).

Elghanayan, Shahrzad. "A Cause for Travel." *Worth* 11, no. 10 (December 2002), p. 46.

———. "Scratch Golfer's Paradise." *Worth* 11, no. 10 (December 2002), p. 44.

Ellison Research. "Most Americans Believe Non-Profits Spend Too Much on Overhead." Ellison Research website. http://www.ellisonresearch.com/releases/20080213.htm (accessed March 5, 2008).

Emerson, Ralph Waldo. *Essays and Lecturers.* Edited by Joel Porter. New York: Library of America, 1983.

Families USA. "Private Health Plans That Service Medicare Provide Lavish Compensation to Executives." "FamiliesUSA.org: The Voice for Health Care Consumers" website, June 24, 2003. http://www.familiesusa.org/resources /newsroom/press-releases/2003-press-releases/press-release-private-health-plans-that-service-medicare.html (accessed April 19, 2004).

Farrell, Christopher. "The Booming Economy Is Greasing Charitable Giving." *Business Week* online, September 15, 2000. http://www.businessweek.com/bwdaily/dnflash/sep2000/nf20000915_565.htm (accessed March 12, 2007).

Federal Trade Commission. "Cigarette Report for 1999." "Federal Trade Commission" website, March 13, 2001. http://www.ftc.gov/opa/2001/03/cigarette.htm (accessed February 13, 2007).

"$575,000 Goes to Charity." *Washington Post* online, November 22, 1986, via Lexis-Nexis, http://web.lexis-nexis.com (accessed August 15, 2006).

Fleming, Mike. "Pallotta Announces End to AIDS Vaccine Rides: Even with Production Fee Forfeited, Beneficiaries to Receive Less Than 10 Percent." *Washington Blade* online, July 5, 2002. http://www.aegis.com/news/wb/2002/WB020702.html (accessed July 29, 2006).

"Foundation Center" website. http://foundationcenter.org/ (accessed 2003).

Four Seasons Hotels and Resorts. "With Proper Care, Delight Will Grow in Any Climate." Print advertisement, February 2007.

Fox, Matthew, ed. *Meditations with Meister Eckhart*. Santa Fe: Bear & Company, 1983.

Franklin, Benjamin. "The Way to Wealth." July 7, 1757. http://itech.fgcu.edu/faculty/wohlpart/alra/franklin.htm (accessed January 29, 2007).

Frazier, Mya. "Costly Red Campaign Reaps Meager $18 Million." *Advertising Age* online, March 5, 2007. http://adage.com/article?article_id=115287 (accessed March 12, 2007).

Frey, Christine, and John Cook. "How Amazon.com Survived, Thrived, and Turned a Profit: E-tailer Defied Predictions It Would Do None of These." *Seattle Post Intelligencer* online, January 28, 2004. http://seattlepi.nwsource.com/business/158315_amazon28.html (accessed March 18, 2004).

Friedman, Lawrence J., and Mark D. McGarvie, eds. *Charity, Philanthropy, and Civility in American History*. Cambridge: Cambridge University Press, 2003.

Frost, Laurence. "Airbus Flight Shows Off Troubled A380." *Washington Post* online, February 7, 2007. http://www.washingtonpost.com/wp-dyn/content/article/2007/02/08/AR2007020801885.html (accessed February 7, 2007).

Gajilan, Arlyn Tobias. "The Business of Charity." "CNNMoney.com" website, March 1, 2002. http://money.cnn.com/magazines/fsb/fsb_archive/2002/03/01/319484/index.htm (accessed October 26, 2003).

Galbraith, John Kenneth. *The Affluent Society*. Boston: Houghton Mifflin Company, 1958.

Gay.com/PlanetOut.com. "Los Angeles Gay Center Cuts 55 Jobs." "Gay.com/PlanetOut.com" website. http://www.planetout.com/news/article.html?2002/03/25/2 (accessed January 26, 2008).

"General Motors Foundation, Inc." "The Foundation Directory Online" website. http://fconline.fdncenter.org/gperl/fdonl_dtgm_show.pl?id=GENE006&row1data=general (accessed March 16, 2004).

George, Jason. "Farm Aid Expenses Eat Away Donations: Only 28% of Revenue from Last Year Made It to Farm Families." *Chicago Tribune* online, September 17, 2005. http://www.chicagotribune.com/news/nationworld/chi-0509170144sep17,1,3227320.story (accessed August 15, 2006).

Getty, Jeff. "Time to Throw Out POZ." *Bay Area Reporter* online, April 20, 2001. http://www.aegis.com/news/bar/2001/BR010417.html (accessed March 26, 2004).

Gilbert, Ron. "AIDS LifeCycle May 2002." "Rbgilbert.com" website. http://www.rbgilbert.com/life/ (accessed March 18, 2004).

Giving Back Fund. "Buy a Calendar & Change the World." Print advertisement. 2004.

Gordon, Dan. "Giving Donors Control." *Stanford Social Innovation Review* on-line, April 1, 2006. http://www.ssireview.org/articles/entry/giving_donors_control/ (accessed February 10, 2007).

Grameen Foundation. "Latest News." Grameen Foundation website. http://www.grameenfoundation.org/?gclid+CPL4yf2v9JECFQo6awodX23nxA (accessed March 4, 2008).

——. "2006 Annual Report." Washington, D.C.: Grameen Foundation, 2006.

Grant, Peter, and Rebecca Buckman. "Fatter Pay Lures University Endowment Chiefs." *Wall Street Journal,* June 27, 2006.

Greene, Stephen G. "Former Irvine Foundation CEO and His Wife Repay Fund for Benefits That Raised Questions." *Chronicle of Philanthropy: The News-paper of the Nonprofit World* online, January 8, 2004. http://philanthropy.com/premium/articles/v16/i06/06004302.htm (accessed March 18, 2004).

Greenlee, Janet S., and Karen L. Brown. "The Impact of Accounting Informa-tion on Contributions to Charitable Organizations." *Research in Accounting Regulations* 13 (1999), pp. 111–125.

Gross, Richard. "Giving in America: From Charity to Philanthropy." In *Char-ity, Philanthropy, and Civility in American History.* Edited by Lawrence J. Friedman and Mark D. McGarvie. Cambridge: Cambridge University Press, 2003, pp. 29–48.

Grossman, Allen, and Liz Kind. "Pallotta TeamWorks." Harvard Business School paper no. N1–302–089, April 12, 2002.

GuideStar Philanthropic Research, Inc. "About GuideStar and Philanthropic Research, Inc." "GuideStar.org" website. http://www.guidestar.org/about/index.jsp?source=dnabout (accessed January 27, 2008).

——. "Financial Statements for the Years Ended December 31, 2006 and 2005." GuideStar Philanthropic Research, Inc., Washington, D.C., March 9, 2007.

——. "Frequently Asked Questions." "GuideStar.org" website. http://www.guidestar.org/help/faq.jsp (accessed January 27, 2008).

Gulfstream. "G550." "Gulfstream" website. http://www.gulfstream.com/g550 (accessed January 28, 2007).

Habitat 500. "History of the Habitat 500." "Habitat 500" website. http://www.habitat500.org/habitat500/Habitat500/history.html (accessed January 26, 2008).

Hager, Mark A. "Current Practices in Allocation of Fundraising Expenditures." *New Direction for Philanthropic Fundraising* 41 (Fall 2003), pp. 39–52.

Hager, Mark, and Janet Greenlee. "How Important Is a Nonprofit's Bottom Line? The Uses and Abuses of Financial Data." *In Search of the Nonprofit Sec-tor.* Edited by P. Frumkin and J.B. Imber. New Brunswick, NJ: Transaction Publishers, 2004, pp. 84–96.

Hall, Holly. "A Charitable Divide." *Chronicle of Philanthropy: The Newspaper of the Nonprofit World,* January 10, 2008, pp. 15–17.

Halliday, Jean. "GM Cuts $600M Off Ad Spend—Yes, Really." *Advertising Age,* February 12, 2007, pp. 1, 25.

Harbert, Nancy. "Charity on Wheels: Riding Your Heart Out, Then Feeling Betrayed." *New York Times* online, November 18, 2002. http://query.ny times.com/gst/fullpage.html?res=9500EFDB1030F93BA25752C1A9649 C8B63 (accessed March 17, 2004).

Hargreaves, Steve. "Exxon Guns for All-Time Profit Record." "CNNMoney .com" website, January 23, 2008. http://money.cnn.com/2008/01/23/news/ companies/exxon_profits/?postversion=2008012313 (accessed January 23, 2008).

Harris, Sam. *The End of Faith*. New York: W.W. Norton & Company, 2004.

Harvard Business School MBA Program. "Financial Aid: Cost Summary." "Harvard Business School MBA Program" website. http://www.hbs.edu/ mba/admissions/costsummary.html (accessed January 28, 2007).

———. "What Is Social Enterprise at Harvard Business School?" "Harvard Business School MBA Program" website. http://www.hbs.edu/socialenterprise/ whatis.html (accessed January 28, 2007).

Hästens Vividus. "How Much Is Great Sleep Worth?" Print advertisement, February 2007.

Hayek, F. A. *The Road to Serfdom*. Chicago: University of Chicago Press, 1944.

Hendricks, Tyche. "AIDS Ride Firm Closes Its Doors: Raised Millions in Bay Area." *San Francisco Chronicle* online, August 25, 2002. http://www.aegis .org/news/sc/2002/SC020812.html (accessed January 11, 2007).

Heredia, Christopher. "Layoffs, Pay Cuts Announced at S.F. AIDS Foundation: Nonprofit Blames Post-Sept. 11 Slump, Costs of Charity Ride." *San Francisco Chronicle*, June 19, 2002.

Herman, Robert D., and David O. Renz. "Nonprofit Organizational Effectiveness: Practical Implications of Research on an Elusive Concept." Midwest Center for Nonprofit Leadership; L. P. Cookingham Institute of Public Affairs; Henry W. Bloch School of Business & Public Administration. University of Missouri—Kansas City, 2002.

"The High Price of Admission: 2006 MBA Programs." *Business Week* online. http://bwnt.businessweek.com/bschools/06/mba_payback.asp (accessed January 28, 2007).

"Highest Paid Athletes, 2004: Andre Agassi." "Forbes.com" website, http:// www.forbes.com/athletes2004/LIR1YUQ.html?passListId=2&pass Year=2004&passListType=Person&uniqueId=1YUQ&datatype=Person (accessed January 29, 2007).

Hillman, James. *A Terrible Love of War*. New York: Penguin Press, 2004.

"History of AIDS/LifeCycle." AIDS/LifeCycle press release. San Francisco, June 5, 2006.

Ho, David. Email to Dan Pallotta, March 11, 2002.

Holland America Line. "Intrigue Your Senses." Print advertisement, February 2007.

Hopkins, Bruce R., "The Law of Fundraising." "Brief of Amici Curiae Public Citizen, Inc., American Charities for Reasonable Fundraising Regulation, Inc., and 174 Other Nonprofit Organizations in Support of Respondents."

The People of the State of Illinois ex rel. James E. Ryan, Attorney General of the state of Illinois v. Telemarketing Associates, Inc., Richard Troia and Armet, Inc., no. 01–1806. Supreme Court of the United States, January 2003, p. 9.

Horowitz, Amy. "O'Reilly Fights Fraud: From Free Press to FOX." *Daily Free Press* online, January 16, 2002. http://media.www.dailyfreepress.com/ media/storage/paper87/news/2002/01/16/Spotlight/Oreilly.Fights.Fraud .From.Free.Press.To.Fox–164581.shtml (accessed May 1, 2004).

Howes, Joshua. "Why They Rode." *Chicago Tribune* online, July 29, 2002. http://ww2.aegis.org/news/ct/2002/CT020711.html (accessed July 29, 2006).

"How We Conducted the Survey: By Old Fashioned Mail and E-Mail, We Contacted 4,800 of 5,700 MBAs from the Class of '92." *Business Week* online, September 22, 2003. http://businessweek.com/@@fEskoGQQ5d7PJyAA /premium/content/03_38/b3850609.htm (accessed January 28, 2007).

The Hunger Project. "Homepage." "The Hunger Project" website. http://thp .org (accessed March 6, 2008).

Ibarguen, Diego. "Some Money Raised for Red Cross' Liberty Fund to Go to Long-Term Plans." *Associated Press State & Local Wire,* October 30, 2001, via Lexis-Nexis, http://web.lexis-nexis.com (accessed August 15, 2006).

Illinois ex rel. Madigan, Attorney General of Illinois v. Telemarketing Associates, Inc., et al., no. 01–1806. Supreme Court of the United States, May 5, 2003.

Illinois Office of the Attorney General. "Report of Individual Fund-Raising Campaign." Solicitor: Pallotta TeamWorks, Inc. Charity: AIDS Cycle, Inc. Solicitation dates: August 1, 2001–July 31, 2002. Campaign description: Bike Ride. Chicago. January 24, 2003.

Independent Sector. "Before *Madigan:* A Brief History of the United States Supreme Court and Charitable Solicitation Regulation." "Independent Sector" website, 2004. http://www.independentsector.org/programs/gr/Ryan history.html (accessed January 5, 2008).

———. "What the Supreme Court's Decision in *Madigan v. Telemarketing Associates* Means for Fundraising." "Independent Sector" website, 2003. http:// www.independentsector.org/programs/gr/ryan.html (accessed January 25, 2008).

Infiniti. "Horsepower Is What Sends You Against the Back of Your Seat." Print advertisement, February 2007.

Innes, Stephen. *Creating the Commonwealth: The Economic Culture of Puritan New England.* New York: W.W. Norton & Company, 1995.

Institute of Design at the Illinois Institute of Technology. "Pallotta Team-Works: How Design Created Economic Value . . . Then Lost It." "Institute of Design at the Illinois Institute of Technology" website, October 10, 2003. http://trex.id.iit.edu/~bschauer/downloads/PTW_casestudy.pdf (accessed January 9, 2007).

Jack Myers Media Business Report. New York City: Myers Publishing, 2005.

Jaffe, Rochelle. "One of Rochelle Jaffe's Letters." "Wheels of Fortune: AIDS Ride Updates 2001/2002—Lawsuits, Loss and Lifecycle" website. http:// members.tripod.com/~homeo/wheels8.html (accessed January 13, 2007).

James Irvine Foundation. "About Irvine: Assets & Financial Information: Asset Size and Allocation." "James Irvine Foundation" website. http://www.irvine.org/about_irvine/assets/size.shtml (accessed January 27, 2008).

———. "About Irvine: Assets & Financial Information: Total Grantmaking." "James Irvine Foundation" website. http://www.irvine.org/about_irvine/assets/total.shtml (accessed January 27, 2008).

———. "About Irvine—History: Overview." "James Irvine Foundation" website. http://www.irvine.org/about_irvine/history.shtml (accessed January 27, 2008).

———. "About Irvine: History—Timeline." "James Irvine Foundation" website. http://www.irvine.org/about_irvine/timeline.shtml (accessed January 27, 2008).

"John Calvin Quotes." "Thinkexist.com" website. http://thinkexist.com/quotes/John_Calvin/ (accessed December 5, 2006).

Jones, Mark. "Tsunami Coverage Dwarfs 'Forgotten' Crises-Research." *Reuters Foundation Alertnet* online, March 10, 2005. http://www.alertnet.org/thefacts/reliefresources/111044767025.htm (accessed February 28, 2007).

"The Joy of Giving." *Economist* online, October 12, 2006. http://www.economist.com/science/displaystory.cfm?story_id=8023307 (accessed October 29, 2007).

"Joy Ride." *Los Angeles Times,* June 13, 2004.

Kadlec, Daniel. "How to Give to the Little Guys." *Time,* November 6, 2006, p. 97.

Kaiser Network. "Critics Say AIDS Rides Place Participant 'Experience' Above Charities." "Kaisernetwork.org" website. http://www.kaisernetwork.org/daily_reports/rep_index.cfm?hint=1&DR_ID=5367 (accessed January 28, 2008).

Kean, Sam. "Charity Ads Are Broadcast During Key Times, Study Finds." *Chronicle of Philanthropy: The Newspaper of the Nonprofit World,* May 31, 2007, p. 51.

Kirby, David. "Neighborhood Report: Greenwich Village/Chelsea—Amid Cheers After AIDS Ride, Costs Are Faulted." *New York Times* online, September 21, 1997. http://query.nytimes.com/gst/fullpage.html?res=9502E0DE1F38F932A1575AC0A961958260 (accessed March 22, 2004).

Knue, Paul. "A Letter from Cincinnati Rider Paul Knue." *Post: World Wide Web Edition of the Cincinnati Post* online, July 10, 1998. http://www.cicnypost.com/bike/paulo71098.html (accessed July 30, 2006).

Kragen, Ken. "Kragen & Company Charity." "Kenkragen.com" website. http://www.kenkragen.com/charity_more.html (accessed January 27, 2008).

Kramer, Mark. "Venture Capital and Philanthropy: A Bad Fit." *Chronicle of Philanthropy: The Newspaper of the Nonprofit World* online, April 22, 1999. http://www.philanthropy.com/premium/articles/v11/i13/13007201.htm (accessed January 3, 2007).

Krishnan, Ranjani, Michelle H. Yetman, and Robert J. Yetman. "Expense Misreporting in Nonprofit Organizations." *Accounting Review* 81, no. 2 (March 2006), pp. 399–420.

Kristof, Kathy M. "Charity Takes Lots of Clarity." *Los Angeles Times* online, December 2, 2007. http://www.latimes.com/business/la-fi-charity2dec02,1,621 4425.story?coll=la-headlines-business (accessed December 4, 2007).

Krugman, Paul. "In Praise of Cheap Labor: Bad Jobs at Bad Wages Are Better Than No Jobs at All." "Slate.com" website, March 21, 1997. http://www .slate.com/id/1918 (accessed February 9, 2007).

Kugler, Sara. "Bill Clinton to Write New Book." *USA Today* online, May 17, 2006. http://www.usatoday.com/life/books/news/2006-05-17-clinton-book _x.htm (accessed February 2, 2008).

Landrover USA. "The Range Rover for 2007." Online advertisement. http:// www.landroverusa.com/us/en/Vehicles/Range_Rover/Overview.htm (accessed January 28, 2007).

Lavelle, Louis, et al. "The Best B-Schools of 2006." *BusinessWeek,* October 23, 2006, pp. 56–57.

Lawson, Katie. "American Red Cross Receives Four Stars from Charity Navigator." "American Red Cross" website, December 5, 2006. http://www.red cross.org/article/0,1072,0_312_5824,00.html (accessed March 12, 2007).

Lee, Madeline. "Foundations Should Listen to Charities." *Chronicle of Philanthropy: The Newspaper of the Nonprofit World,* March 4, 2004, pp. 37–38.

Lenkowsky, Leslie. "The Uphill Battle to Steer Government Aid to Religious Groups." *Chronicle of Philanthropy: The Newspaper of the Nonprofit World* online, July 22, 2004. http://philanthropy.com/premium/articles/v16/i19/ 19004601.htm (accessed November 27, 2006).

"Letter to *SF Weekly* Following Matt's Column." *SF Weekly,* May 2, 2001. "Wheels of Fortune: AIDS Ride Updates 2001/2002—Lawsuits, Loss and Lifecycle" website. http://members.tripod.com/~homeo/wheels8.html (accessed January 13, 2007).

Letts, Christine W., William Ryan, and Allen Grossman. "Virtuous Capital: What Foundations Can Learn from Venture Capitalists." *Harvard Business Review,* March 1997, via *Harvard Business Review* online archive, http://harvard businessonline.hbsp.harvard.edu/b01/en/hbr/hbr_current_issue.jhtml; jsessionid=EWABL3ILJNQYoAKRGWDR5VQBKEoYIISW (accessed January 30, 2007).

Lewis, Nicole. "Charitable Giving Slides: Overall Donations Fall 2.3%, but Some Groups See Big Gains." *Chronicle of Philanthropy: The Newspaper of the Nonprofit World* online, June 27, 2002. http://philanthropy.com/free/articles /v14/i18/18002701.htm (accessed November 11, 2006).

Life Foundation. "2005 Annual Report." Life Foundation, Honolulu, 2005.

———. "2004 Annual Report." Life Foundation, Honolulu, 2004.

Light, Paul C. "Charities Must Make Innovation an Ordinary Act." *Chronicle of Philanthropy: The Newspaper of the Nonprofit World* online, March 12, 1998. http://philanthropy.com/premium/articles/v10/i10/10004201.htm (accessed February 9, 2007).

———. "The Content of Their Character: The State of the Nonprofit Workforce." *Nonprofit Quarterly* online, October 2, 2002. http://www.brookings.edu/views/ papers/light/20021002.htm (accessed June 29, 2006).

——. "Rebuilding Giving." *Worth* online, March 1, 2004. http://www.worth .com/Editorial/Money-Meaning/Philanthropy/Culture-Rebuilding-Giving-2.asp?ht=rebuilding%20giving%20rebuilding%20giving (accessed June 30, 2006).

——. *Sustaining Nonprofit Performance: The Case for Capacity Building and the Evidence to Support It.* Washington, D.C.: Brookings Institution Press, 2004.

Lincoln. "There Was a Time When I Couldn't See the Road Ahead." Print advertisement, February 2007.

Lipman, Harvy. "Americans Give Bigger Share to Charity Than Residents of Other Countries." *Chronicle of Philanthropy: The Newspaper of the Nonprofit World* online, November 22, 2006. http://philanthropy.com/free/update/ 2006/11/2006112202.htm (accessed November 27, 2006).

——. "Charity Executives' Median Pay Is $42,000, Report Says." *Chronicle of Philanthropy: The Newspaper of the Nonprofit World* online, January 10, 2002. http://philanthropy.com/premium/articles/v14/i07/06004902.htm (accessed March 18, 2004).

——. "Unbalanced Pay Scales." *Chronicle of Philanthropy: The Newspaper of the Nonprofit World* online, May 31, 2001. http://philanthropy.com/premium/ articles/v13/i16/16003301.htm (accessed January 28, 2007).

Lipman, Harvy, and Elizabeth Schwinn. "52 Top Executives Are Paid at Least $1-Million." *Chronicle of Philanthropy: The Newspaper of the Nonprofit World* online. June 24, 2004. http://philanthropy.com (accessed August 5, 2004).

"Local Communities Receive More Than $1 Million to Fight Breast Cancer." Avon Foundation press release. Denver, June 26, 2005.

"Local Communities Receive More Than $1.4 Million to Fight Breast Cancer." Avon Foundation press release. Los Angeles, September 18, 2005.

"Local Communities Receive More Than $2 Million to Fight Breast Cancer." Avon Foundation press release. San Francisco, July 10, 2005.

"Local Communities Receive More Than $2,150,000 to Fight Breast Cancer." Avon Foundation press release. Chicago, June 5, 2005.

"Local Communities Receive More Than $2,250,000 to Fight Breast Cancer." Avon Foundation press release. Boston, May 15, 2005.

"Local Communities Receive More Than $2.7 Million to Fight Breast Cancer." Avon Foundation press release. Washington, D.C., May 1, 2005.

"Local Communities Receive More Than $500,000 to Fight Breast Cancer." Avon Foundation press release. Charlotte, NC, April 17, 2005.

"Local and National Communities Receive $3 Million to Fight Breast Cancer." Avon Foundation press release. New York, October 2, 2005.

Lohr, Steve. "A Capitalist Jolt for Charity." *New York Times* online, February 24, 2008. http://www.nytimes.com/2008/02/24/business/24social.html (accessed February 25, 2008).

"Managing: Results of the Salary-Survey Search." *Chronicle of Philanthropy: The Newspaper of the Nonprofit the World* online, 2003. http://philanthropy .com (accessed March 18, 2004).

Manning, Cyril. "Holier Than Thou: A Bitter Battle Between Organizers and Beneficiaries Tears the California AIDS Ride Apart." "Salon.com" website,

February 1, 2002. http://dir.salon.com/story/mwt/feature/2002/02/01/aids_ride/index.html?source=search&aim=/mwt/feature (accessed January 9, 2007).

Manning, Jason. "Hands Across America." "The Eighties Club" website. http://eightiesclub.tripod.com/id312.htm (accessed August 15, 2006).

Massachusetts Office of the Attorney General, Division of Public Charities. "Professional Solicitor's Annual Financial Reports, Form 11A." Solicitor: Pallotta TeamWorks, Inc. Charity: Lesbian and Gay Community Services Center. Solicitation dates: July 1, 2001–June 30, 2002. Boston.

Matthews, Jay. "USA for Africa: The Audit; New Grants Listed for the Hungry, Homeless." *Washington Post,* March 26, 1987, C1, via Lexis-Nexis, http://web.lexis-nexis.com (accessed August 15, 2006).

McCaffrey, Shannon. "Watchdog Faults Red Cross on Sept. 11 Fund-Raising." *Associated Press State & Local Wire,* August 15, 2002, via Lexis-Nexis, http://web.lexis-nexis.com (accessed August 15, 2006).

McCarthy, Kathleen D. "Women and Political Culture." In *Charity, Philanthropy, and Civility in American History.* Edited by Lawrence J. Friedman and Mark D. McGarvie. Cambridge: Cambridge University Press, 2003, pp. 179–198.

McCraw, Thomas K. "It Came in the First Hips: Capitalism in America." In *Creating Modern Capitalism: How Entrepreneurs, Companies, and Countries Triumphed in Three Industrial Revolutions* (Cambridge: Harvard University Press, 1997), via "Harvard Business School" website. http://hbswk.hbs.edu/itm/0896.html (accessed December 16, 2006).

McDaid, Jennifer Davis. Review of *Women's Struggle for Equality,* by Jean V. Matthews. H-Women@msu.edu, May 1998. http://www.holysmoke.org/fem/fem0592.htm (accessed January 23, 2007).

McDougal, Dennis. "$11 Million for Poor From 'Hands.'" *Los Angeles Times* online, June 12, 1986. http://pqasb.pqarchiver.com/latimes/advancedsearch.html (accessed February 5, 2007).

——. "$15 Million for U.S. Poor May Come from 'Hands.'" *Los Angeles Times* online, September 27, 1986. http://pqasb.pqarchiver.com/latimes/advancedsearch.html (accessed February 5, 2007).

——. "Group Asks 'Hands' to Spend Funds." *Los Angeles Times* online, December 24, 1986. http://pqasb.pqarchiver.com/latimes/advancedsearch.html (accessed February 5, 2007).

——. "Hands Across America: Can Ken Kragen Make It Work?" *Los Angeles Times* online, November 24, 1985. http://pqasb.pqarchiver.com/latimes/advancedsearch.html (accessed February 5, 2007).

——. "Hands Across America, May 25, 1986: Hands Bills Paid in Full, but Homeless Still Waiting." *Los Angeles Times* online, November 2, 1986. http://pqasb.pqarchiver.com/latimes/advancedsearch.html (accessed February 5, 2007).

——. "Letting Go a Year Later, Hands Across America Goes Low Profile." *Los Angeles Times* online, May 24, 1987. http://pqasb.pqarchiver.com/latimes/advancedsearch.html (accessed February 5, 2007).

———. "New Deal: Hands Does a Recount." *Los Angeles Times* online, August 25, 1986. http://pqasb.pqarchiver.com/latimes/advancedsearch.html (accessed February 5, 2007).

McDougal, Dennis, and Victor Vale. "Hands Across America's Nonpolitical Status Challenged by Partisan Anti-Hunger Activists Series: Last in a Series Assessing the Continuing Influence of Mega-Events Like Hands Across America on Social Issues." *Los Angeles Times* online, June 19, 1986. http://pqasb.pqarchiver.com/latimes/advancedsearch.html (accessed February 5, 2007).

McFarlan, F. Warren. "Working on Nonprofit Boards: Don't Assume the Shoe Fits." *Harvard Business Review,* November 1, 1999, via *Harvard Business Review* archive, http://harvardbusinessonline.hbsp.harvard.edu/b01/en/hbr/hbr_current_issue.jhtml;jsessionid=EWABL3ILJNQY0AKRGWDR5VQBKE0YIISW (accessed February 10, 2007).

Mercer. "Mercer Issues Annual Study of CEO Compensation at Large US Firms: CEO Pay, Company Performance Show Close Alignment for 2004." "Mercer" website, April 11, 2005. http://www.mercerhr.com/summary.jhtml?idContent=1176860 (accessed January 22, 2007).

Merton, Thomas. *Seeds.* Edited by Robert Inchausti. Boston: Shambhala, 2002.

———. *The Waters of Siloe.* San Diego, CA: Harvest Books, 1949.

Metro Goldwyn Mayer. "2002 Annual Report." Metro-Goldwyn-Mayer, Los Angeles, 2003.

Microsoft Corporation. "2003 Annual Report." Microsoft Corporation, Seattle, 2004.

Miele. "The Smart Silent Type." Print advertisement, February 2007.

Miller, Perry. *The New England Mind: The Seventeenth Century.* Cambridge: Belknap Press of Harvard University Press, 1939.

Miller, Perry. *Orthodoxy in Massachusetts, 1630–1650.* Boston: Beacon Press, 1933.

Miller, Perry, and Thomas H. Johnson. *The Puritans: A Sourcebook of Their Writings, Two Volumes Bound as One.* Mineola, NY: Dover Publications, Inc., 2001.

"Millionaire Has-Beens." "CNNMoney.com" website, June 12, 2003. http://money.cnn.com/2003/06/11/pf/millionaire/millionaires/ (accessed May 1, 2004).

"Minding the Medians." *Business Week* online. http://businessweek.com/magazine/content/03_38/photo_essay/mediantable.htm (accessed January 28, 2007).

Monks.org. "Expansion & Renewal—Gethsemani—History—The Abbey of Gethsemani." "Monks.org" website. http://www.monks.org/hist_gethsemani3.html (accessed January 21, 2008).

Moore, Jennifer, and Grant Williams. "Cultivating Clout." *Chronicle of Philanthropy: The Newspaper of the Nonprofit World* online, June 18, 1998. http://philanthropy.com/premium/articles/v10/i17/1704101.htm (accessed February 14, 2007).

Morello, Carol. "Fundraiser with a Marketer's Touch; Treks Stress 'Human Potential' at Cost to Charities, Some Say." *Washington Post* online, June 20,

2001, http://pqasb.pqarchiver.com/washingtonpost/access/74252206.html
?dids = 74252206 : 74252206&FMT = ABS&FMTS = ABS : FT&fmac =
&date = Jun + 20 %2C + 2001&author = Carol + Morello&desc = Fundraiser
+ With + a + Marketer%27s + Touch (accessed January 29, 2008).

Murphy, Tim. "Anchors Aweigh." *Worth* 11, no. 10 (December 2002), p. 40.

Murphy, Tim, and Kevin O'Leary. "The 2002 POZCARDS." *POZ: Health, Life
& HIV* online, January 2003. http://www.poz.com/articles/163_2929
.shtml (accessed January 11, 2007).

Murray, William H. "Quotes by W. H. Murray: Until one is committed there is
hesitancy. . . ." "Gaia Community" website. http://www.gaia.com/quotes/
WH_Murray (accessed January 28, 2008).

Musbach, Tom. "California AIDS Ride Beneficiaries Pull Out." "Gay.com/
PlanetOut.com" website. http://www.planetout.com/news/article.html?2001
/10/12/3 (accessed January 26, 2008).

———. "Charities Split with AIDS Ride Promoter." "Gay.com/PlanetOut.com"
website. http://www.planetout.com/news/article.html?2002/05/31/2 (accessed January 9, 2007).

Muscular Dystrophy Association, Inc. "Report of Independent Auditors." July
13, 2006.

Nalder, Eric. "CEO's Rewards at Non-Profit." *San Jose Mercury News* online,
April 27, 2003. http://www.bayarea.com/mld/mercurynews/news/special_
packages/5278417.htm (accessed October 27, 2003).

National Alliance to End Homelessness. "Homelessness Counts." "National
Alliance to End Homelessness" website, January 10, 2007. http://www.end
homelessness.org/content/general/detail/1440 (accessed March 2, 2007).

National Cancer Institute. "Screening Mammograms: Questions and Answers."
"National Cancer Institute" website. http://www.cancer.gov/cancertopics/
factsheet/Detection/screening-mammograms (accessed October 28, 2006).

"National Salary Data for Senior IT Management Positions." *Computerworld*
online, 2005. http://www.computerworld.com/html/research/salarysurvey/
2005/senior.html (accessed January 23, 2007).

"The Nation's Major Charity-Watchdog Groups: At a Glance." *Chronicle of Philanthropy: The Newspaper of the Nonprofit World* online, November 28, 2002.
http://philanthropy.com/premium/articles/v15/i04/04002501.htm (accessed
March 17, 2004).

Neil, Dan. "Saleen Machine." *Worth* 11, no. 10 (December 2002), p. 42.

Nelson, Paul D. "Useful, but Limited: What Donors Need to Know About
Rating Services." *Philanthropy* online 18, no. 1 (January–February 2004).
http://www.philanthropyroundtable.org/magazines/2004/january/Rating
%20Services.htm (accessed August 20, 2004).

Newhan, Ross. "Ending on Whimper, No Bang." *Los Angeles Times,* October
26, 2003.

"Nonprofit Groups That Paid Top Officials $1-Million or More." *Chronicle of
Philanthropy: The Newspaper of the Nonprofit World* online, June 24, 2004.
http://philanthropy.com (accessed August 5, 2004).

"The Nonprofit World: Financial and Employment Trends." *Chronicle of Philanthropy: The Newspaper of the Nonprofit the World* online, March 21, 2002. http://philanthropy.com/premium/articles/v14/i11/11003201.htm (accessed January 23, 2007).

"Northeast AIDS Ride: Over 2,300 Riders Registered to Pedal 350 Miles from Bear Mountain, NY to Boston in Northeast AIDSRide, June 20–23, 2002." AIDS Project Los Angeles press release. Los Angeles, June 11, 2002.

Office of Bill Lockyer, Attorney General, State of California. "Attorney General's Summary of Results of Charitable Solicitation by Commercial Fundraisers: March 2001." California Department of Justice, Sacramento, 2001.

——. "Attorney General's Summary of Results of Charitable Solicitation by Commercial Fundraisers: Year Ending 2004." California Department of Justice, Sacramento, 2004.

——. "Attorney General's Summary of Results of Charitable Solicitation by Commercial Fundraisers: Year Ending 2001." California Department of Justice, Sacramento, 2001.

Office of New York State Attorney General Eliot Spitzer. "Charities." "Office of New York State Attorney General Eliot Spitzer" website. http://www.oag .state.y.us/charities/charities.html (accessed July 30, 2006).

Ogilvy, David. *Confessions of an Advertising Man.* London: Southbank Publishing, 2004.

——. *Ogilvy on Advertising.* New York: Vintage Books, 1983.

"100 Best Charities (and 10 Worst)." *Worth* 11, no. 10 (December 2002), pp. 80–95.

"Open Wide, AIDS Ride." *POZ: Health, Life & HIV* online. http://www.poz .com/articles/232_1655.shtml (accessed October 26, 2003).

O'Reilly, Bill. "Unresolved Problem." *O'Reilly Factor,* May 17, 2002, via Lexis-Nexis, http://web.lexis-nexis.com (accessed May 1, 2004).

O'Rourke, P. J. *On "The Wealth of Nations."* New York: Grove Press, 2007.

"Out of the Darkness: Over 2400 Registered (So Far) for Out of the Darkness—A 26-Mile Walk to Benefit the American Foundation for Suicide Prevention, August 17–18, 2002." Pallotta TeamWorks press release. Los Angeles, May 7, 2002.

Pallotta TeamWorks. "Avon Breast Cancer 3-Day: Budget Summary." Pallotta TeamWorks, Los Angeles, 2002.

——. "California AIDS Ride 8—Los Angeles Agreement." Pallotta TeamWorks, Los Angeles, 2000.

——. "California AIDS Ride 8—San Francisco Agreement." Pallotta TeamWorks, Los Angeles, 2000.

——. "Comparisons, Graphs, Data and Photographs." Trial support documentation for Judicial Arbitration and Mediation Services, case no. 1420011424. Pallotta TeamWorks, Los Angeles, 2003.

——. Email to riders, crew, and supporters of the vaccine rides. February 5, 2002.

——. "Out of the Darkness—Contract." Pallotta TeamWorks, Los Angeles, 2002.

———. "Record of Impact 1994–2002." Summary of fundraising results. Pallotta TeamWorks, Los Angeles, 2006.

———. "Rider Information Sheet." Pallotta TeamWorks, Los Angeles, 1998.

———. "2002 Event Catalogue," Pallotta TeamWorks, Los Angeles, 2001.

Parks, David E. "Calvin: The Man and His Doctrine." "Waterford Church of Christ" website. http://www.wcofc.org/deep/calvin%20the%20source%20of%20his%20odoctrin.htm (accessed December 13, 2006).

Parsons, Linda, M. "Is Accounting Information from Nonprofit Organizations Useful to Donors? A Review of Charitable Giving and Value-Relevance." *Journal of Accounting Literature* 22 (2003), pp. 104–115, via ProQuest, ABI/Inform Global. http://www.proquest.com (accessed October 31, 2006).

Passov, Richard. "How Much Cash Does Your Company Need?" *Harvard Business Review,* November 1, 2003, via *Harvard Business Review* archive, http://harvardbusinessonline.hbsp.harvard.edu/b01/en/hbr/hbr_current_issue.jhtml;jsessionid=EWABL3ILJNQY0AKRGWDR5VQBKE0YIISW (accessed February 10, 2007).

Perry, Suzanne. "Average Donation by Individuals fell in 2006." *Chronicle of Philanthropy: The Newspaper of the Nonprofit World* online, January 11, 2007. http://philanthropy.com/premium/articles/v19/i06/06002803.htm (accessed January 28, 2007).

———. "Courting the New Congress." *Chronicle of Philanthropy: The Newspaper of the Nonprofit World,* January 25, 2007, pp. 28, 30.

———"Donations to Victims of 2004 Asian Tsunamis Topped $3-Billion." *Chronicle of Philanthropy: The Newspaper of the Nonprofit World* online, January 11, 2007. http://philanthropy.com/premium/articles/v19/i06/06002801.htm (accessed February 28, 2007).

———. "Interim CEO Resigns from Red Cross." *Chronicle of Philanthropy: The Newspaper of the Nonprofit World,* May 31, 2007, p. 50.

———. "Public Confidence in Nonprofit Groups Slides Back New Survey Finds." *Chronicle of Philanthropy: The Newspaper of the Nonprofit World,* April 3, 2008, p. 12.

Perry, Suzanne, and Elizabeth Schwinn. "Fundraising Costs and Marketing Deals Get New Attention in Congress." *Chronicle of Philanthropy: The Newspaper of the Nonprofit World,* January 10, 2008, p. 18.

Perry, Tony. "Philanthropy That Was Deeply Personal." *Los Angeles Times,* January 31, 2004.

Peters, Geoffrey W. "Madigan v. Telemarketing Associates (Formerly Known as Ryan v. Telemarketing Associates)." "American Charities for Reasonable Fundraising Regulations" website, December 2002. http://gpeters.net/supremecourt.html (accessed March 22, 2004).

Pollak, Thomas H., Patrick Rooney, and Mark A. Hager. "Understanding Management and General Expenses in Nonprofits." Overhead Cost Study Working Paper, presented at Annual Meeting of the Association for Research on Nonprofit Organizations and Voluntary Action, New Orleans, 2001.

Pool, Bob. "AIDS Ride Founder Lays Off L.A. Staff." *Los Angeles Times* online, August 27, 2002. http://www.aegis.com/news/lt/2002/LT020804.html (accessed January 9, 2007).

Porretto, John. "$40 Billion Profit for Exxon." *Beaver County Times & Allegheny Times* online, February 1, 2008. http://www.timesonline.com/articles /2008/02/01/news/top_stories/doc47a3d4061d24d653846165.txt (accessed February 3, 2008).

Porterfield, Amanda. "Protestant Missionaries: Pioneers of American Philanthropy." In *Charity, Philanthropy, and Civility in American History.* Edited by Lawrence J. Friedman and Mark D. McGarvie. Cambridge: Cambridge University Press, 2003, pp. 49–70.

Princeton Survey Research Associates, Inc. "BBB Wise Giving Alliance Donor Expectations Survey: Final Report." PSRAI, Princeton, NJ, 2001.

Prives, Dan. "Charity Standards Proposed by Watchdog Group Are Deeply Flawed." *Chronicle of Philanthropy: The Newspaper of the Nonprofit World* online, April 2002. http://philanthropy.com/premium/articles/v14/i13/1300 6501.htm (accessed March 17, 2004).

Project Inform. "Project Inform Mourns Passing of Board Member and Long-time AIDS Treatment Activist Linda Grinberg." "Project Inform" website, June 3, 2002. http://www.projectinform.org (accessed March 24, 2004).

———. "Staff Bio: Martin Delaney, Founding Director." "Project Inform" website. http://www.projectinform.org (accessed March 23, 2004).

Provenzano, Jim. "Berkeley Man Sues AIDS Ride Organizer." *Bay Area Reporter* online, April 25, 2002. http://members.trpiod.com/~homeo/wheels1 .html (accessed November 22, 2006).

———. "Wheels of Fortune, Part Three: Clif Notes and Big Staffs." *Bay Area Reporter* online, May 7, 1999. http://www.aegis.com/news/bar/1999/ BR990504.html (accessed March 22, 2004).

———. "Wheels of Fortune: AIDS Ride 99 Part 1: AIDS Riders Gear Up for Controversy." *Bay Area Reporter* online, 1999. http://members.trpiod.com/ ~homeo/wheels1.html (accessed November 22, 2006).

Queen Mary 2. "It's Just the Way It Used to Be." Print advertisement,. February 2007.

Quittner, Jeremy. "Breaking the Cycle: Two Top California AIDS Groups Fire Pallotta TeamWorks—AIDS Ride." *Advocate* online, November 20, 2001. http://findarticles.com/p/articles/mi_m1589/is_2001_Nov_20/ai_80116717 (accessed January 6, 2008).

Rand, Ayn. *Atlas Shrugged.* New York: Plume, 1957.

———. *The Virtue of Selfishness: A New Concept of Egoism.* New York: Signet Books, 1961.

Randolph Riley, etc., et al. v. National Federation of the Blind of North Carolina, Inc., et al., no. 87–328. Supreme Court of the United States. June 29, 1988.

Rauch, Jonathan. "'This Is Not Charity.'" *Atlantic Monthly* 300, no. 3 (October 2007), pp. 64–76.

Rodriguez, Olga R. "California: Turnout for AIDS Ride Suffers from Lawsuit, Competing Ride." "The Body: The Complete HIV/AIDS Resource" website, June 3, 2002. http://www.thebody.com/content/policy/art20152.html (July 29, 2006).

Rogers, Julie L. "Foundations Are Burning Out Charity CEO's." *Chronicle of Philanthropy: The Newspaper of the Nonprofit World* online, May 9, 2006. http://philanthropy.com/premium/articles/v18/i10/16003401.htm (accessed February 10, 2007).

Rohmann, Chris. *A World of Ideas: A Dictionary of Important Theories, Concepts, Beliefs, and Thinkers.* New York: Ballantine Books, 1999.

RootsWeb.com "Stearns-L Archives." "RootsWeb.com" website. http://archiver.rootsweb.com/th/read/STEARNS/1996–09/0842036816 (accessed December 16, 2006).

Rosenberg, Barry. "Gulfstream Brings New Visions Here: Of Runways and Product Nomenclature." "Aviationweek.com" website, 2002. http://www.aviationweek.com/shopnews/02nbaa/airfrm01.htm (accessed March 18, 2004).

Rosenman, Mark. "Are There Too Many Nonprofits? The Wrong Debate." Compiled by Heather Peeler. *Foundation News & Commentary*, May–June 200, pp. 47, 49.

——. "McKinsey Study Shows Stunning Lapse in Logic." *Chronicle of Philanthropy: The Newspaper of the Nonprofit World* online, May 29, 2003. http://philanthropy.com/premium/articles/v15/i16/16003401.htm (accessed February 10, 2007).

Salamon, Lester M., ed. *The State of Nonprofit America.* Washington, D.C.: Brookings Institution Press, 2002.

"Salary Survey: National Salary Data for Staff and Entry-Level IT Positions." *Computerworld* online. http://www.computerworld.com/html/research/salarysurvey/2005/entry.html (accessed January 27, 2008).

"Salary Survey: National Salary Data for Middle Management IT Positions." *Computerworld* online. http://www.computerworld.com/html/research/salarysurvey/2005/middle.html (accessed January 27, 2008).

"Salary Survey 2001." *The NonProfit Times* online. http://www.nptimes.com/Feb01/ss_2001.pdf (accessed June 29, 2006).

Salmon, Jacqueline L. "Charities Cut the Fat from Sports Fundraisers." *Washington Post* online, January 20, 2004. http://www.washingtonpost.com/wp-dyn/articles/A54750–2004Jun19.html (accessed January 30, 2008).

Saulny, Susan. "Red Cross Announces Plans for Rest of Disaster Funds." *New York Times,* February 1, 2002, via Lexis-Nexis, http://web.lexis-nexis.com (accessed August 15, 2006).

Schneider, Mica. "The Ever-Costlier MBA Degree." *Business Week* online, January 28, 2007. http://www.businessweek.com/bschools/content/oct2004/bs20041028_5621_bs001.htm (accessed January 28, 2007).

Schwinn, Elizabeth. "Back to Basics: More Charities are Seeking—and Getting—Operating Support." *Chronicle of Philanthropy: The Newspaper of the Nonprofit World,* May 1, 2008, pp. 21–22, 24.

——. "Many Americans Say Charity Overhead Costs Are Too High, Study Finds." *Chronicle of Philanthropy: The Newspaper of the Nonprofit World* online, February 14, 2008. http://www.philanthropy.com/news/updates/ 3972/americans-believe-charity-overhead-costs-are-too-high-study-finds (accessed February 4, 2008).

——. "Rooting Out Errors on Charity Tax Forms." *Chronicle of Philanthropy: The Newspaper of the Nonprofit World* online, March 22, 2007. http://www .philanthropy.com/premium/articles/v19/i11/11003301.htm (accessed March 20, 2007).

Schwinn, Elizabeth, and Ian Wilhelm. "Nonprofit CEO's See Salaries Rise." *Chronicle of Philanthropy: The Newspaper of the Nonprofit World* online, October 2, 2003. http://philanthropy.com/premium/articles/v15/i24/24002701 .htm (accessed April 19, 2004).

Secretary of State of Maryland v. Joseph H. Munson Co., Inc., no. 82–766. Supreme Court of the United States, June 26, 1984, via Lexis-Nexis, http:// web.lexis-nexis.com (accessed June 30, 2006).

Seelye, Katherine Q. and Diana B. Henriques. "A Nation Challenged: The Charity—Red Cross President Quits, Saying That the Board Left Her No Other Choice." *New York Times,* October 27, 2001, via Lexis-Nexis, http:// web.lexis-nexis.com (accessed August 15, 2006).

Shore, William H. *Revolution of the Heart: A New Strategy for Creating Wealth and Meaningful Change.* Foreword by Gloria Naylor. New York: Riverhead Books, 1995.

Silverman, Les. "Are There Too Many Nonprofits? Achieving a Better Balance Between Numbers and Scale." Compiled by Heather Peeler. *Foundation News & Commentary,* May–June 2004, pp. 47, 51.

Silverman, Les, and Lynn Taliento. "What Business Execs Don't Know—but Should—About Nonprofits." *Stanford Social Innovation Review* online, January 22, 2007. http://www.ssireview.org/articles/entry/what_business _execs _dont_know_but_should_about_nonprofits/ (accessed February 10, 2007).

Silverman, Stephen M., and Susan Mandel. "Oprah Winfrey: Wealth Is 'A Good Thing.'" *People* online, April 11, 2006. http://www.people.com/people /article/0,,1182572,00.html (accessed January 29, 2007).

Smallwood, Stephen J., and Wilson C. Levis. "The Realities of Fund-Raising Costs and Accountability." "Philanthropy Monthly" website, September 1977. http://nccsdataweb.urban.org/PubApps/levis/realities.html (accessed August 25, 2006).

Smith, Adam. *The Theory of Moral Sentiments.* Amherst, MA: Prometheus Books, 2000.

——. *The Wealth of Nations.* New York: Modern Library, 2000.

Smith, B. Mark. *A History of the Global Stock Market: From Ancient Rome to Silicon Valley.* Chicago: University of Chicago Press, 2003.

Smith, Ralph. "Many Happy Returns." *Worth* online, August 2, 2004. http://www.worth.com/Editorial/Money-Meaning/Philanthropy/Opportunities-Exposures-Many-Happy-Returns.asp?ht=many%20happy%20returns%20many%20happy%20returns (accessed June 30, 2006).

Smith Barney. "I Am Working Wealth." Print advertisement, February 2007.

Sobel, Robert. *The Big Board: A History of the New York Stock Market.* Washington, D.C.: Beard Books, 1965.

Solomon, John, and Matthew Mosk. "For Clinton, New Wealth in Speeches: Fees in 6 Years Total Nearly $40 Million." *Washington Post* online, February 23, 2007. http://www.washingtonpost.com/wp-dyn/content/article/2007/02/22/AR2007022202189.html (accessed March 3, 2007).

Sommer, Sally J. "When Will Hands Across America Touch the Poor?" *Los Angeles Times* online, February 11, 1987. http://pqasb.pqarchiver.com/latimes/advancedsearch.html (accessed February 5, 2007).

Spartacus Educational. "Massachusetts Bay Colony." "Spartacus Educational" website. http://www.spartacus.schoolnet.co.uk/USABmapM.htm (accessed January 5, 2007).

"Special Report: Executive Compensation." *USA Today* online, April 10, 2006. http://www.usatoday.com/money/companies/management/2006-04-07-ceo-total.htm (accessed January 29, 2007).

"Special Report: 100 Leading National Advertisers Supplement." *Advertising Age,* June 26, 2008, pp. 1–9.

Stafford, Katy. "Making Strides to Save Lives: Charlotte Event Raises $1.6 Million to Help Find New Cures, Improve Care." *Charlotte Observer* online, October 22, 2006. http://www.charlotte.com/mid/observer/news/local/15820383.htm (accessed October 28, 2006).

Staricka, Susan K. "Are There Too Many Nonprofits? A Question of Integrity." Compiled by Heather Peeler. *Foundation News & Commentary,* May–June 2004, pp. 47, 50.

State Division of Consumer Affairs. "Final Accounting Report." Solicitor: Pallotta TeamWorks, Inc. Charity: American Foundation for Suicide Prevention. Solicitation dates: September 1, 2001–August 31, 2002. Campaign description: 26-Mile Walk. Richmond, VA, January 24, 2003.

——. "Final Accounting Report." Solicitor: Pallotta TeamWorks, Inc. Charity: Food and Friends. Solicitation dates: July 1, 2001–June 30, 2002. Campaign description: Bike Ride. Richmond, VA, January 24, 2003.

——. "Final Accounting Report." Solicitor: Pallotta TeamWorks, Inc. Charity: UCLA Foundation. Solicitation dates: February 22, 2001–May 31, 2002. Campaign description: Seven (7) Day Trek on Foot in America. Richmond, VA, January 24, 2003.

——. "Final Accounting Report." Solicitor: Pallotta TeamWorks, Inc. Charity: UCLA Foundation. Solicitation dates: August 1, 2001–July 31, 2002. Campaign description: Three-Day Walk from West Point to the

United Nations Plaza in New York City. Richmond, VA, January 24, 2003.

———. "Final Accounting Report." Solicitor: Pallotta TeamWorks, Inc. Charity: UCLA Foundation. Solicitation dates: August 1, 2001–July 31, 2002. Campaign description: Seven-day Bike Ride from Amsterdam, Netherlands to Paris, France. Richmond, VA, January 24, 2003.

State of California Office of the Attorney General Registry of Charitable Trusts. "Form CF-2: Annual Financial Report." Solicitor: Pallotta Team-Works, Inc. Charity: AIDS Project Los Angeles. Campaign dates: June 2, 2002–June 8, 2002. Sacramento, CA, January 24, 2003.

———. "Form CF-2: Annual Financial Report." Solicitor: Pallotta TeamWorks, Inc. Charity: Liberty Hill Foundation. Campaign dates: August 24, 2002–August 25, 2002. Campaign description: 2-Day Walk. Sacramento, CA, January 24, 2003.

———. "Form CF-2: Annual Financial Report." Solicitor: Pallotta TeamWorks, Inc. Charity: UCLA Foundation. Campaign dates: through August 2, 2002 (contract terminated). Campaign description: Canada–U.S. AIDS Vaccine Ride. Sacramento, CA, January 24, 2003.

———. "Form CF-2: Annual Financial Report." Solicitor: Pallotta TeamWorks, Inc. Charity: UCLA Foundation. Campaign dates: through June 12, 2002 (contract terminated). Campaign description: Experimental AIDS Vaccine Ride. Sacramento, CA, January 24, 2003.

———. "Form CF-2: Annual Financial Report." Solicitor: Pallotta TeamWorks, Inc. Charity: Vista Del Mar Child & Family Services. Campaign dates: July 1, 2001–May 2002. Campaign description: 2-Day Walk. Sacramento, CA, January 24, 2003.

State of New York Department of Law, Charities Bureau. "Professional Fund Raiser: Interim/Closing Statement." Solicitor: Pallotta TeamWorks, Inc. Charity: Fenway Community Health Center and Lesbian and Gay Community Services Center. Solicitation dates: July 1, 2001–June 30, 2002, Albany, NY.

Stehle, Vincent. "Are There Too Many Nonprofits? Consolidation—Crisis or Opportunity." Compiled by Heather Peeler. *Foundation News & Commentary,* May–June 2004, pp. 47, 52.

Steinberg, Richard. "Economic Perspectives on Regulation of Charitable Solicitation." *Case Western Law Review*, 1989, via Lexis-Nexis, http://web.lexis-nexis.com (accessed June 22, 2003).

———. "Should Donors Care About Fundraising?" In *The Economics of Nonprofit Institutions.* Edited by S. Rose-Ackerman. New York: Oxford University Press, 1986.

Stengel, Richard. "Joining Hands." *Time* online. http://www.time.com/time/magazine/article/0,9171,1075101,00.html (accessed February 3, 2008).

Stephenson Jr., Max, and Elisabeth Chaves. "The Nature Conservancy, the Press, and Accountability." *Nonprofit and Voluntary Sector Quarterly* 35, no. 3 (September 2006), pp. 345–366.

Stoll, Michael. "AIDS Group Chops Staff: Top Exec Taking 12 Percent Pay Cut." *San Francisco Examiner,* June 19, 2002.

Storch, Charles. "IRS Eyes Marketing Ploy at Partners in Charity." *Chicago Tribune* online, November 17, 2005. www.chicagotribune.com (accessed February 1, 2008).

Strauss, Gary, and Barbara Hansen. "CEO Pay Soars in 2005 as a Select Group Break the $100 Million Mark." *USA Today* online, April 11, 2006. http://www.usatoday.com/money/companies/management/2006-04-09-ceo-compensation-report_x.htm (accessed January 29, 2007).

Strom, Stephanie. "A Nation Challenged: Charities—Narrowly Drawn Rules Freeze Out Tens of Thousands of Indirect Victims, Report Says." *New York Times,* April 23, 2002, via Lexis-Nexis, http://web.lexis-nexis.com (accessed August 15, 2006).

Strouse, Jean. *Morgan: American Financier*. New York: Harper Perennial Books, 2000.

Summers, Vanessa. "Prosperity NOW: Free Wealth & Success Workshops with Financial Guru Vanessa Summers." Print advertisement, February 2007.

———. "The Sutras of Holistic Wealth: Part One." *Yogi Times,* February 2007, pp. 80–81.

"Super Bowl Ad Cost through the Years: Business of Super Bowl." *MSNBC* online. http://www.msnbc.msn.com/id/16874732/ (accessed February 14, 2007).

Szalavitz, Maia. "No Market for Marketing." *Stanford Social Innovation Review* online, December 1, 2005. http://www.ssireview.org/articles/entry/no_market_for_marketing/ (accessed January 30, 2007).

Teltsch, Kathleen. "Hands-Across-America Pledges Unkept." *New York Times,* August 31, 1986, via Lexis-Nexis, http://web.lexis-nexis.com (accessed August 15, 2006).

Tench, Megan. "AIDS Ride Returns on Different Course." *Boston Globe* online, September 14, 2003. http://www.boston.com/dailyglobe2/257/metro/AIDS_ride_returns_on_different_courseP.shtml (accessed September 14, 2003).

"3rd Annual Pacific Coast Bicycle Ride Raises More Than $100,000 for the American Lung Association of Washington: 39 Lung Health Champions Riding 1,000 Miles to Support Lung Research." American Lung Association of Washington press release. Seattle, 2006.

Tierney, Thomas J. "The Leadership Deficit." *Stanford Social Innovation Review* online, June 1, 2006. http://www.ssireview.org/articles/entry/the_leadership_deficit/ (accessed January 30, 2007).

Tierney, Thomas. "The Nonprofit Sector's Leadership Deficit, Executive Summary." "Bridgespan Group, Inc." website, March 2006. http://www.bridgespangroup.org/kno_articles_leadershipdeficit.html.

———. "The Nonprofit Sector's Leadership Deficit, Executive Summary. "Bridgespan Group, Inc." website, March 2006. http://www.bridgespangroup.org/kno_articles_leadershipdeficit.html.

Tindall, Blair. "The Plight of the White-Tie Worker." *New York Times* online, January 27, 2008. http://query.nytimes.com/gst/fullpage.html?res=9F0CE5D91238F937A35754C0A9629C8B63 (accessed January 27, 2008).

Tinkelman, Daniel. "Breast Cancer Walks: Linking Organizational Stresses and Questionable Accounting Practices." Working paper presented at ARNOVA conference, Philadelphia, PA, November 2007.

———. "Factors Affecting the Relation Between Donations to Not-for-Profit Organizations and an Efficiency Ratio." *Research in Government and Nonprofit Accounting* 10 (1999), pp. 135–161.

Tobin, Gary A. "Getting Megagifts to the Neediest Causes." *Chronicle of Philanthropy: The Newspaper of the Nonprofit World* online, May 1, 2003. http://philanthropy.com/premium/articles/v15/i14/14004901.htm (accessed January 30, 2007).

Tocqueville, Alexis de. *"Democracy in America" and Two Essays on America.* Translated by Gerald E. Bevan. London: Penguin Books, 2003.

"Top U.S. Advertisers by Revenue per Ad Dollar." *Advertising Age* online, 2008. http://adage.com/datacenter/datapopup.php?article_id=118677 (accessed January 27, 2008).

Toyota Motor Corporation. "Driving a Car as Well as a Revolution: Prius 07." Print advertisement, 2007.

"25 Most Generous Young Americans." *Worth* 11, no. 10 (December 2002).

"24th Annual Trek Tri-Island Bicycle Ride." American Lung Association of Washington press release. Seattle, 2006.

"2006 Full-Time MA Profile: University of Chicago, Graduate School of Business." *Business Week* online, 2006. http://businessweek.com/@@Fz50Do QQ3t7PJyAA/bschools/06/full_time_profiles/chicago1.htm (accessed January 28, 2007).

"2003 Celebrity Salary Compensation." "Forbes.com" website, October 20, 2003. http://www. Forbes.com (accessed March 18, 2004).

"2003 CEO Compensation." "Forbes.com" website, October 20, 2003. http:// www. Forbes.com (accessed March 18, 2004).

U.S. Congress, Senate. Committee on Finance. "Charity Oversight and Reform: Keeping Bad Things from Happening to Good Charities," June 22, 2004. Testimony of H. Art Taylor, President & CEO of BBB Wise Giving Alliance, Arlington, VA.

U.S. National BBB.org. "U.S. National BBB.org: Staff." "U.S. National BBB .org" website. http://www.us.bbb.org/WWWRoot/SitePage.aspx?site=113 &id=41018df4-9a11-4ed1-a767-297765eedbf6 (accessed January 26, 2008).

U.S. Office of Personnel Management. "Welcome to the Official One-Stop Source for Information About the Combined Federal Campaign." U.S. Office of Personnel Management website. http://www.opm.gov/cfc/ (accessed March 26, 2007).

United Way. "Alternative Spring Break 2007 (ASB)." "United Way" website. http://national.unitedway.org/ (accessed March 12, 2007).

———. "United Way Homepage." "United Way" website. http://www.united way.org/ (accessed January 26, 2008).

University of Chicago Graduate School of Business. "Full-Time MBA Costs." "University of Chicago Graduate School of Business" website. http://chicago gsb.edu/fulltime/admissions/costs.aspx (accessed January 28, 2007).

working paper presented at the International Conference on Systems Thinking in Management, Philadelphia, PA, 2004.

Winthrop, John. *The Journal of John Winthrop, 1630–1649.* Edited by Richard S. Dunn, James Savage, and Laetitia Yeandle. Cambridge: Belknap Press of Harvard University Press, 1996.

———. "A Model of Christian Charity." 1630. http://religiousfreedom.lib.virginia.edu/sacred/charity.html (accessed November 14, 2006).

Wiscombe, Janet. "Leader of the Pack." *Los Angeles Times Magazine,* May 10, 1998.

Wise, Jeff. "Altruism for Fun and Profit." *New York Times Magazine,* September 7, 1997.

Wolf, Buck. "Great Shakes: 'Hands Across America' 20 Years Later—The Day Oprah, President Reagan, Mickey Mouse and 5 Million Other Americans Joined Hands." *ABC News* online, May 23, 2006. http://abcnews.go.com/Entertainment/WolfFiles/story?id=2044810&page=1 (accessed August 15, 2006).

Wolverton, Brad. "Community Foundations Plan to Spend More on Advertising." *Chronicle of Philanthropy: The Newspaper of the Nonprofit World* online, February 6, 2003. http://philanthropy.com/premium/articles/v15/i08/08003002.htm (accessed February 14, 2007).

———. "Many Americans Are Still Skeptical of Charities, a New Opinion Poll Finds." *Chronicle of Philanthropy: The Newspaper of the Nonprofit World,* September 16, 2004, p. 35.

———. "Rethinking Charity Rules." *Chronicle of Philanthropy: The Newspaper of the Nonprofit World,* July 22, 2004, pp. 31, 33.

———. "Surviving Tough Times: Big Charities Suffer First Drop in Donations in 12 Years." *Chronicle of Philanthropy: The Newspaper of the Nonprofit World* online, October 30, 2003. http://philanthropy.com/premium/articles/v16/i02/02002801.htm (accessed March 17, 2004).

Wood, Tim. "Big Liquor Meets Big Tobacco." "Moneyweb: Your Trusted Friend on the Internet" website, May 31, 2002. http://www.moneyweb.com (accessed March 18, 2004).

Yahoo! Education. "Admissions to Business School: Business School Admissions Tips." "Yahoo!" website. http://education.yahoo.com/college/essentials/articles/biz/bschool-admissions.html (accessed January 28, 2007).

Yaqub, Reshma Memon. "To Give Well, Give Wisely." *Worth* 11, no. 10 (December 2002), pp. 80–95.

Yasuoka, Akira. *"Evolution of the US Retail Securities Market (Volume 1); Financial Institutions Prepare for Retiring Baby Boomers."* New York City: Nomura Research Institute, 2006.

Young, Michael D., Esq. "Partial Final Award and Statement of Reasons." *Pallotta TeamWorks v. Avon Products Foundation, Inc.,* no. 1420011424. Judicial Arbitration and Mediation Services, New York. July 15, 2005.

YouTube. "Supervote: The Super Bowl Commercials Ranked Your Way." "YouTube.com" website, 2007. http://www.youtube.com/superbowl (accessed February 13, 2007).

Zinn, Howard. *A People's History of the United States: 1492-Present.* New York: Harper Collins, 1980.

Zummach, Nicole. "Canada Boasts Second Largest Nonprofit Sector in the World." "CharityVillage.com" website, March 28, 2005. http://www.charity village.com/cv/archive/acov/acov05/acov0510.html (accessed January 29, 2008.)

INDEX

Page numbers in *italics* refer to tables.

Aaron Diamond Center, 193
accountability: comparison of charity
types and, 161; conflicting efficiency
standards, 159–62; in for-profit sector,
174–75; outcomes assessment
approaches, 170–76, 181–82; watchdog
guidelines and, 16–17, 109, 130–37, 172.
See also efficiency measures; infrastructure; outcomes
Adams, Henry, 23
advertising: advantages of advertising for
charities, xiii, 103–4, 106; branding,
108–9; consumer demand, 105–7;
cross-marketing, 205–6; disaster relief
and, 110–12, 155; donated advertising,
102–3; ideological prohibition of in
charity, xii, 100, 102–4, 107, 109; images of success in, 72–77; nonprofit vs.
for-profit approaches to, xiii, 46, 96–
104, 107–10; at Pallotta TeamWorks,
198, 201–7; political transformation
and, 116; return-on-investment, 104–5,
113, *113*; segregation vs. consolidation
of causes, 204–6; self-interests of consumers and, 38–39; special event
fundraising and, 156, 191, 194–95; as
"taking funds from the needy," 39–40,
104; target population as "grassroots,"
104
AIDS Community Donor Action, 198
AIDS Lifecycle, 221–23, *222–23*, 265–
66n120
AIDS pharmaceutical charities, 14
AIDSRides: achievements of, 191–94, 213;
advertising for, *113*, 114; AIDS Lifecycle compared with, 221–23, *222–23*,
265–66n120; Breast Cancer 3-Day

compared with, 154–55; efficiency assessment of, 196–97; "failure" rhetoric
in reviews of, 82–83; Harvard Business
School case study, 191; initial investment in, 86; intangible benefits of,
145–46, 194–95, 200; "most you can
do" approach, 190–91, 199; origin of,
190; overhead, 82–83, 93–94, 143;
overview, xiv–xv, 190; Pallotta Team-
Works collapse and, 216–20; resistance
from nonprofit ideology, 44–45;
smaller charities and, 121–22
AIDS Vaccine Events, net income from,
203
AIDS Vaccine Rides, 154–55, 213–14
altruism: among Harvard Business School
graduates, 70; charity as self-motivated
act, 44, 55–56; compensation and, 53–
56; as destructive of the concept of
benevolence, 45; hope as unacceptable
risk and, 89–90; limits of, 119; moral
authority and, 56; personal security
compared with, 69; scientific studies
of, 45; venture philanthropy and, 119,
122. *See also* compensation; nonprofit
ideology; self-interest
Amazon.com, 94–95
American Cancer Society, 97, 136
American Foundation for AIDS
Research, *99*
American Foundation for Suicide Prevention, 193
American Institute for Research, 100
American Institute of Philanthropy, 132–
33, 135, 159
American Lung Association, 136, 193, 208
American Red Cross. *See* Red Cross